"This publication underscores the vital importance of national mitigation strategies. Ambitious, 1.5°C-aligned national climate plans – covering all sectors and all greenhouse gases—are more critical than ever. Robust tracking of progress through Biennial Transparency Reports is also vital, to guide stronger policy-making, and to identify financing needs and investment opportunities—including through carbon markets under Article 6. Whole-of-government approaches, with meaningful engagement with sector leaders and other key stakeholders, are key to unlocking whole-of-society benefits: among them stronger growth and productivity, more jobs, less pollution and much lower health costs, and more secure and affordable energy. Helping all countries to seize these huge benefits is crucial. This new volume from the IMF is a valuable and timely contribution."

Simon Stiell, *Executive Secretary of the United Nations Framework Convention on Climate Change*

"This volume offers practitioners and scientists a clear framework for designing effective climate mitigation strategies. It shows how carbon pricing, reinforced by targeted sectoral policies, can align emission goals with economic efficiency, fairness, and political realism. For those advancing climate policy, this handbook provides an essential toolkit—to manage competitiveness, navigate distributional challenges, and foster international coordination toward global climate objectives."

Ottmar Edenhofer, *Potsdam Institute for Climate Impact Research, Technical University of Berlin, and Mercator Research Institute of Global Commons and Climate Change*

"Emissions of carbon dioxide and other greenhouse gases have been intricately woven into the fabric of economic activity for more than a century. Successfully addressing climate change requires pulling them out of this intricate weave while recognizing the fragilities of the fabric. No single policy is likely to be successful. The IMF has produced a much-needed guide for policymakers and stakeholders that helps balance the competing interests of cost-effectiveness, fairness, and feasibility. It highlights policy options across the economy, analytical tools to answer key questions, the importance of action, and the value of international cooperation. This book will be a valuable reference for anyone piecing together (or trying to understand) practical and effective national climate policy regimes."

Billy Pizer, *President and CEO, Resources for the Future*

AF872708

"This is an extraordinary resource – a thorough, readable, well-organized, and well-documented survey of climate economics, with a focus on mitigation. The authors frame this as a valuable tool for policy makers, but I will certainly assign sections to my students. The final chapter on dispelling climate myths deserves to be widely circulated."

Catherine Wolfram, *William Barton Rogers Professor in Energy, MIT Sloan School of Management*

"The political, economic, and ethical challenges posed by climate change can be overwhelming. This outstanding book manages to address these challenges comprehensively while remaining highly readable. With close attention to recent empirical findings, it shows how using a combination of policy approaches can significantly mitigate climate change at relatively low cost while respecting concerns about fairness and political constraints. It is an exceptionally valuable reference for policy analysts, decision-makers, university students, and others interested in finding solutions to the climate change problem."

Lawrence H. Goulder, *Shuzo Nishihara Professor of Environmental and Resource Economics, EmeritusStanford University*

Strategies for Climate Mitigation

This book provides a practical, step-by-step guide to help policymakers formulate comprehensive mitigation strategies tailored to their domestic circumstances.

The core of the volume is a discussion of all the key elements of the mitigation strategy, using conceptual frameworks to understand policy options and design issues, as well as numerous quantitative analyses illustrating the effects of different measures across different countries. The discussion within chapters is broken down into a series of key questions, many of which routinely come up in discussions with country authorities and in international fora. Each question contains a concise response and, in many cases, a graphic illustrating the key points. Chapters start with a summary of the main messages and end with suggestions for further reading.

The main target audience for this book is technical staff in finance, environment, and energy ministries grappling with national climate mitigation policy issues. However, the volume will also be a useful reference for individuals in international organizations, research institutes, and universities involved in climate policy analysis, as well as negotiating parties at international climate fora.

Ian Parry is Principal Environmental Fiscal Policy Expert in the Climate Policy Division of the IMF's Fiscal Affairs Department.

Simon Black is an Economist in the IMF's Fiscal Affairs Department, where he specializes in climate change mitigation, carbon pricing, and environmental taxation.

Nate Vernon-Lin is an Economist in the IMF's Climate Policy Division, Fiscal Affairs Department.

Karlygash Zhunussova is an Economist in the IMF's Climate Policy Division, Fiscal Affairs Department.

Strategies for Climate Mitigation

A Handbook for Policy Design

Ian Parry, Simon Black, Nate Vernon-Lin and Karlygash Zhunussova

Routledge
Taylor & Francis Group
LONDON AND NEW YORK

Designed cover image: VectorMine/Getty Images

First published 2027
by Routledge
4 Park Square, Milton Park, Abingdon, Oxon OX14 4RN

and by Routledge
605 Third Avenue, New York, NY 10158

Routledge is an imprint of the Taylor & Francis Group, an informa business

© 2027 International Monetary Fund

Nothing contained in this book should be reported as representing the views of the IMF, its Executive Board, member governments, or any other entity mentioned herein. The views expressed in this book belong solely to the authors.

The right of Ian Parry, Simon Black, Nate Vernon-Lin, and Karlygash Zhunussova to be identified as authors of this work has been asserted in accordance with sections 77 and 78 of the Copyright, Designs and Patents Act 1988.

The Open Access version of this book, available at www.taylorfrancis.com, has been made available under a Creative Commons Attribution-Non Commercial-No Derivatives (CC BY-NC-ND) 4.0 International license.

Any third party material in this book is not included in the OA Creative Commons license, unless indicated otherwise in a credit line to the material. Please direct any permissions enquiries to the original rightsholder.

For Product Safety Concerns and Information please contact our EU representative GPSR@taylorandfrancis.com. Taylor & Francis Verlag GmbH, Kaufingerstraße 24, 80331 München, Germany.

Trademark notice: Product or corporate names may be trademarks or registered trademarks, and are used only for identification and explanation without intent to infringe.

British Library Cataloguing-in-Publication Data
A catalogue record for this book is available from the British Library

ISBN: 978-1-041-27566-4 (hbk)
ISBN: 978-1-041-27560-2 (pbk)
ISBN: 978-1-003-75501-2 (ebk)

DOI: 10.4324/9781003755012

Typeset in Sabon
by SPi Technologies India Pvt Ltd (Straive)

Contents

Figures

Tables

Preface

Climate change is a critical global challenge of our time. The year 2024 was the hottest on record. Scorching heat waves in India, China, and Mexico; torrential downpours and flooding across the United States and East Africa; devastating hurricanes in the Caribbean and forest fires in California. The climate emergency is no longer a distant threat but is our reality. Our warming world is experiencing these impacts with a frequency and severity more rapid than scientists previously expected. Worse, there are uncertain but potentially catastrophic risks of crossing irreversible "tipping point" thresholds in the global climate system. Among those known to scientists include the collapse of major ice sheets, shutting down of ocean circulatory systems, and runaway warming from emissions released from permafrost.

Moreover, climate change poses critical macroeconomic and financial policy challenges for all countries in the coming years and decades. For example, global warming is likely to undermine productivity and growth, affecting fiscal positions and debt trajectories. It will also redistribute income across the globe, which will influence trade patterns and exchange rate valuations. Further, addressing climate change requires macro-fiscal policies which can have broad macroeconomic implications. Climate mitigation policy typically entails significant changes to tax regimes and fiscal frameworks, complemented by structural, regulatory, and spending policies to support a just transition. Lastly, climate change mitigation is a global public good and requires an unprecedented level of cross-country policy cooperation and coordination.

To limit climate damages and risks, with the signing of the Paris Agreement in 2015, almost every country agreed to limit warming to "well below" 2°C, ideally 1.5°C, above preindustrial levels. A decade later, the world is not on track. Even if countries were to fully achieve their emissions targets (in Nationally Determined Contributions, NDCs), this would still fall well short of aligning global emissions in 2030 with even a 2°C, let alone 1.5°C, target.

Yet there are also grounds for cautious optimism. To accelerate global decarbonization, substantive changes in policy are needed across countries, especially in fiscal policy. Fortunately, policymakers have both the tools and the modeling frameworks needed to craft effective, equitable, and administratively practical mitigation strategies that, collectively, can get the world on track to stabilizing the global climate system at manageable cost.

An efficient climate mitigation strategy involves a balance between carbon pricing at the economy-wide level and other policies, like feebates, at the sectoral level. These latter reinforcing instruments are especially important for sectors (like transport and buildings) where a strong price signal is needed to kick-start investments in low-carbon technologies, or sectors (like forestry) where carbon pricing in its pure form may be administratively difficult. Policy packages also need accompanying measures to address impacts on vulnerable households, some firms, and regions. And, depending on the country case, additional elements of the strategy might include public investment in enabling infrastructure, incentives to advance critical technologies, reforms to enhance the responsiveness of energy and financial markets to mitigation policies, and diversification of fiscal revenues away from fossil fuel extraction.

Design of policy packages is critical to ensuring their economic and environmental efficacy as well as their political durability. Because of this, reliable modeling frameworks are needed for assessing the environmental, economic, fiscal, and distributional impacts, and appropriate stringency, of mitigation policies. Fortunately, policymakers in all countries now have a rich set of tools at their disposal to achieve this, including one developed by IMF and World Bank staff that is now available for use by government officials in all member countries.

But beyond domestic climate policy, international coordination will be essential to scaling up global mitigation action. One such approach is for the major emitting countries—which collectively account for most current and historical emissions—to come together and reach a plurilateral agreement on, for example, minimum carbon prices or emissions targets, alongside other agreements such as those on international finance, freer trade for low-carbon technologies, harmonization of standards, and coordinated research and development efforts. Similarly, agreements within global regions could accelerate action, such as among the many countries in the Asia region now moving forward with carbon pricing.

All this is not to underplay the challenges. Comprehensive mitigation strategies need to be carefully calibrated to national circumstances. This includes consideration of the composition and availability of the energy mix, administrative capacity, the contribution of different sectors to emissions cuts, fiscal space, existing policies, resistance from influential groups, and "just transition" considerations to ensure that no one is left behind. And plurilateral agreements will require compromises over who cuts emissions fastest and who pays for and receives financial and technological support.

The challenge remains stark, and the domestic and international politics of climate policy are not easy. But the world's leaders and policymakers need to implement the necessary measures to safeguard the planet for our, and all future, generations. This book aims to set those policies out in clear terms.

Acknowledgments

We are indebted to many people for their help in the preparation of this volume.

Florence Jaumotte and Gregor Schwerhoff provided many thoughtful comments on multiple chapters of this book. Romain Duval and John Spray provided valuable insights on the choice between, and design of, mitigation instruments. Mario Mansour and Samuele Rosa offered practical feedback on the design of fiscal instruments to reduce emissions at the sectoral level. Christina Kolerus provided helpful comments on the modeling of mitigation instruments. Ritu Basu and Fabiana Machado provided valuable material on strategies to enhance the acceptability of mitigation strategies. Hasan Dudu and William Oman provided guidance on improving the discussion of supportive financial, technology, and investment policies. And Dominique Fayad and Gabriel Di Bella provided valuable insights on international coordination of mitigation, finance, and technology. We are also grateful to comments and suggestions from other participants at an internal IMF workshop on a draft version of this book (aside from those just acknowledged), including Ashvin Ahuja, Sandra Baquie, Laila Drissi Bourhanbour, Enrique Chueca, Ding Ding, Gianluigi Ferrucci, Maria Gelrud, Eduardo Camero Godinez, Andrew Hodge, Irena Jankulov, Eva Jenker, Eliakim Kakpo, Amit Kara, Izabela Karpowicz, Dominque Lam, Koshy Mathai, Thornton Matheson, Sonia Munoz, Galen Sher, Frederik Toscani, Bruno Versailles, and Sebastian Weber.

Benjamin Carton, Hugo Rojas-Romagosa, Sneha Thube, and Sebastian Wende provided some of the modeling results and graphics in Chapters 5 and 6. The modeling in these chapters was also supported by Dirk Heine, Daniel Bastidas, Alexandra Campmas, Ira Dorband, Faustyna Gawryluk, Victor Mylonas, Helene Naegele, Christian Schoder, Paulina Schulz, and Stephen Stretton.

We are also grateful to Lukas Adamski, Ximing Dong, Jing Han, and Sunalika Singh for their help in producing many of the graphics in this book. Dora Benedek and Ruud de Mooij supervised work for the volume and provided valuable encouragement and comments. We also thank Lorraine Coffey, Heidi Grauel, and Patricia Loo for assistance in the final preparation of the manuscript.

Authors

Ian Parry is Principal Environmental Fiscal Policy Expert in the Climate Policy Division of the IMF's Fiscal Affairs Department. He worked at Resources for the Future from 1995 to 2010, where he held the Allen Kneese Chair in Environmental Economics. He received a PhD in economics from the University of Chicago in 1993. Parry's research focuses on country-level analysis of comprehensive climate mitigation strategies and their broader fiscal and economic impacts. He also quantifies the broader environmental (e.g., local air pollution) costs of fossil fuel use at the country level and the efficient levels of fuel prices needed to reflect supply and environmental costs.

Simon Black is an Economist in the IMF's Fiscal Affairs Department, where he specializes in climate change mitigation, carbon pricing, and environmental taxation. Before joining the IMF, he was a Climate Economist at the World Bank, a Climate Economist at the UK's foreign ministry, and served as a UK negotiator to the UN's climate body, where he helped negotiate the Paris Agreement. He has also worked in financial sector advisory and economic diplomacy. He holds a Master's degree in International Political Economy from the London School of Economics and a master's degree in International Development (MPA/ID) from Harvard University, where he was a Frank Knox Fellow.

Nate Vernon-Lin is an Economist in the IMF's Climate Policy Division, Fiscal Affairs Department. He conducts research and works with countries on climate change mitigation policies, with specialization in carbon pricing, extractive industries, and the transport sector. Prior to joining the IMF, Vernon-Lin worked at IDinsight, focusing on social protection system design, monitoring, and evaluation in Malawi and Zambia. He holds a Bachelor's degree in Financial Economics from the University of Rochester and a Master's degree in Public Policy from the Harvard Kennedy School.

Karlygash Zhunussova is an Economist in the IMF's Climate Policy Division, Fiscal Affairs Department. She specializes in climate change mitigation, carbon pricing, mitigation policy equivalence, and environmental taxation. Before joining the IMF in 2021, she worked on climate change issues at the World Bank and as a consultant to the government of Kazakhstan on various strategic initiatives. She holds a Master's degree in Public Administration in International Development from Harvard University.

1 Motivation for and Summary of the Volume

The Challenges Facing Policymakers

Climate change is the ultimate global commons problem because emissions released in one country affect all other countries, as well as current and future generations. At the global level, the central issue in climate change mitigation is to get greenhouse gas (GHG) emissions on track with global warming targets in the 2015 Paris Agreement. For a 2°C or 1.7°C target, this requires cutting global GHGs by 25 to 45 percent by 2035, respectively, compared with 2019 levels, and to continue rapidly cutting emissions thereafter. Almost all IMF member countries have committed to cut GHGs in their Nationally Determined Contributions (NDCs) and to achieve net zero emissions by mid-century or thereabouts. Even if current NDCs were fully achieved, however, this would only cut global emissions by 7 percent by 2035, implying a large gap in near-term global mitigation ambition (see Figure 1.1).

At the domestic level, moreover, most countries are largely at or near base camp in terms of implementing strategies to get them on track with emissions commitments. Governments across the globe need comprehensive and effective mitigation strategies that contain costs to the economy, address distributional concerns, navigate the political obstacles to reform, while also being administratively practical.

At first glance, the task seems bewildering:

- There is a wide menu of alternative mitigation instruments, including carbon taxes, emissions trading systems (ETSs), low-carbon technology subsidies and mandates, feebates, performance standards, fuel taxes, and production taxes.
- These instruments have different effects on emissions, fiscal balances, energy prices, household groups, and trade-exposed industries, while also differing in administrative practicality.
- There are a wide range of sectors, each with its own mitigation technologies and policy design considerations, where emissions from multiple gases need to be cut, including power generation, industry, transportation, buildings, agriculture, forestry, extractives, and waste.

DOI: 10.4324/9781003755012-1
This chapter has been made available under a CC-BY-NC-ND license.

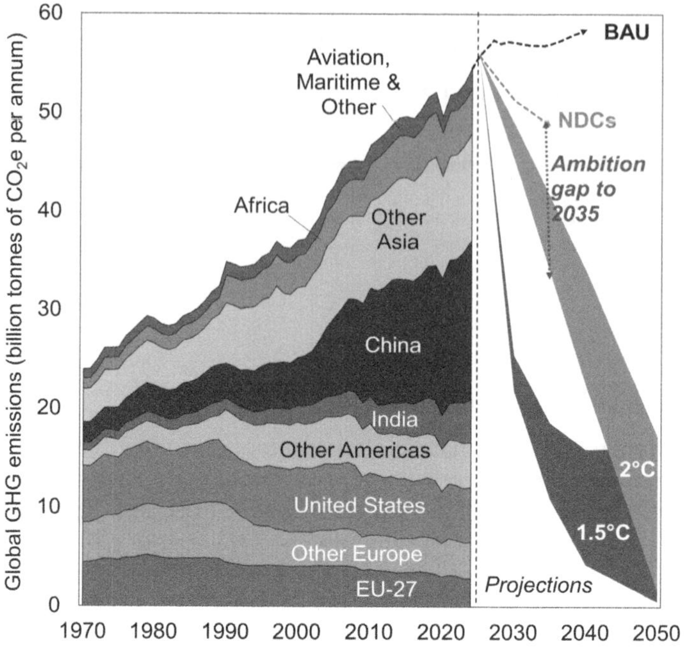

Figure 1.1 Global Mitigation Ambition Gap.

Source: Black et al. (2025).

Note: Includes land use and land-use change emissions. BAU = business as usual; NDCs = Nationally Determined Contributions and show the needed emissions trajectories to meet 2035 targets set either in 2015 or in the most recent submissions. Emissions pathways for temperature goals assume negative global emissions in the latter half of the century and a temporary overshoot of temperature goals—without overshooting allowed, emissions need to be cut to zero even more rapidly.

- Policymakers need practical modeling kits to project economywide and sectoral emissions and the wide-ranging effects of different instruments and options for their stringency and coverage.
- Distributional and competitiveness concerns need to be addressed to enhance acceptability with stakeholders and the public.
- Other elements may be needed such as supporting public investments, measures to advance development, deployment, and production of key technologies, strategies for regulating energy markets, financial market reforms, and (for fossil fuel exporters) revenue and economic diversification strategies.
- Understanding the broader environmental effects of climate mitigation policies, for example, on local air pollution mortality, is also important, as well as the implications of these effects for fuel pricing and other reforms to complement climate mitigation policies.

- And as countries move forward with mitigation policies, they will likely start to cooperate over mitigation policies, requiring practical coordination mechanisms. Countries will need to negotiate equitable ways to better align global mitigation ambition and policy implementation with temperature goals, while supporting it with enhanced climate finance and technology diffusion.

Moreover, appropriate mitigation strategies will vary with national circumstances, including the nature and stringency of emissions targets; the composition of the energy system; administrative capacity; the importance of broader sectors like forestry, agriculture, and extractives; sensitivities to higher energy prices; fiscal space; existing mitigation policies, fuel taxes, and subsidies; and so on. Where to begin?

A Way Forward

The previous issues imply that comprehensive mitigation strategies need to include a variety of different elements, as summarized in Figure 1.2. The centerpiece is the package of mitigation instruments, ideally a balance between economywide carbon pricing and reinforcing instruments (like feebates and performance standards) for each of the emissions-generating sectors. Another element is measures to promote fair distributional burdens across households (for example, through targeted assistance and equitable recycling of carbon pricing revenues) and address competitiveness concerns (through, for example, recycling revenues within the industrial sector or border carbon adjustments). Additional complementary measures might include public investment in infrastructure networks; incentives for R&D in and deployment of critical technologies; reforms to enhance responses in regulated energy markets (like shadow carbon pricing) and financial markets (like climate information); revenue diversification strategies for energy producers; and broader reforms (like fuel price adjustments or local air emissions fees) to simultaneously account for domestic environmental problems. Policymakers also need to contribute to international fora for global action. Modeling toolkits, at country and global levels, feed into all these elements to inform dialogue and policy design.

This volume seeks to provide a practical guide to help policymakers operationalize all the previous elements through both conceptual frameworks for understanding policy options and design issues as well as numerous quantitative analyses illustrating the effects of different measures across different countries. For the most part, these analyses use the Climate Policy Assessment Tool (CPAT), which provides assessments of comprehensive mitigation strategies for all 194 parties to the Paris Agreement.[1] The book synthesizes and refines a large body of analytical and country work developed by IMF staff over the past dozen years[2] and adds many additional policy discussions and analyses.

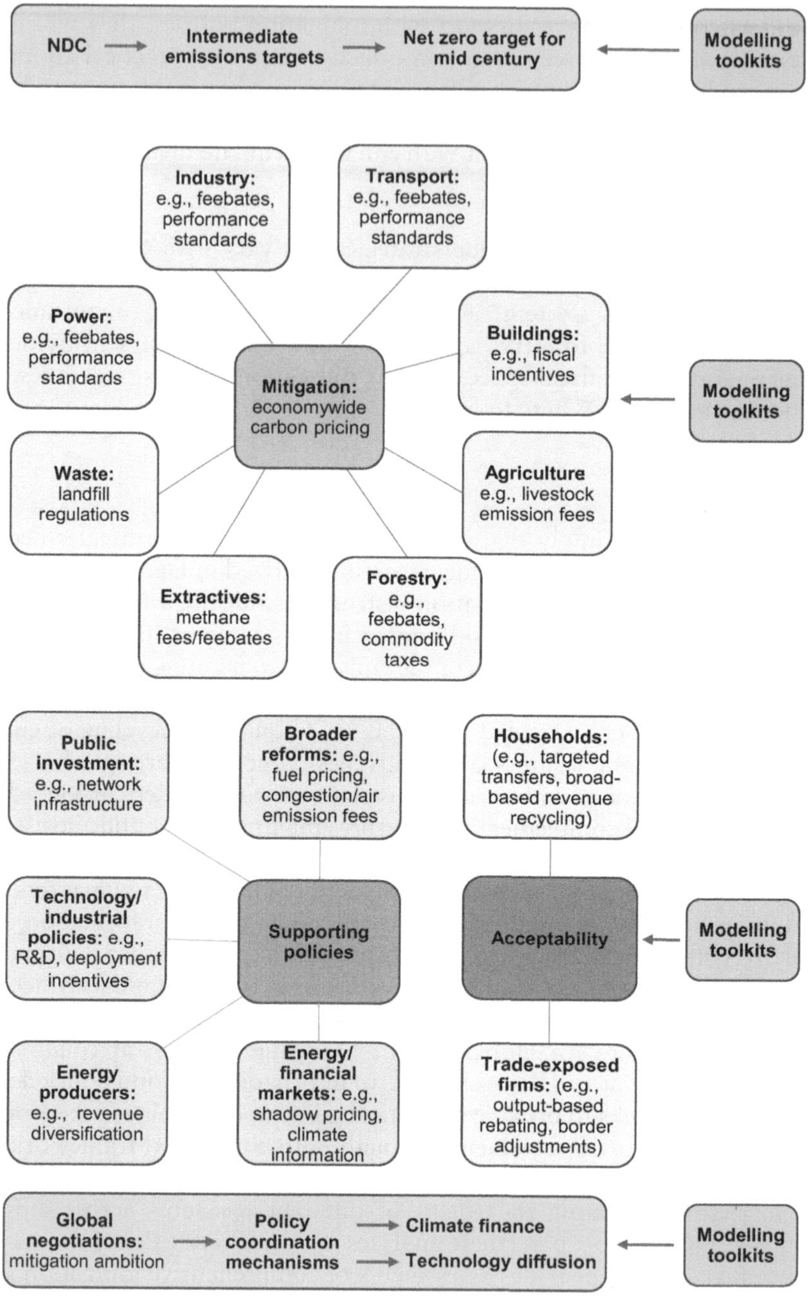

Figure 1.2 Elements of a Comprehensive Mitigation Strategy.

Source: Authors.

Note: NDC = Nationally Determined Contribution.

The discussion within chapters is broken down into a series of key questions, many of which routinely come up in climate policy discussions with country authorities and in international fora. Each question contains a concise response and (given the only too true adage that a picture is worth a thousand words) in many cases a graphic illustrating the key points. Chapters start with a summary of main messages and end with suggestions for further reading. The volume can be skimmed for questions of interest without necessarily reading whole chapters and chapters are largely self-contained and do not need to be read in order.

The main target audience for the book is technical staff in finance, environment, and energy ministries grappling with national climate mitigation policy issues. However, the volume should also be a useful reference for individuals in international organizations, research institutes, and universities involved in climate policy analysis, as well as negotiating parties at international climate fora.[3]

Seven Steps for Crafting a Comprehensive Mitigation Strategy

After providing brief background on the science of global warming, emissions trends, effects of climate change, and the Paris Agreement in Chapter 2, the next seven chapters break down the crafting of comprehensive mitigation strategies into seven steps.

Chapter 3. *A logical first step is to understand the potential behavioral responses by firms and households to reduce energy-related emissions, how the costs to the economy from those responses can be contained, the main policy instruments for promoting these responses and how they work, and how these instruments are best designed, administrated, and combined in a policy package.*

From an economic perspective, economywide carbon pricing should be the centerpiece of mitigation strategies, because it exploits the full range of mitigation responses, achieves emissions reductions at the lowest cost (by equating the cost of the last ton reduced across responses and sectors) while also raising fiscal revenues. There are administrative attractions for implementing carbon pricing midstream through taxes on fuel suppliers or upstream on fuel extractors. ETSs can also work well where capacity is adequate for monitoring power and industrial plant emissions and trading markets—especially if the ETS is supplemented with price floors (to promote price certainty) and allowance auctions (to raise revenues).

Reinforcing mitigation instruments at the sectoral level are, however, needed to complement carbon pricing (or perhaps substitute for it altogether), not least because pricing may face acceptability constraints from its more substantial effect on energy prices. To reduce emissions (rather than address impediments to specific technologies), these supplementary instruments should ideally be neutral with regard to low-carbon technologies and cost-effectively promote a broad range of mitigation responses. Feebates (sliding scales of fees for products/activities with high emissions intensity and rebates for products/activities with low emissions intensity) are a promising option, as are tradable performance (or emissions rate) standards. However, the latter also require fluid trading markets and may not work well for small countries or for the building sector.

Low-carbon technology subsidies and mandates (for example, to promote renewable power generation) focus on a narrower range of responses while (in the former case) imposing fiscal costs and (in the latter case) lacking cost-effectiveness. They may, however, have a role given they are already in place in many countries (and therefore avoid new capacity requirements), and various design features (for example, broadening their scope, using auctions or means-testing to allocate subsidies, or combining mandates with credit trading) can improve their effectiveness, cost-effectiveness, and limit fiscal burdens.

Chapter 4. *Next, it makes sense to develop a more detailed understanding of the main emissions-generating sectors and the applicability of instruments for those sectors to complement economywide policies.* Some messages include the following:

- *Power generation*: Feebates and tradable performance standards are reasonably effective policies for power generation if carbon pricing is constrained (though they have significant capacity needs) and, in some cases, converting electricity taxes to emissions taxes. Renewable policies are reasonably effective when there is limited scope for other mitigation responses (like improving plant efficiency, shifting to nuclear, and from coal to gas).
- *Industry*: Again, feebates and tradable performance standards are fairly effective alternatives to carbon pricing for most industries—low-carbon technology subsidies or mandates are less effective, given the difficulty of encouraging the diverse range of potential low-carbon technologies for the sector.
- *Transportation*: Reinforcing fuel taxes with feebates (for example, integrated into car registration taxes) or performance standards (where administratively feasible for vehicle sellers) promotes more mitigation responses than electric vehicle subsidies and avoid fiscal costs. Ultimately, kilometer-based taxes will be needed to replace revenues from fuel taxes.
- *Buildings*: Incentives for electric heat pumps, insulation upgrades, and rooftop solar might be financed through residential fuel taxes, whereas feebates (linked to energy performance ratings) might be integrated into property tax systems. Performance standards or feebates can also promote energy-efficient household appliances.
- *Forestry*: Nationwide pricing systems penalizing deforestation and rewarding carbon sequestration are ultimately needed but have substantial capacity requirements (for land rights and monitoring emissions). Interim possibilities might include incentives for conservation projects (possibly with funds redirected from farm programs) and taxes on forest products (with rebates for sustainably produced commodities).

- *Agriculture*: For the livestock sector, farmers could be taxed based on self-assessed emissions (linked to farm characteristics) or production taxes could be levied at processor level using default emissions factors for different meat products (with side payments for certified, low emissions-intensity farmers).
- *Extractives*: Methane fees could be integrated into existing business tax regimes based on emissions reporting requirements for firms, or default emissions factors and production levels but allowing low-carbon firms to petition for tax rebates. Alternatively, feebates or performance standards have a role where producers are concerned about competitiveness.
- *Waste*: Emissions pricing is less compelling for the waste sector (due to the limited range of mitigation responses)—instead, regulations can be used to control methane leaks from landfills and perhaps separate organic waste prior to landfill disposal.

Chapter 5. *Using models to quantify, and understand the underlying determinants of, emissions projections and the wide-ranging effects of mitigation policy options is an essential step.*

There is a huge range of models that are used to project emissions and assess the effects of mitigation policies. The IMF and World Bank CPAT model is, however, unique in its coverage of all IMF member countries, comprehensive evaluation of a wide range of mitigation policy instruments against a diverse range of metrics of concern to policymakers, neutral assumptions parameterized to the midrange of results from the broader modeling and empirical literatures, and transparency in terms of how the model works. For example, emissions projections in the model depend on assumptions about GDP growth, the responsiveness of energy demand to income, trend rates of technological progress, and planned investments in the power generation sector. And the emissions effect of CO_2 mitigation policies depends on how they (explicitly or implicitly) affect fuel prices, the price responsiveness of fuel use, and the emissions intensity of electricity. Complementary IMF models (IMF-ENV and GMMET) provide more detail on sectoral investment employment, as well as inflation and other macroeconomic effects.

Some illustrative results from the models, across G20 countries, include the following:

- Carbon pricing has, by far, the largest effect on coal prices, increasing them on average by 100 percent for a \$50 per ton carbon price, intermediate effects on natural gas prices (about 40 percent on average for a \$50 carbon price), and more modest effects on electricity and gasoline prices (about 20 and 15 percent on average, respectively).
- A \$50 carbon price would cut CO_2 emissions by about 10–30 percent below baseline levels in 2030 in most G20 countries.
- Mitigation costs (gross of domestic or global environmental benefits) rise disproportionately with the level of abatement, and vary across countries but are generally manageable, for example, about 0.05 to 0.3 percent of GDP across G20 countries for a 20 percent reduction in CO_2 emissions below baseline levels in 2030 and 0.3–0.9 percent for a 30 percent reduction.

- Potential revenues from carbon pricing are about 0.5 to 1.5 percent of GDP a year across most G20 countries in the near term (though over 2 percent in some cases). Using revenues productively (for example, to reduce tax wedges in factor markets or fund investments for Sustainable Development Goals) can significantly lower the overall costs of carbon pricing.
- Although it may not be feasible to accurately pin down GDP effects of mitigation policies (given the difficulty of accounting for all the potentially relevant factors such as the state of the business cycle and labor market frictions), studies nonetheless suggest effects are generally modest and could be positive or negative, though effects are sensitive to how revenues are recycled.
- Feebates and tradable performance standards for the power generation and vehicle sectors have about 60–90 percent of the effectiveness of pure carbon pricing depending on the country and sector, whereas policies targeted at renewables and electric vehicles tend to have significantly less effectiveness.
- A price equivalent to $70 per ton of CO_2 cuts methane emissions from extractives and agriculture by half and one-quarter, respectively, in 2030. In countries with large forestry emissions, full enforcement of deforestation laws and pricing of emissions from forestry at $100 per ton can reduce emissions by three gigatons (about 6 percent of global GHG emissions).

Chapter 6. *Another step is to choose additional measures to enhance the acceptability of the mitigation strategy, especially the burdens on vulnerable households and firms. This involves use of input–output tables and household surveys (which are integrated into the CPAT model for about 100 countries) to measure the effect of mitigation policies on different groups and a conceptual understanding of alternative measures for ameliorating these effects.*

Carbon pricing tends to impose a burden on low-income households (relative to their consumption) that is similar to or moderately higher than that for wealthier households. To maintain anti-poverty objectives, low-income deciles might be compensated through income support, which typically requires about 15 percent of carbon pricing revenues and leaves the bulk of revenues for general uses (for example, broad tax reductions or public investments) that provide an offsetting boost to the economy and garners political support. Where higher energy prices are still unacceptable politically, feebates and tradable performance may be reasonable alternatives given their smaller effects on energy prices, though they generate no revenues for household recycling.

Carbon pricing moderately (for example, steel) or substantially (for example, cement) increases production costs for energy-intensive industries (principally from charges on their unabated emissions) and it can be difficult, due to international competition, for domestic firms to pass forward most of this cost increase in higher consumer prices. A simple model of trade between countries and their main partners, integrated into the CPAT model, provides estimates of the resulting effects on production and emissions leakage by country and industry. These effects might be addressed through nontrade measures that keep carbon pricing revenues within the industrial sector or use of mitigation instruments (feebates and performance standards) with smaller effects on production costs. Border carbon adjustments are potentially the most robust instrument for addressing competitiveness and leakage under carbon pricing but need careful design to address administrative, legal, and international equity concerns. For agriculture, border adjustments would be more administratively challenging—competitiveness concerns might be addressed through recycling revenues from emissions fees in a subsidy per kilogram of farm output or using feebates.

Chapter 7. *Policymakers also need to consider additional elements in the mitigation strategy that might complement and bolster the environmental effectiveness of mitigation policies, though the appropriateness of these measures varies by country.*

Although there are large investment needs for low-carbon energy transitions, it is efficient to mobilize most of this investment through private markets through explicit or implicit carbon price signals. There is some role for public investment, such as providing infrastructure networks (for example, to enable renewables and electric vehicles), though annualized investment needs can be modest (relative to potential revenues from carbon pricing) and could be financed through user fees at the sectoral level. Supplementary incentives to advance low-carbon technologies may also be needed such as support for basic and applied research (in advanced and large emerging market economies) and deployment incentives, energy efficiency awareness programs, contracts to guarantee carbon pricing, and financing mechanisms to overcome household borrowing constraints. Policymakers may also wish to encourage domestic production of emerging, low-carbon technologies, though ideally instruments would limit trade tensions, fiscal costs, and promote domestic consumption.

Additional measures may also be needed where energy markets are dominated by state-owned enterprises, such as performance standards (to force emissions reductions) and shadow carbon pricing (to guide cost-effective investments). Supportive measures can also lubricate funding from financial markets in response to carbon price signals, such as reporting of firms' carbon footprints, market frameworks for green bonds, and loan guarantees. And the main challenge for energy exporters is to craft comprehensive strategies for transitioning away from dependence on revenues from fuel extraction, rather than perhaps levying carbon taxes on exports or ramping up domestic production.

Chapter 8. *Policymakers also need to understand the implications of the broader environmental costs of fossil fuel use, like local air pollution and side effects of vehicle use, for evaluating climate policies, fuel price reform, and complementary measures.*

Broader environmental effects from fossil fuel use are most efficiently addressed through fine-tuned instruments, such as (direct or proxy) emissions fees for local air pollution or per kilometer tolls on busy roads for traffic congestion. Although their administrative practicality has improved, these policies have yet to be comprehensively implemented—for the interim, it is economically efficient to reflect the full range of (climate and domestic) environmental costs in fuel prices. CPAT provides estimates of the fuel prices to do this by product and sector for most countries, as well as the environmental, fiscal, and economic benefits from price reform, which can be quite large. In the absence of energy price reform, moving ahead with climate mitigation can generate domestic environmental benefits that, up to a point, outweigh the mitigation costs for many countries, so they are better off before even counting climate benefits—indeed there is some scope for factoring local air pollution into feebates or tradable performance standards designed for carbon emissions.

Chapter 9. *A final step is to understand, and constructively contribute to, international dialogue on meeting global temperature goals.*

Global emissions can be aligned with a pathway for limiting global warming to 2°C, with manageable mitigation costs (about 0.5 percent of global GDP) and burdens equitably distributed across advanced and developing countries. A supplementary international policy coordination mechanism is likely needed, however, given obstacles under the Paris Agreement to negotiating greater ambition (because of the large number of parties) and to implementing strong domestic mitigation policies (when countries act unilaterally). The mechanism would need to focus on a limited number of negotiators (large emitters and representatives of country blocs), concrete policy actions, requirements differentiated by development level, and assistance for low-income participants. One possibility is a carbon price floor requirement, which could substantially scale up global mitigation, even with only a handful of key participants. A regional coordination mechanism (for example, among Asian countries moving ahead with carbon pricing schemes) may be more realistic for the nearer term and could be a first step to a broader international agreement.

Pricing schemes will also be needed to decarbonize the international aviation and maritime sectors (to close cost gaps for zero emissions fuels) and, in the case of maritime, need to be globally applied (given the mobility of the tax base)—programs are administratively practical and could mobilize valuable revenues for climate finance. A supplementary global agreement could also be applied to methane emissions from the extractives sector, a natural platform being signatories to the Global Methane Pledge (which seeks to cut global methane emissions by 30 percent by 2030). Advanced and developing countries need to jointly achieve commitments on international climate finance, where the latter have a key role in establishing the carbon price signals for leveraging private investment flows. International cooperation over critical technologies could focus on scaling up public and private research, robust cross-border patenting, lowering trade barriers, preventing market fragmentation for critical minerals, and appropriate governance for geoengineering.

Chapter 10. *The volume concludes by dispelling 50 common myths about climate mitigation using some of the main messages from the volume.*

A Call to Action

The window of opportunity for containing global warming to target levels enshrined in the Paris Agreement is closing rapidly. Although some countries (for example, in Europe) have been in the vanguard, action is falling well short—global emissions are yet to peak, let alone fall rapidly (Figure 1.1). As discussed in this volume, policymakers have the toolkits, in terms of policy elements and supportive modeling, needed for crafting comprehensive mitigation strategies. Careful design is, however, required to effectively reduce emissions from all key sectors, avoid unnecessary costs on the economy or the government budget, address political sensitivities, and limit administrative burdens.

Dynamic political leadership is also needed. Governments can act unilaterally, not least as aggressive action by one leader can often catalyze similar actions in other countries, though policy coordination among governments also has a critical and necessary role in speeding up net zero emissions transitions. We hope this volume provides policymakers with a toolkit which can help them operationalize and coordinate mitigation strategies and scale them up in line with global mitigation needs.

Notes

1 CPAT is available upon request to country authorities.
2 Much of this work has been published in books, reports, and papers. See, for example, Parry, de Mooij, and Keen (2012), Parry, Morris, and Williams (2015), Parry et al. (2014), IMF (2019a, 2019b), and the summary of over 30 other IMF staff publications in Black and others (2023), Table A.IV.1. For related discussion, see Hyman (2023).
3 Adaptation to climate change is beyond the scope (for some discussion, see Aligishiev, Bellon, and Massetti 2022; Bellon and Massetti 2022a, 2022b).

References

Aligishiev, Zamid, Matthieu Bellon, and Emanuele Massetti. 2022. "Macro-Fiscal Implications of Adaptation to Climate Change." IMF Staff Climate Note 2022/02, International Monetary Fund, Washington, DC.

Bellon, Matthieu, and Emanuele Massetti. 2022a. "Economic Principles for Integrating Adaptation to Climate Change into Fiscal Policy." IMF Staff Climate Note 2022/01, International Monetary Fund, Washington, DC.

Bellon, Matthieu, and Emanuele Massetti. 2022b. "Planning and Mainstreaming Adaptation to Climate Change in Fiscal Policy." IMF Staff Climate Note 2022/03, International Monetary Fund, Washington, DC.

Black, Simon, Dora Benedek, Ian Parry, Nate Vernon-Lin, and Sunalika Singh. 2025. "Cutting Emissions, Securing Energy: A Macroeconomic Assessment for COP30." Working paper 25/245, International Monetary Fund, Washington, DC.

Black, Simon, Ian Parry, Victor Mylonas, Nate Vernon, and Karlygash Zhunussova. 2023. "The IMF-World Bank Climate Policy Assessment Tool (CPAT): A Model to Help Countries Mitigate Climate Change." IMF Working Paper 23/128, International Monetary Fund, Washington, DC.

Hyman, Andrew (ed.), 2023. *Mitigation Strategies for Climate Change*. New York, NY: Syrawood Publishing House.

International Monetary Fund (IMF). 2019a. *Fiscal Monitor—How to Mitigate Climate Change*. Washington, DC.

International Monetary Fund (IMF). 2019b. "Fiscal Policies for Paris Climate Strategies—From Principle to Practice." Board Paper, Washington, DC.

Parry, Ian, Ruud de Mooij, and Michael Keen. 2012. *Fiscal Policy to Mitigate Climate Change: A Guide for Policymakers*. Washington, DC: IMF.

Parry, Ian, Dirk Heine, Shanjun Li, and Eliza Lis. 2014. *Getting Energy Prices Right: From Principle to Practice*. Washington, DC: IMF.

Parry, Ian, Adele Morris, and Roberton Williams. 2015. *Implementing a US Carbon Tax: Challenges and Debates*. London, UK: Routledge.

2 A Quick Primer on Climate Change

Main Messages

- Without mitigation action, atmospheric greenhouse gas (GHG) concentrations are projected to double preindustrial levels by around mid-century, irreversibly raising global average temperatures by a predicted 2.3°C above preindustrial levels—warming predictions are, however, subject to significant uncertainties because of risks of poorly understood feedback effects in the climate system.
- Human-induced GHG emissions have so far warmed average planetary temperatures by an estimated 1.2°C.
- CO_2 emissions (mostly from fossil fuels) are the most important GHG but substantially cutting methane emissions (which have much shorter atmospheric lifespans) could yield a one-off cooling in global temperatures.
- Developed and developing countries have a key role in global mitigation efforts. Developing countries account for 70 percent of projected baseline global emissions in 2030 (and more than half of historical emissions), whereas developed countries tend to have higher current and historical per capita emissions.
- Warming is increasing the frequency and intensity of climate damages and risks such as heat waves, shifting precipitation, droughts, wildfires, floods, and hurricanes. Higher CO_2 concentrations are also significantly harming marine life, notably through ocean acidification.
- Risks of crossing tipping point thresholds in the global climate system include, for example, runaway warming because of release of CO_2 and methane from thawing permafrost, collapse of major ice sheets, changes in ocean circulation, and forest dieback. Crossing such thresholds could have dire consequences for human and other life.

DOI: 10.4324/9781003755012-2
This chapter has been made available under a CC-BY-NC-ND license.

- Parties to the Paris Agreement have submitted national emissions targets in their Nationally Determined Contributions (NDCs). Although these targets are intended to be increased in terms of stringency, achieving them would only cut global GHG emissions by 12 percent by 2030 relative to 2019 levels, half of that needed to be on track even with 2°C.
- Parties to the Paris Agreement have variably pledged to achieve net zero emissions by around mid-century (from 2035 at the earliest to 2070 at the latest). However, these long-term targets should not detract from the urgent necessity for strong mitigation action in the near term to achieve temperature goals.

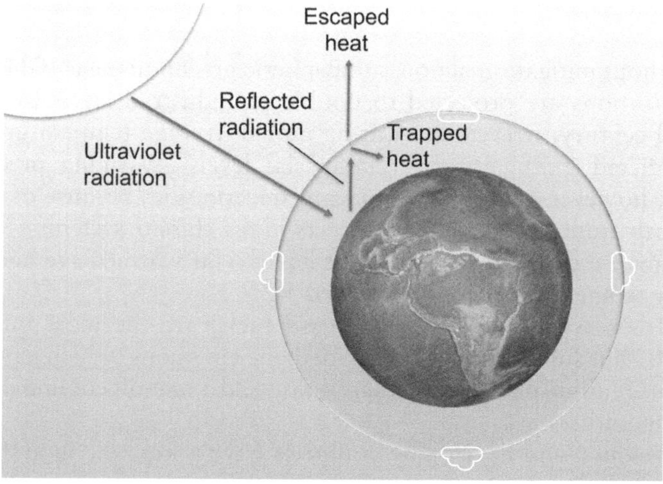

Figure 2.1 Simple Representation of the Greenhouse Effect.

Source: Authors.

Science

What Is the Greenhouse Effect?

The greenhouse effect refers to the trapping and buildup of heat in the atmosphere that warms the Earth's temperature. About 70 percent of incoming solar energy is absorbed by the Earth with 30 percent deflected back toward space, mainly by clouds and ice. Some of the heat flowing back from the Earth's surface is absorbed by GHGs in the atmosphere and then reradiated back toward the Earth's surface (see Figure 2.1).

Most GHGs occur naturally in the Earth's atmosphere, raising the Earth's average surface temperature to about 15°C. Without this natural greenhouse effect, all the heat emitted by the Earth would pass outward into space and the Earth would have an average temperature of about –20°C. The atmospheric concentration of heat-trapping gases is rising, however, because of human activities, which is causing global temperatures to increase.

How Have Global GHG Emissions and Concentrations Changed Over Time and How Might They Change in Future?

Carbon dioxide (CO_2) is by far the most important GHG, and global emissions of this gas have increased dramatically over time. They tripled from 2 billion tons in 1900 to 6 billion tons in 1950, tripled again to 20 billion tons in 1980, and since then have doubled to current levels of about 40 billion tons. In the absence of mitigation policies, global CO_2 emissions are projected to keep rising, albeit more slowly than in recent decades. See Figure 2.2, panel 1 and Chapter 5 for factors underlying emissions projections.

At the same time, the atmospheric concentration of CO_2 has risen 50 percent from about 280 parts (of CO_2) per million (ppm) molecules in 1750 to 420 ppm in 2024—in the past two decades alone concentrations have increased 10 percent.[1] Accounting for other GHGs, the concentration in CO_2 equivalents (see the following section) is about 470 ppm. Without new, or tightening of existing, mitigation policies, CO_2 concentrations alone are projected to reach 550 ppm—that is, about double preindustrial levels—around mid-century. See Figure 2.2, panel 2.

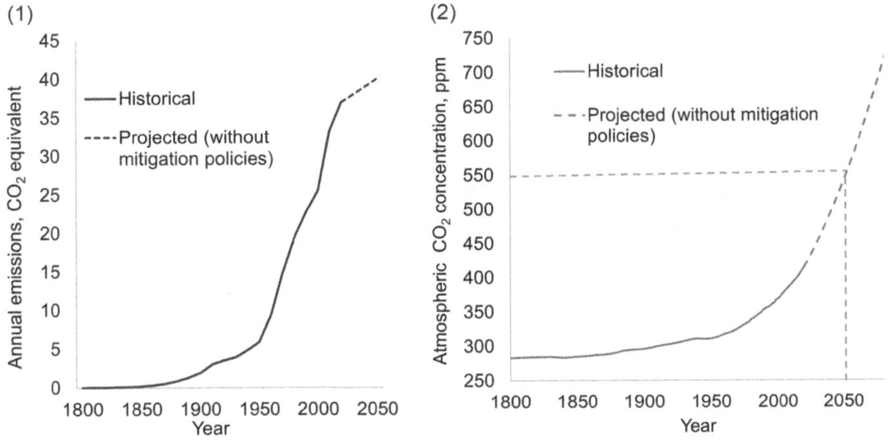

Figure 2.2 Trends in Global CO_2 Emissions and Atmospheric Concentrations. Panel 1. Emissions,[a] Panel 2. Concentrations[b]

Sources: [a]Historical from https://www.statista.com/statistics/264699/worldwide-co2-emissions and projected from authors' modeling (see Chapter 5). [b]IPCC (2022a), scenario Shared Socioeconomic Pathway (SSP) 3–7.0, which corresponds to a case with no additional mitigation policies.

How Much Warming Has Occurred to Date and Is It Human-Made?

Global mean surface temperatures increased (see Figure 2.3) by 1.2°C between 1900 and 2020 (temperatures in 1900 were essentially the same as in preindustrial times). Temperatures increased by 0.5°C between 1900 and 1945, fell back slightly after that (perhaps due to the counteracting offsetting effect of higher atmospheric concentrations of particulates, mainly from fuel combustion, which can reflect incoming sunlight). However, temperatures have increased steadily since then and were 1.3°C higher in 2024 than in 1880. The decade between 2015 and 2024 was the warmest since modern recordkeeping began in 1880 (when weather stations were first emerging around the world).

Temperature trends across the globe are not uniform because of diverse geography. For example, the Arctic is heating up about twice as quickly as the global average in part because melting ice lowers the amount of the sun's energy reflected back into space. In addition, warming is faster in continental

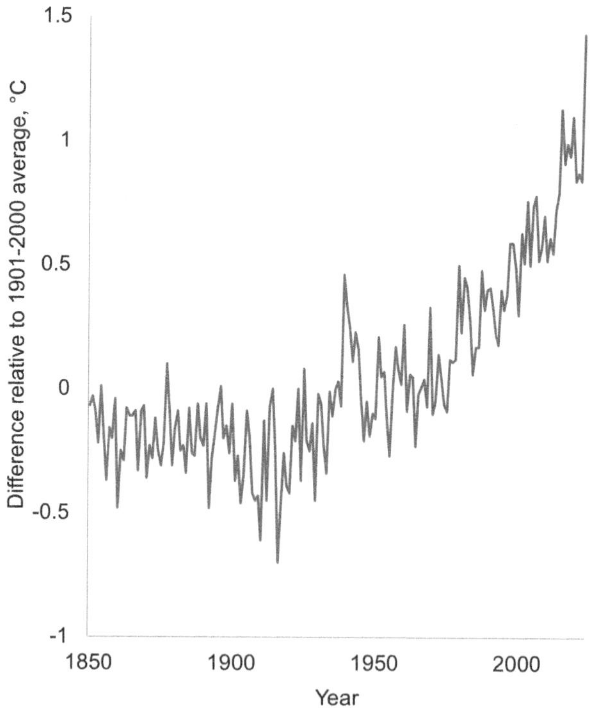

Figure 2.3 Global Average Surface Temperature Trends since 1850.

Source: NOAA (2025).

Note: Figure shows surface temperatures averaged over the globe for the year based on temperature measurements from thousands of weather stations, ship- and buoy-based observations of sea surface temperatures, and temperature measurements from Antarctic research stations. Ground-based temperature measurements are validated with satellite data.

interiors (where soil drying leads to less cooling from evaporation) and slower in coastal regions (because it takes much more heat to warm water than air and land).

Many factors affect the average global temperature in any given year,[2] but the long-term global warming trend largely reflects rising atmospheric GHG concentrations. Other factors explain little of the trend, for example (GCRP 2017, Chapter 2):

- *Solar radiation*: Scientists have measured slight fluctuations in the amount of energy released by the sun over the past few decades and find that they cannot explain long-term warming trends.
- *Volcanic activity*: This activity puts particles into the stratosphere, which deflects incoming sunlight and cools local temperature—a decline in volcanic activity could therefore increase temperatures. Most volcanic particles, however, fall rapidly to earth (within several weeks), so there is little effect on long-term global warming trends.
- *Urban heat island effect*: This refers to local warming from replacing natural land cover with concentrations of pavement and buildings that absorb and retain heat. This effect, however, does not significantly impact overall global warming because scientists adjust for it when measuring global temperature trends.

How Much Warming Is Projected in the Absence of Climate Mitigation Policies?

The Intergovernmental Panel on Climate Change (IPCC) projects that if atmospheric GHG concentrations were stabilized at 450, 550, and 650 ppm of CO_2 equivalent, mean projected warming over preindustrial levels would be 1.6°C, 2.3°C, and 2.9°C, respectively. But there is uncertainty surrounding these projections because the net effect of various feedback mechanisms in the climate system is uncertain.[3] The likely warming range, with 95 percent confidence, for 550 ppm CO_2 equivalent stabilization is estimated at 1.9–2.9°C (leaving aside extreme scenarios). See Figure 2.4. The climate system mostly adjusts to a given increase in atmospheric GHG concentrations within about 10 years (Ricke and Caldeira 2014).

Previous experience suggests that temperature changes of the magnitude projected over this century are associated with radically different climates. For example, at the peak of the past Ice Age 20,000 years ago when global temperatures were only 5°C cooler than temperatures in 1900, glaciers covered a quarter of the Earth's land area, and the global sea level was more than 120 meters lower than today (USGS 2023). Moreover, the rate of projected temperature changes over this century is unprecedented. Over the past 10,000 years, temperatures have only changed by about 0.5°C, providing a stable environment for the natural world and human development. In contrast, without policy action, temperatures are projected to rise by about 0.5°C each decade to 2050.

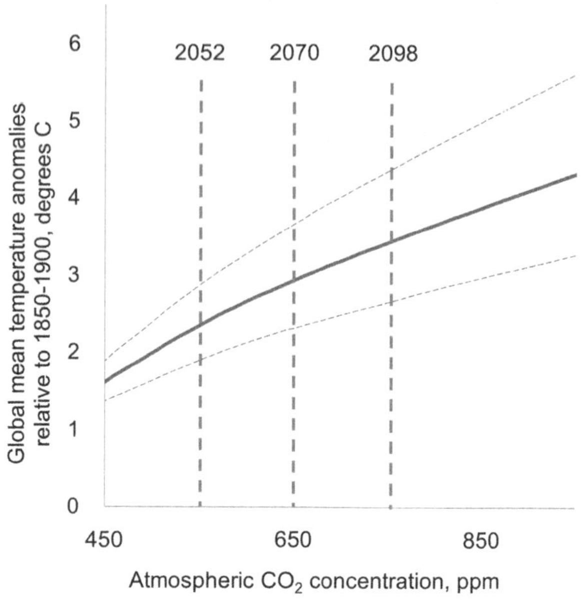

Figure 2.4 Relation between Atmospheric CO_2 Concentrations and Equilibrium Temperature Increases

Source: IPCC (2022a).

Note: The solid and dashed curves indicate the mean projection and 95 percent confidence interval, respectively. Leaving aside extreme warming scenarios, warming is projected to be a logarithmic function of atmospheric concentrations, implying each doubling of concentrations increases warming by the same amount. The vertical dashed lines indicate projected years when higher concentration levels are reached.

Emissions Sources

What Are the Main GHGs Causing Global Warming?

Different GHGs can be compared using global warming potentials (GWPs), which refer to the cumulative change in warming over time caused by an extra ton of the gas relative to a ton of CO_2—usually GWPs are estimated over 100-year time periods. In 2023, global (non-land use) GHG emissions were 52.5 billion tons with CO_2 accounting for 74 percent of the total, methane 18 percent, nitrous oxide 5 percent, and other gases—mostly hydrofluorocarbons (HFCs)—3 percent (Figure 2.5, panel 1).

- CO_2: About half of human-induced CO_2 releases are absorbed by the oceans and biosphere, while the remainder enters the atmosphere. CO_2 is removed from the atmosphere by absorption from the oceans and terrestrial sinks but only very gradually—its atmospheric life is about 300 to 1,000 years (and even this very gradual uptake could decline in future as oceans warm and become more saturated with CO_2). Cutting CO_2 emissions slows the rate of accumulation of the atmospheric stock of CO_2, but (due to its very long atmospheric residence time) does not reduce the stock, and therefore slows temperature rises but does not reduce temperatures.

- *Methane*: Despite its relatively short atmospheric lifespan, about 12 years, methane has a high GWP of 30 or 85 over 100 and 20 years, respectively, because it is far more effective at trapping heat radiated from the Earth than a ton of CO_2.[4] Unlike for CO_2, substantially reducing methane emissions can reduce its atmospheric concentration (because of its short residence time) and thereby lower temperatures and limit the risk of tipping points. For example, cutting methane emissions by half over the next decade could cut global temperatures in 2040 by up to 0.3°C (see Dreyfus et al. 2022, IGSD 2022a, 2022b).
- *Nitrous oxide*: This GHG has an expected atmospheric lifespan of 120 years and is also highly effective at trapping heat—it has a GWP over 100 years of about 270.
- *HFCs*: Like methane, HFCs have a relatively short atmospheric lifespan (15 years) but are highly effective at trapping heat—their GWP over 100 years is 15,000.

Figure 2.5, panel 2 summarizes lifespans and GWPs of different GHGs.

(1)

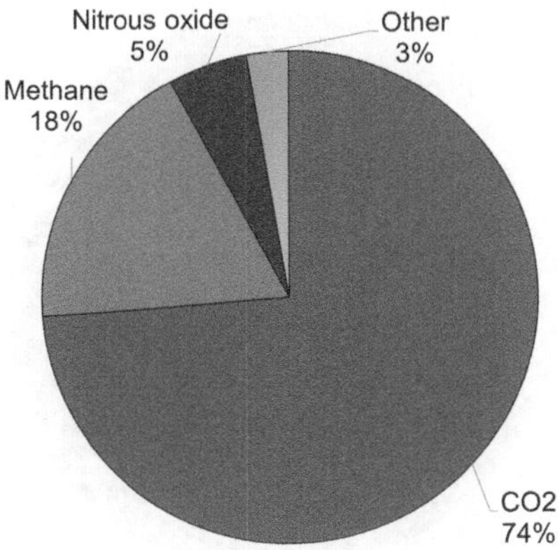

(2)

Gas	Atmospheric lifespan, years	GWP, CO_2 equivalent	
		20 years	100 years
CO_2	300-1,000	1	1
Methane	12	81-83	27-30
Nitrous oxide	120	783	273
Hydrofluoro-carbons	15	43,000	15,000

Figure 2.5 Contribution of Different Gases to CO_2 Equivalent GHG Emissions. Panel 1. Share of Global GHG Emissions by Gas, 2023.[a]* Panel 2. Lifespan and GWP by Gas[b]†

Sources: [a]See Chapter 5. [b]USEPA (2024) and author's extrapolations.

Note: *Other includes (most importantly) hydrofluorocarbons and (less importantly) perfluorocarbons and sulfur hexafluoride. Gases are compared using GWPs over 100 years. †The GWP of a gas is the cumulative change in warming over time caused by an extra ton of the gas relative to a ton of CO_2.

Which Sectors and Fuels Contribute Most to GHG Emissions?

By sector, power generation contributed the most, 32 percent, to global GHG emissions in 2023, and industry accounted for 22 percent, with about two-thirds from fuel combustion and one-third from processes (like conversion of limestone into cement). Transport was the next largest contributor (14 percent), followed by agriculture (13 percent, mostly methane and nitrous oxide), extractives (7 percent from methane), buildings (7 percent), and waste (4 percent, also from methane). By fossil fuel in 2022, coal contributed the most to global CO_2 emissions (41 percent), followed by oil (29 percent) and gas (21 percent). See Figure 2.6, panels 1 and 2. Land use, land-use change and forestry contributed an additional 3.5–4.5 billion tons of CO_2 in 2023, or 7–10 percent of total GHG emissions—these emissions are often excluded from global totals due in part to uncertainties in measuring them (see Chapter 4).

What Activities Cause the Emissions from Each Sector?

Table 2.1 summarizes the main sources of GHGs by sector. In the power, industry, transport, and building sectors, CO_2 emissions are produced from fossil fuel combustion—for example, coal and natural gas, and to some extent oil, may be used in electricity generation and industrial heating, gasoline and diesel are used in transportation, while oil, gas, and biomass may be used for heating buildings.

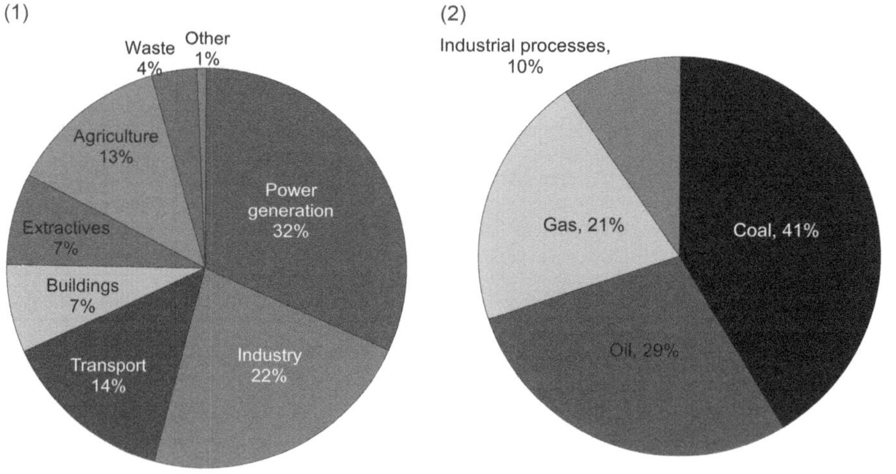

Figure 2.6 Sources of Global (Non-land Use) GHGs and CO_2. Panel 1. GHGs by Sector (2023).[a*] Panel 2. CO_2 by Fuel (2022)[b†]

Sources: [a]GHGs by Sector: IMF Climate Indicators Dashboard (2023); [b]CO_2 by Fuel: IMF Staff Calculation using CPAT (2025).

Note: *In left panel, industry includes CO_2 emissions from fuel combustion (13 percent) and processes (10 percent). Emissions embodied in electricity consumption in buildings and industry are attributed to power generation. †Right panel excludes CO_2 from forestry.

Table 2.1 Causes of Emissions: Main Examples by Sector and Gas

Gas	*Sector*							
	Power	*Industry*	*Transport*	*Buildings*	*Agriculture*	*Forestry*	*Extractives*	*Waste*
CO_2	Coal, gas, oil combustion	Coal, gas, oil combustion; processes (e.g., for cement)	Gasoline, diesel combustion	Oil, gas, biofuel combustion for heating, cooking	Rice paddies, land clearance for crops	Deforestation, degradation (e.g., from fires, disease, illegal logging)	Gas flaring at mines/wells	Waste incineration
Methane	ns	ns	ns	ns	Enteric fermentation, manure storage	ns	Methane venting at mines/wells, leaks from gas infrastructure	Leaks from landfills, wastewater systems
Nitrous oxide	ns	ns	ns	ns	Manure storage; soil tilling	ns	ns	ns

Source: Authors.

Note: ns = not significant.

In the agricultural sector, methane emissions are released from enteric fermentation (digestive processes in cows and sheep) and manure storage contributes to both methane and nitrous oxide emissions—rice paddies and soil tilling also contribute to emissions. In the extractives sector, methane is released from venting (in coal mines and oil wells) and leaks, whereas CO_2 is released when methane is flared (though by reducing methane on net this reduces CO_2 equivalent emissions). Deforestation (clearing of forestland for other uses like farming and urban development) is the main cause of CO_2 releases from the forest sector, though forest degradation (from fires, disease, illegal logging) also contributes. Chapter 4 elaborates on options for reducing the various emissions sources from different sectors.

How Does Emissions Intensity for Fossil Fuels Vary Across Countries and Products?

CO_2 emissions factors per unit of energy, or gigajoule (GJ), for a given fuel product vary very little across countries. But by fuel product, emissions factors per unit of energy are about 25–30 percent lower for gasoline and diesel than for coal and about 30–40 percent lower for natural gas and liquefied petroleum gas than for coal. For road fuels, CO_2 emissions per liter or gallon are about 12 percent higher for diesel than for gasoline. See Table 2.2.

In addition, baseline prices per GJ are lowest for coal and highest for road fuels (see Chapter 5). For both reasons (higher emissions factors and lower baseline prices), pricing CO_2 emissions has a much larger proportionate effect on coal prices than road fuel prices, with natural gas an intermediate case.

Table 2.2 CO_2 Emissions Factors for Fuel Products

Fuel Product	*Unit*	*Tonnes CO_2/Unit*
Coal	GJ	0.096
Natural Gas	GJ	0.056
	1,000 cubic feet	0.053
Liquefied Petroleum Gas	GJ	0.069
	1,000 cubic feet	0.069
Gasoline	GJ	0.068
	liter	0.0024
	gallon	0.0090
Diesel	GJ	0.072
	liter	0.0027
	gallon	0.0102

Source: Authors' modeling (see Chapter 5).

Note: Figures are averages across countries. For coal, emissions factors per ton of output vary significantly with coal type (lignite, anthracite, bitumen, sub-bitumen) but only moderately per unit of energy. For road fuels, emissions factors account for biofuel blending. Figures do not account for upstream methane leaks and CO_2 from flaring. GJ = gigajoule.

Which Country Groups Are Most Responsible for Historical and Future Emissions?

Historically, high-income countries accounted for the majority of annual and cumulative global CO_2 emissions, but this pattern has changed markedly over time, with rapid emissions growth among middle-income countries (like China) and low-income countries (like India), and these trends are set to continue.[5] For example, high-income countries accounted for 57 percent of annual global CO_2 emissions and 62 percent of historical emissions as of 1990, but by 2020 their share in annual emissions had dropped to 36 percent and in cumulative emissions to 50 percent. Under baseline projections (with no change to current mitigation policies), middle- and low-income countries combined account for almost 68 percent of annual global CO_2 emissions in 2030 and 55 percent of cumulative emissions and therefore have a critical role (along with advanced economies) in future global mitigation efforts (see Figure 2.7).

What Countries Contribute the Most to GHGs?

As of 2023, China was the largest emitter of (non-land use) GHGs, contributing 31.5 percent to the global total, followed by the United States (12.3 percent), India (8 percent), Russia (4.4 percent), Brazil, Indonesia, Japan, and Iran (each with global shares of 1.9–2.5 percent). The top 10 and 25 emitters collectively accounted for 67.5 and 81.8 percent of global GHGs. CO_2 accounts for about 70–90 percent of GHGs in most cases, but there are some countries with relatively large agricultural and extractive emissions where non-CO_2 GHGs are about 50 percent or more of their total emissions (Argentina, Brazil, Nigeria, and Pakistan). See Figure 2.8.

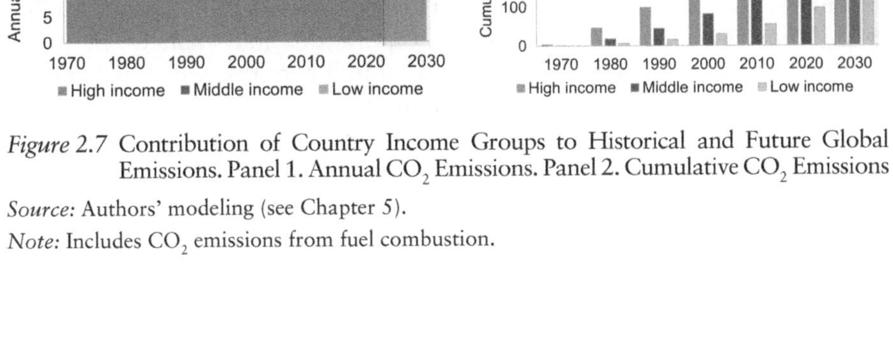

Figure 2.7 Contribution of Country Income Groups to Historical and Future Global Emissions. Panel 1. Annual CO_2 Emissions. Panel 2. Cumulative CO_2 Emissions

Source: Authors' modeling (see Chapter 5).

Note: Includes CO_2 emissions from fuel combustion.

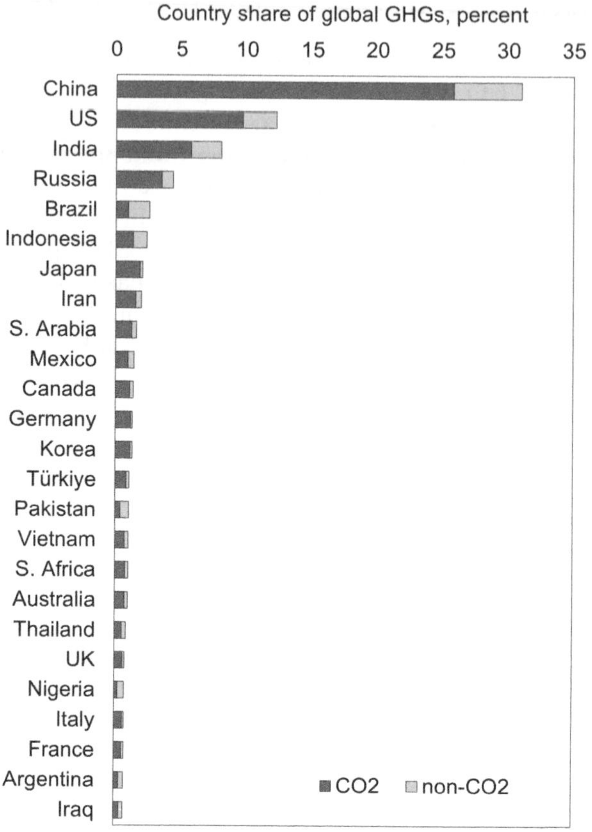

Figure 2.8 Top 25 GHG Emitters, 2023

Source: IMF Staff calculations using Climate Policy Assessment Tool.

Impacts of Climate Change

What Are Some Climatic and Other Impacts of Rising GHG Concentrations?

These include the following:

- *Heat waves*—Higher temperatures can contribute to the frequency and intensity of heat waves by increasing the chances of very hot days and nights.
- *Shifting precipitation*—Increasing evaporation and changes in atmospheric circulation are altering global rainfall patterns, which puts at risk water systems, agriculture, and ecosystems.
- *Droughts*—Risks increase because warming enhances evaporation, which reduces surface water and dries soils and vegetation, making periods with low precipitation even drier.

- *Wildfires*—Greater evaporation on land also creates conditions more prone to wildfires and a longer wildfire season.
- *Floods*—Climate change results in more intense rainfall (warmer air can hold 7 percent more moisture for every 1°C of warming), which increases risks of flooding.
- *Hurricanes*—Warmer sea surface temperatures intensify tropical storm wind speeds, giving them the potential to deliver more damage when they make landfall.
- *Ocean acidification*—Rising atmospheric CO_2 concentrations have caused oceans to become more acidic, which disrupts ocean ecosystems by increasing the rate at which shells of marine life (like corals, clams, oysters) are dissolved.

The severity of all these impacts is projected to rise as the planet continues to warm, not least because higher temperatures increase energy and water vapor in the atmosphere, making weather systems more intense.

What Are the Impacts of Warming on Sea Levels?

Global warming is also causing global mean sea level to rise due to the melting of land-based ice sheets, especially in Antarctica and Greenland,[6] and thermal expansion (as oceans warm, they increase in volume). Projections of future global mean sea level rises are uncertain, varying between about 0.40 and 0.7 meters by late this century if warming reaches 2°C and by 0.6–0.9 meters with 4°C of warming (Fox-Kemper, Hewitt, and Xiao 2021).

For many countries, this gradual sea level rise should be manageable, with investments in sea walls, levees, and flood barriers for valuable coastal areas and withdrawal from other areas prone to inundation. Indeed, with forward-looking adaptation, one study suggests annual costs of sea level rises could be reduced to less than 0.1 percent of GDP (Depsky et al. 2023). Coastal countries (like Bangladesh, Cambodia, China, Egypt, Guyana, Mauritania, Suriname, Thailand, and Vietnam) are highly vulnerable however and risks are existential for many small island states that are no higher than a few meters above sea level. Moreover, sea level rises could be dramatically larger under more extreme scenarios for ice sheet collapses, potentially approaching 2 meters by 2100.

What Are the Risks of Tipping Points in the Climate System?

Tipping points refer to risks of crossing thresholds in the Earth's climate system beyond which abrupt (or nonlinear) changes occur. These risks are not well understood but likely rise exponentially with warming above 1.5°C.[7] Examples include the following (see Table 2.3 for further explanation):

Table 2.3 The Nature of Climate Tipping Points

Risk	*Explanation of Tipping Point*
Permafrost Thawing	Permafrost is a layer of frozen sub-surface soil across a quarter of the Northern hemisphere's land, in Arctic and sub-Arctic regions of Alaska, Russia, and Canada. It preserves organic matter that could decay as global warming causes soils to thaw, thereby releasing more CO_2 and methane.
Collapse of Major Ice Sheets	Warming causes ice sheets to melt, thereby lowering their elevation—temperatures increase with lower elevation so a smaller ice sheet will be warmer at the top. Melting also exposes darker ice underneath which absorbs more solar radiation. Both processes could become self-reinforcing leading to unstoppable melting.
Ocean Circulation	Warm Atlantic currents from the Gulf of Mexico, including the Gulf Stream, cool and partially evaporate as they approach Greenland causing them to sink and slowly spread back southward, marking the completion of their circuit. As the planet warms and sends freshwater from melting ice into the Atlantic, northern water may no longer be salty enough to sink, potentially slowing down or even stopping and reversing the flow with potentially dramatic impacts on temperatures and precipitation.
Forest Die Back	Unprecedented droughts and longer dry seasons are impacting tree growth in the Amazon (which holds a quarter of global land-based carbon) and killing others causing the release of stored carbon. The process is compounded by deforestation, greater fire risk, and reduced precipitation (with fewer trees to soak up water and breathe it back out). If precipitation patterns change too drastically to support flora and fauna the rainforest could eventually transform into a savannah. Global warming is also causing risks of back-to-back runaway wildfire seasons and increased insect infestations in boreal forest land in North America, Scandinavia, Russia, and China (which holds up to 40 percent of land-based carbon), potentially transforming it into grassland and releasing large amounts of CO_2.
Ocean Acidification	Coral reefs are highly productive at sustaining marine life. Twenty percent of reefs have already been lost due to acidification, warming, water pollution, and other factors, and continued increases in acidification as oceans absorb more CO_2 may kill of 90 percent of warmwater reefs by 2100 even if warming is kept to 1.5°C.

Sources: Cheng and Redfern (2022), IPCC (2018), and UNEP (2021).

- *Permafrost thawing*—Frozen soils below the tundra and forests of Alaska, Canada, and northern Russia contain about four times the amount of carbon emitted over the past 200 years. Permafrost thawing (which is already visible) could turn on an (unstoppable) gas tap of CO_2 and methane, which could have a positive (and possibly drastic) feedback effect on global warming.[8]
- *Collapse of major ice sheets*—Full collapse of the Greenland and West Antarctic ice sheets from feedback effects during ice melting could ultimately add about 7 and 5 meters, respectively, to sea level rises if melting becomes reinforcing and they fully collapsed. Given extremely gradual melting processes, however, these risks are more for the deep future (perhaps two centuries or more).
- *Ocean circulation*—This circulation encompasses a wide-reaching network of currents, including the Gulf Stream, spanning the Atlantic Ocean. If the system were to slow significantly or collapse, it could radically influence temperature and precipitation patterns around the world, for example, lowering temperatures in Europe. Evidence suggests the current is already at its weakest state in more than 1,000 years and conceivably could reach a tipping point by mid-century (IPCC 2018; Caesar et al. 2021).
- *Forest dieback*—The Amazon rainforest creates and relies on its own rainfall for survival. Deforestation, increased drought, and wildfire are threatening this process, risking a dieback that could transform it into dry savanna and release its stored carbon. Boreal forests face similar risks.
- *Ocean acidification*—This refers to an increase in the acidity of oceans over an extended period, caused primarily by uptake of CO_2 from the atmosphere. Ocean acidification creates conditions that eat away at the minerals used by oysters, clams, lobsters, shrimp, coral reefs, and other marine life to build their shells and skeletons.

International Policy Architecture and NDCs

What Are the United Nations Framework Convention on Climate Change (UNFCCC) and the Conference of Parties (COP)?

The *UNFCCC* comprises 196 parties (195 countries plus the European Union [EU]) and was established in 1992 to develop a global agreement to respond to climate change which (after the ineffectiveness of smaller agreements like the 1997 Kyoto Protocol) culminated in the 2015 Paris Agreement. The UNFCCC Secretariat, located in Bonn, Germany, facilitates negotiation.

The *COP* is the decision-making body of the UNFCCC, which meets annually and has regular run-up meetings or "intersessionals." Parties are usually represented by heads of state or foreign or environment ministers at the COPs and negotiating teams at the intersessionals. The COP also has its own Presidency (normally the government of where the COP is hosted), which organizes the COP with the UNFCCC Secretariat but generally takes a neutral negotiating stance. Voting by parties is rare in UNFCCC meetings—the body generally acts when consensus is reached.

Although parties are formally independent, most of them negotiate in blocs to be more influential (see Annex 2.1) though only national delegations can vote.[9]

What Are the Mitigation Objectives of the Paris Agreement?

The central objective of the Paris Agreement is to limit future global warming to "well below" 2°C, and ideally to 1.5°C, relative to preindustrial levels.

The Paris Agreement requires parties to voluntarily submit NDCs outlining targets for mitigation and adaptation as well as strategies for implementing them. Parties are also required to report progress on implementing NDCs every two years and from 2020 onward to submit revised targets, expected to be progressively more stringent, every five years under a five-yearly global stock take (which began in 2023) evaluating global mitigation action and ambition.

On equity grounds, given their disproportionately small contribution to historical emissions, lower per capita income, and generally greater vulnerability to climate change, developing countries are generally expected to cut emissions more slowly than developed countries while receiving financial support from advanced economies for their mitigation and adaptation costs. This is known as the principle of "common but differentiated responsibilities and respective capabilities in the light of national circumstances."

As part of the Paris Agreement, developed countries committed to mobilizing $100 billion a year from 2020 onward in climate finance for developing countries with the public/private and mitigation/adaptation splits being unspecified. This finance can help address both equity issues and obstacles to borrowing in developing countries (see Chapter 7). The target was met belatedly in 2022, and at COP29 in 2024 countries committed to a new climate finance goal of $300 billion a year by 2035 (see Chapter 9).

What Are Mitigation Targets in NDCs?

Parties to the Paris Agreement have submitted NDCs[10] though there is no mechanism (like a system of non-compliance penalties) for ensuing mitigation targets are actually achieved (or even credible).

Mitigation targets are heterogeneous (see Table 2.4 for those in G20 countries), varying in terms of the following:

- *Target variables*: Most NDCs (including all those for high-income countries) specify absolute emissions targets, but a few specify targets for the emissions intensity of GDP (India), or the emission reduction below peak, without setting a base year (China, Türkiye). Some NDCs in non-G20 countries specify targets for low-carbon energy or energy efficiency rather than emissions.

Table 2.4 Mitigation Targets for the Paris Agreement, G20 Countries

Country	*Latest Mitigation Target for Paris Agreement*	*Year for Net Zero Target*
Argentina	Net emissions cap of 349 $MtCO_2e$ in 2030	2050
Australia	Reduce GHGs 43% below 2005 by 2030	2050
Brazil	Reduce GHGs 59–67% below 2005 by 2035	2050
Canada	Reduce GHGs 45–50% below 2005 by 2035	2050
China	Reduce GHGs 7–10% below peak by 2035	2060
France	Reduce GHGs 66.25–72.5% below 1990 by 2035	2050
Germany	Reduce GHGs 66.25–72.5% below 1990 by 2035	2045
India	Reduce GHG/GDP 45% below 2005 by 2030	2070
Indonesia	Reduce GHGs 31.89% (43.2%) below baseline in 2030	2060
Italy	Reduce GHGs 66.25–72.5% below 1990 by 2035	2050
Japan	Reduce GHGs 60% below 2013 by 2035	2050
Korea	Reduce GHGs 40% below 2017 by 2030	2050
Mexico	Reduce GHGs 364–404 (332–362) $MtCO_2$ equivalent by 2035	2050
Russia	Reduce GHGs up to 65–67% of 1990 level by 2035	2060
S. Arabia	Reduce GHGs 278 $MtCO_2$ equivalent below 2019 by 2030	2060
S. Africa	Annual GHGs will be in the range of 320–380 $MtCO_2e$ by 2035	2050
Türkiye	Reduce GHGs by 466 $MtCO_2$ equivalent by 2035	2053
UK	Reduce GHGs 81% below 1990 by 2035	2050
US	Reduce GHGs 61–66% below 2005 by 2035	2050

Source: UNFCCC (2024). Link to source: https://unfccc.int/NDCREGNote: Table is updated to November 2025 and includes the US Nationally Determined Contribution (NDC) prior to its announced withdrawal from the Paris Agreement in January 2025. All targets include land-use emissions except Saudi Arabia. The EU-wide target is specified for EU countries. In some cases, net zero targets have been announced but are not yet featured in policy documents.

- *Emissions sources*: Most NDCs target reductions in all GHGs but a few focus exclusively on CO_2. While land-use emissions were often excluded from economy-wide commitments, almost all recent NDC updates include land-use emissions.
- *Nominal stringency*: Emissions reduction goals for 2035 vary between 7–10 and 81 percent among G20 countries (China and the United Kingdom, respectively).
- *Reference years*: Some countries specify emissions reductions relative to 1990 levels, others relative to 2005, and still others relative to projected baseline emissions in 2030 (countries also use different procedures for projecting future baseline emissions).
- *Conditioning on support*: Many developing countries, including two G20 countries, have specified more ambitious targets that are conditional on external support as well as less ambitious, unconditional targets.

Despite these differences, operational methodologies are available for converting NDCs into consistently estimated emissions reduction targets (see Chapter 5).

What Are the Global Mitigation Ambition and Policy Implementation Gaps?

- *Ambition gap*. This refers to the gap between global GHGs if mitigation targets in NDCs were fully achieved and global GHGs needed to be on track with meeting warming goals. Although global ambition has increased by 9 percentage points since 2015, NDCs would still reduce global GHG emissions by only 7 percent relative to 2019 levels—implying ambition gaps of 18 and 38 percent for 2°C or 1.7°C, respectively in 2035 (Figure 1.1).
- *Implementation gap*. This refers to the gap between global GHGs in the baseline (with no new or tightening of existing mitigation policies) and global GHGs needed to be on track with meeting warming goals. Although global GHGs have been somewhat flat since 2019, baseline emissions in 2035 are projected to be 9 percent higher compared with 2019. This implies an implementation gap of about 35 and 55 percentage points for 2°C and 1.7°C, respectively—again (see Figure 1.1).

In short, meeting temperature goals requires countries to specify and implement policies in line with greatly enhanced mitigation commitments (see Chapter 9).

Do 2030 Emissions Targets Matter If Countries Have Made Net Zero Emissions Commitments?

All parties to the Paris Agreement have committed to achieving net zero emissions, typically by 2050 (in some cases, notably China, by 2060, and in others, notably India, by 2070), though most of the commitments have been specified in policy documents or are political targets, rather than being enshrined in law (see Figure 2.9). Net zero allows positive emissions from

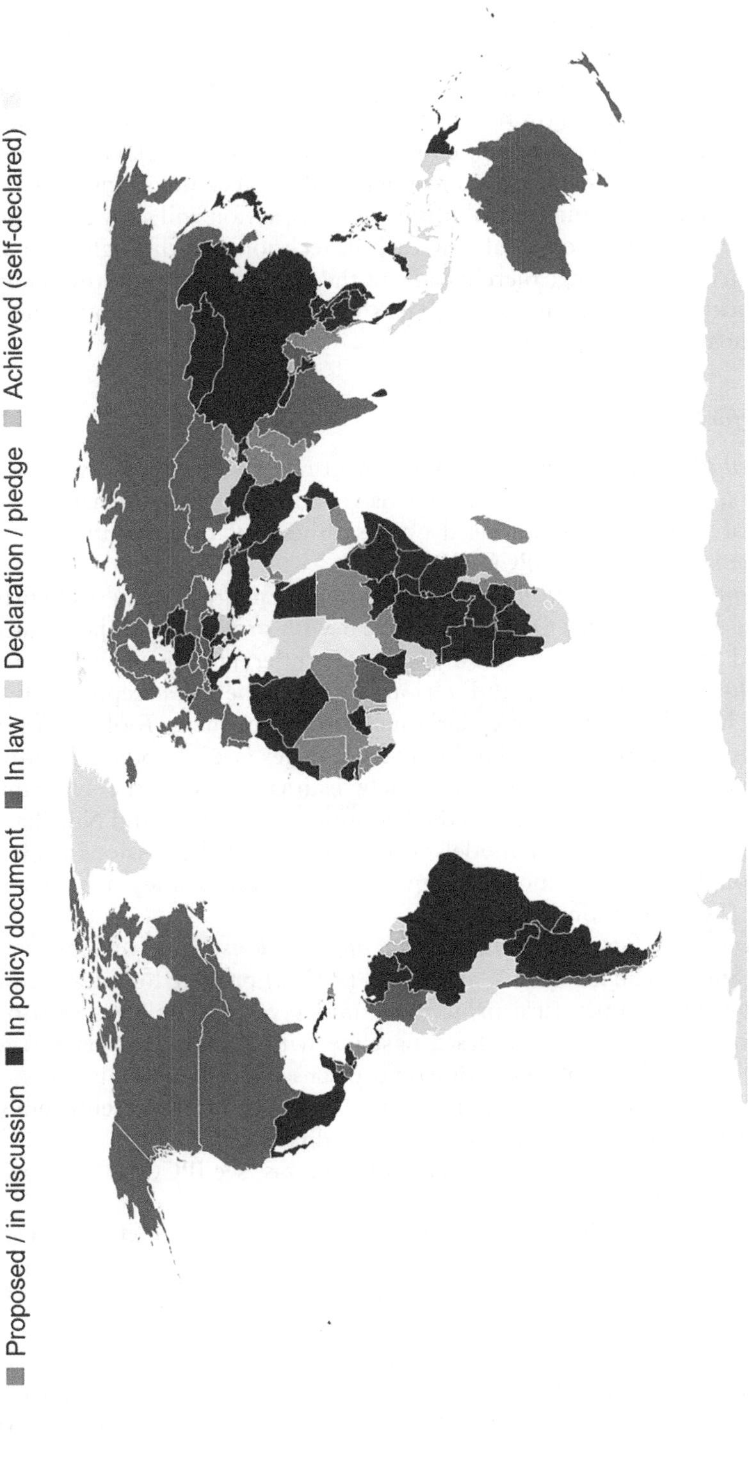

Figure 2.9 Net Zero Emissions Commitments by Country.

Source: https://zerotracker.net and https://ourworldindata.org as of November 2025.

Note: Reflects data prior to the United States' withdrawal from its climate commitments.

some (hard-to-abate sectors) like agriculture so long as they are offset by negative emissions elsewhere, for example, through forest carbon sequestration or direct air capture.

Even if there were reasonable confidence that net zero emissions targets will ultimately be achieved (in reality, their achievement is highly uncertain), the path to net zero also matters. If emissions reductions are delayed till later in the transition, this increases atmospheric GHG accumulations and the eventual amount of warming. In addition, delaying action will slow down the prospective reduction in costs of low-carbon technologies through innovation and learning-by-doing, thereby raising the costs of cutting future emissions. In short, long-range net zero goals should not distract from the need for strong near-term mitigation action.

Suggestions for Further Reading

- *Science of global warming*. IPCC assessment reports, produced every several years, provide the most comprehensive, and detailed, evidence on the science of global warming, based on a synthesis of the available literature—the last report was IPCC (2022a).
- *Global emissions projections*. The International Energy Agency (IEA) produces the *World Energy Outlook* each year with projections of how emissions and the energy system will evolve under different policy scenarios for the world, large countries, and various regions (the latest report is IEA 2024). The IMF World Bank Carbon Policy Assessment Tool generates emissions projections for 200 individual countries (see Chapter 5). Future emissions projections are also routinely estimated using the Dynamic Integrated Model of Climate and the Economy (see Barrage and Nordhaus 2024). Many other energy models also contain global emissions projections though often, for model comparability exercises, they are aligned with the IEA projections.[11]
- *Projections of future atmospheric concentrations and temperature*. Barrage and Nordhaus (2024) and IPCC (2022a) provide long-term concentration and temperature projections under various policy scenarios, though only the former includes a baseline with no new, or changes to existing, mitigation policies. For some discussion of uncertainties surrounding long-range GDP forecasts, a key driver of future baseline emissions, see Christensen, Gillingham, and Nordhaus (2018).
- *Impacts of climate change*: For recent discussions, see IPCC (2022b) and Nordhaus and Moffat (2017).
- *Tipping points*. See Dietz et al. (2021), IPCC (2018), and McKay et al. (2022) for comprehensive discussions of the risks of various tipping points.
- *Paris Agreement*. For overviews of the Paris Agreement, see Stern (2018) and UNFCCC (2016).
- *Emissions commitments in NDCs and global mitigation ambition gaps*. Future emissions implied by countries' NDC targets, and the gaps between emissions targets at the global level and emissions aligned with

temperature goals, are regularly assessed by the United Nations Environment Program, the UNFCCC, and by IMF staff (see UNEP [2025], UNFCCC [2023], and Black et al. [2025] for recent reports).

Annex 2.1 Negotiating Blocs at the UNFCCC

The main negotiating blocs at the UNFCCC are listed in the following section, though their membership may change over time, many countries are members of multiple negotiation blocs (especially large developing countries like China and India), and not all groups are formally recognized by the UNFCCC.[12]

- *European Union*: The EU formally speaks as one bloc, though larger national delegations also negotiate on the sidelines to support EU efforts.
- *Group of 77 and China*: 135 developing countries, designed to promote its members' collective economic interests, founded in 1964. The country holding the Chair of the G-77 in New York (which rotates every year) speaks for the G-77 and China as a whole, though the coalition is a diverse group with differing interests.
- *Alliance of Small Island States*: 39 small island developing states, established in 1990 to consolidate the voices of low-lying islands in addressing global warming.
- *Least Developed Countries*: 48 countries, defined as Least Developed Countries by the UN, regularly work together in the wider UN system to defend their interests, for example about vulnerability and adaptation to climate change.
- *Africa Group*: 54 countries that negotiate together and represent the interests of countries in the region. They are active in and support all aspects of the climate change negotiating process, for instance regarding vulnerability, mitigation, and adaptation to climate change.
- *Brazil, South Africa, India, and China*: This is essentially the Brazil, Russia, India, China, South Africa countries minus Russia (which is classified as a developed "non-annex I" country).
- *The Umbrella Group*: A loose coalition of non-EU developed countries. Although there is no formal list, the Group is usually made up of Australia, Canada, Japan, New Zealand, Kazakhstan, Norway, Russia, Ukraine, the United Kingdom, and the United States.
- *The Arab States*: Comprises 22 countries, including Algeria, Bahrain, Comoros, Djibouti, Egypt, Iraq, Jordan, Kuwait, Lebanon, Libya, Morocco, Mauritania, Oman, Palestine, Qatar, Saudi Arabia, Somalia, Sudan, Syria, Tunisia, United Arab Emirates, and Yemen.
- *Cartagena Dialogue*: This is not a negotiating bloc, but a dialogue of countries working toward an ambitious, comprehensive, and legally binding regime in the UNFCCC, and committed, domestically, to becoming or remaining low-carbon economies. It includes, among others, EU, Chile, New Zealand, Costa Rica, and Colombia.

Notes

1 The last time CO_2 concentrations were this high was several million years ago when global temperatures were 2–3°C warmer and sea levels were 10–20 meters higher (WMO 2024).
2 Including, for example, El Niño, where changes in the Pacific jet stream occurring every several years cause a warming of the central and eastern Pacific Ocean and land temperatures in South America.
3 For example, if (through enhanced evaporation) warming increases high-level cloud cover this tends to deflect incoming sunlight (a cooling effect) but if it increases low-level cloud cover this reflects more heat back to earth (a warming effect).
4 Atmospheric methane concentrations have also increased rapidly by 165 percent over preindustrial levels to 1935 parts per billion in 2023 (WMO 2024).
5 High-, middle-, and low-income refer to countries with annual per capital income above $14,005, between $4,515 and $14,005, and below $4,515, respectively, in 2023 (see https://datahelpdesk.worldbank.org/knowledgebase/topics/19280-country-classification).
6 Melting sea ice in the Arctic (which in the summer has declined 40 percent since 1979) does not itself raise sea levels, but there can be some effect because freshwater is less dense and has greater volume than saltwater.
7 IPCC (2018) and McKay and others (2022). See Gardes-Landolfini and others (2024) and NGFS (2023) for broader discussions of nature-related risks and their financial and macroeconomic implications.
8 Additional quantities of methane could also be released from methane molecules trapped in ice crystals in ocean sediments.
9 For more discussion of the UNFCCC, see https://unfccc.int/process-and-meetings/the-paris-agreement
10 The registry is available at https://unfccc.int/NDCREG. In January 2025 the United States announced its withdrawal from the Paris Agreement. Other non-parties to the Paris Agreement include Iran, Libya, and Yemen.
11 See various modeling exercises at https://emf.stanford.edu/projects
12 For further information, see https://unfccc.int/process-and-meetings/parties-non-party-stakeholders/parties/party-groupings

References

Barrage, Lint, and William Nordhaus. 2024. "Policies, Projections, and the Social Cost of Carbon: Results from the DICE-2023 Model." *Proceedings of the National Academy of Sciences* 121: e2312030121.

Black, Simon, Dora Benedek, Ian Parry, Nate Vernon-Lin, and Sunalika Singh. 2025. "Cutting Emissions, Securing Energy: A Macroeconomic Assessment for COP30." Working Paper 2025/245, International Monetary Fund, Washington, DC.

Caesar, Levke, Gerard McCarthy, David J. R. Thornalley, Niamh Cahill, and Stefan Rahmstorf. 2021. "Current Atlantic Meridional Overturning Circulation Weakest in Last Millennium." *Nature Geoscience* 14: 118–20.

Cheng, Chin-Hsien, and Simon A. T. Redfern. 2022. "Impact of Interannual and Multidecadal Trends on Methane-Climate Feedbacks and Sensitivity." *Nature Communications* 13: 3592.

Christensen, Peter, Kenneth Gillingham, and William D. Nordhaus. 2018. "Uncertainty in Forecasts of Long-Run Economic Growth." *Proceedings of the National Academy of Sciences* 115: 5409–14.

Depsky, Nicholas, Ian Bolliger, Daniel Allen, Jun Ho Choi, Michael Delgado, Michael Greenstone, Ali Hamidi, et al. 2023. "DSCIM-Coastal v1.1: An Open-Source Modeling Platform for Global Impacts of Sea Level Rise." *Geoscientific Model Development* 16 (14): 4331–66.

Dietz, Simon, James Rising, Thomas Stoerk, and Gernot Wagner. 2021. "Economic Impacts of Tipping Points in the Climate System." *Proceedings of the National Academy of Sciences* 118 (34): e2103081118.

Dreyfus, Gabrielle B., Xu Yangyang, Drew T. Shindell, Durwood Zaelke, and Veerabhadran Ramanathanf. 2022. "Mitigating Climate Disruption in time: A Self-Consistent Approach for Avoiding both Near-Term and Long-Term Global Warming." *Proceedings of the National Academy of Sciences* 119 (22): e2123536119. https://doi.org/10.1073/pnas.2123536119

Fox-Kemper, Baylor, Helene T. Hewitt, and Cunde Xiao. 2021. "Ocean, Cryosphere and Sea Level Change, Climate Change 2021: The Physical Science Basis." Contribution of Working Group I to the Sixth Assessment Report of the Intergovernmental Panel on Climate Change, 1211–362. Cambridge University Press, Cambridge, UK.

Gardes-Landolfini, Charlotte, William Oman, Jamie Fraser, Mariza Montes de Oca Leon, and Bella Yao. 2024. "Embedded in Nature: Nature-Related Economic and Financial Risks and Policy Considerations." IMF Staff Climate Note 2024/002, International Monetary Fund, Washington, DC.

Global Change Research Program (GCRP). 2017. *Our Changing Climate*. Washington, DC: US GCRP, Fourth National Climate Assessment.

Institute for Governance and Sustainable Development (IGSD). 2022a. "The Need for Fast Near-Term Climate Mitigation to Slow Feedbacks and Avoid Tipping Points: Critical Role of Short-lived Super Climate Pollutants to Address the Climate Emergency." Background Note, IGSD, Washington, DC.

Institute for Governance and Sustainable Development (IGSD). 2022b. "A Primer on Cutting Methane: The Best Strategy for Slowing Warming in the Decade to 2030." Working Paper, IGSD, Washington, DC.

Intergovernmental Panel on Climate Change (IPCC). 2018. *Global Warming of 1.5°C*. Geneva, Switzerland: IPCC.

Intergovernmental Panel on Climate Change (IPCC). 2022a. "Climate Change 2022: The Physical Science Basis." Contribution of Working Group I to the Sixth Assessment Report of the Intergovernmental Panel on Climate Change. Cambridge University Press, Cambridge, UK.

Intergovernmental Panel on Climate Change (IPCC). 2022b. "Climate Change 2022: Impacts, Adaptation, and Vulnerability." Contribution of Working Group II to the Sixth Assessment Report of the Intergovernmental Panel on Climate Change. Cambridge University Press, Cambridge, UK.

International Energy Agency (IEA). 2024. *World Energy Outlook 2024*. Paris, France: IEA.

McKay, David I., Arie Staal, Jesse F. Abrams, Ricarda Winkelmann, Boris Sakschewski, Sina Loriani, Ingo Fetzer, et al. 2022. "Exceeding 1.5°C Global Warming could Trigger Multiple Climate Tipping Points." *Science* 377: eabn7950.

National Oceanic and Atmospheric Administration (NOAA). 2025. *Climate at a Glance Global Time*. Washington, DC: NOAA, US Department of Commerce. https://www.ncei.noaa.gov/access/monitoring/climate-at-a-glance/global/time-series

Network of Central Banks and Financial Supervisors for Greening the Financial System (NGFS). 2023. *Recommendations toward the Development of Scenarios for Assessing Nature-Related Economic and Financial Risks*. Paris, France.

Nordhaus, William D., and Andrew Moffat. 2017. "A Survey of Global Impacts of Climate Change: Replication, Survey, Methods, and a Statistical Analysis." NBER Working Paper 23646, National Bureau of Economic Research, Cambridge, MA.

Ricke, Katharine L., and Ken Caldeira. 2014. "Maximum Warming Occurs about One Decade after a Carbon Dioxide Emission." *Environmental Research Letters* 9 (12): 124002.

Stern, Todd. 2018. *The Paris Agreement and Its Future*. Washington, DC: Brookings Institution.
United Nations Environment Programme (UNEP). 2021. *United in Science 2021. A Multi-organization High-level Compilation of the Latest Climate Science Information*. Nairobi, Kenya.
United Nations Environment Programme (UNEP). 2025. *Emissions Gap Report 2024: No more Hot Air … Please!* Nairobi, Kenya.
United Nations Framework Convention on Climate Change (UNFCCC). 2016. *Paris Agreement, United Nations Framework Convention on Climate Change*. New York. https://unfccc.int/sites/default/files/resource/parisagreement_publication.pdf
United Nations Framework Convention on Climate Change (UNFCCC). 2023. *Nationally Determined Contributions under the Paris Agreement: Synthesis Report by the Secretariat*. Bonn, Germany: UNFCCC.
United Nations Framework Convention on Climate Change (UNFCCC). 2024. *NDC Registry*. New York https://unfccc.int/NDCREG
United States Environmental Protection Agency (USEPA). 2024. *Understanding Global Warming Potentials*. Washington, DC. https://www.epa.gov/ghgemissions/understanding-global-warming-potentials
United States Geological Survey (USGS). 2023. *Climate*. Washington, DC: USGS, US Department of the Interior. https://www.usgs.gov/science/science-explorer/climate
World Meteorological Organization (WMO). 2024. *WMO Greenhouse Gas Bulletin No. 20*. Geneva, Switzerland: WMO.

3 Choosing and Designing Mitigation Instruments

A First Look at Energy

Main Messages

- Commonly used mitigation instruments include carbon taxes, emissions trading systems (ETSs), feebates, (emissions rate or energy efficiency) performance standards, and low-carbon technology subsidies or mandates.
- Achieving emissions reductions at least cost requires equating the cost of the last ton reduced across behavioral responses by households, firms, and sectors.
- Carbon pricing is potentially the most effective and cost-effective instrument and mobilizes valuable revenue—schemes are proliferating, though with substantial cross-country variation in coverage and prices, and global average prices are far below needed levels.
- There are compelling administrative reasons for applying carbon taxes where fuels enter the economy or where they are extracted (rather than where they are combusted)—tax trajectories can be aligned with emissions targets and periodically updated, while revenues can be used for general purposes and to support vulnerable households.
- ETSs are more administratively complex than taxes and may not be practical for capacity-constrained countries. Permit price volatility can be an issue in ETSs—price floors (and collars) can limit this volatility and help encourage low-carbon investments.
- Sectoral instruments are generally needed to complement explicit carbon pricing, or perhaps substitute for it all together, not least because raising energy prices can be politically difficult (requiring targeted compensation to vulnerable households/firms). A policy package is needed with sectoral mitigation instruments to reinforce carbon pricing and to kick-start transitions for hard-to-abate sectors like transport and buildings.

DOI: 10.4324/9781003755012-3
This chapter has been made available under a CC-BY-NC-ND license.

- Feebates can cost-effectively reduce the emissions intensity of a sector without fiscal costs or significant effects on energy prices—they have been integrated into vehicle tax systems but could be applied to other sectors, including power generation, industry, and buildings.
- Performance standards with credit trading are the regulatory analog of feebates and are commonly applied to vehicles and (in a nontradable form) household appliances. They have, however, moderately higher capacity needs than feebates, require fluid trading markets to be cost-effective, and have limited applicability to buildings.
- Clean technology subsidies are commonly used but promote a narrower range of mitigation responses—design features like financing them through sectoral energy taxes or using auctions for emissions reduction bids and means-testing can improve their effectiveness and cost-effectiveness, while limiting fiscal burdens on the government.
- Clean technology mandates are also narrowly focused, though their effectiveness and cost-effectiveness might be improved by incorporating a broader range of technologies and credit trading provisions.

Mitigation Basics

What Behavioral Responses by Firms and Households Can Reduce Emissions?

Potential opportunities for reducing greenhouse gas (GHG) emissions from major energy sectors (power generation, industry, transport, buildings) and broader sectors (agriculture, forestry, extractives, waste) can be classified as follows (see Table 3.1):

- *Fuel/input switching*: for example, in power generation shifting from coal to gas and from these fuels to renewables and nuclear; in transport shifting from internal combustion engine vehicles (ICEVs) to electric vehicles (EVs); in buildings switching from gas/oil to electric heating and cooking or installing rooftop solar.
- *Energy/production efficiency*: for example, shifting sales from low- to high-fuel economy ICEVs; adopting more efficient heating/cooling equipment, lighting, and appliances in buildings; shifting to more productive livestock herds.
- *Emissions capture*: for example, adopting carbon capture and storage (CCS) technologies at power plant and industrial smokestacks; afforestation or slowing deforestation; collecting methane at fuel extraction sites and landfills.
- *Demand reduction*: for example, conserving on driving, space heating, meat consumption, wood products.

Table 3.1 Classification of Behavioral Responses for Reducing Greenhouse Gas Emissions

Sector		*Examples of Types of Response*			
		Fuel/Input Switching	*Energy/Production Efficiency*	*Emissions Capture*	*Demand Reduction*
Main Energy Sectors	Power (supply side)	Coal→gas; fossil→nuclear, wind, solar, hydro, other renewable	Heat optimization	Carbon capture and storage	na
	Industry	Coal→gas; fossil→electric, hydrogen; clinker substitution	Energy-efficient machinery and processes	Carbon capture and storage	Conserving on use of steel (in vehicles), cement (in construction)
	Transport	Internal combustion engine→electric vehicles	Low→high fuel economy internal combustion engine vehicles	na	Reducing vehicle km traveled
	Buildings	Gas/oil heating/cooking →electric; solar panels	More efficient heating/ cooling, lighting, appliances; insulation	na	Using less heating/ cooling
Broader Sectors	Agriculture	Changing feed to reduce enteric fermentation	Higher productivity livestock breeds	Covering/composting manure, using methane for biogas	Meat → plant-based diet; reducing food waste
	Forestry	na	na	Afforestation, reducing deforestation, forest management	Reducing demand for timber and agricultural products
	Extractives (supply side)	na	na	Capture of vented methane for on-site power or sales; leak detection and repair	na
	Waste	na	na	Collection/flaring landfill gas	Recycling, composting, reducing packaging

Source: Authors.

This chapter mostly focuses on major energy sectors given their generally large share in potential GHG reductions and the proliferation of policies already affecting these sectors.

Conceptually, What Are the Costs of Mitigation Responses?

Costs for the first three types of responses in Table 3.1 reflect the (annualized) costs of switching to cleaner but more expensive inputs and technologies (for example, capital and operating costs of renewable generation less than those for the equivalent amount of coal generation amortized over plant lifetimes), net of any savings from lower lifetime energy costs or utilization/selling of captured emissions. For the fourth response in Table 3.1, costs are the loss of consumer benefits from, for example, driving less or eating less meat than otherwise preferred, less any avoided costs like savings on fuel or food bills.

Marginal abatement cost (MAC) curves are used to conceptualize, and quantify, mitigation costs for behavioral responses. The height of these curves shows, for a given emissions reduction (denoted ΔE in Figure 3.1), the cost from reducing emissions by one extra ton. The MAC curve is upward sloping because it is increasingly costly to cut emissions (for example, coal plants with longer remaining economic lives might need to be closed, while new renewables plants might need to be in less accessible sites with less favorable sunlight and wind). The integral under the MAC curve over the emissions reductions indicates total costs, whereas the average cost curve (which averages over incremental mitigation costs across the range of emissions reductions) lies below the MAC (Chapter 5 provides further discussion of cost measurement).[1] MAC curves tend to shift downward over time because new, less costly technologies to reduce emissions are developed.

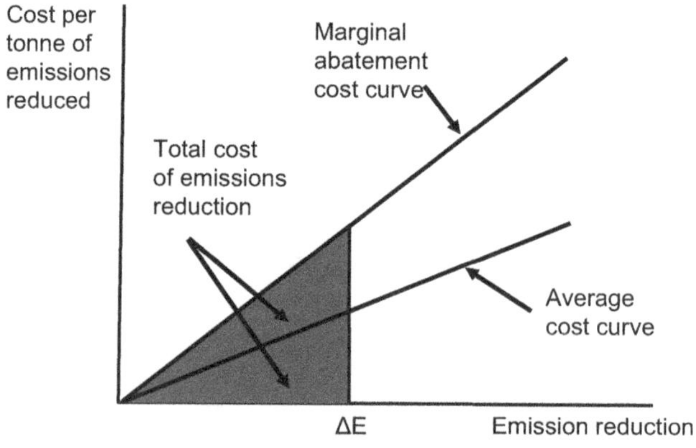

Figure 3.1 Graphical Depiction of Mitigation Costs.

Source: Authors.

What Is the Least Cost Way to Cut Emissions?

Cutting economywide emissions at least cost involves equating the cost of the last ton reduced across responses and sectors. This is illustrated in Figure 3.2, panel 1, where the economywide MAC curve is the envelope, or horizontal summation, of MAC curves at the sectoral level for fuel/input switching and other responses. Reducing economywide emissions by ΔE at least cost involves emissions reductions of ΔE_1 and ΔE_2 from fuel/input switching in industry and power generation, respectively, and so on. If instead, only a limited range of behavioral responses is exploited, costs will be higher for a given total emissions reduction as indicated in Figure 3.2, panel 2, because the narrower policy pushes along a steeper MAC schedule.

The relative position of sectoral MACs varies with country circumstances but will depend on the following:

- *Sectoral share in economywide emissions*—the larger this share, the greater the potential for cutting emissions, and the flatter the MAC curve for this sector; and
- *Emissions price responsiveness*—the MAC curve will also be flatter the more emissions are reduced in response to pricing emissions for the sector, or put another way, the greater the preponderance of low-cost mitigation opportunities for the sector.

For many countries, at least those with significant coal use, the MAC curves for power and industry tend to be flatter than those for buildings and transport, in part because of the larger emissions reductions from cutting coal use compared with cutting oil and gas (see Chapter 5).

In the absence of mitigation policy, households and firms have little incentive to cut emissions, and the (sectoral or economywide) MAC curve will have a zero intercept. More generally, preexisting policies (for example, fuel taxes/subsidies) can affect mitigation costs by shifting MAC curves so they have positive or negative intercepts (see Chapter 8).

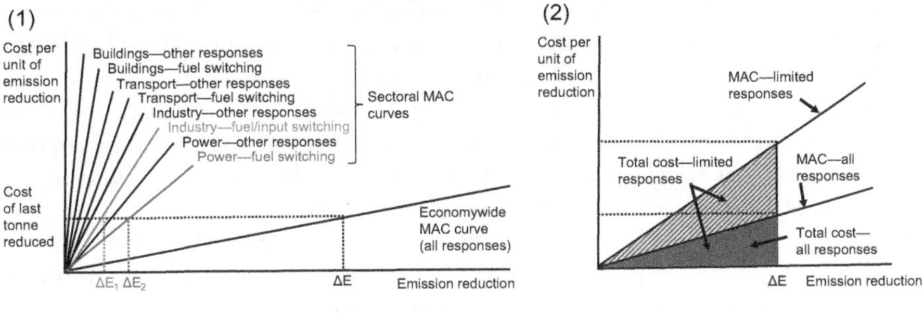

Figure 3.2 Minimizing Mitigation Costs. Panel 1. Reducing Economywide Emissions with Least Cost, Panel 2. Costs with Full and Limited Responses.

Source: Authors

What Are Commonly Used Mitigation Instruments?

Table 3.2 defines commonly used mitigation instruments, provides examples of their application, and classifies them in various ways. Instruments include as follows:

- *Carbon tax*: imposes a charge on the carbon content of fossil fuel supply or (less commonly) emissions when fuels are combusted, usually with the tax rate rising over time;
- *ETS*: requires firms to surrender allowances for their emissions or for the carbon content of fuel supply—the government caps the total quantity of allowances and tightens the cap over time, leaving emissions prices determined in allowance trading markets;
- *Feebate*: applies a sliding scale of fees to products or activities with emissions rates above a pivot point rate and sliding scale of rebates to products or activities with emissions rates below the pivot point;
- *Performance standards*: require firms, products, or fuels to meet an emissions rate or energy efficiency standard—if credit trading is allowed, firms can fall short of the standard by purchasing credits from firms exceeding the standard (under the market clearing credit price the average firm exactly meets the standard);
- *Low-carbon technology subsidy*: subsidy (or tax credit) for a firm or household adopting a low-carbon technology or fuel, for example, a feed-in tariff provides a guaranteed, above-market price for producers using a particular technology; and
- *Technology standards*: specify minimum requirements for use of a low-carbon technology or maximum allowable use of a polluting technology, for example, a renewable portfolio standard specifies minimum production shares for renewable energy.

The previously mentioned instruments can be classified in various ways, including the following:

- *Charging versus non-charging*: this distinction refers to whether the instrument charges unabated emissions for the average firm or household (carbon tax, ETS) or not (all other instruments).
- *Regulatory versus fiscal*: a regulatory policy specifies a quantity for absolute emissions (ETS), rates of emissions or energy efficiency (performance standards), or technologies (technology standard), whereas a fiscal policy specifies a tax or subsidy (all other instruments).
- *Technology neutral or specific*: the latter favors individual technologies (technology subsidies and standards), whereas the former promotes all low-carbon technologies (all other instruments).
- *Responsible ministry*: regulatory and fiscal instruments are typically under the purview of environment/energy and finance ministries, respectively. Some mechanism may be needed to ensure different mitigation policies are coordinated and consistent across different implementing agencies.

Table 3.2 Typology of Commonly Used Pricing and Regulatory Mitigation Instruments for the Energy Sector

Instrument	*Definition*	*Common Examples*	*Classification*			
			Charging/ Non-charging	*Fiscal/ Regulatory*	*Technology Neutral/Specific*	*Usual Ministry Responsible*
Carbon tax	Charge on carbon content of fossil fuels or their emissions	Applied to fossil fuel sales	Charging	Fiscal	Neutral	Finance
Emissions trading system (ETS)	Require firms to hold allowances for emissions or carbon content of fuel supply; the government caps allowances; emissions prices are determined in allowance trading markets.	Applied to large emitters in power and industry	Charging	Regulatory	Neutral	Environment
Feebates	Sliding scales of fees on products/activities with emission rates above a pivot point and rebates for products/activities with emission rates below the pivot point.	Integrated into vehicle registration tax systems	Non-charging	Fiscal	Neutral	Finance

(*Continued*)

Table 3.2 (Continued)

Instrument	*Definition*	*Common Examples*	*Classification*			
			Charging/ Non-charging	*Fiscal/ Regulatory*	*Technology Neutral/Specific*	*Usual Ministry Responsible*
Performance standards	Require firms to meet an emission rate or energy efficiency standard—credit trading may allow firms to fall short of the standard by purchasing tradable credits from firms exceeding the standard.	Applied to industrial firms, appliance sellers, vehicle sales fleets, transportation fuel suppliers	Non-charging	Regulatory	Neutral	Environment
Clean technology subsidy	Subsidy or tax credit for adopting a clean technology or fuel.	Feed-in tariffs or production tax credits for renewables; tax credits for EVs	Non-charging	Fiscal	Specific	Environment/ finance
Technology standard	Specifies minimum requirements for adoption or use of a clean technology or maximum use of a polluting technology.	Renewable portfolio standards for generators; manufacturer sales share requirements for EVs; bans on coal generation or ICEVs	Non-charging	Regulatory	Specific	Environment/ energy

Source: Authors.

Note: Charging/non-charging refers to whether the instrument charges the average firm or household for unabated emissions.

Most of the instruments in Table 3.2 (aside from technology standards or performance standards without credit trading) are also commonly referred to as pricing or market-based instruments, because they provide a price signal to decarbonize. The rest of this chapter discusses the main (administrative and environmental/economic) attributes of all the instruments, with a summary graphic provided in Annex 3.1 (energy pricing is discussed in Chapter 8, whereas production/consumption taxes, which can have a role in specific sectors like agriculture, are discussed in Chapter 4).

Carbon Pricing

Introduction

What Is the State of Carbon Pricing Schemes?

Carbon pricing schemes—carbon taxes or ETSs—are proliferating, having doubled in coverage of global GHG emissions since 2015. As of May 2025, 80 carbon pricing schemes were operating in 52 countries, covering 28 percent of global GHGs. At the national level, there are 31 carbon taxes and 15 ETSs, as well as the EU ETS (covering EU and European Free Trade Association countries). Many subnational pricing schemes are also operating, the largest being California's ETS. See Figure 3.3 and, for more details on individual schemes, Annex 3.2.

The emissions coverage of national carbon pricing schemes varies from below 30 percent in some cases to more than 80 percent in others. And price levels vary from below $5 to over $100 per ton (mostly in European countries). At the global level, the average price across schemes has increased from $7 per ton in 2015 to $19 in 2025. However, given these schemes cover only 28 percent of global GHGs the average price across global GHGs is only $5 per ton, a small fraction of the global carbon price in 2030—upward of $85 per ton (see Chapter 9)—consistent with keeping warming below 2°C.

What Are the Main Rationales for Carbon Pricing?

These include as follows:

- *Emissions reductions*—As charges on carbon emissions are passed forward in higher prices for fossil fuels, electricity, and energy-intensive products, this promotes the full range of behavioral responses for reducing energy-related emissions.
- *Cost-effectiveness*—Carbon pricing is cost-effective if it covers all sectors and fuels because it provides the same incremental reward for reducing CO_2 emissions by an extra ton (the CO_2 price) across all behavioral responses by households and firms (at least leaving aside other policies like fuel taxes—see Chapter 8).
- *Clean investment*—The expectation of a clear, credible, and rising price signal levels the playing field for low-carbon technologies many of which (like renewables plants or electric furnaces for steel) have long-range emissions reductions.

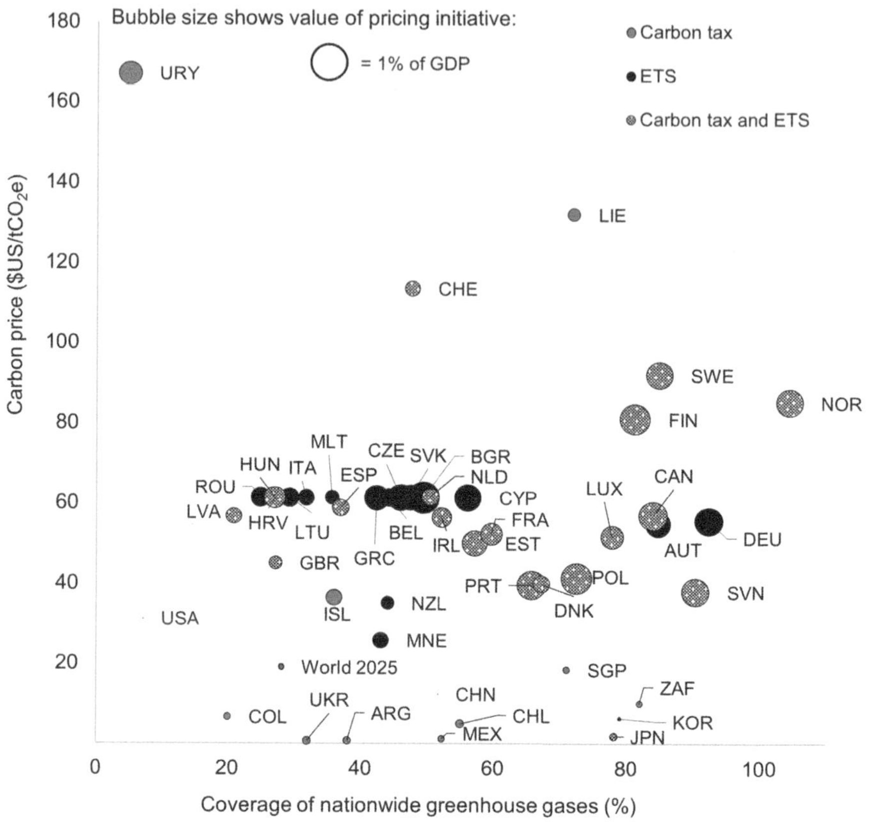

Figure 3.3 Carbon Pricing Schemes at National, Subnational, and Regional Levels, 2025.

Source: WBG (2025a), national sources, and authors.

Note: Prices are expressed in year 2025 US dollars. Data labels in the figure use International Organization for Standardization country codes.

- *Fiscal*—Carbon pricing mobilizes a valuable revenue source for general and distributional objectives, which can be especially appealing in countries where high informality constrains revenue mobilization from broader labor and business taxes.
- *Domestic environmental co-benefits*—Carbon pricing reinforces efforts to reduce the domestic environmental effects of fossil fuel use (see Chapter 8), such as local air pollution mortality (though other mitigation instruments can also generate some of these benefits).
- *Administration*—Carbon pricing can be straightforward administratively, especially if it builds off existing capacity for fuel tax collection, which is well established in most countries.

How Does the Point at Which Carbon Pricing Is Applied Affect Mitigation Responses?

Carbon pricing can be applied at three alternative points in fossil fuel supply chains (see Table 3.3):

- *Upstream*—where fuels are extracted from coal mines and oil/gas wells, though (to price emissions within domestic borders) CO_2 charges should apply to fuel imports and be rebated/exempted for fuel exports.
- *Midstream*—where fuels enter the economy after processing (to remove impurities or distill different fuel products) at refineries, coal "washing" plants, and gas processors or through processed fuel imports.
- *Downstream*—where CO_2 emissions are released from power and industrial smokestacks.

Upstream and midstream pricing systems promote nearly all the behavioral responses for reducing CO_2 emissions, though they need to be combined with (1) downstream incentives to promote emissions capture at power and industrial plants and (2) taxes on industrial inputs like clinker to reduce industrial process emissions. And given the relatively low responsiveness of

Table 3.3 Emissions Effects of Applying Pricing at Alternative Points in Fuel Supply Chains

End Use Sector	*Point of Pricing*	
	Upstream or Midstream	*Downstream*
Power	N: Promotes most responses but supplementary measures needed for carbon capture	A: Promotes all responses (but small emitters are exempt for administrative reasons)
Industry	N: Promotes most responses but supplementary measures needed for carbon capture/process emissions	A: Promotes all responses (but small emitters are exempt for administrative reasons)
Buildings	A: Promotes all responses (but supplementary measures needed given low price responsiveness)	D: Impractical
Transport	A: Promotes all responses (but supplementary measures needed given low price responsiveness)	D: Impractical

Source: Authors.

Note: A indicates an advantage of a pricing point, D a disadvantage, and N neither an advantage nor a disadvantage. Upstream, midstream, and downstream refer, respectively, to points at which fuels are extracted (at oil/gas wells and coal mines), enter the economy (after processing, for example, at refineries), and are combusted (in industrial plants, vehicles, and buildings).

transport and building emissions to carbon pricing (see Chapter 5), supplementary instruments are likely needed for these sectors to be decarbonized by mid-century.

Downstream pricing schemes are impractical for building and transportation emissions—they need to be combined with midstream pricing to cover these sectors. Within the power and industrial sectors downstream pricing promotes all mitigation responses for covered firms (because they price all emissions from fuel combustion and processes coming out of smokestacks net of any captured emissions) but numerous small-scale emitters are exempt to limit administration costs.[2]

Leaving aside some cases of administered energy pricing (see Chapter 7), for the same emissions coverage and price level, carbon pricing will generally have the same effect on energy prices, fuel use, emissions, revenue, and so on, regardless of whether it is imposed upstream, midstream, or downstream. For example, a midstream tax on the carbon content of fuel supply will impose the equivalent increase in costs for using coal, natural gas, and petroleum products as a tax on the emissions released from these fuels.

Do Carbon Taxes and ETSs Have the Same Emissions and Price Effects?

If there were no uncertainty over future MAC curves, then equivalently scaled carbon taxes and ETSs would have the same effect on emissions and emissions prices. In reality, future MAC curves are uncertain (because they vary, for example, with future fuel prices and costs of emerging mitigation technologies)—this means that carbon taxes and ETSs scaled upfront to have the same expected effect on emissions and prices will subsequently have different effects.

In particular, emissions will be fixed under a pure ETS, but emissions prices will be higher or lower than expected if future mitigation costs are higher or lower than expected, respectively. Conversely, the emissions price will be fixed under a carbon tax, but emissions reductions will be lower or higher than expected if future abatement costs are higher or lower than expected. See Figure 3.4.

Carbon Taxes: Design Issues

What Is the Administrative Case for Midstream/Upstream Application of Carbon Taxes?

Several considerations affect the choice of where in the fossil fuel supply chain to apply carbon taxes, including (see Table 3.4 for a summary):

- *Firm capacity*: New capacity requirements for firms are limited when carbon taxes are applied midstream because (in about 160 countries) firms already report fuel sales and remit excises, at least for road fuels. A supplementary payment would be needed based on the carbon content of the fuels and

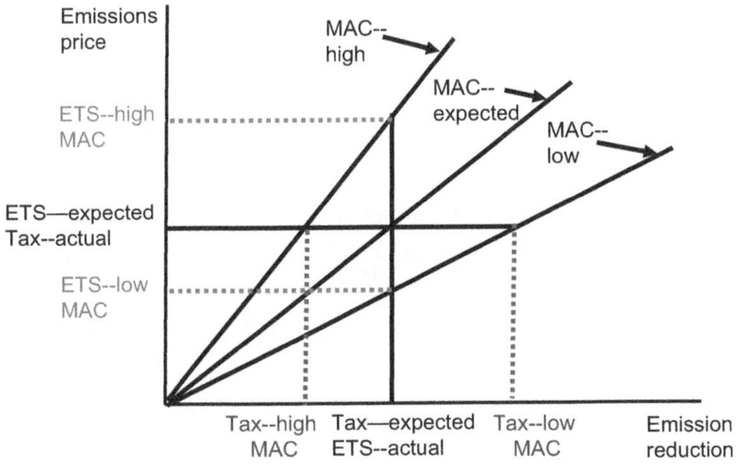

Figure 3.4 Emissions and Price Outcomes under Tax and ETS with Uncertain Mitigation Costs.

Source: Authors.

Note: ETS = emissions trading systems; MAC = marginal abatement cost.

Table 3.4 A Summary of Administrative Issues for Carbon Taxes

Metric	*Upstream (After Extraction)*	*Midstream (After Processing)*	*Downstream (Where Fuel Combusted)*
Additional capacity: firms	A: Fuel output already reported and business tax remitted	A: Fuel output already reported (typically for road fuels and sometimes other fuels) and excises remitted	D: Firms need new capacity to monitor emissions
Additional capacity: government	A: Legal framework for taxpayer registration, returns, payment, audits, dispute resolution in place	A: Legal framework for taxpayer registration, returns, payment, audits, dispute resolution in place	D: Legal framework and training of government staff required
Fuel coverage	A: Can cover all fuels	A: Can cover all fuels	D: Impractical to tax transport and building fuels
Assistance for downstream industries (if no border adjustment)	N: New capacity needed for assistance (e.g., recycling revenue to sector)	N: New capacity needed for assistance (e.g., recycling revenue to sector)	A: Assistance can be provided with same capacity for carbon tax collection

(*Continued*)

Table 3.4 (Continued)

Metric	*Upstream (After Extraction)*	*Midstream (After Processing)*	*Downstream (Where Fuel Combusted)*
Exemptions for small firms	A: Not needed	A: Not needed	D: Needed because large number of firms use fuel inputs and impractical to tax them all
Non-combusted fuels and CCS	N: Compensation needed for non-combustion and payments for CCS (but administratively manageable)	N: Non-combusted fuels could be exempt; compensation needed for CCS (but administratively manageable)	A: Automatically addressed
Number of taxpayers	A: Limited number of mines/wells; number of firms (taxpayers) is smaller still	A: Limited number of wholesalers selling processed fuels	N: Larger number of taxpayers but numbers manageable with small emitters exempt
Ability to fine-tune tax rates to emissions	N: Impurities slightly reduce accuracy of emissions factors; taxes not differentiated by petroleum product	A: Emissions factors reasonably accurate; taxes can vary for different petroleum products	A: Tax is on emissions

Source: Authors based on Calder (2015).

Note: A indicates an advantage of a taxing point, D a disadvantage, and N neither an advantage nor a disadvantage. CCS = carbon capture and storage.

taxes would need to be extended where fossil fuel products are not subject to excise. Capacity requirements are also minimal for upstream collection, given firms already report fuel production and remit business taxes.[3] For a downstream carbon tax, firms would need to start assessing their emissions based on fuel inputs and emissions factors, or installing metering equipment in smokestacks (these requirements could be onerous for small firms).

- *Government capacity*: New government capacity requirements are also minimal under midstream or upstream carbon taxes because legal frameworks for taxpayer registration, returns, payments, audits, and dispute resolution already exist (for excise or business taxes) and could be adapted for a carbon tax. This capacity would need to be established for a downstream carbon tax along with training for administrative staff.

- *Fuel coverage*: As noted earlier, midstream/upstream carbon taxes can comprehensively cover all fuels, whereas downstream taxes can only cover fuel use in the power and industrial sectors.
- *Assistance for downstream industries*: Chapter 6 discusses assistance measures for vulnerable downstream industries (like steel and cement). Aside from border carbon adjustments, these measures are administratively easier under a downstream carbon tax because they can be provided with the same capacity used for collecting the carbon tax—under an upstream/midstream carbon tax they would require separate capacity for implementing them.
- *Exemptions for small emitters*: These are needed for a downstream carbon tax, because most firms across the economy combust fossil fuels and it is not practical administratively to require all of them to report, and remit taxes on, all their facilities' emissions.
- *CCS and non-combusted fuels*: A downstream pricing scheme automatically rewards CCS and does not charge for the carbon in fuels (mainly asphalt and petrochemicals) that are not combusted. However, the future viability of CCS remains uncertain, non-combusted fuels are small,[4] and could be (fully or partially) exempted under a midstream carbon tax (because large firms are responsible for CCS and producing goods with non-combusted fuels, a rebate could be provided with little administration and compliance costs).
- *Number of taxpayers*: Under upstream/midstream carbon taxes, the number of taxpayers is small, given the limited number of refineries, gas processors, coal mines, and oil/gas wells, and that firms usually operate multiple facilities. Under downstream taxation, the number of taxpayers is larger, though the numbers are still modest (relative to those paying other taxes like corporate or personal incomes).[5]
- *Fine-tuning tax rates to emissions*: An upstream carbon tax may involve some inaccuracies in pricing emissions because impurities (prior to processing) slightly lower the emissions per unit of output and these schemes cannot differentiate among refined petroleum products with slightly different emissions intensities—but these are minor problems.

In short, there is little basis for administering a carbon tax downstream—indeed, all but 2 of the 30 national carbon taxes operating in 2025 applied point source, upstream or midstream (see Annex 3.2).

How Should Carbon Tax Trajectories Be Set?

In the academic literature, much attention has been paid to pricing emissions according to the social cost of carbon (SCC) to balance the costs of emissions against the costs of mitigating them. The SCC measures the present value of global damage (for example, to agriculture, coastal activities, ecosystems, human health) from future climate change associated with an extra ton of current CO_2 emissions—one recent study suggests a value of about \$185 per ton (Rennert et al. 2022). The SCC approach has, however, not proven practical for carbon tax design. For one thing, reaching cross-country agreement on SCC values would be challenging, given that estimates are much disputed, being highly sensitive to assumptions about intergenerational discounting and modeling of tipping points and ecological effects. A common carbon price across advanced and developing countries would be at odds with equity principles in the Paris Agreement. And the nature and quantification of the SCC can be difficult to understand and convey to stakeholders and the public.

Indeed, Nationally Determined Contributions (NDCs) are based on emissions or low-carbon energy targets rather than pricing for the SCC. The relevant issue for policymakers is therefore how to align emissions pricing (or more generally a combination of pricing and other instruments) with their NDC targets. As discussed in Chapter 5, the needed pricing can be achieved with some confidence in the near to medium term, using baseline emissions projections and assessments of the responsiveness of emissions to pricing.

For illustration, Figure 3.5 shows estimates of carbon prices consistent with cutting CO_2 emissions below baseline levels in 2030 that roughly average across, and span the range of possibilities for, G20 countries (see Chapter 5). Noteworthy points include the following:

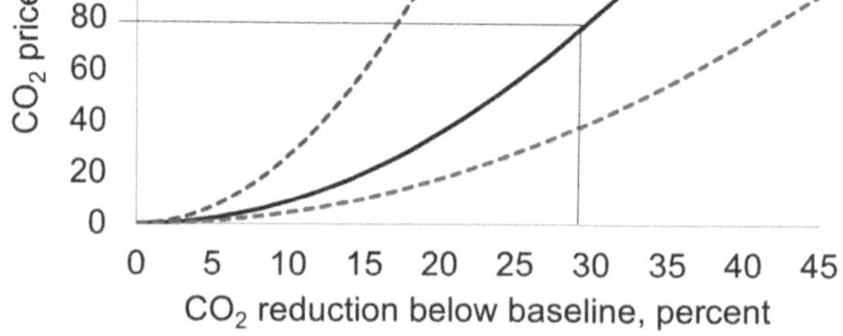

Figure 3.5 Illustrative CO_2 Prices Needed for Emissions Reductions, 2030.

Source: Authors' calculations assuming quadratic marginal abatement cost curves which, in the average case, are parameterized to G20 average figures. The low and high price responsiveness cases approximately span the range of possibilities across individual G20 countries (see Chapter 5).

- On average, emissions prices consistent with cutting emissions by 30 percent below baseline levels are about $80 per ton;
- Prices rise disproportionately with emissions reductions (because low-cost mitigation opportunities are progressively exploited)—for example, an emissions reduction of 15 percent requires on average a price of $20 per ton, whereas a reduction of 45 percent requires a price of $180 per ton; and
- In cases with low and high emissions price responsiveness, a price of $80 per ton cuts emissions by about 15 and 45 percent below baseline levels, respectively.

Tax trajectories may need to be periodically updated with new information (for example, about emissions and energy prices), and these updates can usually be included as part of a budget and related finance bill. There is, however, a trade-off because more discretionary adjustments imply more uncertainty over future prices which can deter low-carbon investment—ideally prices would largely follow fixed rules with only infrequent adjustments.

What Are the Trade-Offs in Using Carbon Tax Revenues for Different Purposes?

Potential revenues from carbon taxes in the near to medium term are typically about 0.5 to 3 percent of GDP, depending on the carbon price and the emissions intensity of GDP (see Chapter 5). These revenues would accrue to finance ministries, and there is much at stake in terms of economic efficiency and distributional outcomes in how they are used for domestic purposes[6]—again see Annex 3.2 on how revenues have been used to date. The discussion here provides some high-level remarks as summarized in Table 3.5 (Chapter 6 provides further discussion).

Table 3.5 Comparing Alternative Domestic Uses for Carbon Tax Revenue

Revenue Use	*Metric*	
	Economic Efficiency	*Income Distribution*
Proportionate Reductions in Personal Income Taxes	A: Improves work/investment incentives, reduces tax evasion/avoidance	D: Disproportionately small benefit to low-income households
Payroll Tax Reductions	A: Improves work incentives, reduces tax evasion/avoidance	N: Approximately distribution neutral for formal workers but some poor households may be informal
Corporate Income Tax Reductions	A: Improves investment incentives, reduces tax evasion/avoidance	D: Disproportionate benefit to wealthier households
Consumption Tax Reductions	A: Improves work incentives, reduces tax evasion/avoidance	N: Approximately distribution neutral

(*Continued*)

Table 3.5 (Continued)

Revenue Use	*Metric*	
	Economic Efficiency	*Income Distribution*
Public Investment	A: Sizable efficiency benefits if strong public investment management	N: Basic education, health, infrastructure may disproportionately benefit poor households
Earmarking for Environmental Spending	N: May be less efficient than general revenue uses	N: Approximately distribution neutral
Deficit reduction	A: Lowers future taxes on work/investment and macro-financial risk	N: Depends on country circumstances
Universal Lump-Sum Transfers	D: Forgoes efficiency benefits	A: Larger benefit (relative to consumption) to low-income households

Source: Authors.

Note: A, N, and D indicate an advantage, neither an advantage or disadvantage, and a disadvantage of the revenue use, respectively.

- *Personal income taxes*—Proportional reductions in personal income tax rates perform well on efficiency grounds by improving incentives for work effort, household saving, and reducing incentives for informal work and tax sheltering (for example, purchasing tax-favored goods). They may do little to help low-income households, however, if most or all their income is below threshold levels for paying tax or they work in the informal sector.
- *Payroll taxes*—Payroll tax reductions will also improve work incentives and reduce informality and some tax sheltering (for example, fringe benefits are exempt from payroll taxes). They also provide more benefits for low-income households with formal jobs than personal income tax cuts (because payroll taxes usually apply to all their wage income) but no benefits to low-income households not participating in formal work effort.
- *Corporate taxes*—Unilateral corporate income tax reductions could have large domestic investment benefits, though mainly at the expense of investment in other countries (given high international mobility of the tax base). Much (perhaps more than half) of the benefit from tax cuts accrues to labor rather than owners of capital given that the net-of-tax return to capital is largely determined in international (rather than domestic) markets (see, for example, Peichl, Siegloch, and Fuest 2017) though on balance the reductions are likely to disproportionately benefit the better off.
- *Consumption taxes*—Cutting general consumption taxes can also improve work incentives (by increasing the purchasing power of labor earnings) and deter broader tax evasion and avoidance. Benefits are approximately proportional for low-income households, including those without formal jobs.

- *Public investment*—Increasing general public investment can provide efficiency benefits if sound budgeting practices prioritize projects with high rates of return. And benefits are skewed to lower-income households if investments focus on basic education, health, and infrastructure needs.
- *Earmarked environmental spending*—Earmarking revenues for environmental investments (for example, for climate adaptation or low-carbon technology infrastructure) can be efficient if such investments are fully integrated into robust public investment management systems (and can protect such spending during fiscal difficulties), but if not, there is a risk of diverting revenue from more efficient uses. Broadly speaking, distributional effects are neutral.
- *Deficit reduction*—It can also be efficient to use carbon tax revenues for deficit reduction because this (slightly) reduces the need for future taxes on households and firms. The benefits to different household groups are, however, opaque and may do little to help the acceptability of carbon taxes.
- *Universal lump-sum transfers*—Returning revenues in equal lump-sum transfers to all households forgoes efficiency benefits (it does not, for example, improve returns to working or investing), but it does favor poor households relative to their income and may help to build support for the tax among households.

There has been much discussion in the academic literature about whether carbon taxes with productive use of revenues can reduce emissions with negative overall costs (before even counting global and domestic environmental benefits). This is possible if revenues are used to cut a particularly distorting tax or fund high-return investments, though the prospect for negative costs diminishes as deeper decarbonization erodes the base of the carbon tax. Conversely, if revenues are not used productively the overall costs of carbon taxes are positive and potentially significant. See Chapter 5 on these issues.

ETSs: Basic Design Issues

What Are the Main Administrative Issues for ETSs?

These include the following:

- *Compliance.* Under ETSs, firms are typically required to submit annual reports on their emissions (subject to third-party verification) and surrender the equivalent number of allowances. Penalties for non-compliance might, for example, be based on some multiple of the prevailing allowance price times the difference between reported emissions and allowance holdings.
- *Point of regulation.* There is less flexibility in the choice of where in the fossil fuel supply chain to apply ETSs than for carbon taxes as the need for enough firms to create a viable market for allowance trading usually implies ETSs should include power generators and industrial firms. This downstream focus may also extend pre-existing regulations for local

pollution and address possible pressures for free allowance allocations from industrial firms, though the same administrative drawbacks for downstream systems as for carbon taxes apply. ETSs could also be extended midstream to transportation, building, and small industrial fuel suppliers (as, for example, under a new ETS in the EU) though with some duplication of existing capacity for fuel excise collection.

- *Capacity requirements*. Firms are required to report their emissions—indeed policymakers need accurate emissions projections to inform appropriate setting of an ETS cap.[7] ETSs also require new capacity for supervising allowance registries and market trading.[8] They may not be viable in countries with limited institutional capacity or where there are too few firms to create fluid allowance trading markets (for example, if power generation is dominated by a state-owned enterprise).

Is Price Volatility under ETSs a Problem?

The certainty over emissions provided by a pure ETS is attractive if policymakers wish to meet an emissions target in a future year. The resulting allowance price volatility can be significant, however (see Figure 3.6 for selected ETSs) which can deter private innovation in, and adoption of, low-carbon technologies, especially those with high upfront costs and long-range emissions reductions. It also causes significant inefficiencies in a dynamic sense, if there are large differences in (discounted) incremental abatement costs at different points in time.[9] Abatement cost uncertainty also tends to imply revenues from auctioned allowances under ETSs will be more volatile than revenues from carbon taxes—see Annex 3.3.

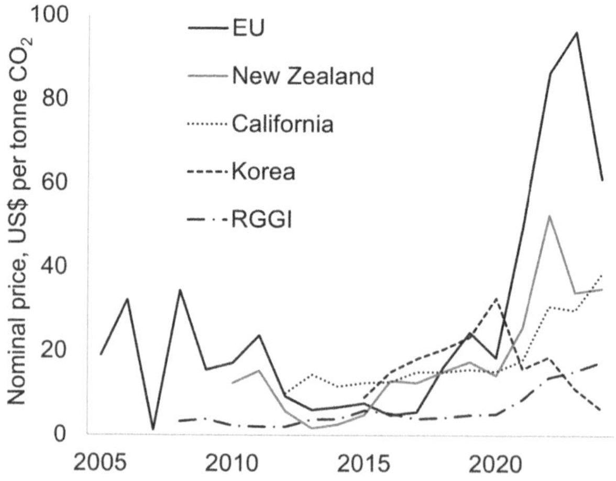

Figure 3.6 Allowance Price Volatility in ETSs.

Source: https://carbonpricingdashboard.worldbank.org/compliance/price

Note: RGGI = Regional Greenhouse Gas Initiative among 11 US states.

How Can Price Volatility Be Addressed?

There are several options for limiting ETS allowance price volatility (see Table 3.6 for a summary), including the following:

Table 3.6 Price Stability Mechanisms for ETSs

Price Stability Measure	*Mechanism*	*Emissions Impacts*	*Price Impacts*	
			Reduces Risk of Low Prices	*Reduces Risk of High Prices*
Price Floor	Sets minimum price for allowance auctions or price at which government will buy back allowances	A: Reduces emissions when binding	A: Yes	D: No
Price Collar	Same as price floor plus sets price ceiling where government sells allowances at this price	N: Reduces emissions when floor is binding; increases emissions when ceiling is binding	A: Yes	A: Yes
Allowance Banking	Firms can bank allowances (when prices are low) for use in future periods (when prices are high)	N: Cumulative emissions unaffected—annual emissions reductions (when firms bank allowances) offset emissions increases (when firms borrow allowances)	N: Partially	N: Partially
Tightening the Cap	If prices are depressed, future allowance caps can be scaled back at a faster rate	A: Reduces trajectory of future emissions	N: Partially	D: No

(*Continued*)

Table 3.6 (Continued)

Price Stability Measure	*Mechanism*	*Emissions Impacts*	*Price Impacts*	
			Reduces Risk of Low Prices	*Reduces Risk of High Prices*
Supplementary Allowance Withdrawals	Permanently or temporarily withdraws allowances from auctions when banked allowances exceed a threshold level	N: Cumulative emissions either unaffected or reduced depending on whether withdrawn allowances are permanently retired or put back into the system later	N: Partially	N: Partially
Linking to other ETSs	Firms can buy/sell allowances on international carbon markets	N: No effect on international emissions—domestic emissions could increase (if firms buy international allowances) or decrease (if firms sell allowances abroad)	N: Partially	N: Partially
Domestic or International Offsets	Firms can buy offset credits for emission reduction projects in domestic sectors beyond the ETS or from other countries	D: Increases domestic/global emissions if domestic/international offsets not fully additional	D: No	A: Yes

Source: Authors.

Note: A, N, and D indicate an advantage, neither an advantage or disadvantage, and a disadvantage of the price stability mechanism, respectively.

- *Price floors*: These can be implemented by specifying minimum bid prices at allowance auctions or by the government buying back allowances from the market when prices fall to the floor level—either way allowances are withdrawn, thereby reducing emissions, when the floor price is binding. Ideally, the floor price is exogenous and rises predictably at a default rate over time (as, for example, in California).
- *Price collars*: These combine a price floor with a price ceiling, where the latter involves the government selling extra allowances to the market when prices reach a trigger level, thereby relaxing the cap and increasing emissions.
- *Allowance banking*: This allows firms to bank allowances (when emissions prices are low) for later use (when prices are higher). This mechanism does not affect cumulative emissions—it does reduce (but not eliminate) allowance price volatility, while increasing variability in annual emissions.
- *Tightening the cap*: If prices are depressed, future emissions caps can be scaled back more rapidly thereby raising future emissions prices.
- *Supplementary allowance withdrawals*: For example, the EU's Market Stability Reserve withdraws allowances from auctions when the accumulation of banked allowances in the ETS reaches a threshold level—initially, withheld allowances were put back into the system later, though a subsequent reform allows for their permanent withdrawal. This measure smooths, but does not eliminate, price volatility.
- *Linking to other ETSs*: Linking a domestic ETS to an ETS in another country or region implies that domestic emissions prices are determined, at least partially, on international markets (or fully if the domestic market is small relative to the international market). A broader (international) allowance market helps to limit price volatility without affecting global emissions (domestic emissions are increased or decreased depending on whether the domestic country is a net importer or exporter of allowances).
- *Domestic or international offsets*: Allowing firms under an ETS to purchase credits for emissions reduction projects in sectors outside the ETS, or in other countries, helps to reduce the risk of high emissions prices, because the supply cost of offsets effectively creates a ceiling on allowance prices. A major concern with offsets, however, is that they may not be fully additional (see Chapter 9) in which case they will on net *increase* domestic or global emissions.

In short, an exogenous price floor is the most robust mechanism for truncating the risks of low emissions prices and can be extended to a price collar if there are concerns about the risks of high emissions prices.

Are ETSs Compatible with Overlapping Mitigation Instruments?

ETSs need to be designed to be compatible with overlapping instruments like feebates, which may be needed to enhance effectiveness in an acceptable way (see the following section), renewables policies, or incentives to advance low-carbon technologies (see Chapter 7). If these overlapping policies are superimposed on top of a pure ETS, they reduce emissions prices but not emissions (which are fixed by the ETS cap). Underpinning the ETS with a floor price can improve compatibility, however—where the price floor binds, overlapping instruments will cause allowances to be removed from the system, thereby lowering emissions. Alternatively, the sequence of future ETS emissions caps can be tightened over time to account for the effect of overlapping instruments.

What Are the Trade-Offs across Alternative Allowance Allocations?

There are three main options for allocating ETS allowances, including as follows (see Table 3.7 for a summary):

Table 3.7 Trade-offs Across Alternative Allowance Allocations

Metric	*Allowance Allocation under ETS*		
	Free	*Auctioned—General Revenue*	*Auctioned—Earmarked Revenue*
Household Incidence	D: Rents accrue to better off households through windfall profits to firms	A: Revenues can be recycled equitably to households	N: Investments benefiting low-income households could be targeted
Environmental Impact	D: Could retard exit of polluting firms	N: No impact	A: Clean infrastructure investments can reduce emissions/ lower cost of meeting emissions cap
Competitiveness	A: Free allocation to industry mostly compensates for higher production costs	D: Does not address burdens on energy-intensive trade-exposed firms	D: Does not address burdens on energy-intensive, trade-exposed firms
Economic Efficiency	D: No efficiency benefit	A: Revenues can be used to cut distorting taxes or fund general investment	N: Earmarked spending may be less efficient than general revenue uses
Political Acceptability	A: Helps to address opposition from firms (but not households)	N: General revenue recycling may garner some support	N: May garner support from recipients of earmarked funds

Source: Authors.

Note: A, N, D indicate an advantage, neither an advantage or disadvantage, and a disadvantage of an allocation mechanism, respectively.

- *Free allocation*—where allowances are freely given to firms based on historical benchmarks (for example, previous production multiplied by the emissions intensity of relatively low-carbon firms in the industry). This allocation can provide some compensation to firms with limited scope for passing forward higher production costs in consumer prices because of international competition (see Chapter 6) but for other firms the permit rents create windfall profits, which ultimately accrue to shareholders who are generally concentrated in higher-income groups, worsening distributional outcomes.[10] Although granting free allowances may help to build political support from firms in the early stages, the approach also forgoes economic efficiency benefits from productive revenue recycling and may retard the exit of older, emissions-intensive firms because valuable free allocations are lost if firms shut down.
- *Auctioning*: With allowances sold at auction, governments collect revenues which could be used for assisting low-income households and productive general purposes. Some revenues might also be used to compensate firms for competitiveness losses, though this diverts revenues from the general budget.
- *Earmarking*: Alternatively, allowance revenues might be earmarked for climate-related spending such as supportive low-carbon technology infrastructure networks (see Chapter 7), assistance programs for households and workers, or adaptation investments. Earmarking may, however, not be the most efficient use of the revenues and it does not address competitiveness concerns.

In practice, in the early phases of ETSs (for example, EU, Korea), allowances have been freely allocated to affected firms to help build support for the program, whereas in other ETS cases (for example, California, Germany) allowances have been auctioned from the start. Where allowances in ETSs are auctioned, the revenues are often earmarked for environmental spending—this applies, at least partially, in 39 of the 44 countries in Annex 3.2.

Feebates and Performance Standards

Why Are Supplementary Sectoral Mitigation Instruments Needed?

There are several reasons why sectoral mitigation instruments are generally needed, to complement and reinforce carbon pricing, or perhaps substitute for it altogether, though the appropriate policy varies according to the rationales (see Table 3.8):[11]

- *Constraints on carbon pricing*. There are likely political acceptability constraints on the level of carbon prices because of the burden of higher energy prices on households (though targeted measures can help, see Chapter 6). Where this applies, ideally a combination of reinforcing sectoral instruments is needed to mimic, insofar as possible, the behavioral responses of higher carbon prices—ideally, a technology-neutral combination with uniform implicit emissions prices across sectors.

Table 3.8 Rationales for Sectoral Mitigation Instruments and Their Design

Rationale		*Needed Policy Response*		
		Type of Instrument	*Technology Neutral or Specific*	*Implicit Emissions Prices across Sectors/Technologies*
Constraints on Carbon Pricing	Acceptability	Combination of non-charging instruments across sectors to mimic many of the behavioral responses of carbon pricing	Neutral	Uniform across sectors
	Long-term credibility	Extra incentive for long-lived, low-carbon investments	Specific	Higher for specific technology
Adjustment Costs in Hard-to-Abate Sectors	Transport	Extra incentive for EVs (or other zero-emission vehicles)	Neutral	Higher for transport
	Buildings	Net zero requirements for new structures; extra incentive for retrofitting old structures (e.g., for heat pumps, insulation, solar panels)	Neutral	Higher for buildings
Additional Sectoral Targets	Emissions	Supplementary carbon price or similar instrument	Neutral	Higher for sector
	Technology-specific	Incentive targeted at the technology (e.g., renewables, EVs)	Specific	Higher for specific technology
Additional Market Impediments		Tailored to impediment (e.g., transitory incentive for new technology with learning-by-doing spillovers)	Specific	Higher for specific technology

Source: Authors.

Note: EV = electric vehicle.

In addition, commitments to carbon pricing into the deep future may lack some certainty or credibility (for example, because governments may change) which can deter specific investments in long-lived, low-carbon technologies. This could rationalize extra incentives (like subsidies) targeted at such investments, though these should be limited to technologies with demonstrated capacity for significantly cutting emissions at reasonable cost (which may apply, for example, to renewable generation, electric steel production, and rooftop solar).

- *Adjustment costs in hard-to-abate sectors.* Extra high explicit, or implicit, carbon prices may be needed, even in the near term, to kick-start investment in certain hard-to-abate sectors to get them on track with decarbonization by mid-century—smoothing the investment over time, rather than bunching it all in future periods, will lower the present value of decarbonization costs. Even so, decarbonization is backloaded in these sectors, and there is a greater need for complementary instruments given carbon pricing has less certainty in the deeper future.

In transportation, for example, decarbonization by 2050 implies that all new vehicle sales should be EVs by, say, 2035, if vehicles have 15-year lifespans. Ramping up EV sales shares progressively over time, rather than rapidly going from near zero sales to 100 percent sales just before 2035, will reduce adjustment costs (for example, the cost of building a new ICEV factory now, but then subsequently retrofitting it to produce EVs, is costlier than building an EV factory in the first place). Current fuel taxes by themselves are unlikely to induce this rapid transition to EVs, implying a need for supplementary incentives.

Similarly in the building sector, it is less costly to make new structures net zero emissions (through a combination of, for example, roof/window/wall insulation, electric heating, and rooftop solar), rather than building an emissions-intensive structure and subsequently retrofitting it to become net zero. And given the long life of buildings (typically 50 years or more) retrofitting the existing stock will also be needed for mid-century decarbonization—progressively retrofitting old buildings over a longer period also lowers adjustment costs, for example, given constraints on specialized labor.

- *Additional sectoral targets.* Besides economywide targets, many governments also specify sectoral targets for emissions, or penetration of specific technologies like renewables and EVs (see Chapter 4). To the extent sectoral targets require extra effort, even when economywide targets are met, additional incentives are needed, either technology neutral (for a sectoral emissions target) or specific (for a technology target).
- *Additional market impediments.* Even with high carbon pricing, the development and deployment of low-carbon investments may be hindered by additional market impediments, such as the inability of early adopters of a new technology to capture learning-by-doing benefits at their own firm that spill over to other firms subsequently adopting the technology. These impediments generally warrant tailored measures, however (like transitory incentives for the diffusion of specific new technologies), and are discussed in Chapter 7.

What Are the Pros and Cons of Feebates?

Feebates (linked to emissions rates) are a technology-neutral policy and have several attractions, including the following (see Table 3.9):

Table 3.9 Attributes of Feebates and Performance Standards

Attribute	*Instrument*	
	Feebate	*Performance Standard*
Effectiveness	N: Reduces emissions intensity but does not exploit demand responses (e.g., reduced driving)	N: Reduces emissions intensity but does not exploit demand responses; impractical for some sectors (e.g., buildings)
Cost-effectiveness	A: Automatically cost-effective across responses promoted	N: Cost-effective if fluid credit trading markets
Administration	N: Involves new capacity for monitoring emissions and where feebates do not build off existing taxes	D: Involves new capacity for monitoring emissions and trading markets
Uncertainty: Price	A: Price certainty can promote clean technology innovation and adoption	N: Prices uncertain but less volatile than for ETS (volatility can be further reduced by combining with price floors and ceilings)
Uncertainty: Emissions	N: Emissions uncertain but feebate price can be periodically adjusted	A: Certainty over emission rates
Revenue	N: Recommended design is revenue neutral	N: No revenue impact
Political Economy	A: Can be more politically acceptable than carbon pricing as no new charge on average firm or household	A: Can be more politically acceptable than carbon pricing as no new charge on average firm or household
Competitiveness/ Leakage	A: Limited as average firm is not charged for unabated emissions	A: Limited as average firm is not charged for unabated emissions
Compatibility with Other Instruments	A: Compatible with overlapping instruments	N: Overlapping instruments do not reduce emission rates (though standards can be set or adjusted accordingly)

Source: Authors.

Note: A indicates an advantage of an instrument, D a disadvantage, and N neither an advantage nor a disadvantage.

- *Effectiveness*: Feebates promote the full range of behavioral responses for reducing the emissions intensity of a sector. In transportation, for example, they promote shifting from ICEVs to EVs and to more fuel-efficient vehicles among ICEVs, whereas EV incentives promote only the first response.
- *Cost-effectiveness*: A feebate is automatically cost-effective, given the reward for reducing emissions by an extra ton (through lower fees or higher rebates) is the same across all behavioral responses—a combination of feebates for different sectors is cost-effective if emissions prices are harmonized across the schemes.
- *Certainty*: Feebates provide price predictability, because the government specifies the future trajectory of emissions prices.
- *Acceptability*: Because they do not impose a new tax burden on the average household or firm, feebates likely have greater political acceptability than carbon pricing (see Chapter 6).
- *Competitiveness*: Similarly, competitiveness effects are limited because feebates do not charge the average firm for unabated emissions (again see Chapter 6).
- *Compatibility*: Feebates are compatible with overlapping policies—indeed if combined with regulatory standards, feebates provide ongoing incentives to exceed the standard.

Compared with carbon taxation, feebates have some drawbacks. They (1) are less effective because they do not promote demand responses (for example, they do not encourage people to drive less); (2) do not provide a fiscal benefit, at least if the pivot point is aligned with (recent) market-average emissions rates; (3) involve higher administrative costs because they must be applied downstream (for example, on generators, steel producers, vehicle sellers), requiring new capacity for monitoring emissions and (in some sectors) for applying fees/rebates; and (4) involve multiple policies (for different sectors) compared with one (economywide) policy.

What Are the Pros and Cons of Performance Standards?

Performance standards are the regulatory analog of feebates and share many of their attractions, though there are some drawbacks and other differences (Table 3.9):

- *Cost-effectiveness*: For a particular sector, a performance standard is cost-effective if credit trading is allowed and markets are fluid (with large numbers of potential participants).
- *Administration*: This is a little more burdensome because credit trading markets need to be supervised.
- *Uncertainty*: Performance standards create certainty over emissions rates (or energy efficiency), but not absolute emissions, because the latter vary

with changes in production levels. Emissions prices are uncertain, but less so than under a pure ETS—shifts in demand for electricity, steel, cement, and so on over the business cycle affect emissions prices in the latter case but not the former. Performance standards can also be combined with price collars (on credit trading markets) to further limit price volatility.

- *Compatibility*: Overlapping instruments do not affect emissions rates in the presence of binding performance standards, though standards can be modified accordingly. Nonetheless, simultaneous application of feebates and performance standards sometimes applies for the vehicle sector (see Chapter 4) and might be rationalized by the instruments reinforcing one another—performance standards ensure minimum targets for future emissions rates are met, while the feebate provides ongoing incentives for firms to exceed an emissions rate standard.

How Can Feebates Be Implemented in Different Energy Sectors?

The following section (summarized in Table 3.10) explains how feebates could apply to the main energy sectors (Chapter 4 provides more details and applications to broader sectors).

Table 3.10 Applying Feebates to Energy Sectors

Sector	*Base for Fee/Rebate*	*Fee Formula*	*Capacity Requirements*
Transport	Per vehicle (e.g., where taxes apply at the border) or average emission rates for sellers' fleets. Separate feebates with harmonized prices could apply to light- and heavy-duty vehicles.	CO_2 price × (CO_2/km of vehicle – pivot point CO_2/km) × average lifetime km driven	Firms: report CO_2 rates of individual vehicles or their sales fleet. Government: integrate feebate into vehicle registration taxes.
Industry	Industry output (e.g., tons of steel, cement). Separate feebates (with harmonized prices) could apply to different industries	CO_2 price × (firm CO_2 rate – pivot point CO_2 rate for industry) × firm production	Firms: report CO_2 rates per unit of output. Government: establish tax collection/ payment capacity for firms.

(*Continued*)

Table 3.10 (Continued)

Sector	*Base for Fee/Rebate*	*Fee Formula*	*Capacity Requirements*
Power	Power generation output, kWh	CO_2 price × (average CO_2/kWh across firm's plants – pivot point CO_2/kWh) × production	Firms: report emission rates per unit of output. Government: establish tax collection/ payment capacity for generators
Buildings: Appliances	Sales of refrigerators, air conditioners, light bulbs, washing machines, etc.	Example refrigerators: price per kWh × (kWh per cubic foot cooled – pivot point kWh per cubic foot cooled) × cubic feet of unit sold	Firms: report average energy efficiency of product sales. Government: establish tax collection/ payment capacity for firms
Buildings: Structures	Energy efficiency or CO_2 rating	kWh or CO_2 price × (rated kWh or CO_2 per square foot – pivot point kWh or CO_2 per square foot) × square foot of residence	Government (usually subnational): classifies buildings according to energy efficiency or CO_2 ratings and integrates feebate into property taxes

Source: Authors.

- *Transportation.* To date, feebate-type schemes have most commonly been applied to transportation. First-time vehicle sales would be subject to fees/ rebates equal to the product of (1) a CO_2 price, (2) the difference between their CO_2 emissions rate per kilometer (km) and a pivot point emissions rate, and (3) average lifetime vehicle km driven. Capacity requirements may be minimal, given information on emissions rates by vehicle model and vintage is generally available, and feebates imply a recalibration of vehicle taxes which already apply in many countries. Feebates could apply on an individual vehicle basis (when tariffs are collected at the border) or to average emissions rates of manufacturers' sales fleets. Subsidies for EVs under a feebate would decline over time as the average vehicle emissions rate declines, which is appropriate because the cost differential between EVs and their ICEV counterparts declines over time.

- *Industry*. Firms within an industry would be subject to a fee/rebate given by the product of (1) a CO_2 price, (2) the difference between their CO_2 per unit of output and a pivot point emissions rate for the industry, and (3) firm output. A separate scheme is needed for different industries (like steel, cement, and chemicals) but the emissions prices across schemes can be harmonized. Where the number of firms is limited, emissions benchmarks could be set exogenously, rather than on recently observed industry emissions rates, to deter firms colluding to keep their emissions rates high to influence future pivot points.
- *Power*: Generators would be subject to a fee equal to the product of (1) a CO_2 price, (2) the difference between the CO_2 per kilowatt hour (kWh) averaged across their plants and a pivot point CO_2 per kWh, and (3) their electricity production. Feebates require new capacity for monitoring CO_2 emissions rates for power generators (unless capacity is already in place for an ETS) and applying the system of fees/rebates.
- *Buildings*: Feebates could promote adoption of energy-efficient appliances by applying fees on product sales in proportion to the difference between energy consumption rates of the products (like kWh per cubic foot cooled for refrigerators) and a pivot point energy consumption rate. To encourage energy or CO_2 saving by retrofitting existing buildings, feebates could also be linked to energy or CO_2 performance ratings (in countries where this information is available) and integrated into property taxes (though this may require administration at the subnational level).

How Would Performance Standards Work for Different Energy Sectors?

Performance standards could also be applied to most energy sectors:

- *Transportation*: Standards would apply to the average CO_2 per km of firms' sales fleets. With credit trading, net credit purchases by firms would be the difference between their average emissions rate and the standard, multiplied by number of vehicles sold and perhaps scaled by lifetime vehicle km traveled.
- *Industry and power*: Emissions rate standards per unit of output could be applied to different industries or power generators. With credit trading, net credit purchases by firms would be the difference between their CO_2 per unit of output and the relevant standard multiplied by the firm's output. Credit trading across firms within, and across different industries, would promote cost-effective emissions reductions through a single credit trading price. Cases where there are a limited number of firms may not, however, be good candidates, given risks of gaming credit markets.
- *Buildings*: Performance standards are not practical for promoting building upgrades, but they could be applied to sellers of household appliances in proportion to the difference between energy consumption rates and a market-wide energy consumption rate—indeed energy efficiency standards commonly apply already, though often without the flexibility provided by credit trading (see the following section).

Technology Standards and Subsidies

How Common Are Low-Carbon Technology Subsidies and Standards?

Table 3.11 summarizes use of technology subsidies and standards across G20 countries for the power, transport, and building sectors (these policies are less common for industry). Some noteworthy points include as follows:

- *Power generation*: Countries commonly use both low-carbon technology subsidies and standards to promote renewables. All but five G20 countries apply feed-in tariffs (at either national or subnational level) and all but seven apply production or investment tax credits to promote renewables. Ten G20 countries have renewable portfolio standards, while six have announced bans on coal use by a future date.
- *Transportation*: Fourteen G20 countries promote EVs through subsidies, although in half of these cases they are the rebate side of a broader feebate policy, while seven countries have announced bans on sales of ICEVs by a certain future date.
- *Buildings*: All but four G20 countries apply building codes, that is, minimum requirements for how structural systems, plumbing, heating, ventilation/air conditioning, natural gas systems, and other aspects of residential and commercial buildings should be designed and constructed. And 12 countries apply fiscal incentives for retrofitting (for example, subsidies for insulation, heat pumps, and rooftop solar). However appliances are regulated by performance standards rather than subsidies and mandates.[12]

How Do Low-Carbon Technology Subsidies Compare with Feebates?

If subsidies promote all the main possibilities for adopting cleaner technologies, they can act like the rebate side of a broader feebate. Even so, as already mentioned, they promote a narrower range of behavioral responses for reducing emissions, because they do not charge for fossil fuel emissions. Whereas the fee part of a feebate generates revenues to offset outlays on the rebate part, there is no revenue offset for low-carbon technology subsidies—indeed the more effective they are at reducing emissions, the larger their fiscal cost. And picking which technologies to subsidize upfront can lead to significant inefficiencies when there is uncertainty over the costs of future, alternative technologies, although this is less of a concern with rapid declines in the costs of key technologies like renewable generation, EVs, and rooftop solar.

Subsidy approaches may still have a significant role, however (in conjunction with other instruments to address the mitigation responses they miss). For example, they may have political appeal given they benefit from a compact constituency, they do not require emissions monitoring capacity, and careful design can limit their fiscal costs (see the following section). Other attributes in Table 3.9 are similar for feebates and low-carbon technology subsidies.

Table 3.11 Clean Technology Subsidies and Standards by Sector, G20 Countries 2022

Country	*Power Generation*				*Transportation*		*Buildings*	
	Feed-in tariff	*Renewable Portfolio Standard*	*Investment or Production Tax Credits*	*Future Coal Bans*	*EV Subsidies*	*Future Bans on Gasoline/ Diesel Vehicle Sales*	*Building Codes*	*Fiscal Incentives for Retrofitting*
Argentina	●	●	●					
Australia	○	●			●		●	
Brazil			●					
Canada	○	○	●	●	feebate	●	●	●
China	●	●	●		feebate	●	●	●
France	●		●	●	feebate	●	●	●
Germany	●		●	●	feebate	●	●	●
India	○	●	●		●			
Indonesia	●	●	●		●			
Italy	●		●	●	feebate	●	●	●
Japan	●				feebate	●	●	
Mexico			●				●	●
Russia	●				●		●	●
Saudi Arabia							●	●
South Africa		●					●	●
South Korea		●	●	●	●		●	●
Türkiye	●				●		●	●
UK	○	●		●	feebate	●	●	●
US	○	○	●,○		●		●	

Source: Black et al. (2022), various annexes.
Note: ● = national; ○ = subnational.

How Do Design Features Affect the Attributes of Low-Carbon Technology Subsidies?

Key choices in the design of subsidy schemes can improve (or worsen) their attributes (Table 3.12 provides a summary):

- *Financing the subsidy by sectoral energy taxes*: For example, funding EV subsidies through surcharges on gasoline/diesel vehicles; subsidies for insulation, heat pumps, and rooftop solar through surcharges on residential natural gas; and renewables subsidies through taxes on electricity or fossil generation. These financing schemes eliminate the fiscal burden on the general budget, while enhancing environmental effectiveness by also penalizing use of fossil fuels. They may be difficult politically, however, because the taxes are more visible, or more concentrated on influential constituencies, than central government financing.
- *Auctions for (certified) low-carbon technology investment bids*: Under this scheme, firms would bid for contracts to develop renewable energy sites or adopt low-carbon technologies with funding prioritized to firms offering the lowest bid for a particular contract and third-party verification of contracts. This helps allocate funding to the most cost-effective investments, while minimizing fiscal costs for achieving a given low-carbon energy target (not least because it avoids windfall gains for investments that would have occurred without the policy). This is generally how renewable energy auctions work with contracts awarded to firms bidding the lowest guaranteed price.
- *Auctions for emissions reduction bids*: In this case firms bid for payments to cut their emissions with the bid consisting of the payment per ton of CO_2 reduced and the emissions reduction. This has similar advantages to low-carbon technology bids though allows for a broader range of behavioral responses to cut emissions.
- *Linking subsidies to local content requirements*: For example, limiting subsidies for renewable technologies or EVs to domestic producers, the main motivation being to promote domestic production. These requirements likely reduce the environmental effectiveness of the subsidy by precluding purchase of low-carbon technologies from abroad and may induce trading partners to retaliate with their own trade-distorting measures.
- *Guaranteed prices*: Guaranteeing prices for renewable electricity above market levels provides a stronger incentive for renewable generation when market-determined electricity prices are low (implying a wider gap between the guaranteed and market price) and vice versa when market prices are high. In contrast, a fixed subsidy per unit of renewable generation is more cost-effective in a dynamic sense because it provides the same incremental incentive for renewable generation at different points in time.

Table 3.12 Implications of Design Features for Clean Technology Subsidies

Design Feature	*Examples*	*Implications of Design Feature*			
		Effectiveness	*Cost-effectiveness*	*Fiscal Burden on General Budget*	*Trade Distortion/ Competitiveness*
Finance Subsidy by Sectoral Energy Taxes	Residential gas tax (building upgrades), gasoline/diesel surcharge (EV subsidies), fossil electricity tax (renewable subsidies)	A: Penalizes fossil technologies	N: Maintains cost-effectiveness	A: Eliminates fiscal burden	N: Neutral
Auctions for clean technology bids	Renewable energy auction (power); bids for low-carbon investments (industry)	N: No effect on emissions for a given (technology or emissions) target	A: Promotes most cost-effective investments	A: Limits fiscal costs (e.g., avoids funding non-additional investments)	N: Neutral
Auctions for Emission Reduction Bids	$ per ton bids for emissions reductions (power, industry)	A: Rewards broader range of responses to reduce emissions	A: Promotes most cost-effective investments	A: Limits fiscal costs (e.g., avoids funding non-additional investments)	N: Neutral
Link Subsidy to Local Content Requirements	Renewable technologies, EVs only receive subsidy if produced domestically	D: Limits supply of clean technologies	N: Maintains cost-effectiveness	A: Reduces fiscal cost	D: Distorts trade; competitiveness gain may be offset by retaliation
Guaranteed Prices	Feed-in tariffs for renewable generation equal to difference between target price and market generation price	N: Effectiveness stronger/weaker when market price low/high	D: Not cost-effective over time with volatility in market prices	N: Fiscal costs higher/lower when market price high/ low	N: Neutral

Source: Authors.

Note: A indicates an advantage of a reform feature, D a disadvantage, and N neither an advantage nor a disadvantage. Design features are compared relative to a simple subsidy per unit for low-carbon technology funded by the general government budget.

How Do Technology and Tradable Performance Standards Compare?

Analogous to the comparison between technology subsidies and feebates, low-carbon technology standards promote a narrower range of mitigation responses than tradable performance standards. Moreover, technology standards are not cost-effective in the sense that they force the same requirement on all firms regardless of whether it is relatively costly for them to meet the requirement.

However, an attraction of standards is that—if credible—they can achieve a given outcome, such as phaseouts of coal generation, ICEVs, and fossil-based home heating with high certainty. Credibility requires, however, that (1) governments enforce these bans (for example, through sufficient penalties for non-compliance) and (2) there is minimal perceived risk of the government backtracking on the ban (for example, in response to public opposition or if the cost of meeting it is higher than initially anticipated).

Technology mandates are also less onerous from an administrative perspective than tradable performance standards as (1) monitoring compliance with technology requirements is generally easier than monitoring emissions and (2) there are no trading markets to supervise.

How Do Design Features Affect the Attributes of Technology Standards?

Three design features might improve the cost-effectiveness, or effectiveness, of technology mandates:

- *Credit trading*: This would allow firms to fall short of a low-carbon technology standard by purchasing credits (for example, for renewable energy generation) from firms exceeding the standard, which reduces total mitigation costs across firms for the same industry-wide standard.
- *Combining standards with fees/subsidies*: Alternatively, allowing firms to pay out-of-compliance fees for falling short of a standard in proportion to the shortfall, while providing proportional subsidies to firms exceeding the standard, can have similar benefits.
- *Broadening the definition of the standard*: Broadening the range of allowable technologies to comply with the standard can facilitate more aggressive emissions reductions by making (in combination with credit trading) it behave more like a tradable performance standard. For example, if power generators obtain full credit for wind/solar, hydro, and nuclear generation, and partial credit for natural gas or fossil fuels with CCS, this promotes a much wider range of mitigation responses compared with a standard for wind/solar only (Krupnick et al. 2010).

Suggestions for Further Reading

- *Country databases on mitigation policies*. The IEA's Policies and Measures Database (https://www.iea.org/policies) provides information on past, existing, and planned mitigation policies at a granular level. The Climate

Action Tracker website (https://climateactiontracker.org) provides a high-level overview of major mitigation policies by sector for over 40 countries.

- *General discussions of mitigation instruments.* For broader discussions of mitigation policy options, see Chateau, Jaumotte, and Schwerhoff (2024) and Krupnick et al. (2010)—the latter provide detailed discussions of a wide range of policy instruments for reducing greenhouse gases and oil use along with detailed modeling of their effects in a US context. On mitigation policy options in Latin America and the Caribbean, see Ivanova, Kozack, and Muňoz (2024).
- *Carbon pricing schemes.* The World Bank publishes an annual report discussing developments in, and the state of, carbon pricing schemes at regional, national, and subnational levels (the latest report is WBG 2025b) and its Carbon Pricing Dashboard (WBG 2025a) provides a readily searchable database with details on each scheme. Tietenberg (2013) discusses lessons learned from experiences with carbon pricing.
- *Carbon taxes.* Timilsina (2022) provides an overview of academic literature on carbon taxes. For detailed discussions of administrative and other design issues needed to implement carbon taxes, see Calder (2015), Metcalf and Weisbach (2009), Marron and Toder (2014), and Sorensen, Aav, and Whyte (2024). An edited volume (see Parry, Morris, and Williams 2015) provides chapters on the main design issues relevant for implementing a carbon tax (in the US context). For some country-specific discussions, see, for Canada, Murray and Rivers (2015), Parry and Mylonas (2018) and for Sweden, Andersson (2019). UN (2021) discusses carbon taxes in a developing country context.
- *ETSs.* Tietenberg (2006) provides an in-depth discussion of design issues for ETSs. On reforms to strengthen the EU ETS, see Hepburn and Teytelboym (2017) and for experiences with ETSs more generally, see Schmalensee and Stavins (2017). MacDonald and Parry (2024) discuss experiences with ETSs in the Asia-Pacific region.
- *Tax versus ETS.* For discussions comparing the general attributes of carbon taxes and ETSs, see, for example, Goulder and Schein (2013), Hepburn (2006), Metcalf (2009), Parry, Black, and Zhunussova (2022), and Stavins (2022).
- *Feebates and tradable performance standards.* For a general discussion of feebates and how they can be implemented in different sectors, see Parry (2021). For some discussion of price stability mechanisms for tradable performance standards, see Wang, Pizer, and Munnings (2022). Goulder et al. (2022) discuss China's performance standard for the power sector.
- *Policy instruments for renewables.* On the design of subsidy schemes for renewables, see Löschel and Schenker (2017).

Annex 3.1 Summary Comparison of Mitigation Instruments

Table A3.1 provides a summary comparison of most of the instruments discussed in this chapter and how they rank against various metrics, including political acceptability and competitiveness which are discussed in Chapter 6.

Table A3.1 Attributes of Alternative Mitigation Instruments

Metric	*Mitigation Instrument*					
	Carbon Tax	*ETS*	*Feebates*	*Performance Standards*	*Technology Mandates*	*Technology Subsidies*
Administrative Practicality	A: Straightforward (e.g., as extension of fuel taxes)	N: Requires capacity for monitoring emissions and trading markets	N: Requires capacity for monitoring emissions	N: Requires capacity for monitoring emissions and trading markets	A: Monitoring compliance is straightforward	A: Monitoring compliance is straightforward
Effectiveness	A: Cost-effectively promotes all responses for reducing emissions	A: Cost-effectively promotes all responses for covered sectors/firms	N: Cost-effectively promotes all responses for reducing emissions intensity	N: Promotes all responses for reducing emissions intensity and cost-effectively if fluid trading	D: Promotes narrow range of responses	D: Promotes narrow range of responses
Uncertainty: Price	A: Price certainty can promote clean technology innovation and adoption	N: Price volatility can be problematic; price floors/collars, and cap adjustments can help	A: Announced trajectory for feebate price provides price certainty	N: Less volatile than ETS and price stability measures can help	A: Not applicable	A: Announced trajectory for subsidy rates provides price certainty
Uncertainty: Emissions	N: Emissions uncertain but tax rate can be periodically adjusted	A: Certainty over emissions levels	N: Emissions uncertain but CO_2 price and pivot point can be updated	A: Emissions standard can be aligned with emission rate targets	N: Leaves uncertainty over emissions	N: Leaves uncertainty over emissions

(*Continued*)

Table A3.1 (Continued)

Metric	*Mitigation Instrument*					
	Carbon Tax	*ETS*	*Feebates*	*Performance Standards*	*Technology Mandates*	*Technology Subsidies*
Revenue: Efficiency	A: Revenue accrues to finance ministry for general purposes	N: Free permit allocation lowers revenue and tendency for earmarking auctioned revenues	N: Recommended design is revenue neutral	N: Revenue neutral	N: Revenue neutral	D: Loses revenue
Revenue: Distribution	A: Revenues can be recycled to make overall policy distribution neutral or progressive	D: Free allowance allocation/ earmarking limits options for distributional objectives	N: Limited distributional impacts	N: Limited distributional impacts	N: Limited distributional impacts	D: Risk of subsidies (e.g., for EVs, solar panels) benefiting better off
Political Acceptability	D: Politically challenging; use of revenues and communications critical	A: Free allocation can increase acceptability	N: Revenue neutrality helps with acceptability	N: Revenue neutrality helps with acceptability	N: Revenue neutrality helps with acceptability	A: Can be popular with firms/ households
Competitiveness	N: Additional measures needed to address competitiveness	N: Additional measures needed to address competitiveness	N: Revenue neutrality helps but not robust for deep decarbonization	N: Revenue neutrality helps but not robust for deep decarbonization	N: Revenue neutrality helps but not robust for deep decarbonization	A: Competitiveness impacts neutralized as subsidy (over) compensates for abatement cost

Source: Authors.

Note: A indicates an advantage of an instrument, D a disadvantage, and N neither an advantage nor a disadvantage.

Annex 3.2 Additional Information on Carbon Pricing Policies Table A3.2

Table A3.2 Details of Carbon Pricing Instruments, 2025

Country/ Region	*Year Introduced*	*Coverage of Energy Sectors*				*Coverage, All GHGs (Percent)*	*Price, $/ Tonne*	*Revenue/ Rent, % GDP*	*Point of Tax/ Regulation*	*Revenue Use*
		Power	*Industry*	*Transport*	*Buildings*					
Carbon Taxes										
Albania	2008	✓	✓	✓	✓	73	13	0.00	Downstream	General budget
Argentina	2018	✓	✓	✓		38	1	0.04	Upstream	General budget
Chile	2017	✓	✓			55	5	0.04	Downstream	General budget
Colombia	2017	✓	✓	✓	✓	20	7	0.03	Upstream	Environmental spending
Singapore	2019	✓	✓			71	18	0.03	Point source	General budget, environmental spending
South Africa	2019	✓	✓	✓	✓	82	10	0.02	Point source	General budget
Ukraine	2011	✓	✓		✓	32	1	0.04	Point source	Environmental spending
Uruguay	2022		✓	✓		5	167	0.37	Upstream	General budget, environmental spending
ETSs										
EU	2005	✓	✓			38	61	0.26	Point source	General budget, environmental spending
Australia	2023	✓	✓	✓		27	22	0.00	Point source	N/A
Austria	2005, 2023	✓	✓			85	55	0.43	Upstream	General budget, environmental spending

(*Continued*)

Table A3.2 (Continued)

Country/ Region	*Year Introduced*	*Coverage of Energy Sectors*				*Coverage, All GHGs (Percent)*	*Price, $/ Tonne*	*Revenue/ Rent, % GDP*	*Point of Tax/ Regulation*	*Revenue Use*
		Power	*Industry*	*Transport*	*Buildings*					
Belgium	2005	✓	✓			44	61	0.22	Point source	General budget, environmental spending
Bulgaria	2005	✓	✓			49	61	0.69	Point source	General budget, environmental spending
Croatia	2005	✓	✓			27	61	0.24	Point source	General budget, environmental spending
Cyprus	2005	✓	✓			56	61	0.49	Point source	General budget, environmental spending
China	2013–2021	✓	✓			52	12	0.00	Point source	Environmental spending proposal
Czech Republic	2005	✓	✓			46	61	0.48	Point source	General budget, environmental spending
Germany	2005, 2021	✓	✓	✓	✓	92	56	0.54	Point source, Upstream	Environmental spending
Greece	2005	✓	✓			42	61	0.42	Point source	General budget, environmental spending
Indonesia	2023	✓				24	1	0.00	Point source	General budget
Italy	2005	✓	✓			32	61	0.17	Point source	General budget, environmental spending
Kazakhstan	2013	✓	✓		✓	43	1	0.00	Point source	General budget
Korea	2015	✓	✓	✓	✓	79	6	0.01	Point source	Environmental spending

Lithuania	2005	✓	✓			29	61	0.24	Point source	General budget, environmental spending
Malta	2005	✓	✓			36	61	0.12	Point source	General budget, environmental spending
Montenegro	2022	✓	✓			43	26	0.17	Point source	Environmental spending
New Zealand	2008	✓	✓	✓		44	35	0.11	Point source, Upstream	General budget, environmental spending
Romania	2005	✓	✓			25	61	0.24	Point source	General budget, environmental spending
Slovakia	2005	✓	✓			47	61	0.44	Midstream	General budget, environmental spending
US	2009–2023	✓	✓	✓	✓	7	31	0.00	Point source, Upstream	General budget, direct transfers, env. spending
Hybrid										
Canada	2007–2022	✓	✓	✓	✓	84	57	0.56	Point source, Upstream	Tax cuts, environmental spending
Denmark	1992, 2005	✓	✓	✓	✓	67	40	0.20	Point source, Upstream	Payroll tax cuts, environmental spending
Estonia	2000, 2005	✓	✓			57	50	0.43	Point source	General budget, environmental spending

(Continued)

Table A3.2 (Continued)

Country/ Region	*Year Introduced*	*Coverage of Energy Sectors*				*Coverage, All GHGs (Percent)*	*Price, $/ Tonne*	*Revenue/ Rent, % GDP*	*Point of Tax/ Regulation*	*Revenue Use*
		Power	*Industry*	*Transport*	*Buildings*					
Finland	1990, 2005	✓	✓	✓	✓	81	81	0.64	Point source, Upstream	Income tax cuts, environmental spending
France	2005, 2014	✓	✓	✓	✓	60	52	0.33	Point source, Upstream	General budget, environmental spending
Hungary	2005, 2023	✓				27	61	0.31	Point source	General budget, environmental spending
Iceland	2005, 2010	✓	✓	✓	✓	36	37	0.16	Point source, Upstream	General budget
Ireland	2005, 2010	✓	✓	✓	✓	52	56	0.27	Point source, Upstream	General budget, environmental spending
Japan	2010–2012	✓	✓	✓	✓	78	2	0.04	Up & Downstream	Environmental spending
Latvia	2004, 2005	✓	✓			21	57	0.17	Point source, Upstream	General budget, environmental spending
Liechtenstein	2005, 2008	✓	✓	✓	✓	72	132	0.11	Point source, Upstream	General budget
Luxembourg	2005, 2021	✓	✓	✓	✓	78	52	0.36	Point source, Upstream	General budget, environmental spending
Mexico	2014, 2020	✓	✓	✓	✓	52	1	0.03	Point source, Upstream	General budget
Netherlands	2005, 2021	✓	✓			50	62	0.20	Point source	General budget, environmental spending
Norway	1991, 2005	✓	✓	✓	✓	105	85	0.50	Point source, Upstream	General budget

Poland	1990, 2005	✓	✓	✓	✓	72	41	0.66	Point source	General budget, environmental spending
Portugal	2015, 2005	✓	✓	✓	✓	66	40	0.56	Point source, Upstream	General budget, environmental spending
Slovenia	1996, 2005	✓	✓	✓	✓	90	38	0.52	Point source, Midstream	General budget, environmental spending
Spain	2005, 2014	✓	✓		✓	37	59	0.19	Point source, Upstream	General budget, environmental spending
Sweden	1991, 2005	✓	✓	✓	✓	85	92	0.49	Point source, Upstream	Income tax cuts, environmental spending
Switzerland	2008	✓	✓		✓	48	113	0.16	Point Source, Aviation, Upstream	Tax cuts, direct transfers, environmental spending
UK	2013, 2021	✓	✓			27	45	0.11	Point Source, Aviation, Upstream	General budget, payroll tax cuts

Source: WBG (2025a), Government sources.

Note: Includes subnational schemes. Revenue/rent excludes revenue loss from erosion of prior fuel tax bases. For Canada, Mexico, Switzerland, and the United States not all subnational schemes cover the sector. Most recent data is used, where available.

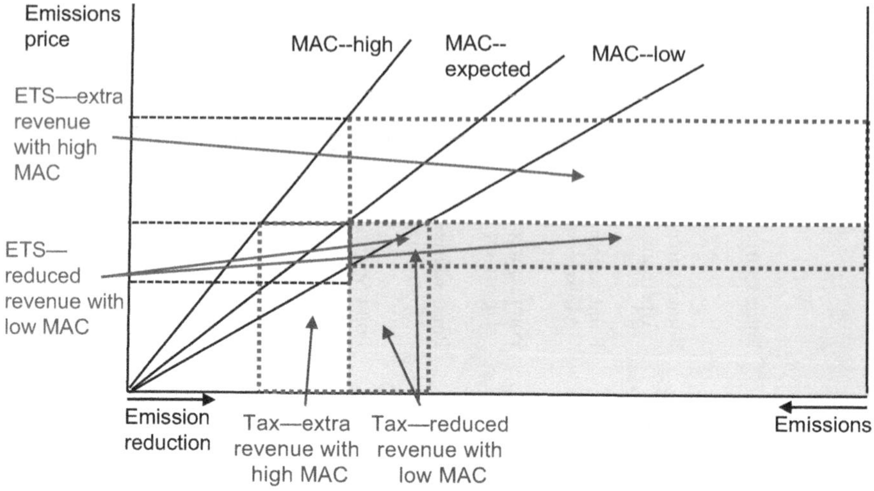

Figure A3.1 Revenue Volatility under Carbon Taxes and ETS.

Source: Authors.

Note: Shaded rectangle shows revenues under carbon tax and ETS with the expected MAC curve. ETS = emissions trading systems; MAC = marginal abatement cost.

Annex 3.3 Why Are Revenues More Volatile under ETSs Than Carbon Taxes?

If there we no uncertainty over future MAC curves, then (equivalently scaled) carbon taxes and ETSs with (full) allowance auctions yield the same revenues—indicated by the shaded rectangle in Figure A3.1. With uncertainty over MAC curves, however, revenues tend to be more volatile under ETSs. This is because volatility in emissions prices (under an ETS) affects revenues collected across the entire tax base whereas volatility in emissions (under a carbon tax) implies modest changes in the size of the tax base but not the tax applied to the base. Again, see Figure A3.1, where the increased/reduced revenues from a higher- or lower-than-expected MAC curve are likely larger under the ETS than the carbon tax.

Notes

1 For simplicity, MAC curves are drawn as smooth and linear throughout this volume. In practice, MAC curves might have flat portions (if there are lumpy investments at the economywide level) and marginal costs likely rise at an increasing (rather than constant) rate with more abatement.

2 For example, facilities with annual CO_2 emissions below 25,000 tons are exempt in the California, EU, and Korean ETSs.

3 Sometimes a hybrid of midstream and upstream collection might be most practical. For example, the same firms might extract and process fuels (especially for coal), whereas some fuels are not processed (for example, when dry gas is put into the distribution pipeline directly from the wellhead). Working out the most practical points to maximize tax coverage is, however, routine for tax administrations.

4 See Calder (2015). One hundred percent of the carbon in asphalt is stored but substantially less for chemical feedstocks (about 60 percent) and lubricants (only 10 percent).
5 In the United States, for example, the number of taxpayers under upstream/midstream and downstream carbon pricing would be about 1,500 and 12,000, respectively (Calder 2015).
6 A small portion might go to international climate finance (see Chapter 9).
7 In the initial stage of the EU ETS, the EU did not have reliable information about firms' emissions before the market started and largely defined allocations based on (inflated) industry projections—CO_2 prices crashed following the first round of emissions verifications in 2005 showing actual emissions were well below the emissions cap (see Hintermann 2010).
8 This includes guarding against fraud which, for example, might take the form of allowance thefts by phishers posing as registry administrators (Nield and Pereira 2011).
9 See Fell, MacKenzie, and Pizer (2012). At the global level, uncertainty over annual emissions is less of a concern, given their small effect on the accumulated atmospheric stock of CO_2, and therefore the small likelihood that extra emissions in any given year will cause the crossing of tipping points in the climate system (see Newell and Pizer 2003).
10 See Parry (2004). The government might ultimately appropriate a minor portion of the rents through corporate and personal income/capital gains taxes on windfall profits.
11 For further discussion of instrument synergies across countries, see D'Arcangelo et al. (2024).
12 More generally clean technology subsidies and mandates might include a range of policies which have relatively limited emissions impacts, such as subsidies for geothermal heat pumps, low carbon fuel standards, and ethanol mandates.

References

Andersson, Julius J. 2019. "Carbon Taxes and CO_2 Emissions: Sweden as a Case Study." *American Economic Journal: Economic Policy* 11: 1–30.

Black, Simon, Danielle N. Minnett, Ian W.H. Parry, James Roaf, and Karlygash Zhunussova. 2022. "A Framework for Comparing Climate Mitigation Policies Across Countries", IMF Working Paper 22/254, https://doi.org/10.5089/9798400228285.001

Calder, Jack. 2015. "Administration of a U.S. Carbon Tax." In *Implementing a U.S. Carbon Tax: Challenges and Debates*, edited by Ian Parry, Adele Morris, and Roberton C. Williams III. New York, UK: Routledge.

Chateau, Jean, Florence Jaumotte, and Gregor Schwerhoff. 2024. "Climate Policy Options: A Comparison of Economic Performance." *Energy Policy* 192: 114232.

D'Arcangelo, Filippo M., Tobias Kruse, and Mauro Pisu, 2024. "Identifying and Tracking Climate Change Mitigation Strategies with a Cluster-Based Assessment." *npj Climate Action* 3: 86.

Fell, Harrison, Ian MacKenzie, and William A. Pizer. 2012. "Prices versus Quantities versus Bankable Quantities." *Resource and Energy Economics* 34: 607–23.

Goulder, Lawrence H., Xianling Long, Jieyi Lu, and Richard D. Morgenstern. 2022. "China's Unconventional Nationwide CO_2 Emissions Trading System: Cost-Effectiveness and Distributional Impacts." *Journal of Environmental Economics and Management* 111: 102561.

Goulder, Lawrence H., and Andrew R. Schein. 2013. "Carbon Taxes versus Cap and Trade: A Critical Review." *Climate Change Economics* 4: 1–28.

Hepburn, Cameron. 2006. "Regulation by Prices, Quantities, or Both: A Review of Instrument Choice." *Oxford Review of Economic Policy* 22 (2): 226–47.

Hepburn, Cameron, and Alexander Teytelboym. 2017. "Reforming the EU ETS: Where Are We Now?" In *Energy Tax and Regulatory Policy in Europe: Reform Priorities*, edited by Ian Parry, Karen Pittel, and Herman Vollebergh, 1–29. Cambridge, MA: MIT Press.

Hintermann, Beat F. 2010. "Allowance Price Drivers in the First Phase of the EU ETS." *Journal of Environmental Economics and Management* 59: 43–56.

Ivanova, Anna, Julie Kozack, and Sònia Muñoz, eds. 2024. *Climate Change Challenges and Opportunities in Latin America and the Caribbean*. Washington, DC: International Monetary Fund.

Krupnick, Alan J., Ian Parry, Margaret Walls, Tony Knowles, and Kristin Hayes. 2010. *Toward a New National Energy Policy: Assessing the Options*. Washington, DC: Resources for the Future and National Energy Policy Institute.

Löschel, Andreas, and Oliver Schenker. 2017. "On the Coherence of Economic Instruments: Climate, Renewables, and Energy Efficiency Policies." In *Energy Tax and Regulatory Policy in Europe*, edited by Ian Parry, Karen Pittel, and Herman R. J. Vollebergh, 135–62. Cambridge, MA: MIT Press.

MacDonald, Margaux, and Ian Parry. 2024. "Policy Options for Climate Change Mitigation: Emissions Trading Schemes in Asia-Pacific." IMF Working Paper 24/155, International Monetary Fund, Washington, DC.

Marron, Donald B., and Eric J. Toder. 2014. "Tax Policy Issues in Designing a Carbon Tax." *American Economic Review* 104: 563–68.

Metcalf, Gilbert E. 2009. "Market-Based Policy Options to Control US Greenhouse Gas Emissions." *Journal of Economic Perspectives* 23: 5–27.

Metcalf, Gilbert E., and David Weisbach. 2009. "The Design of a Carbon Tax." *Harvard Environmental Law Review* 3: 499–556.

Murray, Brian C., and Nicholas Rivers. 2015. "British Columbia's Revenue-Neutral Carbon Tax: A Review of the Latest 'Grand Experiment' in Environmental Policy." *Energy Policy* 86: 674–83.

Newell, Richard G., and William A. Pizer. 2003. "Regulating Stock Externalities under Uncertainty." *Journal of Environmental Economics and Management* 45: 416–32.

Nield, Katherine, and Ricardo Pereira. 2011. "Fraud on the European Union Emissions Trading Scheme: Effects, Vulnerabilities and Regulatory Reform." *European Energy and Environmental Law Review* 20 (6): 255–89.

Parry, Ian. 2004. "Are Emissions Permits Regressive?" *Journal of Environmental Economics and Management* 47: 364–87.

Parry, Ian. 2021. "The Critical Role of Feebates in Climate Mitigation Strategies." In *No Brainers and Low-Hanging Fruit in National Climate Policy*, edited by Francesco Caselli, Alexander Ludwig, and Frederick Van Der Ploeg, 217–44. London, UK: Center for Economic Policy Research.

Parry, Ian, Simon Black, and Karlygash Zhunussova. 2022. "Carbon Taxes or Emissions Trading Systems? Instrument Choice and Design." IMF Staff Climate Note 2022/006, International Monetary Fund, Washington, DC.

Parry, Ian, Adele Morris, and Roberton Williams, eds. 2015. *Implementing a US Carbon Tax: Challenges and Debates*. London, UK: Routledge.

Parry, Ian, and Victor Mylonas. 2018. "Canada's Carbon Price Floor." IMF Working Paper 18/42, International Monetary Fund, Washington, DC.

Peichl, Andreas, Sebastian Siegloch, and Clemens Fuest. 2017. "The Incidence of Corporate Taxation and its Implications for Tax Progressivity." *VOXEU*. https://cepr.org/voxeu/columns/incidence-corporate-taxation-and-its-implications-tax-progressivity

Rennert, Kevin, Frank Errickson, Brian C. Prest, Lisa Rennels, Richard G. Newell, William Pizer, Cora Kingdon, et al. 2022. "Comprehensive Evidence Implies a Higher Social Cost of CO_2." *Nature* 610: 687–92.

Schmalensee, Richard, and Robert Stavins. 2017. "Lessons Learned from Three Decades of Experience with Cap-and-Trade." *Review of Environmental Economics and Policy* 11: 59–79.

Sorensen, Aksel, Enriko Aav, and Graham Whyte. 2024. "Developing and Administering a Carbon Tax." IMF Technical Note, International Monetary Fund, Washington, DC.

Stavins, Robert N. 2022. "The Relative Merits of Carbon Pricing Instruments: Taxes versus Trading." *Review of Environmental Economics and Policy* 16. https://doi.org/10.1086/717773

Tietenberg, Thomas H. 2006. *Emissions Trading: Principles and Practice.* 2nd ed. New York, NY: Resources for the Future.

Tietenberg, Thomas H. 2013. "Reflections—Carbon Pricing in Practice." *Review of Environmental Economics and Policy* 7: 313–29.

Timilsina, Govinda R. 2022. "Carbon Taxes." *Journal of Economic Literature* 60: 1456–502.

United Nations (UN). 2021. *Handbook on Carbon Taxation for Developing Countries.* New York, NY: United Nations (UN).

Wang, Banban, William A. Pizer, and Clayton Munnings. 2022. "Price Limits in a Tradable Performance Standard." *Journal of Environmental Economics and Management* 116: 102742.

World Bank Group (WBG). 2025a. *Carbon Pricing Dashboard.* Washington, DC. https://carbonpricingdashboard.worldbank.org

World Bank Group (WBG). 2025b. *State and Trends of Carbon Pricing: International Carbon Markets 2025.* Washington, DC.

4 A Closer Look at Emissions-Generating Sectors and Appropriate Policies

Main Messages

- Feebates and tradable performance standards are reasonably effective policies for power generation if carbon pricing is constrained and, in some cases, converting electricity taxes to emissions taxes. Direct subsidization and other forms of support to renewables are reasonably effective when there is limited scope for other mitigation responses (like improving plant efficiency, shifting to nuclear, and from coal to gas).
- For the industrial sector, if carbon pricing is constrained (even with competitiveness measures), feebates and tradable performance standards are reasonably effective and have similar administrative capacity requirements as emissions trading systems. Low-carbon technology subsidies and mandates are less effective, given the diverse range of potential low-carbon technologies for the sector.
- For transportation, fuel taxes and carbon pricing need to be reinforced with additional instruments, ideally feebates (integrated into registration fees) or performance standards (where administratively feasible) for vehicle sellers, which is preferable to incentives for electric vehicle purchases alone. For heavy-duty vehicles, integrating feebates into annual circulation taxes is a better approach. In the long term, because the base of energy taxation declines with electrification of the vehicle fleet, fuel tax revenues will need to be replaced and driving externalities managed, ideally by transitioning to kilometer-based charging systems.
- For buildings, incentive programs may be needed for electric heat pumps, insulation upgrades, and rooftop solar. These could be financed through residential fuel taxes, whereas feebates linked to energy or emissions performance assessments for buildings could be integrated into property tax systems. Performance standards or feebates can also promote more energy-efficient household appliances.

DOI: 10.4324/9781003755012-4
This chapter has been made available under a CC-BY-NC-ND license.

- For forestry, nationwide pricing systems penalizing deforestation and rewarding carbon sequestration are ultimately needed but have heavy capacity requirements related to monitoring and land rights. Interim possibilities might include incentives for conservation projects (building off payments for environmental services programs) and taxes on forest commodities (with rebates for sustainably produced products).
- For agriculture, livestock farmers could be taxed based on self-assessed emissions (linked to farm characteristics), or production taxes could be levied at the processor level using default emissions factors with side payments for certified, low emissions-intensity farmers. Feebates, at either farm or processor level, are another possibility.
- Methane fees could be integrated, in a revenue-neutral way, into existing business tax regimes for extractives based on emissions reporting requirements for firms, or default emissions rates but allowing low-emissions firms to petition for tax rebates. Feebates or performance standards have nearly similar effectiveness to pricing and may have fewer political and legal barriers.
- Emissions pricing is less suitable for the waste sector, where regulations are needed to control methane leaks from landfills and perhaps to separate organic materials from landfill trash.

Power

Emissions Sources and Current Policies

How Do Power Generation Mixes and CO_2 Emissions Differ across Countries?

Across G20 countries (see Figure 4.1, panel 1), the mix of power generation fuels in 2022 varied dramatically. For example, coal accounted for over half of power generation in four cases (China, India, Indonesia, South Africa) but was 5 percent or less in six cases (Argentina, Brazil, Canada, France, Saudi Arabia, the United Kingdom). In nine cases, natural gas was 25 percent or more of power generation, whereas nuclear was less than a fifth of generation in all cases aside from France and Korea. Hydro was between 5 and 20 percent of generation in 12 countries but accounted for over 60 percent of generation in Brazil and Canada. And wind and solar together accounted for 7–33 percent across all cases except Indonesia, Russia, and Saudi Arabia.

CO_2 emissions rates (averaged across generation fuels) were typically between about 0.1 and 0.7 tons per megawatt hour in 2022 (Figure 4.1, panel 2). And (see panel 3) power sector emissions accounted for over 50 percent of economy-wide CO_2 emissions in South Africa and China, between 40 and 50 percent in six cases (for example, India, Korea, Japan), between 25 and 40 percent in six cases, and less than 15 percent in three cases (Brazil, Canada, France).

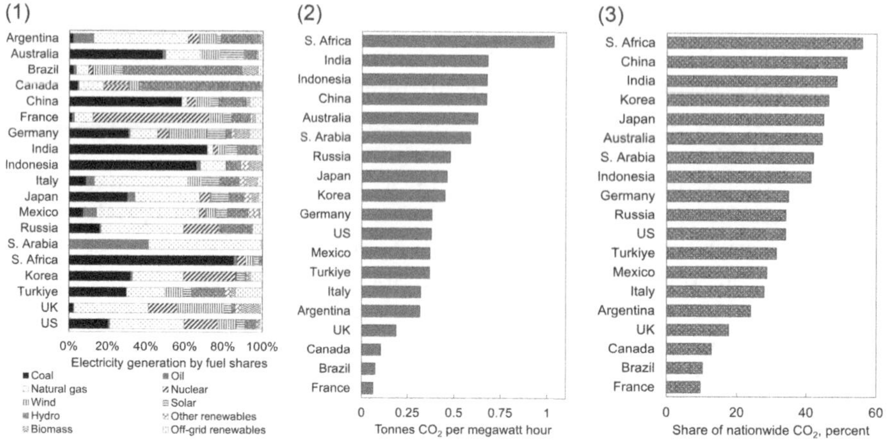

Figure 4.1 Power Generation Mixes and Emissions, G20 Countries, 2022. Panel 1. Generation Mix, Panel 2. CO_2 Emissions Rate, Panel 3. Power Generation Share in Economywide CO_2.

Source: Authors using Climate Policy Assessment Tool (CPAT).

What Are the Prospects for Low-Carbon Technologies?

Earlier modeling studies suggested that future decarbonization of the power sector would (at the global level) require a mix of technologies, including wind/solar, nuclear, fossil technologies with carbon capture and storage (CCS), and biomass with CCS. More recent modeling, however, suggests a much larger role for wind and solar, reflecting their rapidly declining costs, ample availability of sites, and options for addressing intermittency.[1]

Figure 4.2 indicates, for selected countries, the levelized costs (or annualized lifetime capital and operating costs) of new power generation technologies, as of 2022. Some noteworthy points include:

- The levelized costs of new coal generation were about 8–36 cents per kWh.
- Wind and solar were cheaper than coal in all selected countries except for India due to low variable costs.
- Natural gas is largely competitive with, or more competitive than, coal generation (aside from India)—it may have a role as a bridge fuel, but substantially expanding its capacity could ultimately result in stranded assets (given the eventual need for full decarbonization).
- Hydro has broadly similar costs to wind and solar but most viable sites are already developed (and flooding new sites can be environmentally harmful and require population relocation).[2]
- Nuclear fission is sometimes less costly than renewables but (notwithstanding technological progress on small module reactors) constraints to scaling it up include long construction times, limited uranium reserves, concerns about radioactive waste disposal, and risks of nuclear accidents.[3]

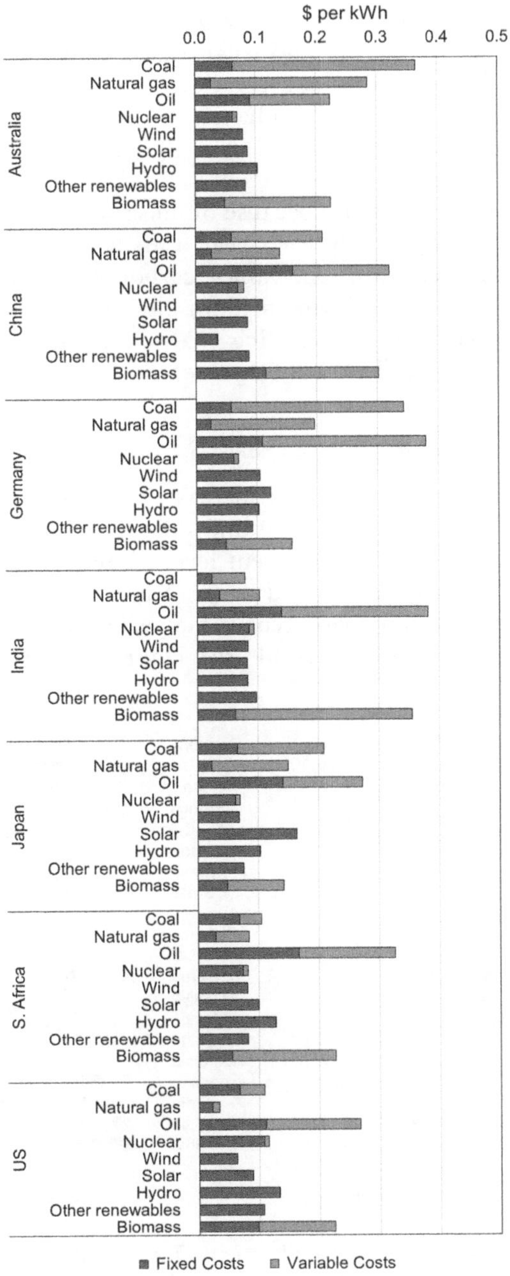

Figure 4.2 Levelized Cost of New Generation by Fuel Type, G20 Countries, 2022.

Source: Authors using CPAT.

Note: Levelized fixed costs include capital, decommissioning, storage, fixed operations and maintenance, and transmission costs. Levelized variable costs include variable operations and maintenance, and fuel costs.

- Biomass (from dedicated crops or agricultural and forest residues) is typically more costly than wind and solar and its production may compete with land for food or forest conservation—it could, however, have some future role because biomass production absorbs CO_2 from atmosphere which can then be captured with CCS at the generation plant.

CCS is excluded from the figure because of uncertainties over the amount of CO_2 that can be stored safely each year and its future cost. Despite the improving competitiveness of renewables, carbon pricing or similar policies are needed to help level the playing field for all low-carbon technologies and to accelerate the retirement of existing coal plants before the end of their economic lifetimes (typically about 50 years).

What Targets and Policies Apply to the Power Sector?

Most G20 countries have targets for increasing the share of renewable generation—typically up to between 30 and 80 percent or more in 2030. In terms of increasing shares above recent levels, however, countries with the most ambitious targets include Indonesia, Saudi Arabia, and the United Kingdom with targets to increase renewable generation shares by about 30 percentage points or more to 2030 (see Figure 4.3, panel 1). To make

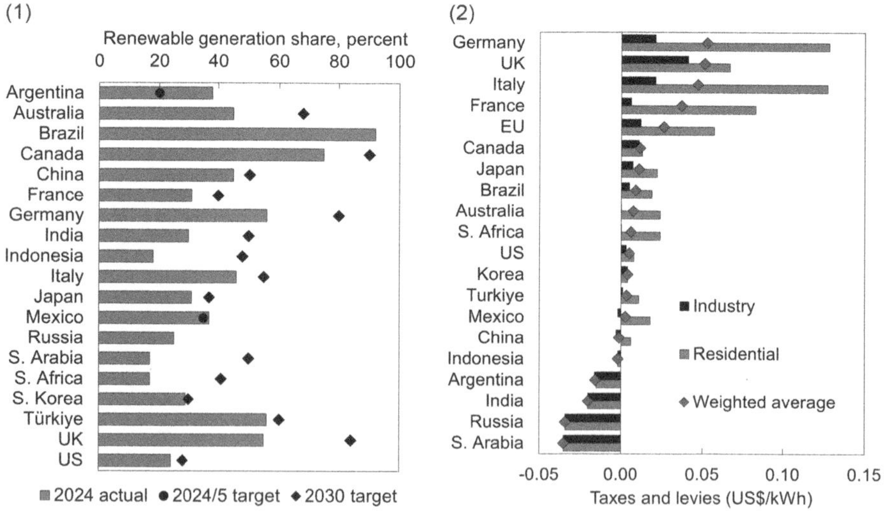

Figure 4.3 Renewables Targets and Electricity Taxes and Levies, G20 Countries. Panel 1. Renewable Targets.[a]* Panel 2. Electricity Taxes and Levies 2024[b†].

Sources: [a]Updated from Parry et al. (2022a). [b]Updated from Black et al. (2023).

Note: *Renewable targets for China and United Kingdom are for 2080 and 2035, respectively, and are interpolated to 2030. The US target was abandoned in 2025. †Taxes include VAT for residential electricity use. Levies include charges such as renewable and capacity taxes.

headway on these targets (mainly at national but also subnational level), 14 G20 countries have implemented feed-in tariffs, 12 have investment or production tax credits, 10 have renewable portfolio standards, and 6 have bans on future coal use (see Table 3.11).

Four European countries levy taxes and other fees on electricity consumption up to about 4 cents per kWh in 2024 (averaging over residential and industrial use)—in some cases, revenue from (a portion of the fees) fund renewable energy subsidies. However, six G20 countries significantly subsidized electricity consumption (for example, through holding down regulated prices below supply costs or providing targeted electricity bill relief) with subsidies between 1.5 and 4 cents per kWh. In 11 other G20 countries, electricity consumption is subject to only modest taxes or subsidies. In most cases, residential consumers pay higher similar taxes mostly due to the VAT. See Figure 4.3, panel 2.

Are Higher Electricity Prices from Carbon Mitigation at Odds with Electrification of Other Sectors?

Figure 4.4 shows the percentage increase in power demand in 2030 relative to baseline power demand, from an illustrative scenario where 25 percent of vehicles, 33 percent of buildings, and half of steel production are electrified in line with a global emissions pathway limiting warming to 2°C. In total, power demand increases by about 5 to 25 percent above the baseline, with most additional demand from buildings followed by transportation. Electrification of steel adds little to power demand.

Under carbon pricing consistent with 2°C, there would be a reduction in current sources of power demand because of higher electricity prices that, in seven cases, more than offsets the potential increase from electrification. The offsetting reduction would however be smaller under non-pricing policies, even with pricing there is a significant increase in electricity demand on net, and these estimates leave aside additional electricity demand from artificial intelligence datacenters. Some countries may, therefore, need to significantly expand generation capacity while power is decarbonized.

Electrification is one among several mitigation options for other sectors (albeit the most important, at least for vehicles and buildings) and striking a cost-effective balance across all responses requires providing the same incremental reward for emissions cuts across the responses without any subsidies for individual responses. If power sector emissions are not priced at the same level as in other sectors this implicitly subsidizes the power sector, which could cause excessive electrification for other sectors relative to other mitigation responses—it can also undermine decarbonization of the power sector itself.

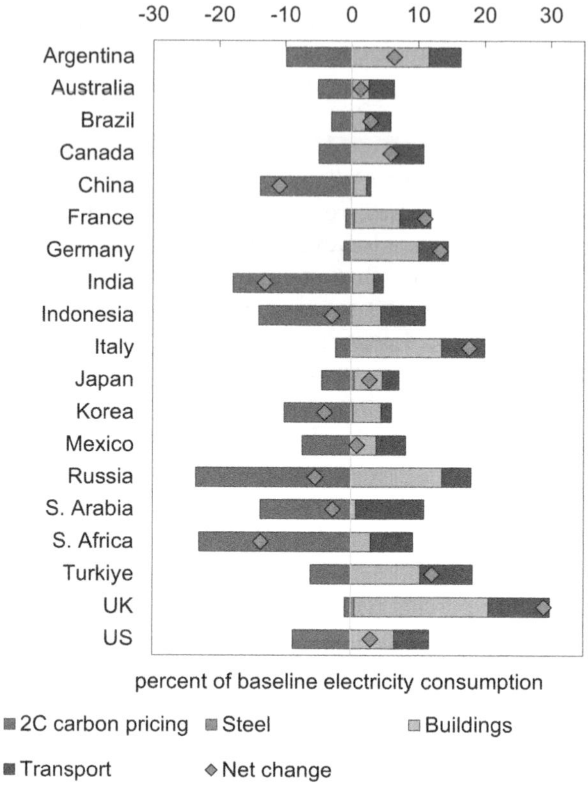

Figure 4.4 Extra Power Demand from Electrification of other Sectors, Illustrative Scenarios for G20 Countries, 2030.

Source: Authors.

Note: Assumes 50 percent of steel production is from electric arc furnaces, 25 percent of driving is from electric vehicles, and 33 percent of heating is from heat pumps. Carbon pricing consistent with 2°C is assumed to be $75 per tonne in 2030.

Choice of Mitigation Instruments

What Mitigation Responses Are Promoted by Alternative Instruments for Power Generation?

Table 4.1 distinguishes eight mitigation responses, including four types of fuel switching, production efficiency (for example, heat optimization), emissions capture, and two demand responses, namely off-grid solar and energy efficiency investments/behavioral changes by households and firms. Responses promoted by different instruments are as follows:

Table 4.1 Responses Promoted by Alternative Mitigation Instruments for the Power Sector

Mitigation Response		*Policy Instrument*						
		Carbon Pricing	*Feebate/ Performance Standard: Generators*	*Renewable Portfolio Standard: Generators*	*Fiscal Incentives for Solar/Wind: Generators/ Households*	*Fuel-Specific Performance Standard*	*Electricity Tax*	*Coal Tax*
Fuel Switching	Fossil → Wind, Solar	A	A	A	A	D	D	N
	Fossil → Hydro, Other Renewable	A	A	A	D	D	D	N
	Fossil → Nuclear	A	A	D	D	D	D	N
	Coal → Gas/Oil	A	A	D	D	D	D	A
Production Efficiency		A	A	D	D	A	D	N
CCS		A	A	D	D	D	D	D
Demand Reduction	Off Grid Solar	A	D	D	A	D	A	N
	Energy Efficiency, Behavioral Change	A	D	D	D	D	A	N

Source: Authors.

Note: A, N, and D indicate where a response is fully promoted, partially promoted, and not promoted, respectively. CCS = carbon capture and storage.

- *Carbon pricing.* Pricing CO_2 emissions from the power sector will promote all mitigation responses.[4]
- *Feebates or performance standards.* Applied at the generator level promote all responses, aside from the two demand reductions. These policies can be applied to smokestack emissions, or to generation fuels scaled by their respective emissions factors, expressed per unit of production.
- *Renewable portfolio standard.* Applied at the generator level, this policy promotes only two of the fuel-switching responses (with all renewables counted). If, however, the standard was generalized so nuclear was credited as a zero-carbon fuel, and (for cases where coal generation is significant) partial credits were awarded for gas/oil generation, the policy could promote all four fuel-switching possibilities (partial credits could also promote CCS).
- *Fiscal incentives for solar/wind.* Applied at the generator and household level, these incentives would promote two of the behavioral responses. Subsidies could be extended to promote shifting to other renewables, nuclear, and from coal to gas/oil, though this would increase fiscal costs.
- *Fuel-specific performance standard.* This approach has been adopted in China where individual coal and natural gas generators are subject to emissions rate standards (Annex 4.1). The policy does not, however, promote shifting from coal to gas plants because the latter are subject to stricter standards than the former, and it does not provide crediting for renewables—the main response promoted by the policy is production efficiency improvements (Black et al. 2024). Setting a common emissions rate standard for all generators and allowing them to purchase credits from renewable and nuclear generators would promote the full range of fuel-switching responses.
- *Electricity taxes.* Pure electricity taxes (on production or consumption) promote only the two demand responses. Converting them into emissions taxes on generators would promote the full range of mitigation responses without a new tax burden on households and firms, though this would require significant administrative capacity given that in most cases excises are levied on end users rather than generators. For example (dividing the electricity excises in Figure 4.3 by CO_2 emissions rates from Figure 4.1), current electricity taxes exceed \$400 per ton of CO_2 in France, Germany, Italy, and the United Kingdom.
- *Coal tax.* This may be a reasonable alternative to emissions taxes where coal is a major share of generation, though it promotes partial responses in most cases, because pricing emissions from all fossil fuel generation is more effective than pricing them from coal alone.

How Would Feebates and Performance Standards Affect the Costs of Generation Technologies?

Figure 4.5, panel 1 indicates the effect on generation costs from an illustrative feebate with price of \$75 per ton of CO_2 and alternative pivot points of 0.25,

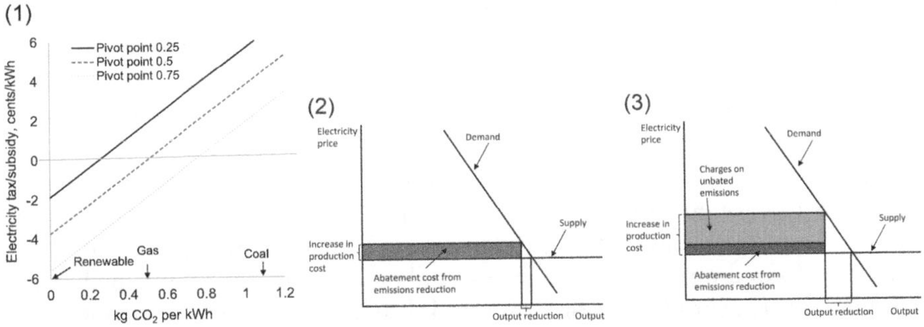

Figure 4.5 Illustrative Feebate and Comparisons with Carbon Pricing. Panel 1. Illustrative Feebate, Panel 2. Demand/Cost Effects of Feebate, Panel 3. Demand/Cost Effects of Carbon Pricing.

Source: Authors.

Note: Assumes CO_2 price of $75 per ton of CO_2.

0.5, or 0.75 kg CO_2 per kWh of generation. For example, for the midrange pivot point, renewables would receive a subsidy of 4 cents per kWh, coal would be subject to a tax of 5 cents per kWh, whereas natural gas plants would receive a small initial subsidy, though this would progressively decrease and become a fee (whereas subsidies for renewables would decline), as the pivot point is updated with declines in the industry average emissions rate over time. Effects on generation costs would be the same for an equivalently scaled tradable performance standard.

Revenue-neutral feebates and performance standards would have a modest effect on production costs and production levels—firms incur abatement costs but, on average, no charge on their remaining emissions. In contrast, under carbon pricing, the increase in production costs is generally higher, because firms are charged for unabated emissions through tax payments or allowance purchases. To achieve the same total emissions reduction, feebates and performance standards would therefore need to reduce emissions intensity by more than under carbon pricing to compensate for the former's smaller effect on production levels. As indicated in Figure 4.5, panels 2 and 3, abatement costs from reducing emissions intensity (and total abatement costs) are therefore larger under emissions-equivalent feebates/performance standards.

Is There a Role for Renewables Incentives?

Appropriate strategies for power sector decarbonization will vary with national circumstances like acceptability of pricing, the relative potential of different mitigation responses, and administrative considerations. Where there are acceptability constraints on higher electricity prices, feebates or tradable performance standards are a potentially promising alternative. And some demand responses might be promoted without higher electricity prices through complementary measures (such as those discussed in the following

"Buildings" section). Feebates and performance standards may, however, have significant capacity requirements in cases where generators' emissions rates are not currently monitored, although the necessary capacity can likely be built because there are a limited number of power plants and they likely already report their electricity output.

Alternatively, a focus on renewables policies may be appropriate if there is limited scope for emissions reductions from efficiency improvements, expanding nuclear, or shifting among different fossil fuel technologies, and where capacity for administering renewable policies is already established. Some design features should be borne in mind, however (applying principles from Table 3.12):

- *Scope*: defining renewables broadly (beyond on-grid wind and solar to include hydro, biomass, off-grid solar) can promote a wider range of mitigation responses.
- *Flexibility*: under a renewable portfolio standard, credit trading provisions or fees/subsidies for falling short/going beyond the standard can improve cost-effectiveness.
- *Subsidy bases*: defining production subsidies as a fixed amount per unit of output rather than the difference between a target price and prevailing electricity prices avoids the incentive being distorted by market price fluctuations.
- *Investment versus production subsidies*: focusing subsidies on new investment, rather than on production, can limit fiscal costs—as could transforming production subsidies into a feebate.[5]
- *Auction mechanisms*: where subsidies are targeted on new investment, awarding contracts to lowest-cost bidders (subject to third-party verification) can also limit costs on the economy and fiscal costs on the government.

Complementary reforms to enhance the effectiveness of power sector mitigation policies (like technology policies, market design, and infrastructure upgrades) are discussed in Chapter 7.

Industry

Emissions, Mitigation Opportunities, and Current Policies[6]

What Are the Sources of Industrial Emissions?

Across G20 countries, industry accounted for between about 15 and 30 percent of nationwide (non-land use) CO_2 emissions in 2023. Within industry, and taking a simple average across G20 countries, (iron and) steel, cement, and chemicals accounted for 26, 29, and 15 percent of CO_2 emissions and all other industries combined (for example, aluminum, textiles, pulp/paper) 30 percent, though there is substantial variation in these shares by country (see Figure 4.6.)

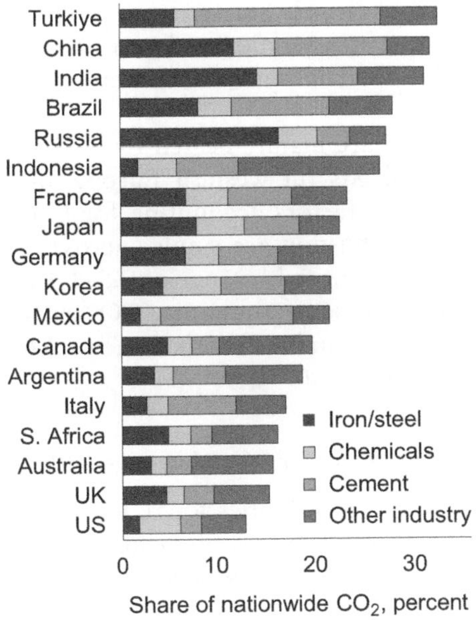

Figure 4.6 Contribution of Industry to Nationwide CO_2 Emissions, 2023.

Source: Parry et al. (2025).

Most industrial emissions are from fossil fuel combustion used in heating processes, but some are also from the chemical decomposition of feedstocks, for example, limestone used in production of clinker for cement (which causes about half of total emissions from cement production), coke used in smelting iron ore, and natural gas or coal used in ammonia production.

Approximately 45 percent of global steel is used for structures, 20 percent for industrial equipment, 18 percent for consumer products, 13 percent for infrastructure, and 10 percent for vehicles. Cement is used in gluing together sand, gravel, and stone to make concrete. Ammonia production makes up 45 percent of global chemical emissions, followed by methanol (27 percent), and other high-value chemicals like ethylene (28 percent). Most ammonia is used in fertilizers; methanol is used, for example, in plastics, fabrics, adhesives, paint, pharmaceuticals, and pesticides; and ethylene is used, for example, to produce bins, buckets, crates, bottles, piping, food packaging, trash liners, and bags.

How Does the Emissions Intensity of Production Vary by Industry?

Steel: About 70 percent of global steel production is from traditional, usually coal-fed, blast furnaces and 30 percent from newer electric arc furnaces using recycled steel—the former are concentrated in Asia and eastern Europe and the latter in western Europe and the United States. Blast furnaces generate about 1.6 tons of CO_2 per ton of steel on average (but with a range of 1.0 to 2.3

across countries) whereas electric arc furnaces produce about 0.3 tons (for example, from on-site power generation and use of coal for chemical purposes) or about 0.8 tons in China and India given their coal-intensive power generation.

- *Cement*: Cement kilns are mainly heated by coal (globally and in China and India) or natural gas (in western Europe and the United States). Overall, CO_2 emissions factors accounting for limestone decomposition processes and fuel combustion are similar across countries at about 0.9 tons CO_2 per ton of cement (with range of 0.8–1.1 across countries).
- *Chemicals*: Taking the case of ammonia, CO_2 emissions factors average about 3 tons per ton of ammonia (with range of 2.6 to 3.7 depending, in part, on the heating fuel used).

What Are the Main Opportunities for CO_2 Mitigation in the Industrial Sector?

There is a diverse range of possibilities for reducing emissions in the industrial sector, though large uncertainties often surround their future costs and viability. Opportunities include (see Table 4.2):

- *Electrification (for heating)*: although electric arc furnaces are well established, they are constrained by limited availability of scrap steel. For primary steel (made from iron ore), cement, and chemicals, all of which require intense heat (of about 1,000–1,500°C) electric furnaces are coming closer to market with innovation. Electrolysis of material inputs is also a possibility for cement.
- *Input switching*: for heating fuels, input switching might include shifting from coal to gas (for cement) or from fossil fuels to green hydrogen (or possibly other fuels like biofuels)—green hydrogen is produced by water electrolysis using renewable electricity. Input switching might also include, for cement manufacture, partial substitution away from clinker (currently about 75–85 percent of cement) to other feedstocks (like volcanic ash, ground limestone, broken glass).
- *Emissions capture*: in principle technologies could be applied to (new or existing) coal blast furnaces, cement kilns, and chemical processes, to separate CO_2 from waste gases (or also during production in cement kilns) but this remains a rarity because of its expense, not least because of the infrastructure and geological sites required for transporting and disposing of CO_2.
- *Production efficiency*: for example, using state-of the-art technologies or, in cement, shifting from wet to dry kilns with preheaters feeding off the kilns, can reduce fuel and feedstock inputs per unit of production.
- *Demand reductions*: steel might be partially substituted with wood or polymers in buildings or plastic in cars; wood or stone might be used in place of concrete; greater use of fillers (like burnt clay or wastes from fly ash and slag) might partially substitute for cement in concrete production; and chemical demand might be reduced through, for example, more use of organic fertilizers or reusable shopping bags.

Table 4.2 Mitigation Opportunities in the Industrial Sector

Type of Response	*Examples*		
	Steel	*Cement*	*Chemicals*
Electrification (for Heating)	Blast furnace → electric furnace using recycled steel or iron ore as feedstocks	Electric kilns and electrolysis of material inputs are future possibilities	Fossil fuels → electric furnaces
Input Switching	Heating: fossil fuels → green hydrogen	Heating: fossil fuels → green hydrogen, coal → gas. Feedstock: partially substituting volcanic ash, ground limestone, other materials for clinker	Heating: fossil fuels → green hydrogen
Emissions Capture	Potentially applicable to new/existing blast furnaces	Potentially applied during or after combustion to extract CO_2 from exhaust gases	Using organic compounds to separate CO_2 from the gas stream
Production Efficiency	State-of-the art technology	State-of-the-art technology; wet → dry kilns with preheaters feeding off the kilns	State-of-the art technology
Demand Reduction	Buildings: steel → wood, fiber-reinforced polymer; cars: steel → plastics for trunk lids, body panels, floor panels, fuel tanks	Concrete → wood, stone; optimizing mix of cement/fillers in concrete	Fertilizers: chemical → organic; shopping bags: single use plastic → reusable

Source: Parry et al. (2025).

Note: Unlike steel, cement recycling is not generally practical because demolition waste is of low value (and is mostly used as gravel for roads and other infrastructure).

What Mitigation Instruments Have Been Applied to Industrial Emissions to Date?

As of 2024, industrial emissions were subject to carbon pricing in nearly 50 countries. This includes 30 countries participating in the EU ETS, six other countries with ETSs (for example, Korea, New Zealand, the United Kingdom), and carbon taxes in seven cases (for example, Colombia, Chile, Singapore, South Africa). See Annex 3.2.

Experiences with feebates and performance standards for industry are limited, but this may change. Canada's federal carbon pricing backstop includes a performance standard for industry, China plans to extend some form of performance standard to industry, and the Netherlands has implemented a feebate variant for the industrial sector (Annex 4.1 discusses each program). These policies were motivated by the need to price emissions, while also containing production cost increases—conceivably other countries will adopt similar programs in place of, or in combination with, carbon pricing.

Low-carbon technology subsidies have been uncommon for the industrial sector. The United States introduced federally funded tax credits for low-carbon industrial technologies (like green hydrogen), often with requirements that technologies are produced locally, although many tax credits were subsequently reversed.

Choice of Mitigation Instruments

What Are the Pros and Cons of Applying Carbon Pricing to the Industrial Sector?

Carbon pricing is well suited for the industrial sector because it can provide a predictable price signal (to promote long-lived, low-carbon technologies) and is technology neutral (which is important given uncertainties over which technologies will prove most cost-effective in future). ETSs applied to smokestack emissions promote all behavioral responses to reduce emissions, whereas carbon taxes applied midstream to fossil fuels can be combined with taxes on feedstocks like limestone or clinker and rebates for emissions capture.

The drawback of carbon pricing is its more substantial effect on production costs, and hence competitiveness (see Chapter 6 for more discussion). Unit production costs increase through three channels (see Figure 4.7):

- *Abatement costs*—from reducing the (direct) emissions intensity of production (through the first four responses in Table 4.2), indicated by the shaded triangle under the marginal abatement cost schedule;
- *Charges on unabated emissions*—tax payments or allowance purchases paid on remaining (direct) emissions per unit of output, indicated by the larger shaded rectangle; and
- *Higher electricity input costs*—charges on (indirect) emissions embodied in electricity inputs (the product of emissions per unit of generation, electricity per unit of industrial production, and the price on power sector emissions), indicated by the smaller shaded rectangle.[7]

Charges on unabated emissions are large relative to abatement costs, though their relative size declines with deeper abatement levels.

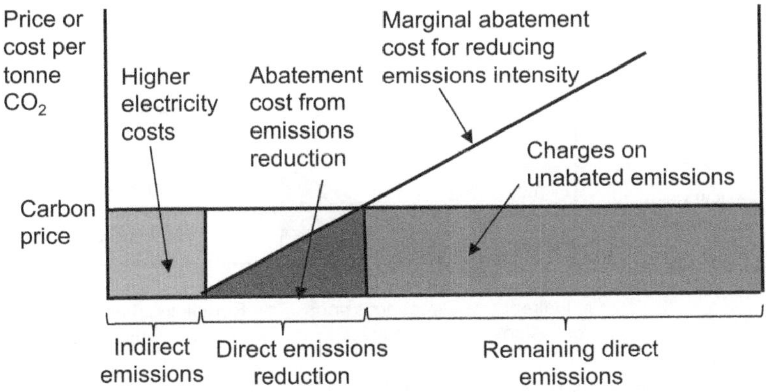

Figure 4.7 Production Cost Increases under Carbon Pricing.

Source: Authors.

Note: Emissions are defined per unit of production. Carbon price is assumed the same for direct industry emissions and indirect emissions embodied in electricity inputs.

Are Feebates and Performance Standards a Good Alternative, or Complement, to Carbon Pricing?

A feebate would involve the government specifying an emissions rate pivot point for each major industry (based, for example, on the previous year's industry average emissions rate) and firms reporting both their emissions and output and paying fees or receiving rebates accordingly. Fluid credit trading markets, across firms within and across industries, are also needed for performance standards to be cost-effective.[8]

Feebates and performance standards are a promising option where carbon pricing is politically constrained because they cost-effectively promote all mitigation responses in Table 4.2 aside from in the last row, while typically having smaller effects on production costs (see Figure 4.8). Abatement costs are larger for the same total emissions reduction (given the need to push harder on reducing emissions intensity of production to compensate for the smaller effect on reducing production levels), but there are no charges on remaining emissions for the average firm. Increases in electricity input costs are also generally smaller if feebates or performance standards are applied to the power sector rather than pricing instruments.

Is There a Role for Technology Subsidies or Mandates?

Realistically, low-carbon technology subsidies cannot promote (and cost-effectively) the full range of behavioral responses for reducing emissions intensity (in the first four rows of Table 4.2) because this would require a different subsidy payment for every small and major technology adjustment across firms and industries. More likely, subsidies would be limited to

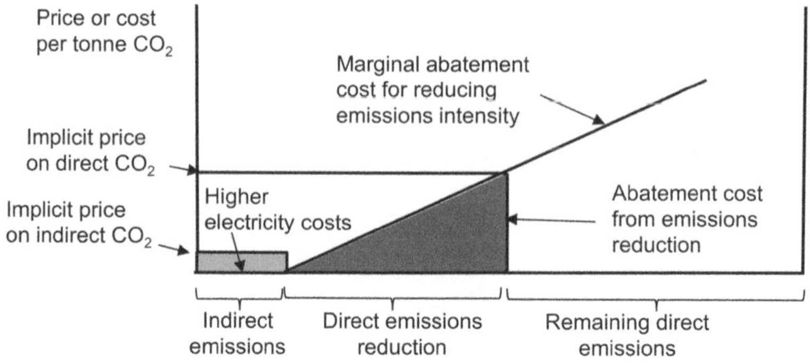

Figure 4.8 Production Cost Increases under Feebates and Performance Standards.

Source: Authors.

Note: Emissions are defined per unit of production.

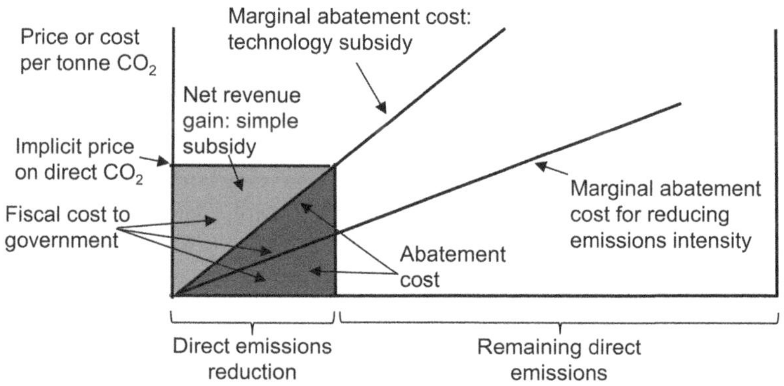

Figure 4.9 Production Cost Impacts of Technology Subsidies.

Source: Authors.

Note: Emissions are defined per unit of production. Figure shows impacts of subsidy per ton of CO_2 reduced.

major observable technologies (like green hydrogen, electrification, and emissions capture) though they would still push against a steeper marginal abatement cost schedule than feebates and performance standards and involve higher abatement costs per unit of production for the equivalent emissions reduction (see Figure 4.9). They also involve a fiscal cost on the government.

Although they affect competitiveness in the opposite direction to carbon pricing (a key concern for trading partners), in quantitative terms the effects on relative competitiveness are likely modest. For one thing, the base of the subsidy is the emissions reduction (which is generally smaller than remaining emissions—the relevant base for carbon pricing) and the subsidy payment is at least partly offset by the extra abatement costs (again see Figure 4.9).

As noted in Chapter 3, if policymakers are pursuing a subsidy approach, a promising model is the auction bid, although it does involve significant administrative and compliance costs. This is operating in the Netherlands (NEA 2020), where industrial firms make bids for subsidies to cover the costs of adopting low-carbon technologies—bids specify the CO_2 reductions and the requested subsidy per ton of CO_2 reduced. Subsidies are allocated to firms from a fixed government budget and prioritized to firms with the lowest bids per ton of CO_2 reduced. This approach: (1) limits fiscal costs, because funding requests (subject to third-party verification) are meant to cover, not overcompensate for, mitigation costs; (2) promotes cost-effectiveness, because firms with the lowest cost per tonne CO_2 reduced are prioritized for funding; and (3) limits competitiveness concerns, because the program has an approximately neutral effect on production costs.

Mandates for specific technologies are not well suited to the industrial sector given the: (1) diverse range of potential mitigation technologies; (2) uncertainty over which technologies will be the most cost-effective in future; and (3) differences in the costs of adopting a particular technology across firms in an industry (for example, retrofitting a steel plant with an electric furnace may be less costly for an older plant due for a major refurbishment).

Transport

Emissions, Mitigation Opportunities, and Current Policies

What Are the Sources of Emissions from Transportation Systems?

CO_2 emissions from domestic transportation systems accounted for between about 10 and 40 percent of economywide CO_2 emissions across G20 countries in 2024 (international transport emissions are discussed in Chapter 9). Within transportation, most (at least 80 percent) of emissions are from road vehicles—the remainder is from domestic rail, shipping, aviation, and alternative fuel (like natural gas) vehicles. Within road transport, the share of emissions from gasoline vehicles, mainly light-duty vehicles, varies widely from about 10 percent (Türkiye) to 70 percent (Mexico), whereas the remainder is almost all from diesel vehicles (mainly heavy-duty trucks, buses, and diesel cars). See Figure 4.10. Diesel cars have higher fuel economy than their gasoline counterparts but per liter of fuel combustion emit about 12 percent more CO_2 emissions.

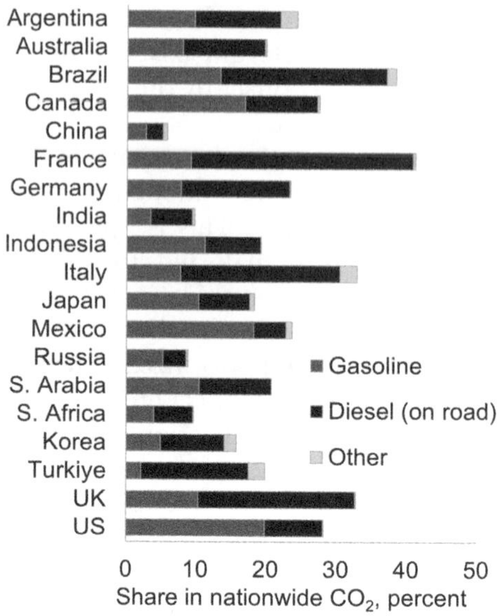

Figure 4.10 Contribution of Transportation Vehicles to Nationwide CO_2 Emissions, 2024.

Source: Authors' calculations using CPAT.

Note: Diesel includes cars, trucks, and buses. Other includes domestic aviation, rail, shipping, and alternative fuel (for example, natural gas) vehicles.

What Are the Main Behavioral Responses for Reducing Transportation Emissions?

Responses can be classified as follows:

- *Vehicle sales*: the main channel for decarbonizing light-duty vehicles over the longer run is shifting sales from internal combustion engine vehicles (ICEVs) to electric vehicles (EVs). EV sales shares for new vehicles have been expanding rapidly in many countries (Figure 4.11), though various technological and infrastructure obstacles to electrification need to be addressed (see Annex 4.2). In the near to medium term, however, while ICEVs are still being sold, another important response is to shift sales from low- to high-fuel economy ICEVs (including hybrids), as well as technological modifications at vehicle manufacturers to raise the fuel economy of new ICEVs (like improved engine efficiency or reduced vehicle weight).
- *Used vehicles*: there is limited scope for reducing CO_2 emissions in used light-duty vehicles given the fixed stock at a point in time. There are, however, possibilities to turn the fleet over faster by accelerating the scrappage rate for older, emissions-intensive vehicles.
- *Km driven per ICEV*: reducing the driving intensity of existing ICEVs can also contribute to reducing CO_2 emissions, though again there are limitations to this response.

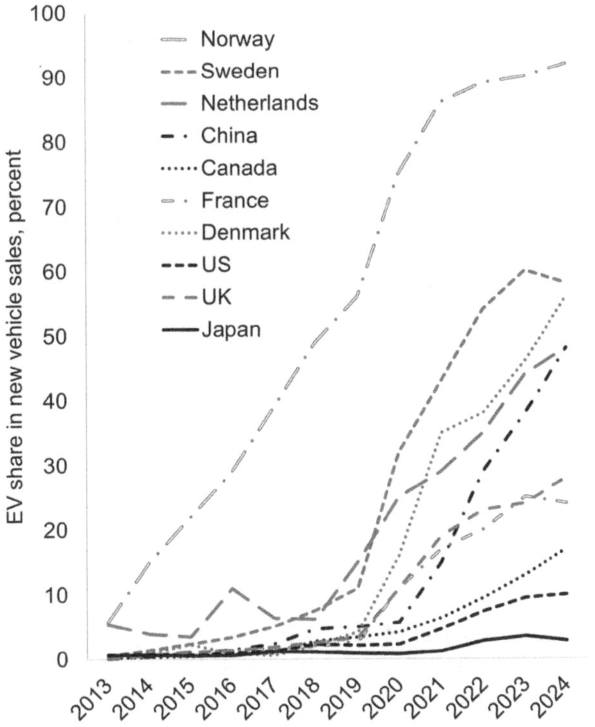

Figure 4.11 Shares of EVs in New Car Sales over Time, Selected Countries.

Source: IEA (2024).

Note: Includes all EVs, including plug-ins and hybrids.

What Are the CO_2 Emissions Intensities and Costs of Different Vehicle Types?

Emissions for passenger EVs using electricity produced with natural gas and coal emit about 50 and 90 percent, respectively, per kilometer driven relative to a comparable ICEV. For freight, emissions per kilometer for EVs are 25 percent higher and 40 percent lower when powered by coal and natural gas, respectively. Moreover, the energy efficiency of freight EVs is expected to fall relative to ICEVs over time, resulting in a similar emissions intensity between ICEVs and coal-powered freight EVs by 2030[9] (see Figure 4.12, panel 1). The time of day when charging occurs also affects the electricity price, load on the electricity network, and emissions generated in producing electricity—home charging is generally done in the evening (when baseload generation from coal might be more likely), whereas public stations are used earlier in the day.

Currently, the lifecycle costs (excluding purchase taxes/subsidies) of new EVs are mostly about a third higher than for their ICEV counterparts across selected countries shown in Figure 4.12, panel 2, mainly reflecting much higher battery costs for EVs but also relative prices of gasoline, diesel, and electricity. The exception is China where EVs are only about 5 percent costlier than ICEVs.

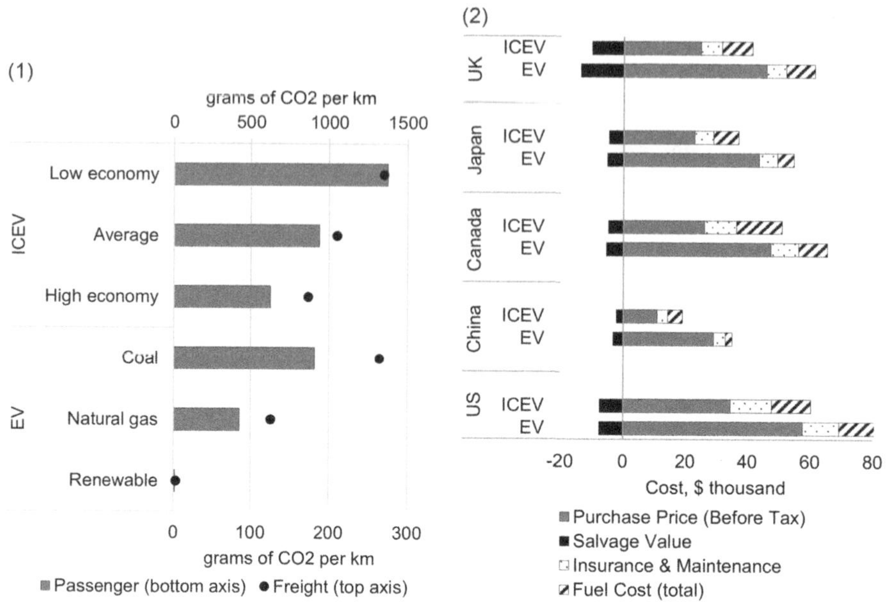

Figure 4.12 Emissions Intensities and Costs of Alternative Vehicle Types. Panel 1. CO_2 Emissions per km.[a]* Panel 2. Lifetime Vehicle Costs[b]†.

Sources: [a]IMF staff calculations using IEA (2019, 2024). [b]IMF staff calculations using IEA (2024).

Note: *For passenger vehicles, high, average, and low fuel economy for ICEVs generally reflect averages for small cars, small SUVs, and large SUVs. Fuel economy for passenger EVs reflects that of a small SUV. †Lifecycle costs are estimated for a medium-sized car.

What Are the Main Policies to Reduce Vehicle Emissions?

These include the following:

- *Fuel taxes*: Nine G20 countries impose gasoline excises equivalent to about $150 per ton CO_2 or more (up to $400 per ton). In most cases, however, diesel fuel taxes, expressed in CO_2 equivalents, are noticeably lower than gasoline taxes. Some countries impose fuel excises equivalent to less than $50 per ton CO_2, and in some cases, countries continue to subsidize road fuels (see Figure 4.13, panel 1).
- *Performance standards*: These policies are sometimes imposed on sellers of light-duty vehicles in the form of requirements for average CO_2 per km, or average fuel economy, across sales fleets. One or other of these policies applies nationally in nine G20 countries, and at the EU level, and has been progressively tightened over the past two decades. Standards in 2020 varied from the equivalent of about 100 grams CO_2 per km in EU countries and Korea to 125 grams CO_2 per km in Brazil and are scheduled to continue tightening (see Figure 4.13, panel 2). Low-carbon fuel standards are applied in some cases—their main effect is to increase blending of biofuels with gasoline and diesel.

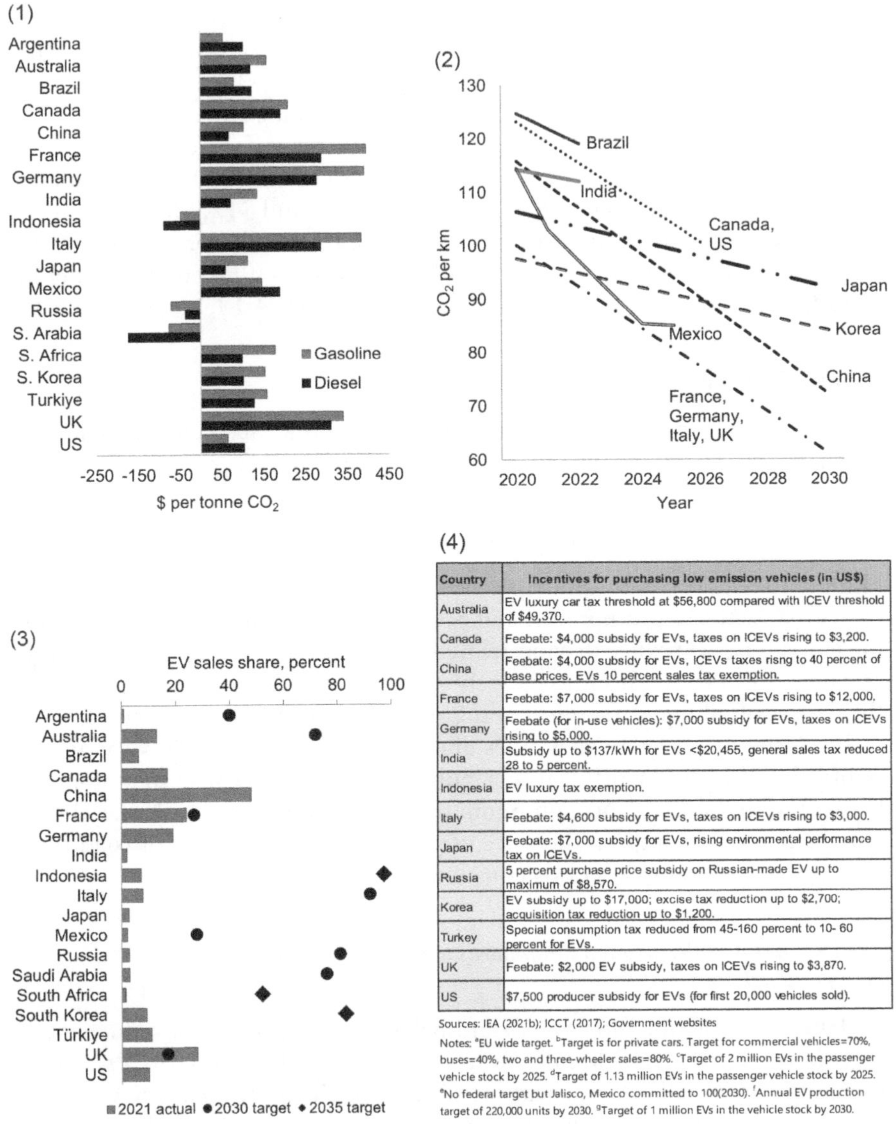

Country	Incentives for purchasing low emission vehicles (in US$)
Australia	EV luxury car tax threshold at $56,800 compared with ICEV threshold of $49,370.
Canada	Feebate: $4,000 subsidy for EVs, taxes on ICEVs rising to $3,200.
China	Feebate: $4,000 subsidy for EVs, ICEVs taxes risng to 40 percent of base prices. EVs 10 percent sales tax exemption.
France	Feebate: $7,000 subsidy for EVs, taxes on ICEVs rising to $12,000.
Germany	Feebate (for in-use vehicles): $7,000 subsidy for EVs, taxes on ICEVs rising to $5,000.
India	Subsidy up to $137/kWh for EVs <$20,455, general sales tax reduced 28 to 5 percent.
Indonesia	EV luxury tax exemption.
Italy	Feebate: $4,600 subsidy for EVs, taxes on ICEVs rising to $3,000.
Japan	Feebate: $7,000 subsidy for EVs, rising environmental performance tax on ICEVs.
Russia	5 percent purchase price subsidy on Russian-made EV up to maximum of $8,570.
Korea	EV subsidy up to $17,000; excise tax reduction up to $2,700; acquisition tax reduction up to $1,200.
Turkey	Special consumption tax reduced from 45-160 percent to 10- 60 percent for EVs.
UK	Feebate: $2,000 EV subsidy, taxes on ICEVs rising to $3,870.
US	$7,500 producer subsidy for EVs (for first 20,000 vehicles sold).

Sources: IEA (2021b); ICCT (2017); Government websites

Notes: [a]EU wide target. [b]Target is for private cars. Target for commercial vehicles=70%, buses=40%, two and three-wheeler sales=80%. [c]Target of 2 million EVs in the passenger vehicle stock by 2025. [d]Target of 1.13 million EVs in the passenger vehicle stock by 2025. [e]No federal target but Jalisco, Mexico committed to 100(2030). [f]Annual EV production target of 220,000 units by 2030. [g]Target of 1 million EVs in the vehicle stock by 2030.

Figure 4.13 Main Policies to Reduce Light-Duty CO_2 Emissions, G20 Countries. Panel 1. Fuel Taxes.[a] Panel 2. Performance Standards.[b] Panel 3. EV Targets.[c] Panel 4. Feebates and Other Vehicle Taxes[d†].

Sources: [a]See Chapter 8. [b]Parry et al. (2022b). [c]Updated from Parry et al. (2022b). [d]Parry et al. (2022b).

Note: [†]For Germany, circulation incentives are converted to the equivalent incentives for new vehicles. Policies are up to date as of 2022.

- *EV sales targets*: Fifteen G20 countries have targets for phasing in (light-duty) EVs or phasing out ICEVs—indeed 10 countries have pledged to fully ban ICEVs in new vehicle sales by 2030 or 2035 (see Figure 4.13, panel 3).
- *Vehicle taxes/subsidies*: Nine G20 countries include some elements of fee-bates in light-duty vehicle registration tax systems (for new and imported used vehicles) with EV subsidies varying between $2,000 and $7,500 and fees for high emitters rising to between $3,000 and $12,000, whereas five other G20 countries just have EV subsidies. Unusually for light-duty vehicles, Germany imposes annual circulation incentives linked to CO_2 per km rather than incentives for new vehicles (see Figure 4.13, panel 4).

Options for Policy Reform

Table 4.3 summarizes the attributes of different policy instruments, while the following discussion provides some elaboration.

Should Policymakers Raise Fuel Taxes?

Higher fuel taxes have multiple economic and practical benefits. They (1) cost-effectively promote the full range of behavioral responses for reducing emissions; (2) reduce driving-related externalities (see Chapter 8); (3) raise revenue; and (4) are administratively straightforward (fuel taxes are among the easiest of all taxes to collect and are well established in most countries).

But large increases in fuel taxes above current levels can be very difficult politically (and frequently cause a public backlash), because they impose a highly visible burden (through pump prices) on motorists, while diesel taxes may be passed through to the price of goods with a high share of road transport costs (for example, goods consumed in rural areas).

Are Feebates and Performance Standards a Reasonable Alternative to Higher Fuel Taxes?

Feebates promote the most important behavioral responses for reducing CO_2 emissions (shifting vehicle sales to more efficient ICEVs and to EVs), can be integrated into vehicle registration taxes (which apply in most countries) once capacity for measuring vehicle emissions rates is established, and should be politically easier than fuel taxes (although the price of emissions-intensive ICEVs increases, prices fall for low-emissions ICEVs and EVs and feebates avoid new tax burdens for the average motorist).

Feebates do not, however, promote retirement of in-use, CO_2-intensive vehicles. They can slightly increase km driven per ICEV through lowering fuel costs per km[10] and (depending on design) can be revenue neutral—in fact, on net, they can moderately reduce revenue because of base erosion for preexisting fuel taxes. Operationally, (tradable) performance standards are like feebates (for a given reduction in average vehicle CO_2/km they have

Table 4.3 Attributes of Alternative Policies for Reducing CO_2 Emissions from Vehicles

Metric	*Policy Instrument*					
	Fuel Taxes	*Feebate (New Vehicles)*	*Performance Standard (New Vehicles)*	*EV Subsidy (New Vehicles)*	*EV Mandate (New Vehicles)*	*Circulation Taxes on CO_2/km (Used Vehicles)*
Effectiveness: Vehicle Sales	A: Promotes more efficient ICEVs; ICEVs → EVs	A: Promotes more efficient ICEVs; ICEVs → EVs	A: Promotes more efficient ICEVs; ICEVs → EVs	N: Does not promote more efficient ICEVs	N: Does not promote more efficient ICEVs	N: Indirectly promotes more efficient ICEVs; ICEVs → EVs
Effectiveness: Used Vehicles	A: Promotes retirement of CO_2 intensive vehicles	D: No effect	D: No effect	D: No effect	D: No effect	A: Promotes retirement of CO_2 intensive vehicles
Effectiveness: km Driven Per ICEV	A: Reduces km driven (moderately)	D: Slightly increases km driven	D: Slightly increases km driven	N: No effect	N: No effect	A: Reduces km driven (moderately)
Fiscal	A: Raises revenue	N: Modest revenue loss (from erosion of fuel tax base)	N: Modest revenue loss (from erosion of fuel tax base)	D: Sizable fiscal cost	N: Modest revenue loss (from erosion of fuel tax base)	A: Raises revenue
Administration	A: Well established in most countries	N: Can be integrated into vehicle registration taxes but capacity needed to monitor emission rates	D: Requires new capacity to monitor emission rate of sales fleets and trading markets	N: Can be integrated into vehicle registration taxes but capacity needed to monitor emission rates	D: Requires new capacity for monitoring EV sales (and possible trading markets)	N: Can be integrated into circulation taxes where they apply
Political Acceptability (Households)	D: Large fuel tax increases can be very difficult	N: Some ICEV buyers worse off/ EV buyers better off	N: Some ICEV buyers worse off/ EV buyers better off	A: EV buyers better off	N: Modest change in relative vehicle prices	D: Large circulation tax increases can be very difficult

Source: Authors.

Note: A, D, and N denote an advantage, a disadvantage and neither an advantage nor disadvantage, respectively. ICEV = internal combustion engine vehicle; EV = electric vehicle.

equivalent effects on relative vehicle prices) but require new capacity for monitoring trading markets as well as emissions rates—for practical purposes they need to be applied to dealers' sales fleets (whereas feebates can alternatively apply to individual vehicles when registration taxes are levied).

Given the multiple benefits of fuel taxes but likely constraints on their acceptability, mitigation strategies for transportation will need a balance between fuel taxes and reinforcing instruments like feebates and performance standards to achieve the stronger price signals on CO_2 emissions needed to promote transitions to EVs.

What Is the Role of Subsidies and Mandates?

EV subsidies are similar to the rebate side of a feebate, so they do not promote shifting among ICEV vehicles and they impose fiscal costs. They may, however, have greater acceptability than feebates because they lower the price of EVs without increasing the price of emissions-intensive vehicles and (unlike performance standards) do not require capacity for monitoring trading markets. In reality, there is a continuum between EV subsidies and feebates because subsidies may be combined with some additional taxes on ICEVs but perhaps not enough to offset the subsidy outlays.

The emissions effects of tradable EV sales share mandates for vehicle dealers are similar to EV subsidies. They do not impose a new fiscal cost on the government, but the flip side is that they likely have lower acceptability than subsidies because they do not compensate households and firms for the costs of shifting the sales mix to EVs (firms exceeding the requirement get a modest subsidy through credit sales and vice versa for firms falling short of the requirement). They also require some capacity for monitoring credit trading markets.

There is less focus nowadays on biofuel subsidies or mandates for road vehicles (such as ethanol derived from corn, cellulosic ethanol derived from plants, and bio-diesel derived from soybeans). This is because: (1) there are limits (typically 10 percent) on the extent they can be blended with gasoline and diesel; (2) they divert land from forestry or agriculture; (3) the policy focus has shifted to EVs given their improving competitiveness and potential for fully eliminating emissions; and (4) biofuels have greater value in international aviation and maritime (see Chapter 9) than road transport.

Is There a Role for Annual Circulation Taxes to Promote Decarbonization of Light-Duty Vehicles?

In principle, over the longer term if there are adequate incentives to shift first vehicle purchases to fuel-efficient ICEVs and EVs there is no need for additional incentives applied to used vehicles. Alternatively, instead of incentives applied at the time of vehicle sales, annual circulation taxes could be applied, linked to the CO_2 emissions rate of in-use vehicles (inferred from vehicle inspection data or tables on average emissions rates by model and vintage)—households should consider these incentives when comparing lifecycle costs of ICEVs and EVs when purchasing vehicles. Annual circulation taxes are, however, opaque and uncertain (because of uncertainty over future tax schedules and how long households will keep vehicles) compared with immediate purchase taxes/subsidies and in this regard provide a weaker signal for low-carbon vehicle transitions.

During the course of the transition, however, incentives are also needed to accelerate the retirement of existing, emissions-intensive ICEVs.[11] This could be done through circulation taxes but there may be constraints on both administration (if annual vehicle taxes are not presently collected) and acceptability (if there is resistance from households to retroactively raising taxes on high emissions vehicles that were not anticipated at the time of purchase). In this case, subsidies for replacing an old ICEV with an EV may be a more practical approach.[12]

What Are the Distributional Concerns with Vehicle Feebates and Fuel Economy Standards?

Policies to lower the price of EVs and raise the price of ICEVs may have distributional concerns given that EVs are currently expensive and disproportionately purchased by the wealthy. In addition, EVs may be a less promising option for the rural poor given ICEVs may have higher fuel economy when driven in rural areas and these households may have high costs to accessing charging networks. There are some counteracting factors, however:

- The concerns are largely transitory—as the market share for (new and used) EVs grows, more EV models will become available at lower prices, and new vehicle subsidies should progressively phase out.
- Vehicle tax systems often include an ad valorem element related to vehicle prices which implies more of this tax component is paid on more expensive vehicles (including high-end EVs).
- A feebate can disproportionately raise the price of luxury vehicles (which may have poor fuel economy because their bigger, more powerful engines require more fuel to accelerate) which are disproportionately used by the wealthy.
- The EV subsidy component of a feebate could be means-tested or the government could subsidize an EV leasing program.
- The rural poor might be assisted with subsidies for swapping an ICEV for a (used) EV.

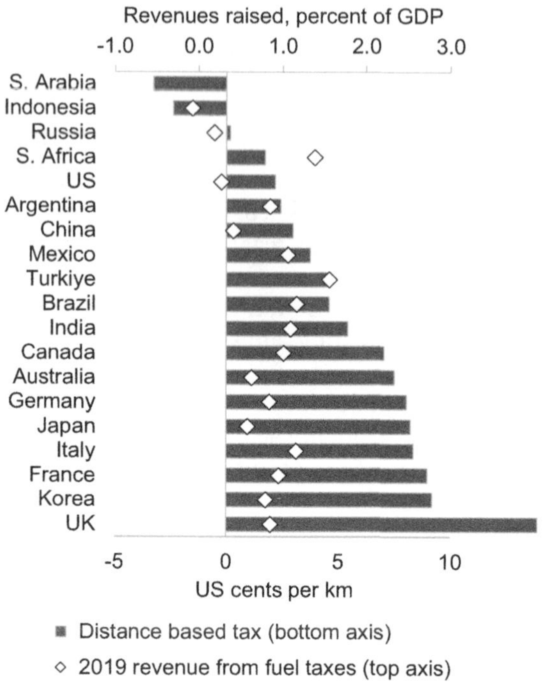

Figure 4.14 Maintaining Transportation Tax Revenues with Kilometer-Based Taxes.

Source: Authors using CPAT.

Note: Figure shows current fuel tax revenues (excluding VAT) and distance-based tax that would raise equivalent revenue.

What Can Replace the Erosion of Fuel Tax Revenues?

The transition away from ICEVs will progressively erode the base of fuel taxes which have been a valuable government revenue source, about 0.5–1.5 percent of GDP in most G20 countries in 2019 (see Figure 4.14).

A promising option to maintain transportation revenues—while preserving robust incentives for low-carbon vehicle transitions—is to transition to km-based taxes for all vehicles. This would provide a stable revenue source (invariant to changes in vehicle emissions rates)—across G20 countries, km-based charges (applied nationwide at a uniform rate to light- and heavy-duty vehicles) of about 4–8 cents per vehicle km could raise the same revenue (as a percent of GDP) in 2030 as fuel taxes in 2019 (Figure 4.14). Ultimately, km-based taxes could be fine-tuned to effectively manage road congestion, which can be severe for urban peak driving (see Chapter 8 for further discussion).[13] Distance-based taxes have the added benefit of being more difficult to avoid—this is especially important in small countries and for freight vehicles where there is a concern that drivers will refuel in neighboring countries with lower fuel prices.

What Are Appropriate Policies for Heavy-Duty Trucks and Other Transport Vehicles?

Electrification of heavy trucks hauling inter-city freight is becoming a possibility (IEA 2021), but applying feebates and performance standards to truck sales is administratively more complex and less effective than for light-duty vehicles. For example, freight companies might assemble trucks themselves after separately purchasing an engine, a vehicle, and a trailer—tailoring feebates and performance standards to each of these components may not be feasible. Moreover, there is more scope for behavioral responses to reduce CO_2 from used trucks—for example, modifying or swapping engines, changing the amount of freight per vehicle km, and adjusting vehicle km driven. Taxing diesel fuel promotes all behavioral responses for reducing truck emissions, but there may be constraints on the political acceptability of higher taxes (for example, opposition from trucking companies) and high taxes promote cross-border refueling and the black market (for example, re-selling to truckers of diesel fuel initially purchased for off-road vehicles not subject to high taxes).

Alternatively, a feebate might be integrated into an annual circulation tax applied to (large) trucking companies, if data were collected on the CO_2 (or fuel efficiency) per ton km of trucks and output in terms of ton km.[14] Taxes would be proportional to the product of a CO_2 price, annual ton km, and the difference between their CO_2 emissions rate per ton km and pivot point emissions rate. A higher CO_2 price would create stronger incentives for the full range of behavioral responses to cut CO_2 emissions from new and used trucks, while a higher pivot point would limit overall tax burdens on freight companies.

As regards other domestic transport vehicles (trains, buses, ships, tractors, industrial cranes) a feebate applied to first-time sales seems a reasonable approach given limited scope for cutting emissions of the in-use fleets and potentially thin markets for credit trading among suppliers under a tradable performance standard.

Should Transit Fares Be Subsidized to Reduce CO_2 Emissions?

There is a solid economic rationale for subsidizing passenger fares for urban bus and rail systems at both peak and off-peak periods, but this is largely because of other rationales than CO_2 reductions (Parry and Small 2009). One rationale is potentially large economies of scale from expanding transit service, such as reduced passenger time lost at transit stops (where service frequency is increased), reduced costs of accessing transit systems (with greater density of the service network), and increased load factors for transit vehicles. Another rationale is reduced road congestion, to the extent peak-period drivers are diverted onto transit. CO_2 benefits tend to be less important given, for example, that some of the increased transit ridership is not from people who would otherwise have driven, and the lower value of CO_2 reductions per avoided car trip relative to congestion benefits in highly congested urban centers.

Buildings

Emissions, Mitigation Opportunities, and Current Policies

What Are the Sources of Emissions from Buildings?

Natural gas use in buildings accounted for between 0 and 15 percent of nationwide CO_2 emissions across G20 countries in 2022, oil use between 0.2 and 5.5 percent, while there is a significant amount of coal use in limited cases (China, South Africa, and Türkiye). Indirect emissions from residential electricity use were significant in all countries, between 2.3 and 14.3 percent (see Figure 4.15, panel 1).

At least in EU countries (where data are available) space heating is usually the biggest source of residential energy consumption, accounting for between about 30 and 75 percent of consumption, followed by lighting/appliances and water heating, and generally small amounts of use for cooling and cooking (see Figure 4.15, panel 2.)

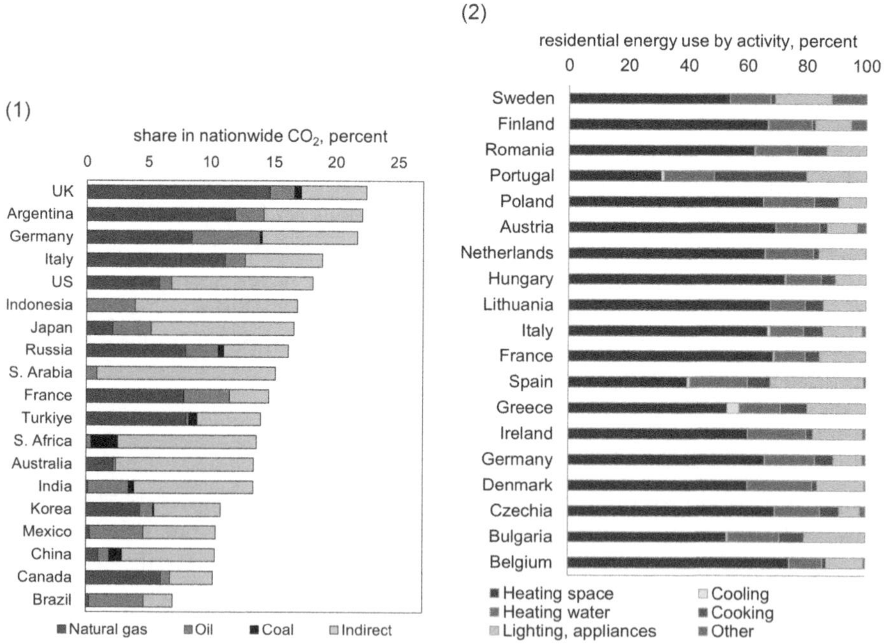

Figure 4.15 Shares of CO_2 Emissions and Energy Use in Buildings, Selected Countries. Panel 1. Share of Building Fuels in Nationwide CO_2, G20 Countries, 2022.[a] Panel 2. Household Energy Consumption by Activity, Selected EU Countries, 2021[b†].

Sources: [a]Authors' calculations using CPAT. [b]Eurostat.

Note: [†]Indirect is CO_2 emissions embodied in electricity use. Biomass emissions, which can be a significant heating source in developing countries, are excluded (because emissions are attributed to deforestation and other land-use activities).

How Energy Efficient Are Building Stocks?

The energy efficiency of buildings can vary dramatically across new structures, existing structures that have been refurbished, and older (non-refurbished) buildings. Many countries compile data on the energy performance of buildings, where assessments are based on factors like insulation, heating systems, lighting, and renewable energy sources (this reporting may be required when buildings are sold or rented). In the EU and the United Kingdom, for example, labels A, B, C, D, and E correspond to annual energy use of below 50, 50–90, 91–150, 151–230, and 231–330 kWh per square meter, respectively. In EU countries, typically about 40–60 percent of the residential building stock has a ranking of E or below, whereas 10 percent or less have a rating of B or above (see Figure 4.16), suggesting substantial opportunities for refurbishments to cut energy consumption. For example, a shift from E or less to A could reduce energy consumption of a building by about 85 percent.[15]

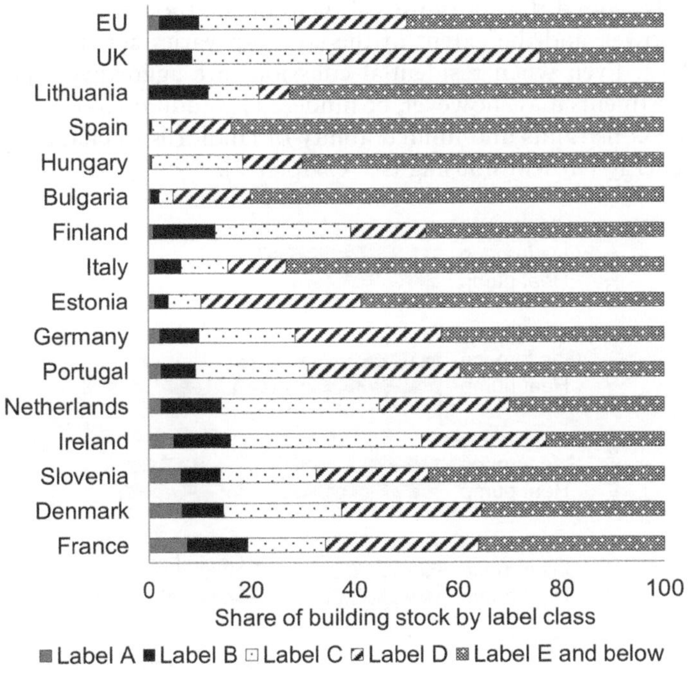

Figure 4.16 Distribution of Building Stock by Energy Performance Class, 2019.

Source: Arregui et al. (2020).

Note: Ratings A, B, C, D, and E correspond to annual energy use of below 50, 50–90, 91–150, 151–230, and 231–330 kWh per square meter, respectively. The United Kingdom refers to England and Wales.

What Behavioral Responses Can Reduce Building Emissions?

Given the very gradual turnover of the residential building stock (typically about 2 percent a year) and that most existing buildings have low energy efficiency, policies need to target both existing and new buildings. Opportunities include:

- *Input shifting*—including switching to rooftop solar and replacing gas/oil heating with electric heat pumps, as well as gas-burning with electric stoves.
- *Efficiency*—including better roof, wall, and window insulation; more efficient heating and cooling equipment; more efficient lighting and appliances; and digitalization to "smart" homes (for example, automatic temperature adjustments based on occupancy, time of day, and weather conditions).
- *Demand responses*—including, for example, turning down the heating, switching off lights, having shorter showers, less frequent use of dishwashers, washing machines, and dryers.

The upfront costs of a residential heat pump (including installation) tend to significantly exceed those from fossil fuel boilers, though lifecycle operating costs are lower, and the extent of the cost gap varies across countries—see Figure 4.17. Even when residential emissions are aggressively priced, heat pump investments may, however, be hindered by additional impediments like borrowing constraints and limited ability of landlords to charge rent premiums for energy-efficient housing (see Chapter 7).

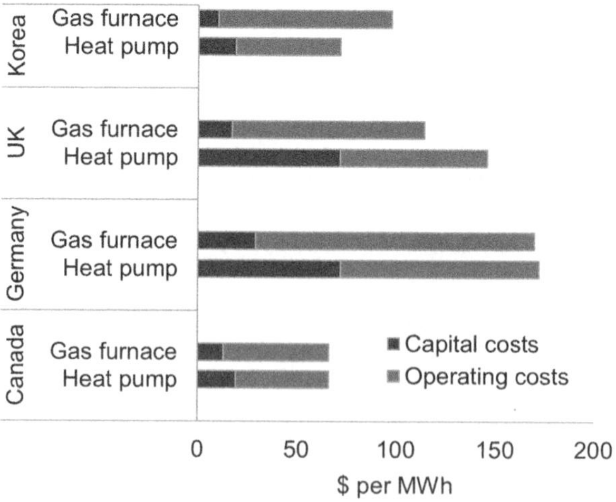

Figure 4.17 Lifecycle Costs of Heating/Cooling Systems, 2021.

Source: Authors' calculations using IEA (2022a), Figure 3.1.

Note: Heat pump is for air-to-air system and excludes subsidies.

What Are the Main Targets and Policies to Reduce Building Emissions?

Four G20 countries have ambitious targets for cutting emissions from the existing residential building stock (France, Germany, Italy, and Japan), whereas nine others have targets for new buildings to be net zero,[16] or nearly net zero by 2030 or thereafter (see Figure 4.18, panel 1).

As noted in Chapter 3, countries typically use multiple instruments to reduce energy use in buildings, such as:

- *Performance standards*: for example, energy efficiency standards for household appliances, minimum energy performance requirements for rented buildings.
- *Technology subsidies*: for example, fiscal incentives for heat pumps, insulation upgrades, and rooftop solar.
- *Technology standards*: for example, phasing out the use of fossil fuel heating systems in new buildings and building codes specifying design requirements to reduce energy needs for space heating.

In addition, about half of the nearly 50 pricing programs summarized in Annex 3.2 cover building fuels. Despite this, however, residential natural gas and oil use are subject to significant CO_2 equivalent taxes in only a handful of G20 countries (see Figure 4.18, panel 2).

(1)

Country	Target
	All new buildings net zero emissions by 2030.
China	Green buildings to account for 50 percent of new urban buildings.
France	Reduce building sector emissions 44 percent below 2020 emisisons by 2030; EU legislation requires all new buildings to be nearly zero energy.
Germany	Reduce building sector emissions 43 percent below 2020 emisisons by 2030; EU legislation requires all new buildings to be nearly zero energy.
India	Reduce energy use for new commercial buildings 50 percent by 2030.
Indonesia	Reduce energy intensity ≥ 1 percent per year till 2025.
Italy	Reduce building sector emissions 25 percent below 2020 emisisons by 2030; EU legislation requires all new buildings to be nearly zero energy.
Japan	Reduce building sector CO2 emissions 66 percent below 2013 levels by 2030. All new houses net zero emissions by 2030.
Mexico	Reduce energy consumption for all buildings 3.7 percent a year 2031-2050.
Russia	5 percent purchase price subsidy on Russian-made EV up to maximum of $8,570.
Korea	All new buildings net zero emissions by 2030.
UK	Reduce CO2 emisisons for all new buildings 75-80 percent by 2030.
US	All new buildings net zero emissions by 2030.

(2)

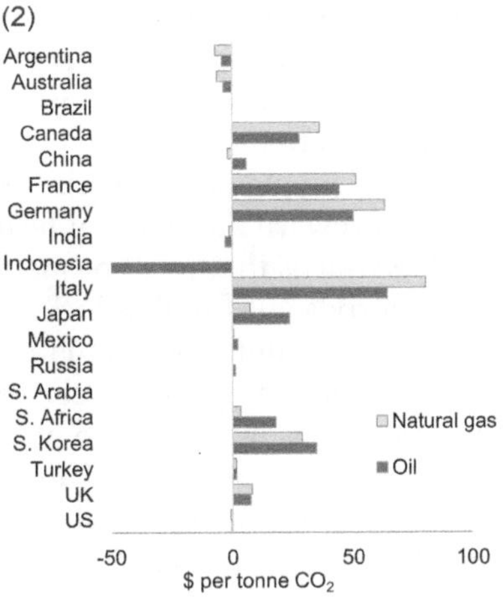

Figure 4.18 Building Emissions Targets and Residential Fuel Taxes/Subsidies, G20 Countries, 2023. Panel 1. Emissions Targets.[a] Panel 2. Fuel Taxes in CO_2 Equivalent[b†].

Sources: [a]Parry et al. (2022a). [b]See Chapter 8.

Note: [†]Targets are up to date as of 2022.

Options for Policy Reform

Do Technology Subsidies Make Sense for the Building Sector?

Given wide dispersion in the costs and energy savings from low-carbon technology retrofits (heat pumps, insulation, and rooftop solar) across existing buildings (varying, for example, with the size of structures and local climate), a subsidy approach is more flexible than a mandatory approach where the latter imposes uniform technology or energy efficiency requirements across all households, regardless of their costs. But the fiscal costs of technology subsidies can be substantial.

One possibility is to finance subsidies for low-carbon technology investments through higher taxes on building fuels. For the equivalent emissions reduction, this requires a smaller increase in fuel taxes than relying on fuel taxes alone, or smaller subsidies than relying on subsidies alone, because the incentive for the low-carbon technology investment is the combined effect of the fuel tax and the subsidies rather than just the fuel tax or just the subsidy.[17]

How Might Property Tax Reform Promote Building Decarbonization?

Most countries impose property taxes, and these could be linked to energy performance ratings to promote refurbishments of the building stock—one possibility is to integrate a feebate into existing property taxes. Figure 4.19 provides an illustration where a fee equal to $0.05 per kWh per square meter is applied to the difference between the energy consumption rate per square meter of a building and that for the average building (taken to be 140 kWh per square meter from the EU average in 2019). In this illustration, a property of size 100 square meters (about the average in France and Germany) would receive a rebate of $500 per year for a class A rating (defined in the previous section) while paying an extra tax of $700 for a class E rating. Better still would be to link the feebate to CO_2 (rather than energy) per square meter to reward adoption of heat pumps and rooftop solar.

One issue is that most property taxes are levied at local level with the primary purpose of funding local public services. Although the aim of the feebate (which could be mandated or otherwise incentivized by the national government) is to promote carbon-saving investments, designing it to be revenue neutral is important to prevent undermining local funding. This can be achieved by updating the pivot point in line with improving energy efficiency of the building stock, which lowers rebates for high-performance buildings over time while raising fees for low-performance buildings.[18]

What Policies Can Promote Energy Efficiency of Household Appliances?

As noted in Chapter 3, many countries apply minimum energy efficiency standards to a wide range of appliances but without credit trading

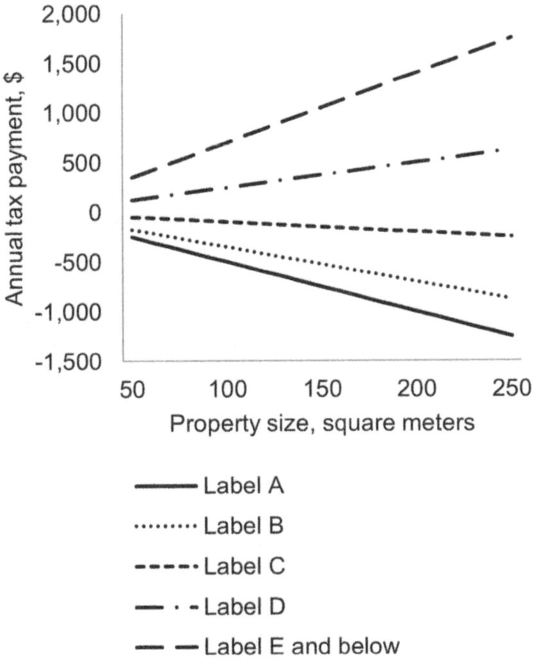

Figure 4.19 Illustrative Property Tax Adjustments under Feebate.

Source: Authors' calculations.

Note: Assumes price of $0.05 per kWh per square meter and pivot point energy consumption rate of 140 kWh per square meter (based on 2019 EU average). Energy performance labels correspond to those in Figure 4.15.

provisions that could promote cost-effectiveness across different models, firms, and products—this may reflect significant administrative costs from setting up and monitoring trading markets across diverse firms and products.

A feebate approach could promote cost-effectiveness without the need for trading markets. This would involve taxes on products with relatively low energy efficiency, in proportion to the difference between their energy consumption rate and a pivot point consumption rate, and subsidies for relatively efficient models in proportion to the difference between the pivot point and their consumption rate. For example, refrigerators would receive a fee/rebate according to the difference between kWh per cubic foot cooled and a pivot point kWh per cubic foot cooled.[19] To take another example, fees/rebates could be applied to air conditioners in proportion to the difference between their kWh per BTU of heat removed and a pivot point kWh per BTU of heat removed.

Forestry

Emissions and Mitigation Opportunities

What Are the Sources of CO_2 Emissions from the Forestry Sector?

Human activities affect CO_2 emissions from the forestry sector through various activities, including the following (see Mendelsohn et al. 2012):

- *Deforestation*—about 10 million hectares of deforestation occur each year with about 90 percent of the change because of burning forests for agricultural land, especially in tropical regions.[20] Mature tropical forests have the highest carbon density, with carbon storage of about 300 tons of CO_2 per hectare.
- *Degradation*—this is activities that permanently diminish the biological wealth of a forest without converting the land for other purposes, including fires, diseases, pests, climate change, and illegal logging (which can result in bare clearings, new roads, and ravaged vegetation and undergrowth).
- *Afforestation*—planting of trees on agricultural and abandoned land that can support forests naturally.[21] Afforestation has more potential for the longer term because it takes decades for trees to grow large enough to store substantial amounts of carbon. There are up to 2 billion hectares of agricultural land worldwide which in principle could be converted back to forestland.
- *Forest management*—converting forestland to plantations could sequester more carbon through, for example, planting larger trees, lengthening rotations, fertilizing, tree thinning, and reducing risks of disease and fires.

Four countries accounted for 70 percent of global CO_2 emissions from deforestation between 2018 and 2022—Brazil (38 percent), Indonesia (21 percent), Bolivia (6 percent), and Malaysia (5 percent) (see Figure 4.20). Deforestation/degradation net of afforestation currently accounts for about 12 percent of global CO_2 emissions though net emissions tend to decline over time as deforestation opportunities are progressively exhausted.[22]

Policy Options

What Policies Can Promote Forest Carbon Storage?

Nationally Determined Contributions contain commitments to reduce deforestation or expand forest coverage (see Table 4.4) but are often vague about specific policy instruments to achieve these objectives. The choice of mitigation instruments should be informed by drivers of deforestation, administrative considerations, and effects on those whose livelihood depends on the forests. Policy options include:

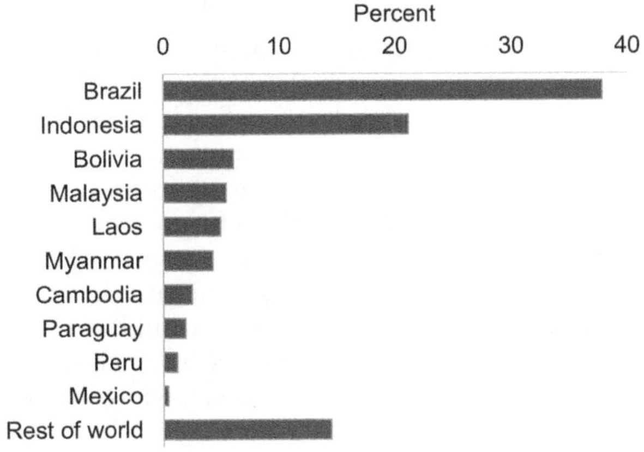

Figure 4.20 Global CO_2 Emissions from Deforestation, 2018–22.

Source: WRI (2023).

Table 4.4 Mitigation Commitments for Large Deforestation Emitters

Country	*Objectives and Measures for Forestry*
Brazil	Zero illegal deforestation by 2028, restore 12 million hectares of forests by 2030, and achieve net zero deforestation by 2050.
Indonesia	Ban on primary forest clearance; reduce deforestation/degradation; restore ecosystem functions; sustainable forest management.
Bolivia	By 2030, reduce deforestation to 80% compared to the baseline and in National Protected Areas to 100%.
Malaysia	Measures to promote forest carbon storage not specified.
Laos	Increase forest cover to 70% of land area.
Myanmar	Reduce deforestation by 25% (50% conditional on external support) by 2030.
Cambodia	Halve deforestation rates by 2030.
Paraguay	Laws prohibit conversion of areas with forest in the Eastern Region.
Mexico	Achieve zero net deforestation by 2030.

Source: UNFCCC (2024).

Note: Where applicable, more ambitious targets conditional on external finance are in parentheses.

- *Nationwide emissions pricing or feebates*: these programs are potentially effective for forestry but have rarely been applied not least because capacity for measuring carbon storage by land parcel is only recently emerging and property rights may not be clearly defined in key areas. Feebates and pricing systems are operationally very similar in the specific case of forestry. In a feebate, a nationwide system of fees and rebates would be applied to landowners according to the difference between stored carbon on their property in a baseline period and current carbon storage. A carbon tax that penalized deforestation while negatively taxing (or subsidizing) afforestation and forest management would work the same way. Under an ETS, as in New Zealand, firms are given allowances for increasing carbon storage relative to a baseline level, while they purchase allowances for reducing carbon storage. See Annex 4.3 on design issues for pricing programs and the New Zealand ETS.
- *Payments for forest conservation or environmental services*: Subsidies could be provided to landowners for afforestation or forest preservation projects with compliance subject to third-party verification. More generally, Payment for Environmental Services (PES) programs compensate for multiple environmental benefits (such as carbon storage, sustaining biodiversity, soil conservation, preventing floods, and land degradation). Annex 4.3 discusses experiences with PES programs which mainly operate in African, Asian, and Central/South American countries.
- *Commodity taxes*: Where harvesting a commodity like timber, palm oil, or cocoa is a key driver of deforestation, an option might be to tax the commodity but allow suppliers to petition for rebates if they demonstrate the commodity was produced sustainably.
- *International offsets*: forestry plays a prominent role in international markets for offset projects though, from a global perspective, offsets are not a mitigation instrument because they reallocate mitigation effort away from offset buyers to offset sellers rather than increase the overall level of mitigation (see Chapter 9).

How Do Instruments Compare in Terms of Effectiveness and Fiscal Impacts?

Table 4.5 compares attributes of the policies discussed in the previous section. Feebates or pricing schemes would cost-effectively promote afforestation, enhanced forest management, and reduced deforestation on privately owned land at the nationwide level.

In contrast, project-based PES programs would be less effective because they forgo many carbon sequestration opportunities (only a limited number of landowners will be enrolled). Indeed, if the program diverts production of agricultural or forest commodities this could encourage (by upward pressure on commodity prices) deforestation elsewhere in the country (a nationwide feebate or pricing program would penalize this extra deforestation). Additionally, there may be an issue if a forestry project would have gone ahead anyway (without the payment) due, for example, to possible

Table 4.5 Comparing Attributes of Alternative Policies for Increasing Forest Carbon Storage

Metric	*Policy Instrument*			
	Feebate/Pricing (National)	*Payments for Environmental Services (Project Based)*	*Timber or Commodity Tax (National)*[a]	*International Offsets for Afforestation/Avoided Deforestation (Project Based)*
Effectiveness: Behavioral Responses	A: Promotes all responses for forest carbon storage	N: Only promotes subset of afforestation projects	D: Does not promote afforestation or deter deforestation for non-logging purposes	D: Only promotes subset of projects; reductions attributed to offset buyer; does not reduce global emissions
Effectiveness: Additionality	A: Additionality not relevant as baseline observed	N: Risk that projects would have gone ahead without offset payment	A: Effectiveness: additionality	N: Risk that projects would have gone ahead without offset payment
Cost-effectiveness	A: Equalizes incremental mitigation costs across responses/landowners	D: No mechanism to promote cost-effectiveness	N: Rebates provide partial mechanism for cost-effectiveness	D: No mechanism to promote cost-effectiveness
Leakage (Domestic)	A: Penalizes leakage	D: Does not penalize leakage	N: Addresses leakage from logging	D: Does not penalize leakage
Government Revenue	N: Feebate can be revenue neutral, pricing can raise revenue	D: Loses revenue	A: Raises revenue	N: Raises modest revenue if government (rather than landowner) sells projects
Administrative Requirements	D: Monitoring carbon storage, capacity for applying fees/rebates, well-designed property rights at forestry/farm border	D: High transaction costs to contracting projects hinders scaling up	A: Timber/commodity volumes easier to monitor than carbon storage; onus on firms to demonstrate sustainability for rebates	D: High transaction costs to contracting projects hinders scaling up
Impact on Forest Users	N: Creates winners and losers	A: Households/communities with ownership rights benefit	D: Commodity suppliers worse off if taxes cannot be passed forward in higher prices	A: Households/communities with ownership rights benefit

Source: Authors.

Note: A, D, and N denote an advantage, a disadvantage and neither an advantage nor disadvantage of an instrument, respectively.

[a] Providing tax relief for sustainably produced timber could provide a broader range of responses for forest carbon storage.

commercial benefits from (sustainable) plantation forests. The program also loses revenue and, without funding allocation through auctions (see Chapter 3), may not prioritize cost-effective projects. The cost-effectiveness of PES programs can potentially be improved by requiring the landowner to cover all land rather than just chosen parcels (for example, see Izquierdo-Tort, Jayachandran, and Saavedra 2024).

A pure tax on sales of timber or forest products discourages deforestation from logging but other responses—afforestation, enhanced forest management, reducing deforestation from agricultural land conversion—are not promoted. Providing rebates for timber or commodity suppliers demonstrating sustainable forestry deters some deforestation/degradation, including illegal logging.

International offsets generally have similar attributes to PES. One difference is that they avoid a fiscal cost on the government (and could raise modest revenues if governments are selling offsets) though CO_2 reductions count toward meeting emissions commitments in the offset buying, rather than domestic, country.

Do Administrative Constraints Preclude Feebates or Similar Programs for Forestry?

Administrative requirements for feebates or similar pricing programs can be substantial and include:

- *Monitoring carbon storage.* Satellite imagery can measure forest coverage, but aerial photography, drones, and on-the-ground sampling may also be needed to assess carbon storage per hectare of forested land which varies with tree species, land productivity, selective harvesting, and so on.[23] The Readiness Fund of the Reducing Emissions from Deforestation and Forest Degradation (REDD+) program is helping tropical and sub-tropical developing countries build capacity for measuring inventories of carbon storage for different land parcels and their regular updating. In the interim, default emissions factors for different classes of forest and deforestation might be used—Table 4.6 provides an illustration for Papua New Guinea.
- *Capacity for applying policies.* Registries assigning land parcels (specifically, forestland potentially subject to deforestation/degradation and land potentially convertible to forest land) to identifiable landowners need to be established, as well as capacity for administering fees/rebates or pricing programs (perhaps building off any existing capacity for business taxes, VAT, or receipt of farm assistance).
- *Well-defined property rights.* Feebates or pricing programs would apply to private landowners, but in tropical areas only about 15 percent of forestland is privately owned.[24] Administrative costs might be contained by establishing clear property rights for large landowners at the forestry/agricultural border. A key challenge, however, is the possibility of overlapping interests in tropical forests—timber companies or the government may have the right to harvest timber while local inhabitants have rights to hunt wildlife, collect firewood, and graze animals.

Table 4.6 Emissions Factors for Deforestation and Degradation: Example of Papua New Guinea

Land-Use Subdivision	*Emissions Factors, Tons CO_2/Hectare/Year*		
	Deforestation (Primary Forest)	*Deforestation (Degraded Forest)*	*Forest Degradation*
Low-Altitude Forest on Plains/Fans	527	345	182
Low-Altitude Forest on Uplands	527	345	182
Low Montane Forest	307	201	106
Montane Forest	306	201	106
Montane Coniferous Forest	306	201	106
Dry Seasonal Forest	287	188	99
Littoral Forest	527	345	182
Seral Forest	527	345	182
Swamp Forest	527	345	182
Savannah	287	188	99
Woodland	287	188	99
Shrub	169	111	58
Mangrove	493	323	170
Plantation Forest	354	232	122

Source: https://pngreddplus.org/wp-content/uploads/2024/04/FRL2.pdf.

Note: Montane, littoral, and seral refer, respectively, to forests that are high altitude, near shore, and immature (growth following, for example, fire or disease) forests.

For many countries therefore, feebates and pricing programs may be a medium- to longer-term option. Where capacity is limited, commodity taxes or PES programs may be more realistic for the interim (these programs also may require more limited capacity improvements). In some cases, funding for the latter may come from partially redirecting existing farm support programs which are substantial in many countries (Figure 4.21)—besides limiting new fiscal burdens, this may reduce emissions through curbing excessive farm output.

Can Zero Deforestation Requirements for Commodity Suppliers Substitute for Forest Mitigation Policies?

Some government and private groups try to discourage deforestation by placing restrictions on commodities that are not produced sustainably. For example, the EU Deforestation-Free Products Regulation requires EU-registered companies to ensure imported agricultural commodities have not been produced on land deforested after 2020, while under the 2009 G4 Agreement, the four largest international meat-packing companies in Brazil exclude suppliers producing on recently deforested areas.

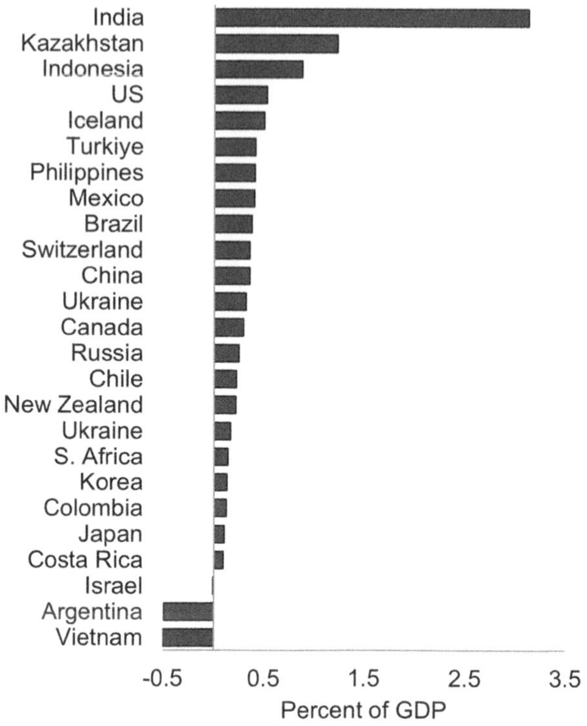

Figure 4.21 Total Agricultural Support, 2021.

Source: OECD (2022).

Note: Estimates mainly reflect the combined effects of producer and consumer supports.

Although these initiatives can have significant benefits (for example, Levy et al. 2023), they should complement, rather than substitute for, forest mitigation policies, given limitations on their effectiveness. For example, the G4 mostly excludes production for domestic consumption, small-scale packagers, and indirect suppliers (like those selling juvenile cattle to other farms)—and it provides no incentives for afforestation or enhanced forest management.

Agriculture

Emissions and Mitigation Opportunities

What Are the Sources of Agricultural Greenhouse Gases Emissions by Activity?

In 2021, global GHG emissions from agriculture were 6 billion tons of CO_2 equivalent (excluding emissions from land-use change, agricultural vehicles, and transport of farm products) with the main sources as follows (see Figure 4.22).

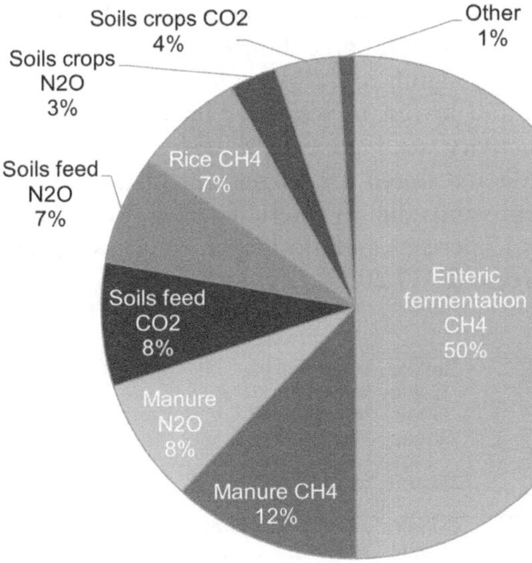

Figure 4.22 Global Agricultural GHG Emissions by Activity, 2021.

Source: FAO (2023).

Note: Assumed CO_2 equivalents for CH_4 and N_2O are 27 and 273, respectively. Excludes emissions from land-use change, agricultural vehicles, and transport of farm products. CH_4 = methane; N_2O = nitrous oxide.

- *Enteric fermentation*—methane emissions from digestive processes in livestock were by far the biggest emissions source, accounting for half of agricultural emissions.
- *Manure storage*—decomposition of manure under anaerobic conditions (which often occurs in intensive farming) accounted for another 20 percent of emissions, with 12 percent from methane and 8 percent from nitrous oxide.
- *Fodder crops*—like soy accounted for 15 percent of emissions, with about half each from CO_2 (for example, when microbes break down carbon compounds in dead crops, especially after tilling) and nitrous oxide (for example, from mineral fertilizers and as bacteria produce nitrate).
- *Rice cultivation*—flooded rice fields produce methane-emitting bacteria by preventing oxygen from penetrating the soil, and the resulting methane emissions contributed 7 percent to agricultural GHGs.
- *Crops for human consumption*—contributed 7 percent to emissions through release of nitrous oxide and CO_2 from soils.

What Are the Most Emissions-Intensive Farming Activities?

Globally, GHG emissions rates (including fodder crop emissions) are relatively high for ruminants[25] like buffalo, cattle, goats, and sheep, between 110 and 160 kg of CO_2 equivalent per kg of output, and relatively low for nonruminants like pigs and poultry (45 and 23 kg of CO_2 equivalent per kg of output, respectively). For emissions-intensive livestock, methane is typically about 60–75 percent of the total greenhouse gas emissions. Emissions intensities do, however, vary significantly by region and are generally highest in sub-Saharan Africa and lowest in western Europe, in part reflecting differences in herd productivity (see Figure 4.23).

Overall beef cattle accounted for 55 percent of the 70 percent of global agricultural GHG emissions due to enteric fermentation and manure storage in 2022—dairy was 17 percent, buffalo 15 percent, pigs 5 percent, and goats/sheep another 5 percent (FAO 2023).

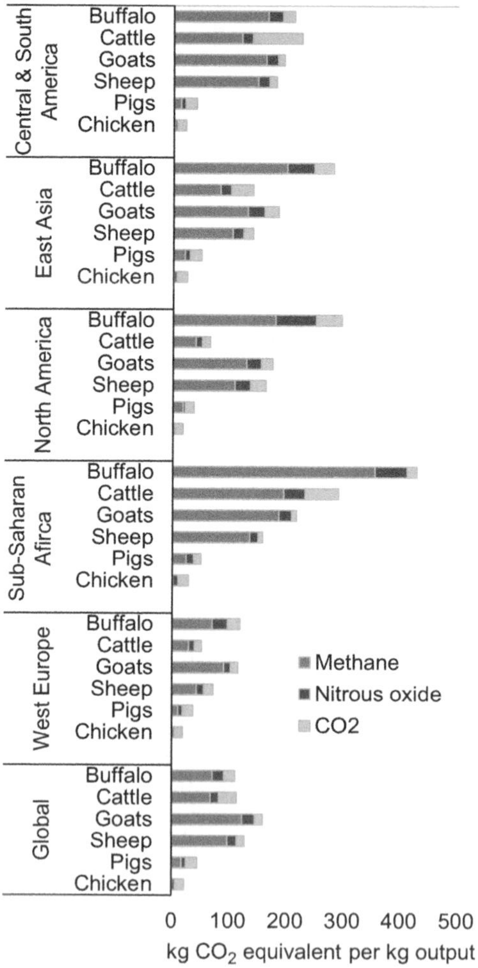

Figure 4.23 GHG Intensity by Livestock Type and Region, 2015.

Source: FAO (2024).

Note: Includes emissions from fodder crops.

Table 4.7 Mitigation Opportunities in the Agricultural Sector

Type of Response	*Examples*	
	Livestock	*Crop*
Higher Quality Inputs	More digestible feeds (e.g., better quality grasses), food additives (e.g., seaweed).	Higher quality soils, machinery, and seeds/ seedlings.
Production Efficiency	Better genetics/ reproductive practices, selective breeding, better medical care, reduced time to slaughter weight.	Intercropping, high-density and precision farming, optimized fertilizer use, hardier crops, more efficient water use.
Emissions Capture	Covering/composting manure, converting manure into biogas.	Soil management (e.g., manure application on cropland, use of cover crops, no-till farming). Draining rice paddies.
Demand Reduction	Beef/other ruminants → pork/chicken → plant-based food. Reducing meat demand.	Reducing food demand and waste.

Source: IPCC (2019), www.epa.gov/agstar/practices-reduce-methane-emissions-livestock-manure-management#one.

What Are the Main Opportunities for GHG Mitigation in the Agricultural Sector?

Opportunities include (see Table 4.7):

- *Higher quality inputs*: more digestible feeds to reduce enteric fermentation might include better quality grasses and food additives like seaweed.
- *Production efficiency*: measures to reduce herd size per unit of output might include better genetics and reproductive practices, selective breeding, better medical care, reduced time to slaughter weight, and barn modernization, whereas crop yields might be improved with, for example, intercropping, high-density and precision farming, optimized fertilizer use, and hardier varieties.
- *Emissions capture*: this includes technologies for covering and composting manure or capturing and using biogas produced by adding methane digestors to manure. It also includes enhanced soil management practices to capture CO_2, including more application of manure on cropland, crop rotation, greater use of cover crops, non-tilling, maintaining permanent pasture, and periodic draining to reduce water intensity of rice paddies.

- *Demand reductions*: the overall demand for food is relatively unresponsive to higher food prices, but there is significant scope for reducing emissions through changing the composition of food production—shifting away from beef to pigs and poultry, shifting from livestock to crop-based production, and reducing food waste (Batini 2021).

Policy Options

Is It Practical to Price Agricultural Emissions?

In principle, livestock farmers could be required to assess and report their own emissions (based, for example, on herd type and size, feed intake and type, and manure management system, along with default emissions factors[26]) and remit taxes accordingly. Small farms could be exempt to contain administrative costs. This pricing program is more realistic where data reporting systems for farm characteristics are already in place, third-party checks of emissions reports (using satellite imagery or on-the-ground inspections) are feasible, and farm registries are established for existing taxes or subsidies. For example, this type of pricing approach is under consideration in Ireland, the Netherlands, and New Zealand and implemented in Denmark. Feebates are another possibility where farmers are charged according to the difference between their emissions per kg of output and a pivot point emissions rate for the industry or specific products.[27] An emissions tax, or feebate, is likely more practical than an ETS for the livestock sector because of significant transaction costs in the latter case.[28]

Administrative costs may, however, preclude pricing programs in many cases where there is no existing data collection and tax/payment capacity to build off. In many African countries, for example, capacity for tax collection is severely constrained by large shares of informal or subsistence agriculture, whereas in many Latin American countries (Argentina is a notable exception), governments do not collect business taxes, administer farm support programs, or have data on farm-level outputs.

Could Production or Consumption Taxes Play a Role Where Emissions Pricing Is Impractical?

A production tax, differentiated by livestock product, may be an administratively practical alternative to emissions pricing. The tax could be collected at the farm level, alongside business taxes or VAT where they exist, or alternatively, at the processor level (again alongside business tax or VAT) with exemptions for imports (but not exports) to focus it on emissions released within national borders. Again, feebates that tax/subsidize products with high/low emissions intensity are another possibility.

The tax or feebate could depend on default emissions rates for different livestock products. Individual farmers might be allowed to petition for a side payment if they demonstrate through establishing their own (verifiable) emissions reporting that their emissions rate is below the default rate—this provision would promote more of the mitigation responses in Table 4.7 without the government supervising emissions reporting for all farmers.

Another option is consumer taxes per kg on meat products which impose the same charge on imported, as domestically produced, consumption and exclude domestic exports, and might be applied to food processors and importers, collected at the same time as VAT.[29] As discussed in Chapter 6, however, these taxes may be largely passed forward to domestic consumers, thereby reducing domestic demand and net imports, without much effect on domestic production—consumption taxes may make sense for countries whose trading partners have relatively high environmental costs per unit of production.

What Are Practical Mitigation Policies for Agriculture and Forestry in Developing Countries?

Agriculture is dominated by small-scale informal farming in lower-middle and low-income countries and accounts for about 40 and 60 percent of economywide employment with productivity of about one-half and one-quarter of that in high-income countries, respectively (WBG 2024). The productivity of forestry and agriculture is intertwined—higher agricultural productivity reduces demand for land input, while shade from forests can raise the productivity of crops like coffee and cocoa (by keeping soils more fertile and moist) and cattle grazing (for example, by reducing risk of heat stress).

As mentioned in the previous section, there may be a role for PES programs and (where commodities are major drivers of deforestation and there are a limited number of identifiable suppliers) commodity taxes. Besides improving production efficiency (ideally in conjunction with transfer of know-how on advanced farming techniques from high-income countries) other mitigation possibilities for developing countries include promoting low-carbon cooking—improving agricultural households' access to electricity and efficient stoves and fuels to reduce CO_2 and methane emissions from wood and biomass combustion.[30] They also include promoting community forest management which can lead to more sustainable forest management practices (see Fischer et al. 2023).

Extractives

Emissions and Mitigation Opportunities

How Are Methane Emissions from Extractives Measured?

There are two approaches to measuring methane emissions:

- *National inventory (bottom-up)*—which is used for submissions to the United Nations Framework Convention on Climate Change and is based on fuel production and methane emissions factors accounting for local characteristics (like surface versus underground mining).[31]
- *Atmospheric observations (top-down)*—which uses, for example, remote sensing from towers, aircraft, drones, and (most importantly) satellites to monitor emissions of regions. Atmospheric observations can be mapped to individual facilities where they are spatially distinct and small in number (which may apply to coal and conventional onshore oil/natural gas production).[32]

Which Extractive Activities Contribute Most to Methane Emissions?

Figure 4.24 shows global methane emissions from extractives broken down by activity and, for selected countries, the emissions rates. Some noteworthy points include:

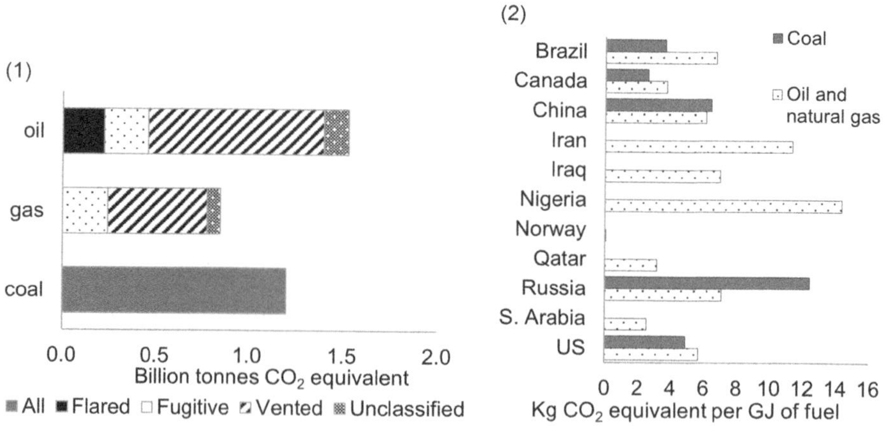

Figure 4.24 Sources of Methane Emissions by Extractive Activity. Panel 1. Sources of Extractive Emissions by Activity, 2023.[a]* Panel 2. Emissions Rates by Fuel, Selected Countries, 2023[b].

Sources: [a]Updated version of Parry et al. (2022b) using IEA (2024). [b]Updated version of Parry et al. (2022b), Annex 4.1, using IEA (2024).

Note: *Most coal-related methane emissions come from operational underground (rather than abandoned or surface) mines.

- Globally oil, natural gas, and coal operations each contributed about one-third to methane emissions from extractives in 2023.
- About 95 percent of these emissions are upstream (from mine mouth or wellhead) and 5 percent midstream (from fuel processing and distribution).
- Venting (intentional release of unwanted methane to lower explosion risks) accounts for all emissions from coal and most emissions from oil and gas. For oil, the remaining emissions are split between flaring and fugitive (unintended methane release), whereas for gas they are all fugitive with about one-third of fugitive emissions occurring midstream.
- Methane emissions factors vary across fuels and countries with, for example, the type of well/mine, equipment, and extent of flaring. For coal, emissions in CO_2 equivalent were about 3 kg per gigajoule (GJ) of energy in Canada and 12 kg in Russia and for oil/natural gas they varied from less than 1 kg in Norway to 14 kg in Nigeria. By contrast, CO_2 emissions from fuel combustion are much larger (about 100, 70, and 60 kg per GJ for coal, oil, and natural gas, respectively—see Table 2.2).

What Are the Main Opportunities for Reducing Methane Emissions Rates from Extractives?

Opportunities include the following:[33]

- *Flaring*: a ton of flared methane releases about 3 tons of CO_2, implying a reduction in the (hundred year) global warming potential of methane by 90 percent, though the CO_2 emissions stay in the atmosphere far longer and flaring is often incomplete.
- *Methane capture*: degasification wells can be drilled into coal seams to decrease water pressure, allowing coalbed methane to be released and collected, whereas in oil wells air might be mixed with water to remove the methane. Collected methane can be compressed and used for power generation at extraction sites, sold to the natural gas grid or mobile processing units, or reinjected into wells.
- *Leak detection and repair*: this identifies (for example, using gas-imaging cameras or ultrasonic detectors) and then fixes fugitive emissions.
- *Other measures*: these might include replacing natural gas pumps and upgrading distribution infrastructure like compressor seals.

Methane emissions could also be reduced through reducing production levels, but this is not cost-effective given that even high emissions fees only modestly increase production costs—for example, a \$70 CO_2 equivalent fee increases production costs only 1 to 13 percent of wellhead prices across fuels and selected countries in Figure 4.25.

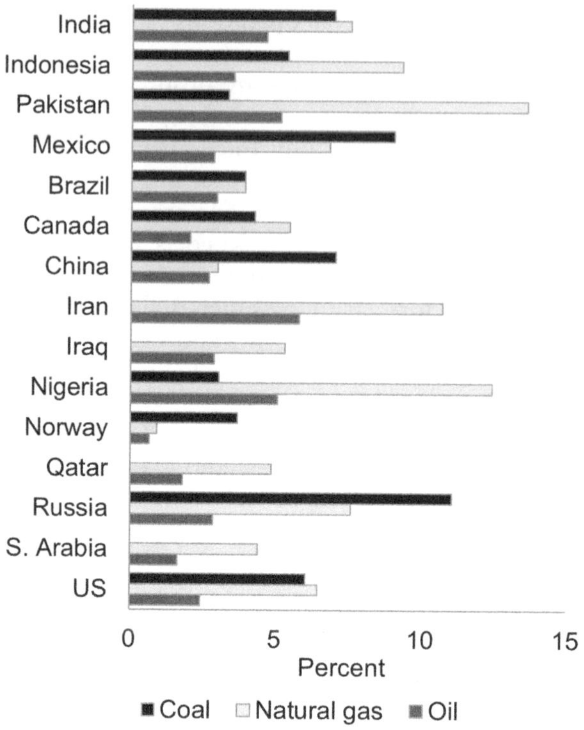

Figure 4.25 Production Cost Increases for \$70/ton CO_2 Equivalent Methane Fee Selected Countries, 2030.

Source: Parry et al. (2022b) using updated data.

Policy Options

How Practical Are Methane Fees for the Extractives Sector?

Methane taxes would cost-effectively promote all behavioral responses for reducing emissions from extractive activities. These taxes are most practical where:

- Upstream fiscal regimes are already established, which is the case in essentially all energy-producing countries—production taxes related to methane emissions rates could be integrated into this component of the fiscal regime; and
- The spatial dispersion of firms facilitates use of atmospheric metering technologies. In fact, most oil and natural gas sector regulators already monitor venting and flaring, and a methane tax could build on this capacity.

The fee, however, needs to be modified when firm-level emissions are not directly observed. Possibilities include:

- *Taxes on self-reported emissions*—where firms install their own emission-monitoring capacity (subject to third-party verification) and remit taxes based on reported emissions. Norway provides a good prototype—see Annex 4.4.
- *Proxy emissions taxes*—where taxes are levied on reported production levels, multiplied by default emissions factors based on observable characteristics like installed equipment, drilling technique, and reservoir type. Importantly, firms could be allowed to petition for tax rebates by demonstrating (through their own self-reported and verified emissions) their emissions rates are below the default rate—rebates might also be linked to the use of technologies like methane capture. Default emissions factors could be based on zero-mitigation scenarios or worst-performing firms to ensure that all firms have incentives to cut their emissions.

Should Methane Fees Be Revenue Neutral?

Fiscal regimes for extractives share the resource rent between tax revenues and firm profits—a higher tax take lowers exploration, development, and production incentives. Implementing methane fees in a revenue-neutral way—that is, using the revenues to reduce production-based or other distortive elements of the broader fiscal regime—will preserve this balance and help to alleviate concerns that methane fees will cause investors to migrate to other countries.

In reality, however, new revenues from methane fees are not that large relative to those from existing fiscal regimes for extractives—about 1–6 percent of projected revenues for a methane fee of \$70 in CO_2 equivalent in 2030 (Parry et al. 2022b, Figure 11)—implying a relatively modest amount at stake in whether revenues are recycled to the sector. There is also a risk of reducing overall government take if the government struggles to administer the methane fee or larger than expected emissions reductions occur. Given that production-based taxes provide a relatively stable and easy-to-administer revenue source, the government should take caution in reducing royalties or other production taxes as methane pricing is introduced but could consider changes to more distortive taxes like those on inputs. There may also be scope in some countries to convert less efficient taxes on unused natural gas (for example, royalties that include vented or flared natural gas in the base like in Brazil and the United States or taxes on per volume of flared natural gas, such as in Nigeria) to emissions taxes.

How Do Methane Fees Compare with Other Mitigation Instruments?

In principle, existing ETSs for CO_2 emissions from the energy sector could be extended to methane emissions from extractives. This approach, however, is less amenable to being revenue neutral for extractive industries, involves extra capacity for monitoring trading among all extractive firms, and might raise concerns about the credibility of trading allowances across CO_2 and methane given uncertainties in measuring methane. And for many countries, implementing a separate ETS for extractives may not include sufficient firms to create viable trading markets. Similar concerns would arise with a tradable performance standard for the extractives sector (Australia and Alberta in Canada expand the number of participating firms by including extractives in tradable performance standards that cover all industries).

In contrast, feebates with pivot points equal to the average methane emissions rate of gas, oil, or coal producers could have appeal because they are automatically revenue neutral for the average firm without the need to adjust broader elements of the fiscal regime. Feebates are most effective when firms self-report emissions, but they could also be linked to default emissions factors related to observable mitigation technologies or production methods.

Although technology mandates, for example, for methane capture technologies, do not seem well suited for the extractives sector, at least in cases where the costs and feasibility of the technology vary considerably across facilities (for example, with site-specific options for use of captured gas), they are often used because of their low administrative costs. One option is to rebalance mitigation policies from mandates to pricing once the government can ensure accurate measurement of emissions at the operator level, which may take several years—for example, this could mean maintaining requirements for proven, low-cost abatement activities (such as leak detection and repair) coupled with emissions pricing.

Super emitters—large facilities with chronic leakage rates (for example, because of damaged or poorly maintained pipeline infrastructure) and which can usually be detected through atmospheric measurement—are best addressed with emergency measures such as immediate shutdowns or large penalties. As regards emissions from previously abandoned mines and wells, these could be capped (with public funding or liability for previous operators), whereas firms currently operating sites could be subject to capping requirements when the site is shut down. Decommissioning plans and provisions should include activities to plug methane sources and, in the case of already abandoned projects, governments can pay for plugging of leaky abandoned wells and mines (as, for example, in the United States).

Waste

What Are Emissions Sources from the Waste Sector?

Across G20 countries, waste emissions typically account for about 2–5 percent of non-land use GHGs, though more than 10 percent in a couple of cases—see Figure 4.26. Sources of these emissions include:

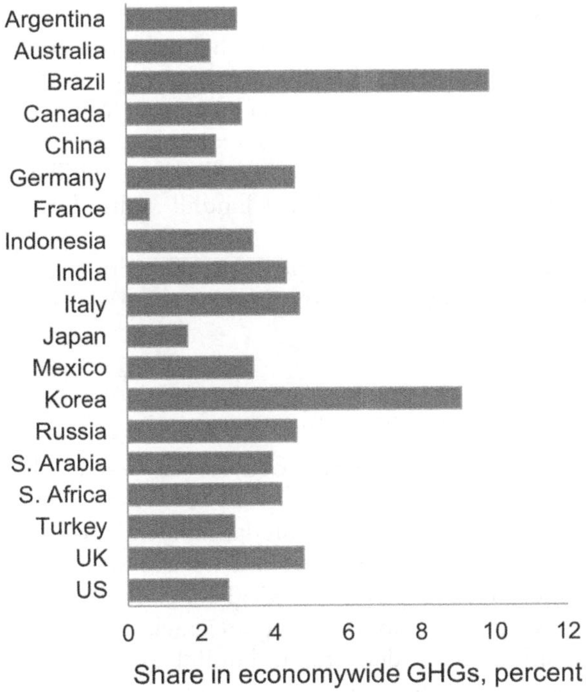

Figure 4.26 Shares of Waste in Nationwide GHG Emissions, 2023.

Source: Authors' calculations using CPAT.

- *Landfill leaks*: methane is generated because buried organic waste decomposes without oxygen.
- *Incineration*: flaring methane emissions from landfills produce CO_2 emissions.
- *Wastewater system leaks*: domestic and industrial activities discharge organic materials into wastewater systems which break down without oxygen, releasing methane.

Globally, landfill, incineration, and wastewater leaks account for about 70, 10, and 20 percent of waste emissions, respectively (UNEP 2021).

What Are the Opportunities for Reducing Methane Emissions from Waste Systems?

Opportunities include:

- *Reducing organic inputs to landfills*—this includes the following: (1) reducing organic waste from households and firms through composting (which avoids methane generation by breaking down organic waste with oxygen) and reducing demand for (and waste of) food and other organic products; and (2) separating organic waste from other trash (for compost or conversion to commercial products like biogas) prior to deposit in landfills.

- *Mitigating landfill emissions*—this includes the following: (1) covering landfills to reduce methane releases (for example, with a biologically active cover to break down methane); and (2) collecting landfill gas (for example, through perforated pipes sent down landfill wells) for safe disposal or commercial use.
- *Treating wastewater*—for example, installing treatment systems (to decompose organic waste with oxygen) or covered lagoons (to capture methane releases).

Is There a Role for Taxes in Reducing Waste Emissions?

Unlike for other sectors, taxes on waste emissions—even if they were administratively practical—would not promote all behavioral responses for reducing emissions. For example, a tax on landfill emissions would promote control technologies at the landfill site but not responses to reduce organic inputs to the site (because it is impractical for landfill operators and trash collectors to pass a tax on embodied methane back to households and firms). And taxes per unit of waste delivered to landfills (for example, by manufacturing, construction, and food processing companies)—which are common in practice to charge for landfill operating costs[34]—only reduce the volume of waste (not the share of it from organic material or emissions released at the landfill).

For the waste sector specifically, a regulatory approach (mandating mitigation responses at waste sites) may be more natural given: (1) waste sites are typically managed by municipalities (rather than private firms); (2) the limited range of behavioral responses for reducing emissions; and (3) the infeasibility of finely tuned fees on methane.

Suggestions for Further Readings

- *All sectors.* For general discussions of mitigation policy instruments for different sectors, see, for example, Arregui et al. (2020) and Krupnick et al. (2010).
- *Power generation.* For a general discussion of mitigation policy instruments for reducing power generation emissions, see Cleary and Palmer (2022) and Palmer, Sweeney, and Allaire (2010) and for a survey of literature on power sector decarbonization, see Schwerhoff (2024). Recent reports on the costs of solar and wind generation include IRENA (2023) and Way et al. (2022). Cai et al. (2024) discuss scaling up renewable generation in the specific case of sub-Saharan Africa.

- *Industry*. Krupnick et al. (2021) discuss various policy options at the industrial level, while Capelle et al. (2023) discuss mitigation issues at the firm level.
- *Transportation*. Small (2010) provides an overview of the main mitigation policy instruments for reducing emissions from passenger vehicles with modeling results for the United States. See Anderson and Sallee (2016) for further discussion. Harrington and Krupnick (2012) discuss complications in regulating the fuel efficiency (or emissions rates) of heavy-duty trucks. On electric vehicle transitions and policies, see Briceno-Garmendia, Qiao, and Foster (2022) and Davis and Sallee (2020).
- *Buildings*. On the (disappointing) experiences with residential energy efficiency programs in the United States, see Alcott and Greenstone (2017) and Fowlie, Greenstone, and Wolfram (2018).
- *Forestry*. See Daigneault et al. (2022) on future emissions for the forestry sector. For further discussion of policies to promote forest carbon storage and their emissions effects, see Favero, Mendelsohn, and Sohngen (2017), Mendelsohn, Sedjo, and Sohngen (2012), Parry (2020). Kulindwa (2016) discusses experiences with PES programs in Tanzania.
- *Agriculture*. Henderson, Frezal, and Flynn (2020) provide a survey of mitigation policies in the agricultural and forestry sectors across different countries. See Ricci et al. (2024) and Funke et al. (2022) for some discussion of agricultural emissions fees and meat taxes, respectively.
- *Extractives*. UNEP (2021) provides an in-depth assessment of options for mitigating methane emissions from the extractive sector, whereas Parry et al. (2022b) discuss practical fiscal policies for reducing methane emissions and quantitative estimates of the environmental, fiscal, and economic effects across different countries. UNEP (2024) reports progress on monitoring methane emissions.

Annex 4.1 Examples of Industrial Performance Standards and Feebates

This annex discusses examples of Tradable Performance Standards (TPSs) and feebates applied to the industrial sector in Canada, China, and the Netherlands.[35]

- *Canada*. Provinces and territories in Canada were required to have a carbon charging system, with the carbon price ramping up progressively from CAN$10 per ton of CO_2 in 2019. A federal carbon pricing backstop system applied in provinces/territories that requested it or that did not meet the federal standard. The backstop had two components: (1) a fuel charge and (2) a TPS for facilities in energy-intensive trade-exposed industries (with annual emissions exceeding 50 kilo tons of CO_2 equivalent), known as the Output-Based Pricing System (OBPS). The OBPS is still in place, but the fuel charge was suspended in April 2025. The OBPS currently applies in Manitoba, Prince Edward Island, Yukon, Nunavut, and partially in Saskatchewan (Ontario and New Brunswick recently transitioned from the OBPS to regional versions). The OBPS sets an annual emissions-intensity standard for each facility based on (70 percent of) the production-weighted average emissions intensity of all large-emitting facilities producing similar products across Canada. Facilities exceeding the standard are subject to fees on their excess emissions (in line with federal pricing), although those emitting less than their standard earn credits they can sell or bank for future use.

- *China.* In January 2021, China launched a nationwide TPS (building off pilot carbon market programs in eight regions) applying to over 2,100 power generators with annual CO_2 emissions by 26 kilo tons and covering nearly 40 percent of nationwide GHGs. Allowances are allocated freely to covered entities according to production levels of coal- and gas-fired power plants and predetermined emissions-intensity benchmarks (in tons of CO_2 per megawatt hour for electricity and or per gigajoule of heat generation) covering only coal- and gas-fired power plants and with no cap on total emissions. The current allowance allocation plan defines four benchmark categories, three for coal-fired and one for gas power plants. Trading prices remain relatively low at the equivalent of about $8 per ton with low liquidity and volume. The Chinese government intends to extend the program to industry, including petrochemicals, chemicals, building materials, iron and steel, non-ferrous metals, paper, and domestic aviation.
- *The Netherlands.* In January 2021, the Netherlands introduced a levy on industrial CO_2 emissions equal to any positive difference between an escalating target price (rising to €125 per ton by 2030) and the prevailing EU ETS price. The levy applies to emissions over and above a pivot point emissions rate based on the cleanest 10 percent of firms in the industry at the EU level. Companies with emissions rates below the pivot points can sell credits to other firms where the levy is binding.

Annex 4.2 Technological Obstacles to EV Transitions

EV sales growth has been encouraged by several factors, including: (1) a rapid decline in vehicle prices because of lower battery costs; (2) lower maintenance and running costs (electricity costs per km driven in EVs are much lower than fuel costs per km in ICEVs);[36] (3) an increase in driving range; (4) improvements in charging technology and reductions in charging time; (5) expansion of charging infrastructure; (6) an increase in the number of makes and models of EVs; and (7) growing familiarity among consumers and mechanics with the technology (see, for example, Adler, Peer, and Sinozic 2019, Sanguesa et al. 2021).

Several barriers to widespread adoption of EVs remain (though technologies are continually advancing):

- *Vehicle price*: as of 2030, EVs are more expensive (because of high battery costs) than conventional vehicles with similar capabilities.
- *Range anxiety*: remains a concern for consumers who drive long distances (EV range is typically 200–350 km with a full charge) or lack access to chargers—EV driving range also is reduced in very cold conditions.[37]
- *Recharging time*: fully charging the battery pack can take several hours and even a "fast charge" to 80 percent capacity can take 30 minutes.
- *Uncertainties*: these surround EV reliability, battery lifetimes, maintenance costs, resale values, and the relative future prices of electricity and gasoline.
- *Bulk and weight*: battery packs are heavy (about 200 kg) and take up considerable vehicle space.
- *Security for critical materials*: batteries contain critical materials like lithium, whereas electric motors require rare-earth elements. Demand for these materials is growing as EV production (and other technologies like wind turbines) ramps up. Impediments to rapid expansion of such materials include limited reserves, supply lags, political risks, industrial concentration, and shortages of the water needed to extract lithium (IEA 2021, IMF 2023).
- *Charging infrastructure*: extra generation capacity is needed to accommodate rising demand for EVs, whereas in remote locations it can be difficult to install charging stations because of a lack of access to the electrical grid.[38]

Annex 4.3 Further Details on Mitigation Policies for Forestry

Main Design Issues for Forest Sector Feebates and Pricing Programs

Major design issues include:

- *Baselines*. Carbon storage baselines should be historical or extrapolated forward from historical measures—most obviously Reducing Emissions from Deforestation and Forest Degradation (REDD+) approved inventories—rather than future land use, because the latter may lead to perverse incentives to clear land before feebates and pricing programs are implemented.
- *Payment formulas*. A key challenge is the risk that increased carbon storage may not be permanent due, for example, to fires, diseases, pests, and windstorms—in addition, trees in forestry projects may be subsequently and intentionally cleared by the landowner (for example, during period of high meat prices). One-off upfront payments for carbon storage projects do not address this problem—they would need to be combined with complex repayment systems if carbon storage is subsequently reduced. Similarly, scaling back upfront payments because of the risk of impermanence does not provide ongoing future incentives to maintain the carbon storage investment. A better approach is annual "rental," payments which would be converted into fees if the carbon storage project were reversed in future (see, for example, Sedjo and Marland 2003).

- *Exemptions.* Partial exemptions from fees may be warranted for tree cutting where the wood is processed for furniture or houses, because the carbon emissions (released at the end of the product life) will be delayed by several decades or more.
- *Linking to pricing in the energy sector.* At least initially, it likely makes sense to keep CO_2 pricing in the forestry sector decoupled from pricing in the energy sector. For example, one concern with including forestry in the New Zealand ETS is that abundant supplies of projects for converting marginal sheep farming into forestland have contained ETS allowance prices, thereby preventing a price high enough to mobilize major low-carbon technology investments in the energy sector.

New Zealand's Pricing Program for Forestry

New Zealand is the first country to implement a nationwide pricing program for the forestry sector through its ETS covering energy, waste, and forestry. Landowners implementing afforestation/reforestation projects can be eligible for credits which can be sold on the allowance market, whereas landowners must purchase allowances if there is deliberate or accidental deforestation on their land.[39]

ETS forestry participants are entitled to receive one carbon credit or New Zealand Unit per ton of CO_2 removed because the forest grows each year for registered post-1989 forestland, for either introduced or native species. To be eligible for credits, landowners must convince regulators that the forest will reach 30 percent canopy cover and 5 meters in height within a reasonable time period. Forest owners also need to repay their units earned if the forest is harvested or if they exit the program. For illustration, for a plot of 10 hectares planted in 2022, (fast-growing) pines would earn an average of about 220 credits per year through to 2050, exotic hardwoods about 200 credits per year, and native forest about 75 credits a year.

There are two situations when land can be considered deforested. First, the land is converted, for example, to land for pasture or housing. Second, the land does not meet certain criteria within set time frames (for example, for stockpiling rates per hectare and growth rates of trees on the land).

PES Programs

PES and similar incentive programs have been widely implemented in Africa, Central and South America, and Asia. Overall, the effects of these programs are mixed with some programs generating significant environmental, social, and economic benefits, whereas others have little or negative effects—see Table A4.1 for some examples in Africa. Based on numerous assessment studies,[40] challenges faced by the programs may include:

Table A4.1 Payments for Environmental Services: Examples from Africa

Country and Project	*Main Outcomes*	*Impact*		
		Environmental	*Social*	*Economic*
Kenya: Field trials with communities in Western Kenya	Auction- and performance-driven PES was more successful than reforestation contracted by Kenyan Forestry Service. Poor households made up majority of participants. Approach might be difficult to scale up.	Positive	Positive	not assessed
Madagascar: Makira REDD+ Project	Participation of households was not equitable. Households that are most at risk from cyclones could not participate because they do not own permanent rice plots. Carbon stocks were enhanced by avoided deforestation. Carbon revenue brought minor benefits (construction of three schools).	Positive	Negative	Positive
Mozambique: Gorongosa National Park (The Carbon Livelihoods Project)	The PES increased participating households' income. There was a modest decrease in the use of forest resources for subsistence by households. Male-headed and richer households were favored by the project.	Not significant	Negative	Positive
Mozambique: N'hambita Community Carbon Project	Over five years more than 500,000 trees were planted by farmers, expecting to sequester 82,000 tonnes of CO_2.	Positive	not assessed	not assessed
Rwanda: Nyungwe National Park	Decrease in human activity after the PES implementation. Most interviewees thought that the project was fair (all households receiving the same payment). Household wealth seemed to be the same for control and treatment groups, only the very poorest perceived to be negatively impacted (those dependent on bamboo).	Not significant	Positive	Not significant

(*Continued*)

Table A4.1 (Continued)

Country and Project	*Main Outcomes*	*Impact*		
		Environmental	*Social*	*Economic*
Tanzania: The Uluguru Mountains	No changes can be demonstrated in forest cover and forest disturbance during the initial pilot period. Income of farmers improved, and they were able to invest into roofs and seeds, school fees, etc. Poorer households were not able to participate much because they have less land available to enroll.	Not significant	Not significant	Negative
Tanzania: Morogoro, payments for watershed services	Payments received by the participating upstream farmers for sustainable land management practices contributed to 20% of their annual cash income. Crop yields and the monetary value of land increased (due to better practices such as terracing).	Not significant	Positive	Positive
Uganda: Program by Chimpanzee Sanctuary and Wildlife Conservation Trust	In villages where PES was implemented, tree cover declined by 4.2% in two years, which is less than the 9.1% decline in control villages. There was no detectable leakage. There was no statistically significant effect on participants' consumption or other measures of economic well-being.	Positive	Not significant	Not significant

Sources: Brimont et al. (2015), Hegde and Bull (2011), Gross-Camp et al. (2012), Jindal, Kerr, and Carter (2012), Lopa et al. (2012), Khalumba et al. (2014), Jayachandran et al. (2017), Kwayu, Paavola, and Sallu (2017), Favretto et al. (2020), and www.conservationeffectiveness.org/datavis/?strategy=2.

Note: Effects are based on statistical analyses in the various studies listed previously. See the weblink for details on PES programs in Central and South America and Asia.

- *Effectiveness*: Although contracts under PES programs can be renewed, this is typically not a requirement, and landowners may be free to deforest their land after a contract has ended.
- *Coverage*: Small and medium farmers may be precluded from PES programs because of limited funding or insecure land tenure.
- *Targeting*: Programs may not target high-priority lands, such as biological corridors, given their voluntary nature.
- *Institutions*: Security of land rights and land-use planning are prerequisites for PES projects but in many developing countries, land is owned by communities (for example, villages, tribes) rather than individual households.
- *Compensation*: Payments may need to be linked to the value of the alternative uses of forests (such as conversion to agricultural land) to provide incentives for participation.
- *Funding*: Programs need to be supported from the general budget (for example, in Costa Rica the budgetary costs are about 0.2 percent of GDP funded by a surcharge on gasoline), levies in the forestry sector, or external donor support.
- *Enforcement*: Monitoring, reporting, and verification, providing regular assessments of whether environmental services paid for by PES programs are in place (for example, tracking forest coverage and carbon sequestration through satellites, drones, and so on), are critical to the success of the program.

PES Pilots in Tanzania[41]

In 2009, a REDD+ program facilitated by several non-government organizations piloted PES programs for forest conservation in several districts of Tanzania. The villagers were informed about the program and received benefits for participation (like improved charcoal stoves, construction of village offices, grants for phones and bicycles in Kilosa district). Overall, the project was economically viable with an internal rate of return of almost 50 percent, but there were a number of difficulties.

Clarifying land rights and demarcation of village borders was the first step though the process was slow (six years in some cases) and demarcation led to border conflicts in some villages. Indeed, some villagers were afraid to lose land to the program, whereas others equated land ownership to the right to use resources. Each participating village was required to have a land use or forest management plan and to set aside land for productive and protective purposes which led to some internal conflicts (especially where residents had to be relocated from forest reserves to villages). Some participants were dissatisfied with the compensation structure because they were not compensated for lost income from reduced access to the forests. There were also conflicts between charcoal burners, who more heavily relied on forest resources, and other villagers. The long-term effects of the pilots remain unclear because the pilots were limited in duration and the program organizers did not have power to prevent increased deforestation in areas outside pilots. Transaction costs were significant (about $1.7 per hectare conserved) with monitoring, reporting, and verification accounting for about half of the costs.

Annex 4.4 Methane Taxes in Norway

The Norwegian government imposes a tax, currently equivalent to about $50 per ton of CO_2 equivalent, on methane emissions from oil and natural gas operators on the Norwegian Continental Shelf. Firms are required to measure and report their emissions and remit taxes to the Norwegian Petroleum Directorate. Several factors were favorable to the implementation of the methane tax, including the following:

- Upstream operations on the shelf account for about 95 percent of the methane emissions from the sector.
- There are close links between the government and the industry: although there are about 30 firms paying the tax, the largest by far is Equinor, in which the government has a two-thirds share.
- Firms use similar equipment, and their output is homogeneous, which facilitates procedures for consistently calculating emissions across firms.
- While developing guidelines for emissions data collection and reporting, Norwegian regulators held extensive consultations with industry, research institutions, and other actors capable of independently verifying emissions measurement.

The Norwegian model for emissions reporting may pave the way for future implementation of methane taxes in other countries.

Notes

1 Including use of natural gas and hydro to counteract supply variability, grid integration across large geographical areas, energy storage from batteries and pumped hydro, and time-of-day pricing (facilitated by digitalization) to shift demand to periods of higher supply. See Schwerhoff et al. (2024).
2 Geothermal is another possibility but is available only in very limited areas and cannot always be safely exploited.
3 Nuclear fusion may be a possibility for the latter half of the century.
4 When power sectors are heavily regulated, carbon pricing can still be integrated into generation investment decisions, the dispatch merit order, and end-user tariffs, promoting all behavioral responses (WBG, ICAP and IEA 2024).
5 Investment subsidies are cheaper than production subsidies if the government's cost of capital is lower than that of the private sector.
6 Unless otherwise noted, figures in this subsection are from Parry et al. (2025).
7 These costs might be reduced if firms switch to more electricity-efficient equipment.
8 Where the number of firms is limited, trading may not be viable, and firms may have perverse incentives to inflate current emissions if future pivot points or standards are based on previously observed industry averages. For these cases, pivot points and standards could instead be based on exogenous benchmarks.

9 EV manufacturing is more energy-intensive than for ICEVs (due especially to the batteries), but ideally, this should be addressed through broader policies for fossil fuels rather than adjusting EV incentives.

10 This is termed the rebound effect—see, for example, Small and Van Dender (2007) for some discussion.

11 Indeed, vehicle fleets in some developing countries are largely made up of used vehicle imports from Europe, Japan, and the United States implying a much older average vehicle age than for developed countries (UNEP 2020).

12 See Linn (2020) for guidance on improving the cost-effectiveness of scrappage subsidies.

13 To compensate for the loss of fuel tax revenues, Iceland, Israel, and New Zealand have recently introduced, or plan to introduce, distance-based road charges on EVs, whereas in Europe most countries impose fees on public charging stations. See OECD (2024).

14 These data might be collected, for example, during routine inspections at truck weighing stations.

15 See Arregui et al. (2020). Energy performance ratings may, however, differ from actual energy consumption because the latter varies with behavioral responses like thermostat settings.

16 A net zero building is an energy-efficient building that produces its own carbon-free electricity (through rooftop solar or geothermal) or procures carbon-free electricity from the grid.

17 Another possibility is to use a feebate approach where subsidies for heat pump installations are financed by fees on fossil furnaces—the heat pump subsidy will start large but decline, whereas the tax on fossil furnaces will start small and rise as the market share of heat pumps rises over time.

18 The property tax would not encourage behavioral responses among households (like turning down the thermostat) for a given energy rating but it would promote investments to improve the energy rating which likely produce the larger energy savings.

19 To illustrate, if the pivot point consumption rate were 5 kWh/month, and the feebate price was $30 per kWh/month, then a refrigerator with an energy consumption rate of 8 kWh/month would be subject to a tax of $90, whereas a refrigerator with an energy consumption rate of 2 kWh/month would receive a $90 subsidy.

20 https://ourworldindata.org/agricultural-land-by-global-diets.

21 Afforestation is tree planting on land not recently covered with forest, whereas reforestation is tree planting, or allowing trees to regrow, on land recently covered with forest (the distinction between the two is ignored here).

22 Significant uncertainties, however, surround current and projected forestry emissions (see, for example, Schwingshackl et al. 2022).

23 For example, the annual sequestration rate for a typical New England forest is 0.5 tons per hectare, a southern pine plantation is 1 ton, and a moist tropical forest could be as high as 11 tons (Mendelsohn et al. 2012).

24 Most is owned or managed by national and subnational governments (for example, Whiteman, Wickramasinghe, and Piña 2015).

25 Animals with more than one stomach where plant-based food is fermented before digestion.

26 For example, based on IPCC (2006) guidelines.

27 A product-specific pivot point may have appeal in countries with significant livestock production because using an industry average pivot point would result in high taxes on livestock, which could cause leakage concerns since meat products can be traded internationally.

28 While large farms might employ specialized staff for buying, selling, and hedging emissions allowances at minimal additional cost, much of the sector may be characterized by small farms where participation in allowance trading markets might significantly increase overheads.

29 Administrative difficulties in determining the emissions intensity of imported products would need to be addressed. Meat taxes have been proposed in Denmark, Germany, and the Netherlands.

30 In 2022, only 30 and 15 percent of rural households in low-income countries had access to electricity and efficient cooking technologies, respectively (WBG 2024).

31 See www.ipcc-nggip.iges.or.jp/public/2006gl and www.ipcc-nggip.iges.or.jp/public/2006gl/pdf/2_Volume2/V2_4_Ch4_Fugitive_Emissions.pdf

32 Atmospheric observations suggest methane emissions have been larger than implied by inventory approaches due mainly to super emitters (see the following section) that are not well captured by the latter approach (IEA 2022b).

33 See also IGSD (2022) and *IEA* (2023). Direct atmospheric removal of methane using soaking materials might be a future possibility, though systems must process much larger quantities of air than for CO_2 capture (requiring far more energy) given methane is 200 times less abundant in the atmosphere (Jackson et al. 2021).

34 See www.eea.europa.eu/data-and-maps/figures/overview-of-landfill-taxes-on

35 For more details, see www.canada.ca/en/environment-climate-change/services/climate-change/pricing-pollution-how-it-will-work/output-based-pricing-system/overview.html; IEA (2022a); https://carbonmarketwatch.org/2020/12/21/what-can-we-learn-from-the-dutch-national-carbon-tax

36 The number of engine elements is much smaller in an EV than in an ICEV (the former do not need cooling circuits, gearshifts, clutches, or noise mitigation technologies), implying lower maintenance costs and less risk of breakdowns.

37 Cabin heat for an EV diverts energy from the battery (ICEVs automatically produce waste heat).

38 There are three types of charging stations for countries like the United States: standard electric outlets delivering 120V alternating current (AC) mostly in homes; upgraded chargers using 240V AC, which can be installed at most homes, workplaces, and public areas; and fast chargers using 480V Direct Current (DC) applied directly to a vehicle's battery (without using an AC/DC converter).

39 See www.mpi.govt.nz, www.carboncrop.nz.

40 Summarized at www.conservationeffectiveness.org/datavis/?strategy=2. Costa Rica was the first country to implement a PES program—for some discussion, see www.fonafifo.go.cr/en and Carter (2020).

41 This discussion is based on Kulindwa (2016).

References

Adler, Martin, Stefanie Peer, and Tanja Sinozic. 2019. "Autonomous, Connected, Electric Shared Vehicles (ACES) and Public Finance: An Explorative Analysis." *Transportation Research Interdisciplinary Perspectives* 2: 100038.

Alcott, Hunt, and Michael Greenstone. 2017. "Measuring the Welfare Effects of Residential Energy Efficiency Programs with Self-Selection into Program Participation." Becker Friedman Institute for Research in Economics Working Paper 2017-05, University of Chicago, Chicago, IL.

Anderson, Soren, and James Sallee. 2016. "Designing Policies to Make Cars Greener." *Annual Review of Resource Economics* 8: 157–80.

Arregui, Nicolas, Ruo Chen, Christian H. Ebeke, Jan-Martin Frie, Daniel Garcia Macia, Dora M. Iakova, Andreas Jobst, et al. 2020. "Sectoral Policies for Climate Change Mitigation in the EU." IMF Departmental Paper 2020/014, International Monetary Fund, Washington, DC.

Batini, Nicoletta. 2021. *The Economics of Sustainable Food: Smart Policies for Health and the Planet.* Washington, DC: Island Press and International Monetary Fund.

Black, Simon, Anthony Liu, Natalija Novta, James Roaf, and Karlygash Zhunussova. 2024. "Reform of the Emissions Trading System (ETS) in China." IMF Selected Issues Paper, Washington, DC.

Black, Simon, Antung A. Liu, Ian W.H. Parry, Nate Vernon-Lin. 2023. "IMF Fossil Fuel Subsidies Data: 2023 Update." IMF Working Papers 2023/169, Washington, DC.

Briceno-Garmendia, Cecilia, Wenxin Qiao, and Vivien Foster. 2022. *The Economics of Electric Vehicles for Passenger Transportation.* Washington, DC: World Bank.

Brimont, Laura, Driss Ezzine-de-Blas, Alain Karsenty, and Angélique Toulon. 2015. "Achieving Conservation and Equity Amidst Extreme Poverty and Climate Risk: The Makira REDD+ Project in Madagascar." *Forests* 6: 748–68.

Cai, Kaihao, Thibault Lemaire, Andrea Medici, Giovanni Melina, Gregor Schwerhoff, and Sneha Thube. 2024. "Harnessing Renewables in Sub-Saharan Africa: Barriers, Reforms, and Economic Prospects." IMF Staff Climate Note 2024/005, International Monetary Fund, Washington, DC.

Capelle, Damien, Divya Kirti, Nicola Pierri, and German Villegas Bauer. 2023. "Mitigating Climate Change at the Firm Level: Mind the Laggards." IMF Working Papers 2023/242, International Monetary Fund, Washington, DC.

Carter, Anna J. 2020, "Effectiveness, Equity and Ethics of Costa Rica's Payment for Environmental Services Program." College of Arts & Sciences Senior Honors Theses, Paper 212, University of Louisville, Louisville, KY.

Cleary, Kathryne, and Karen Palmer. 2022. "An Overview of Federal Climate Policy Options to Reduce Emissions from the US Power Sector." Federal Climate Policy Toolkit, Resources for the Future, Washington, DC.

Daigneault, Adam, Justin S. Baker, Jinggang Guo, Pekka Lauri, Alice Favero, Nicklas Forsell, Craig Johnston, et al. 2022. "How the Future of the Global Forest Sink Depends on Timber Demand, Forest Management, and Carbon Policies." *Global Environmental Change* 76: 102582.

Davis, Lucas W., and James M. Sallee. 2020. "Should Electric Vehicle Drivers Pay a Mileage Tax?" *Environmental and Energy Policy and the Economy* 1: 65–94.

Favero, Alice, Robert Mendelsohn, and Brent Sohngen. 2017. "Using Forests for Climate Mitigation: Sequester Carbon or Produce Woody Biomass?" *Climatic Change* 144, 195–206.

Favretto, Nicola, Stavros Afionis, Lindsay C. Stringer, Andrew J. Dougill, Claire H. Quinn, and Hery Lisy Tiana Ranarijaona. 2020. "Delivering Climate-Development Co-Benefits through Multi-Stakeholder Forestry Projects in Madagascar: Opportunities and Challenges." *Land* 9: 157.

Fischer, Harry W., Ashwini Chhatre, Apurva, Duddu, et al. 2023. "Community Forest Governance and Synergies among Carbon, Biodiversity and Livelihoods." *Nature Climate Change* 13: 1340–47.

Food and Agriculture Organization of the United Nations (FAO). 2023. *Emissions Totals*. Rome. www.fao.org/faostat/en/#data/GT

Food and Agriculture Organization of the United Nations (FAO). 2024. *Livestock Emission Data at a Glance.* Rome. https://foodandagricultureorganization.shinyapps.io/GLEAMV3_Public/

Fowlie, Meredith, Michael Greenstone, and Catherine Wolfram. 2018. "Do Energy Efficiency Investments Deliver? Evidence from the Weatherization Assistance Program." *The Quarterly Journal of Economics* 133(3): 1597–644.

Funke, Franziska, Linus Mattauchy, Inge van den Bijgaartz, H. Charles J. Godfray, Cameron Hepburn, David Klenert, Marco Springmann, et al. 2022. "Toward Optimal Meat Pricing: Is It Time to Tax Meat Consumption?" *Review of Environmental Economics and Policy* 16: 219–40.

Gross-Camp, Nicole D., Adrian Martin, Shawn McGuire, Bereket Kebede, and Joseph Munyarukaza. 2012. "Payments for Ecosystem Services in an African Protected Area: Exploring Issues of Legitimacy, Fairness, Equity and Effectiveness." *Oryx* 46: 24–33.
Harrington, Winston, and Alan Krupnick. 2012. "Improving Fuel Economy in Heavy-Duty Vehicles." Discussion Paper 12-02, Resources for the Future, Washington, DC.
Hegde, Ravi, and Gary Q. Bull. 2011. "Performance of an Agro-forestry Based Payments-for-Environmental-Services Project in Mozambique: A Household Level Analysis." *Ecological Economics* 71: 122–30.
Henderson, B., C. Frezal, and E. Flynn. 2020. "A Survey of GHG Mitigation Policies for the Agriculture, Forestry and Other Land Use Sector." OECD Food, Agriculture and Fisheries Papers, No. 145, Organization for Economic Cooperation and Development, Paris.
Institute for Governance and Sustainable Development (IGSD). 2022. "A Primer on Cutting Methane: The Best Strategy for Slowing Warming in the Decade to 2030." Working paper, IGSD, Washington, DC.
Intergovernmental Panel on Climate Change (IPCC). 2006. *2006 Guidelines for National Greenhouse Gas Inventories*. Geneva: Intergovernmental Panel on Climate Change.
Intergovernmental Panel on Climate Change (IPCC). 2019. *Climate Change and Land: An IPCC Special Report on Climate Change, Desertification, Land Degradation, Sustainable Land Management, Food Security, and Greenhouse Gas Fluxes in Terrestrial Ecosystems*. Geneva.
International Energy Agency (IEA). 2019. *Fuel Economy in Major Car Markets*. Paris: International Energy Agency.
International Energy Agency (IEA). 2021. *Policies to Promote Electric Vehicle Deployment. Global EV Outlook 2021*. Paris.
International Energy Agency (IEA). 2022a. *The Future of Heat Pumps: World Energy Outlook Special Report*. Paris.
International Energy Agency (IEA). 2022b. *Methane Tracker 2020*. Paris. www.iea.org/reports/methane-tracker
International Energy Agency (IEA). 2023. *Global Methane Tracker 2023*. Paris. www.iea.org/reports/global-methane-tracker-2023
International Energy Agency (IEA). 2024. *Global EV Data Explorer*. Paris. www.iea.org/data-and-statistics/data-tools/global-ev-data-explorer
International Monetary Fund (IMF). 2023. *World Economic Outlook: Navigating Global Divergences*. Washington, DC: International Monetary Fund.
International Renewable Energy Agency (IRENA).2023. *Renewable Power Generation Costs in 2022*. Masdar City: International Renewable Energy Agency.
Izquierdo-Tort, Santiago, Seema Jayachandran, and Santiago Saavedra. 2024. "Redesigning Payments for Ecosystem Services to Increase Cost-Effectiveness." NBER Working Paper Series: 32689, National Bureau of Economic Research, Cambridge, MA.
Jackson, Robert B., Sam Abernethy, Josep G. Canadell, Matteo Cargnello, Steven J. Davis, Sarah Féron, Sabine Fuss, et al. 2021. "Atmospheric Methane Removal: A Research Agenda." *Philosophical Transactions of the Royal Society*. https://doi.org/10.1098/rsta.2020.0454
Jayachandran, Seema, Joost de Laat, Eric F. Lambin, Charlotte Y. Stanton, Robin Audy, and Nancy E. Thomas. 2017. "Cash for Carbon: A Randomized Trial of Payments for Ecosystem Services to Reduce Deforestation." *Science* 357 (6348): 267–73.
Jindal, Rohit, John M. Kerr, and Sarah Carter. 2012. "Reducing Poverty through Carbon Forestry? Impacts of the N'hambita Community Carbon Project in Mozambique." *World Development* 40: 2123–35.

Khalumba, Mercelyne, Tobia Wünscher, Sven Wunder, Mirjam Büdenbender, and Karin Holm-Müller. 2014. "Combining Auctions and Performance-Based Payments in a Forest Enrichment Field Trial in Western Kenya." *Conservation Biology* 28: 861–66.

Krupnick, Alan J., Ian W. H. Parry, Margaret Walls, Tony Knowles, and Kristin Hayes, 2010, *Toward a New National Energy Policy: Assessing the Options*. Washington: Resources for the Future and National Energy Policy Institute.

Krupnick, Alan, Joshua Linn, Richard D. Morgenstern, and Dallas Burtraw. 2021. "An Overview of Federal Policy Options for Reducing Greenhouse Gas Emissions from the US Industrial Sector." Federal Climate Policy Toolkit, Resources for the Future, Washington, DC.

Kulindwa, Kassim (ed). 2016. *Lessons and Implications for REDD+: Implementation Experiences from Tanzania*. Dar es Salaam, Tanzania: E&D Vision Publishing.

Kwayu Emmanuel J., Jouni Paavola, and Susannah M. Sallu. 2017. "The Livelihood Impacts of the Equitable Payments for Watershed Services (EPWS) Program in Morogoro, Tanzania." *Environment and Development Economics* 22: 328–49.

Levy, Samuel A., Federico Cammelli, Jacob Munger, Holly K. Gibbs, and Rachael D. Garrett. 2023. "Deforestation in the Brazilian Amazon Could Be Halved by Scaling up the Implementation of Zero-Deforestation Cattle Commitments." *Global Environmental Change* 80: 102671.

Linn, Joshua. 2020. "How Targeted Vehicle Scrappage Subsidies Can Reduce Pollution Effectively." Issue Brief, Resources for the Future, Washington, DC.

Lopa, Dosteus, Iddi Mwanyoka, George Jambiya, et al. 2012. "Towards Operational Payments for Water Ecosystem Services in Tanzania: A Case Study from the Uluguru Mountains." *Oryx* 46: 34–44.

Mendelsohn, Robert, Roger Sedjo, and Brent Sohngen. 2012. "Forest Carbon Sequestration." In *Fiscal Policy to Mitigate Climate Change: A Guide for Policymakers*, edited by I. Parry, R. de Mooij, and M. Keen, 89–102. Washington, DC: IMF.

Netherlands Enterprise Agency (NEA). 2020. *SDE++ 2020 Stimulation of Sustainable Energy Production and Climate Transition*. Utrecht, The Netherlands: Netherlands Enterprise Agency.

Organisation for Economic Cooperation and Development (OECD). 2022, *Agricultural Policy Monitoring and Evaluation 2022: Reforming Agricultural Policies for Climate Change Mitigation*. Paris, https://doi.org/10.1787/7f4542bf-en

Organisation for Economic Cooperation and Development (OECD). 2024. *Pricing Greenhouse Gas Emissions 2024: Gearing up to Bring Emissions Down*. Paris: OECD.

Palmer, Karen, Richard Sweeney, and Maura Allaire. 2010. "Modeling Policies to Promote Renewable and Low-Carbon Sources of Electricity." Working paper, Resources for the Future, Washington, DC.

Parry, Ian. 2020. "The Rationale for, and Design of, Forest Carbon Feebates." In *Designing Fiscal Instruments for Sustainable Forests*, edited by Dirk Heine and Erin Hayde under the guidance of Garo Batmanian, 137–58. Washington, DC: World Bank.

Parry, Ian, Simon Black, Danielle Minnett, Victor Mylonas, and Nate Vernon. 2022b. "How to Cut Methane Emissions." IMF Staff Climate Note 22-008, International Monetary Fund, Washington, DC.

Parry, Ian, Simon Black, Danielle Minnett, James Roaf, and Karlygash Zhunussova. 2022a. "A Framework for Comparing Climate Mitigation Policies across Countries." IMF Working Paper 22/254, International Monetary Fund, Washington, DC.

Parry, Ian, Simon Black, Danielle Minnett, and Karlygash Zhunussova. 2025. "Policies to Decarbonize Industry while Addressing Competitiveness and Carbon Leakage." IMF Staff Climate Note, International Monetary Fund, Washington, DC, forthcoming.

Parry, Ian, and Kenneth A. Small. 2009. "Should Urban Transit Subsidies Be Reduced?" *American Economic Review* 99: 700–724.

Ricci, Mattia, Ignacio Perez Dominguez, Jordan Hristov, Toon Vandyck, and Stijn Van Houtven. 2024. "Pricing GHG Emissions in Agriculture: Accounting for Trade and Fairness for Effective Climate Policy." *European Commission*, JRC13978. https://publications.jrc.ec.europa.eu/repository/bitstream/JRC139782/JRC139782_01.pdf

Sanguesa, Julio A., Torres-Sanz Vicente, Piedad Garrido, Francisco J. Martinez, and Johann M. Marquez-Barja. 2021. "A Review on Electric Vehicles: Technologies and Challenges." *Smart Cities* 4: 372–404.

Schwerhoff, Gregor. 2024. "The Economics of Decarbonizing Electricity Production." Working Paper 2024/213, IMF, Washington, DC.

Schwerhoff, Gregor, Jaden Kim and Augustus J. Panton. 2024. "Energy Security and The Green Transition." Working Paper 2024/6, IMF, Washington, DC.

Schwingshackl, Clemens, Wolfgang A. Obermeier, Selma Bultan, Giacomo Grassi, Josep G. Canadell, Pierre Friedlingstein, Thomas Gasser, et al. 2022. "Differences in Land-Based Mitigation Estimates Reconciled by Separating Natural and Land-Use CO_2 Fluxes at the Country Level." *One Earth* 5 (12): 1367–76. https://doi.org/10.1016/j.oneear.2022.11.009

Sedjo, Roger, and G. Marland. 2003. "Inter-Trading Permanent Emissions Credits and Rented Temporary Carbon Emissions Offsets: Some Issues and Alternatives." *Climate Policy* 3: 435–44.

Small, Kenneth A. 2010. "Energy Policies for Automobile Transportation: A Comparison Using the National Energy Modeling System." Working Paper, Resources for the Future, Washington, DC.

Small, Kenneth A., and Kurt Van Dender. 2007. "Fuel Efficiency and Motor Vehicle Travel: The Declining Rebound Effect." *The Energy Journal* 28: 25–52.

United Nation Environment Programme (UNEP).2020. *A Global Overview of Used Light Duty Vehicles: Flow, Scale and Regulation*. Nairobi, Kenya: UNEP.

United Nations Environment Program (UNEP). 2024. *Invisible but Not Unseen: How Data-Driven Tools Can Turn the Tide on Methane Emissions – If We Use Them.* Nairobi, Kenya: UNEP and Climate and Clean Air Coalition.

United Nations Environment Programme (UNEP). 2021. *Global Methane Assessment: Benefits and Costs of Mitigating Methane Emissions*. Nairobi, Kenya: UNEP and Climate and Clean Air Coalition.

United Nations Framework Convention on Climate Change (UNFCCC). 2024. *NDC Registry*. New York, NY https://unfccc.int/NDCREG

Way, Rupert, Matthew C. Ives, Penny Mealy, and J. Doyne Farmer. 2022. "Empirically Grounded Technology Forecasts and the Energy Transition." *Joule* 6: 2057–82.

Whiteman, Adrian, Anoja Wickramasinghe, and Leticia Piña. 2015. "Global Trends in Forest Ownership, Public Income and Expenditure on Forestry and Forestry Employment." *Forest Ecology and Management* 352: 99–108.

World Bank Group (WBG). 2024. *World Development Indicators*. Washington, DC. https://databank.worldbank.org

World Bank Group (WBG), International Carbon Action Partnership (ICAP), and International Energy Agency (IEA). 2024. "Carbon Pricing in the Power Sector." https://openknowledge.worldbank.org/server/api/core/bitstreams/2478e925-31e3-45eb-bb00-127c25cc43a2/content

World Resources Institute (WRI). 2023. *Global Forest Watch*. Washington, DC. https://www.wri.org/initiatives/global-forest-watch

5 Understanding the Effects of Climate Mitigation Policies

Main Messages

- Understanding the full effects of climate mitigation policies requires modeling. Ideally, models should cover all IMF member countries, all emissions-generating sectors, major policy instruments, and metrics of concern to policymakers, with results that are transparent and broadly in line with the large energy modeling literature and empirical evidence on behavioral responses.
- Emissions projections depend on GDP growth, responsiveness of energy demand to income, planned investments in generation technologies, trend rates of technological progress, and future energy prices. Ideally, baseline projections are based on midrange assumptions for these factors, while sensitivity analyses can identify the ranges of possible outcomes.
- Modeling carbon pricing provides a useful benchmark indicating the least-cost way to achieve emissions targets. If other instruments are used, they could contain costs by mimicking, insofar as possible, the pattern of emissions reduction outcomes in this benchmark.
- Carbon pricing has varying effects on energy prices. Its largest effect is on coal prices, which rise by an average of 100 percent for a \$50 carbon price in 2030. Effects on natural gas prices are more modest at about 40 percent on average for a \$50 carbon price, and even smaller on electricity and gasoline prices, at about 20 and 15 percent on average, respectively.
- The emissions effect of carbon pricing in the energy sector depends on changes in fuel prices, the responsiveness of fuel use to higher prices, and the emissions intensity of fuels. A \$50 carbon price, for example, would cut CO_2 emissions by about 10 to 30 percent below baseline levels in 2030 in most G20 countries.

DOI: 10.4324/9781003755012-5
This chapter has been made available under a CC-BY-NC-ND license.

- Potential revenues from carbon pricing are about 0.5 to 1.5 percent of GDP a year across most G20 countries in the near term (though over 2 percent in some cases) and would peak at about 5 percent of GDP on price trajectories consistent with zero emissions transitions.
- Mitigation costs rise disproportionately with the level of abatement and vary across countries depending, for example, on the emissions intensity of GDP. However, they are generally manageable, at about 0.05 to 0.3 percent of GDP across G20 countries for a 20 percent reduction in CO_2 emissions below baseline levels in 2030 and 0.3–0.9 percent for a 30 percent reduction.
- Moreover, for developing countries, if carbon pricing is the main mitigation instrument and most revenues are used productively (for example, to fund investments with favorable benefit–cost ratios), the overall costs of mitigation can be negative.
- GDP effects of carbon pricing are difficult to pin down accurately, though (at least for pricing to date) empirical and modeling studies suggest effects are modest and of ambiguous sign if revenues are mostly used for productive purposes.
- Across most G20 countries, feebates and tradable performance standards (TPSs) for the power generation and vehicle sectors have about 70–90 percent, and 50–70 percent, respectively, of the effectiveness of pure carbon pricing, whereas narrower policies targeted at renewables and electric vehicles have significantly lower effectiveness.
- Half and a quarter of methane emissions from fossil fuel production and agriculture can be reduced at a cost of $70 per ton or less of CO_2 equivalent, respectively. Feebates achieve about 90 percent of these emissions reductions. Forestry emissions could be reduced by over 3 billion tons globally by 2035 with a carbon price of $100 per ton, coupled with strong enforcement of existing policies.

Modeling Frameworks

What Are Desirable Features of Models for Evaluating Mitigation Strategies?

Ideally, models should include the following:

- *Comprehensive and consistent country coverage*: To provide specific guidance for each IMF member country and to compare outcomes across different countries, with and without mitigation policies.
- *Baseline projections and mapping of Nationally Determined Contributions (NDCs)*: Baseline projections to illustrate how emissions, fuel use by sector, energy prices, and so on evolve in future without changes in mitigation

policies, while commitments in NDCs should be mapped to emissions reductions below future baseline levels to gauge needed policy responses.

- *Full range of mitigation policies*: To compare the effects of all the main mitigation policy options discussed in Chapters 3 and 4.
- *Sectors and gases*: All the main emissions-generating sectors (power, industry, transport, buildings, agriculture, forestry, extractives, waste) and the different gases, so targets and policies for individual sectors and gases can be analyzed.
- *Metrics for policy evaluation*: The full range of effects of interest to policymakers from each policy such as effects on greenhouse gas (GHG) emissions, fuel use, energy prices, revenue, economic costs, GDP, domestic environmental problems, distributional incidence across household income groups, and production costs in trade-exposed industries.
- *Parameterization*: Key assumptions underlying projections and responses to policies that are approximately in the midrange of those implied by the broader energy modeling literature and empirical evidence.
- *Transparency and sensitivity analysis*: The model should be able to transparently convey the key underlying factors driving different results and given uncertainty over key parameters (like fuel price responsiveness) and inputs (like future energy prices), provide for quick sensitivity analysis indicating outcomes under alternative scenarios.
- *Preexisting policies*: Key existing energy and climate policies, like fuel taxes and subsidies, that might influence the emissions, fiscal, cost, and other effects of mitigation policies.
- *Accessibility*: Ideally the model should be accessible to users with relatively low setup costs.

How Does the IMF and World Bank CPAT Address These Features?

CPAT is a user-friendly, spreadsheet model, jointly developed by IMF and World Bank staff, available for use by government officials.[1] It is routinely used by IMF staff for a diverse range of analyses and reports on mitigation policy (see Annex 5.1) and, increasingly, by policymakers. The model provides country-specific analysis for over 200 countries while incorporating the desirable features listed in the previous section (see Table 5.1). For these purposes, the model is streamlined, often summarizing, for example, basic relationships between fuel intensity and prices rather than distinguishing all the technological responses underlying this relationship. See Annex 5.2 on caveats to the model.

CPAT converts all mitigation targets into a single, comparable metric—required emissions reductions against future or historical baseline emissions. It also accommodates all the policies in Chapter 3 as well as additional policies (like fossil fuel subsidy reform, removal of favorable VAT treatment of fuels, energy price liberalization, and combinations of these and other policies) and has full coverage of sectors and gases in the main energy model, and supplementary models for other sectors. For each policy, CPAT assesses

Table 5.1 Attributes of CPAT

Desirable Modeling Feature	*How CPAT Addresses Feature*
Country Coverage	Over 200 countries with full set of data for each country. Provides consistent cross-country comparisons of baselines and policy effects.
Baseline Projections and NDCs	Projections based on most recent observed emissions and projected forward by fuel/ sector using GDP projections, income elasticities for energy products, trend rates of efficiency improvements, and future energy price scenarios. NDC pledges are mapped to emissions reductions below baseline and historical levels.
Mitigation Policies	Carbon taxes, ETSs, energy efficiency/emission rate regulations, feebates, clean technology subsidies/mandates, electricity/fuel taxes, fossil fuel subsidies, energy price liberalization, removals of preferential VAT for fuels, combinations of policies.
Sectoral Coverage	Main module covers power, industry, transport, and buildings. Supplementary models cover agriculture, extractives, forestry, and waste.
Metrics for Policy Evaluation	Impacts on energy production/consumption, prices, trade; GHG and local emissions; GDP and economic welfare; revenue; incidence across households (income deciles, within deciles, urban/rural); incidence across industries; domestic environmental co-benefits (e.g., local air pollution mortality).
Parameterization	Parameterized so projections and policy responses are approximately in the midrange of those from broader energy modeling literature and empirical evidence on responsiveness of fuel use to prices and income.
Sensitivity Analysis/Transparency	Key model parameters and inputs are easily adjusted in the dashboard. Results presented rapidly through a chart-driven interface, allowing for experimentation in designing policy reforms.
Current Policies	Includes country- and sector-specific estimates of prices, taxes/subsidies, and carbon pricing for fuels and electricity.
Accessibility	Spreadsheet model has user friendly dashboard.

Source: Authors.

Note: ETS = emissions trading scheme; NDC = Nationally Determined Contribution.

effects on all the metrics noted in the previous section and some others (household and industry incidence is available for 100 countries—see Chapter 6). The model also includes a (regularly updated) country-specific database on prices, taxes, and subsidies by fuel product/sector.

How Does CPAT Compare with Other Climate/Energy Models?

There are numerous other energy/climate models (see Suggestions for Further Readings) which, to varying degrees, include considerable detail and disaggregation on technologies, sectors (including those beyond energy), and adjustment of capital stocks—collectively, they provide critical information on how mitigation policies work. At the same time, these models often focus on one, or a subset, of countries or regions, incorporate a limited range of policy options and metrics for evaluating them, and their data and computational requirements can make them difficult to access and transfer to other countries. Moreover, the key underlying factors that drive results—like the responsiveness of fuel use to income and prices—are not always transparent in these models.[2] Results also vary significantly across models depending, for example, on assumptions about the future availability and costs of various low-carbon technologies and other model characteristics and judging which models provide the more likely future scenarios can be difficult. It can therefore make sense to average over predictions and responses from a broad suite of commonly used models, rather than relying exclusively on one specific model.

CPAT is transparent with results explained in terms of basic economic concepts familiar to policymakers. It is also parameterized so that emissions projections and responses to policies are approximately in line with those from the mid-point of the broader energy modeling literature (see, for example, Stern and Stiglitz 2017) and are consistent with voluminous evidence on the responsiveness of fuel use to income and prices (see the following section). At the same time, other models can provide alternative analytical frameworks and more information about sectoral investment, employment, and output effects, inflation, trade, or perhaps more granular mitigation policies that are beyond the scope of simpler models.

For example, IMF-ENV is an alternate model for mitigation and transition analysis in the IMF. It is a global, multi-region, multi-sector recursive dynamic computable general equilibrium (CGE) model providing comprehensive analyses of energy production and consumption and linking of GHGs to specific economic activities. This makes the model suitable for examining the macroeconomic and sector-specific effects of single or overlapping energy and climate mitigation policies at both national and global levels. The model simulates effects on energy demand and supply, GHG emissions, macroeconomic variables, sectoral outcomes, employment, investment, and trade, among other factors. Another IMF model is the Global Macroeconomic Model for the Energy Transition (GMMET), a large-scale, dynamic microfounded, model which builds off the IMF's main macroeconomic model, and can be used to assess the inflation and other macroeconomic effects of climate mitigation policies (for China, the United States, and country blocs). IMF-ENV and GMMET are described (along with recent applications) in Annex 5.3 and some results from the models are presented later in this chapter.

What Are the Modules in CPAT?

CPAT's core is an energy model distinguishing 17 fossil and non-fossil fuels and four sectors—power, industry, transport, and buildings, with transport and industry split into various sub-sectors (see Table 5.2). Sectors are consistent with reporting conventions in the United Nations Framework Convention on Climate Change (UNFCCC) so, for example, building emissions include those from residential/public/commercial buildings and energy use in forestry/agriculture, whereas emissions from industrial buildings are included in industry.

CPAT contains three other modules which assess the effects of mitigation policies on household and industry groups, local air pollution mortality, and broader externalities (like congestion) in the transport sector (discussed in Chapter 8). In addition (as discussed in the following section and in Chapter 6), supplementary models linking to CPAT assess policies for extractives, agriculture, and forestry, as well as the trade effects of mitigation policies and the dynamics of low-carbon vehicle transitions.

Table 5.2 Fuels and Sectors in CPAT Energy Module

Fuels	*Sectors*	
	Main	*Sub*
Coal	Power	na
Natural Gas Gasoline Diesel Kerosene	Domestic transport	Road Rail Shipping Aviation
LPG	Buildings	na
Jet Fuel Other Oil Products Electricity Wind Solar Hydro Other Renewables Nuclear Biomass	Industry	Iron/steel Cement Chemicals Other metals (e.g., aluminum) Machinery Other manufacturing Construction Fuel transformation and transport Other energy use

Source: Authors.

Note: LPG = liquefied petroleum gas.

How Do Users Navigate CPAT?

The CPAT user interacts with the "Dashboard," which is a chart-driven, user-friendly interface. The user selects the country, mitigation instrument, policy stringency over time and its sectoral/fuel coverage, and complementary instruments. Revenues from mitigation policies can be recycled in broader tax reductions, public spending or investment, or household transfers. Within seconds, the user sees the main results in key charts (for example, effects on emissions, revenue, GDP, households by income group, local air pollution mortality, and economic welfare) and numerous more detailed charts. CPAT does not require any external data, and users can adjust various inputs (such as domestic energy prices, fuel price responsiveness).

Developing Baseline Energy Scenarios

What Are Data Sources for Fuel Use, Emissions, Prices, and Fuel Taxes/Subsidies?

The first step in developing a baseline scenario (with no change to any current mitigation policy) is assembling recent data on fuel use, emissions, fuel prices, and fuel taxes/subsidies by sector. CPAT uses the following data.

- *Fuel use*: The main source for fuel use is the International Energy Agency's (IEA) World Energy Balances which compiles data for most countries submitted annually by national authorities.[3]
- *Emissions*: CO_2 emissions by sector and fuel use can be calculated from fuel inputs and CO_2 emissions factors—CPAT uses IEA data on these factors, though they vary very little by country (see Chapter 2, Table 2.2 for standard values).[4]
- *Prices*: Using the right prices in the baseline is important to assess the effects of policies, like carbon pricing, which change prices relative to their baseline levels. CPAT's comprehensive database on retail or wholesale prices for households or industry/power generators by fuel product, sector, and country is compiled (and regularly updated) from IMF and World Bank country economists, supplemented by other sources (Black et al. 2023).
- *Taxes/subsidies*: Prices reflect supply costs plus the combined effect of any fuel excises or subsidies, carbon taxes, emissions trading schemes (ETSs), and (for household fuels) general consumption taxes. Fuel taxes/subsidies, including carbon pricing, can be computed by the difference between fuel prices and supply costs—see Table 5.3.

In CPAT, for oil, which is traded in well-integrated international markets, supply costs (the costs of consuming the product domestically rather than selling it abroad) are measured by the import/export price (for fuel importing/exporting countries, respectively), with adjustments for transportation,

Table 5.3 Computing Fuel Taxes or Subsidies

Fuel Tax/Subsidy = Retail or Wholesale Fuel Price – Supply Cost (Including Margins)		
Estimation	Data collected at country level (e.g., by IMF country teams)	*Traded products, oil*: import or export price *Nontraded products, electricity*: domestic production cost *Partially traded products, coal, gas*: weighted average of domestic and international prices

Source: Authors.

processing, and distribution margins. For electricity (largely a nontraded product), the supply cost is the domestic production cost, including margins. For coal and natural gas (where global markets are partially integrated) supply costs are an average (weighted by production shares) of domestic/international (margin-inclusive) prices. CPAT's default assumption is that supply costs and taxes/subsidies are constant in real terms in the baseline (the user can adjust this assumption) but domestic prices respond to changes in future international energy prices (see the following section).

How Do Prices and Supply Costs for Energy Products Vary by Product and Country?

Figure 5.1 shows this information for energy products in G20 countries for 2024. Some noteworthy points are:

- *Coal*: Supply costs for coal vary significantly across countries (for example, with accessibility, coal quality, productivity, labor costs) from about \$1.5 per gigajoule (GJ) of energy (in Russia) to \$11 per GJ (in Japan). User prices approximately covered supply costs in 13 countries and substantially exceeded them in cases where emissions from coal are subject to significant carbon pricing (Canada, EU countries, Korea, and the United Kingdom).
- *Natural gas*: Supply costs for natural gas also vary substantially by country (given the fragmentation of international markets and costs to ship/process liquefied natural gas), from about \$3 per GJ in Russia to \$20–30 per GJ (for example, in gas-importing European countries). Again, prices generally reflect, or significantly exceed, supply costs (Russia and Saudi Arabia are exceptions). In some cases, supply costs are noticeably larger for households than industrial users while prices are typically about the same, or somewhat lower for industrial consumers (reflecting, for example, simpler distribution networks and lack of VAT).
- *Electricity*: Supply costs for electricity in 2024 varied between about 10 and 30 cents per kWh (because of variation in labor, capital, and fuel

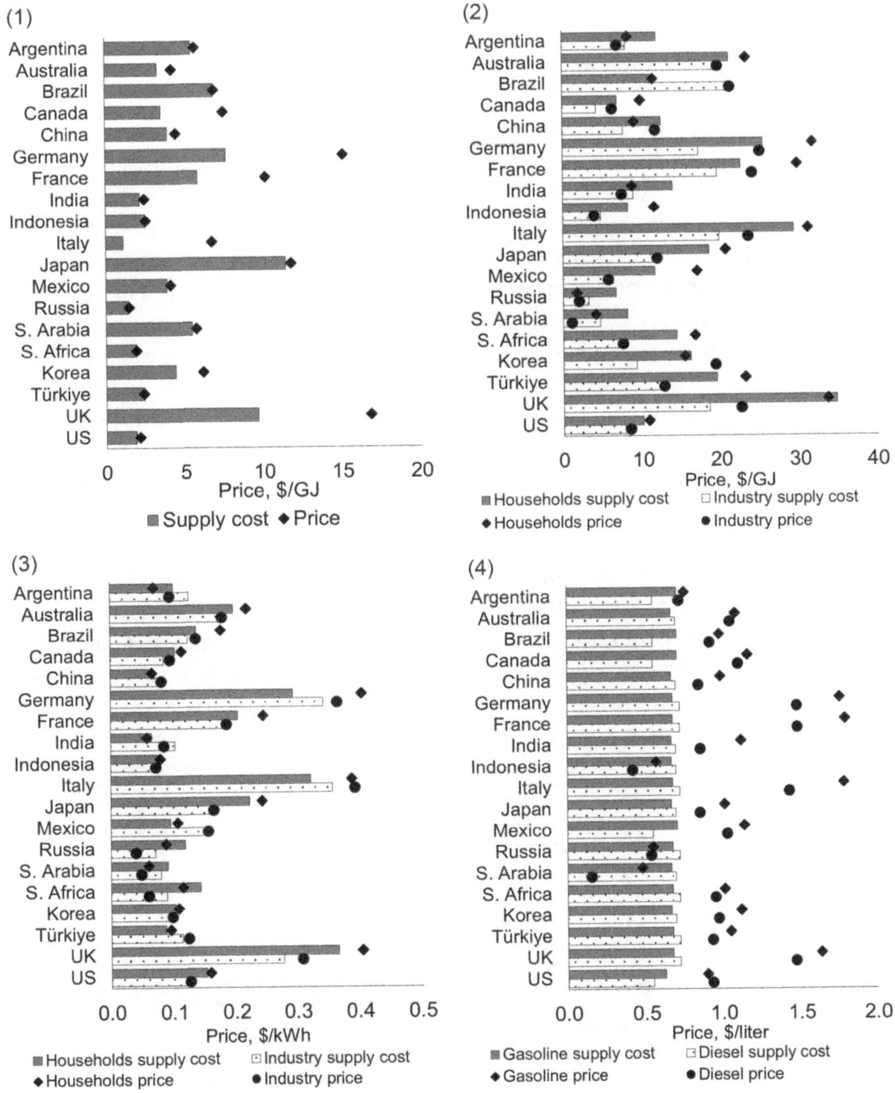

Figure 5.1 Prices and Supply Costs by Energy Product, G20 Countries, 2024. Panel 1. Coal, Panel 2. Natural Gas, Panel 3. Electricity, Panel 4. Road Fuels.

Source: IMF (2024).

costs) with costs similar for households and industry. Prices were somewhere between moderately lower and moderately higher than supply costs.

- *Road fuels*: There is little variation in supply costs for road fuels across countries, because international markets for petroleum products are well integrated. Road fuel prices significantly exceed supply costs in most cases, and typically more so for gasoline than for diesel, though Indonesia, Russia, and Saudi Arabia subsidize fuel use.

How Can Baseline Fuel Use and Emissions Be Projected?

Projections can be made accounting for the following factors:

- *GDP growth.* In CPAT, GDP projections for the next five years are from the IMF's *World Energy Outlook* and then extended assuming gradual convergence between developed and developing country growth rates.
- *Income elasticities of energy demand.* These parameters summarize the change in demand for energy products per 1 percent increase in income (or GDP). If income elasticities are below one this causes the energy intensity of GDP to fall over time (given other factors).[5] CPAT differentiates income elasticities by energy product and per capita income using relationships that are best statistical fits from over 250 empirical studies for different fuels and countries. Income elasticities rise at very low levels of per capita income (for example, because more people become connected to power grids), peak at per capita income of about $3,500, then decline before flattening out—income elasticities are mostly about 0.5–0.8 (see Figure 5.2).
- *Trend rates of technological change.* Improving energy efficiency (for example, because newer more efficient factories and vehicles replace older capital) will also lower the energy intensity of GDP. Based on typical assumptions in other models, CPAT assumes energy efficiency increases between 0.5 percent a year (in the industrial and building sectors where

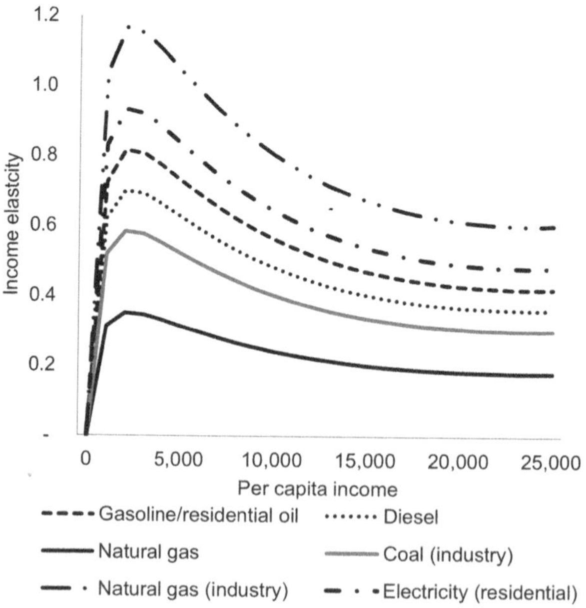

Figure 5.2 Estimated Relationships between Income Elasticities for Energy Products and Income.

Source: Authors.

Note: Estimated relationships are from Black et al. (2023), Annex 1, based on statistical analysis of 250 empirical studies.

capital turnover is gradual) and 1 percent in the vehicle sector (where capital turnover is faster). CPAT also assumes modest improvements in the productivity of coal and oil power plants (0.5 percent a year because new plants tend to be close to maximum thermal efficiency), higher for natural gas, nuclear, and hydro (1 percent a year), and higher still for renewables (5 percent a year given their rapidly declining costs).

- *Future fossil fuel prices.* Future fuel prices are given by current prices plus the product of real changes in future international prices and (historically estimated) pass-through rates to domestic prices (typically 60–100 percent). International energy price projections are based on averaging over IMF and World Bank projections (differentiated by region in the case of natural gas)—they progressively decline about 15 below 2024 levels for coal and oil out to 2030 while increasing about 40 percent for natural gas.

In developing baseline scenarios, a standard approach among modelers is to assume no new, or tightening of existing, mitigation policies because this provides a low-carbon benchmark against which scenarios with enhanced mitigation policies can be compared.

How Do Emissions Projections Vary Across Countries?

Figure 5.3 shows projections of baseline growth in baseline economywide CO_2 emissions between 2021 and 2030 for G20 countries, decomposed by changes in GDP, the energy intensity of GDP, and the CO_2 intensity of energy.

- *GDP*: GDP is projected to grow rapidly by about 40–80 percent in China, India, Indonesia, Saudi Arabia, and Türkiye, though by a more moderate 8–25 percent in most other G20 countries.
- *Energy intensity of GDP*: This is projected to decrease significantly by about 5–20 percent across countries, mainly reflecting below-unitary income elasticities and improving energy efficiency.
- *CO_2 intensity of energy*: This declines by up to about 15 percent reflecting, in particular, penetration of renewable generation technologies because of their improving competitiveness.

On net, baseline CO_2 emissions in G20 countries are projected to expand significantly between 2021 and 2030 in some cases (about 25 and 50 percent in Indonesia and India, respectively), more moderately (up to about 12 percent) in seven cases while declining moderately in others.

How Do Fuels and Sectors Contribute to Future Baseline CO_2 Emissions?

By fuel product (Figure 5.4, panel 1), oil accounts for about 40–60 percent of baseline energy-related CO_2 emissions in 2030 for most G20 countries (though is notably smaller in China, South Africa, and Russia). Coal accounts for 65–75 percent of projected CO_2 emissions in China, India, and South Africa but less than 10 percent in eight other G20 countries. Natural gas

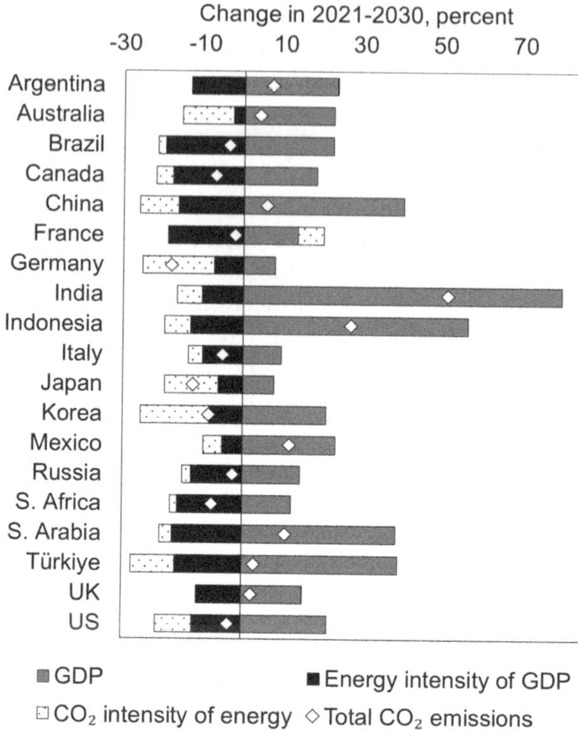

Figure 5.3 Drivers of Baseline CO_2 Emissions, 2021–30.

Source: Authors using Climate Policy Assessment Tool (CPAT).

Note: Countries with fossil fuel subsidies (for example, Saudi Arabia) are assumed to reduce them by half to 2030, which reduces the energy intensity of Gross Domestic Product (GDP).

accounts for less than 10 percent of projected CO_2 emissions in India, Indonesia, and South Africa but about 30–50 percent in most other cases.

By sector (Figure 5.4, panel 2), power generation accounts for about 25–50 percent of projected CO_2 emissions in 10 cases but about 15 percent or less in six cases (for example, Brazil and France where power is largely generated from hydro and nuclear, respectively). Industry's contribution ranges between 20 and 30 percent for most countries. Transport typically accounts for about 25–45 percent of projected CO_2 emissions, with high shares in cases like Brazil and France (the flip side of their low-carbon power sectors) and the United States (where vehicles are used intensively and have relatively low fuel economy). The share of buildings (and some other sources) in emissions is less than 20 percent in 13 cases, though shares are higher in colder countries like the United Kingdom and Germany.

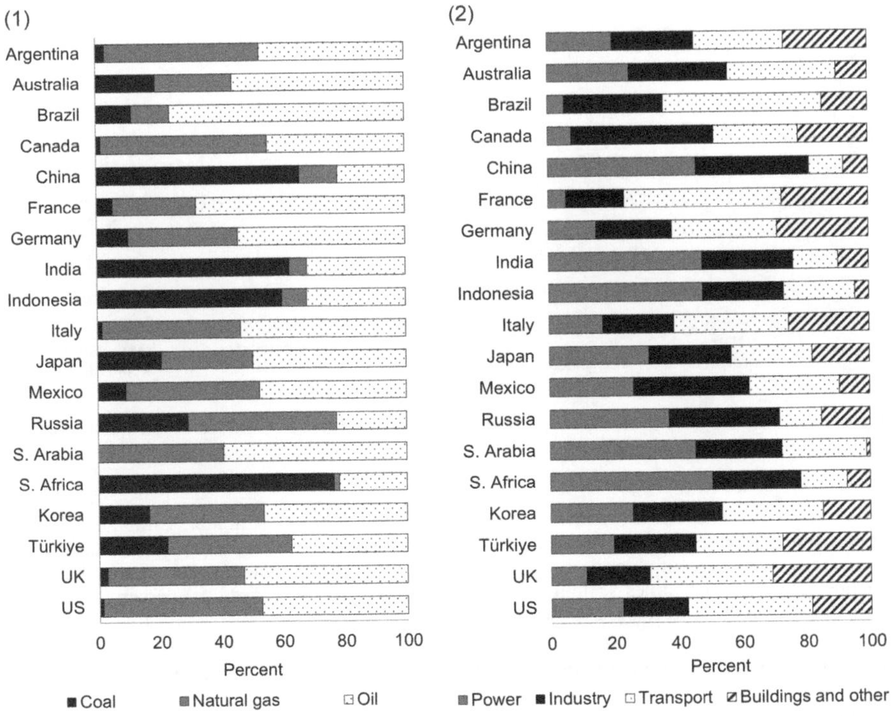

Figure 5.4 Baseline CO_2 Emissions by Fuel and Sector, G20 Countries, 2030. Panel 1. Fuels, Panel 2. Sectors.

Source: Authors using CPAT.

Note: "Buildings and other" includes energy consumption in households, services, public buildings, food and forestry, and military sectors.

How Sensitive Are Emissions Projections to Alternative Assumptions?

Emissions projections are moderately sensitive to alternative scenarios for key underlying factors—see Figure 5.5, which shows results for combined emissions in 2030 from the six largest CO_2 emitters. Varying international energy prices between minus and plus 50 percent (relative to baseline prices) has most effect, increasing combined CO_2 emissions by 8 percent or reducing them by 4 percent compared with baseline emissions. Under scenarios for GDP growth rates that are 50 percent below and 50 percent above those in the baseline, changes in CO_2 emissions are 6 percent in either direction and similarly for income elasticities. Emissions projections are less sensitive to assumptions about fuel price responsiveness and trend rates of technological change.

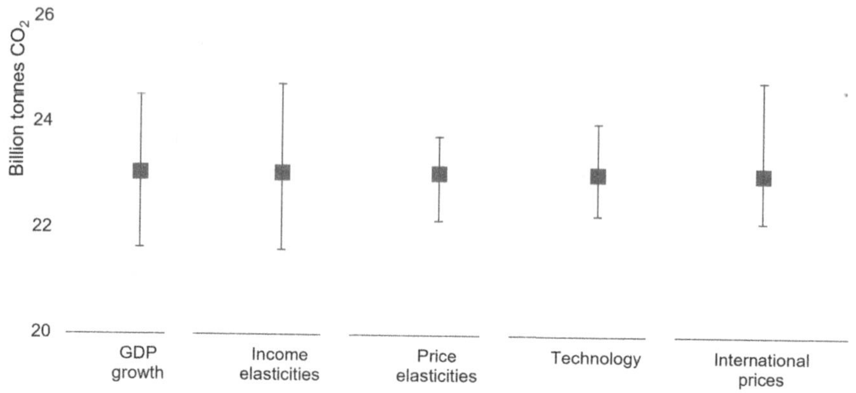

Figure 5.5 Sensitivity of CO_2 Projections for Large Emitters to Alternative Assumptions, 2030.

Source: Authors using CPAT.

Note: Effect on baseline CO_2 emissions in 2030 in six countries (Canada, China, the United States, India, Japan, Mexico). Top bars: GDP growth, income elasticities, and price elasticities all increased 50 percent relative to baseline; technology development slows renewables cost decline rate and renewables scale-up rate; international prices reduced 50 percent relative to baseline. Lower bars reverse these assumptions.

How Are Mitigation Commitments Mapped into Emissions Reductions?

This can be done by comparing economywide emissions in 2030 if a country's NDC target is met with 2030 baseline emissions. CPAT converts all quantifiable, economywide mitigation targets for all GHGs into percent reductions in CO_2 equivalents relative to 2030 (non-land use) baseline levels (see the following section on baseline projections for other GHGs).

Figure 5.6 shows estimated emissions reductions implied by NDCs (listed in Chapter 2, Table 2.4) for G20 countries. In most cases, countries have significantly tightened their targets since 2015 and are now committed to GHG reductions of about 25–40 percent below baseline levels in 2030. China's NDC is less ambitious, however, and in five cases NDCs have already been achieved (that is, the target is met under baseline emissions projections from CPAT).

Developing a Least-Cost Mitigation Scenario

Why Is a Least-Cost Reference Scenario Useful?

The least-cost way to achieve a given emissions target is to equate the incremental cost of reducing emissions across responses and sectors (subject to meeting the target) which can be achieved through economywide carbon pricing (see Chapter 3). Although policymakers may use a combination of instruments (with or without pricing), and additional instruments are needed to address broader market impediments (see Chapter 7), analyzing a reference scenario with carbon pricing is important:

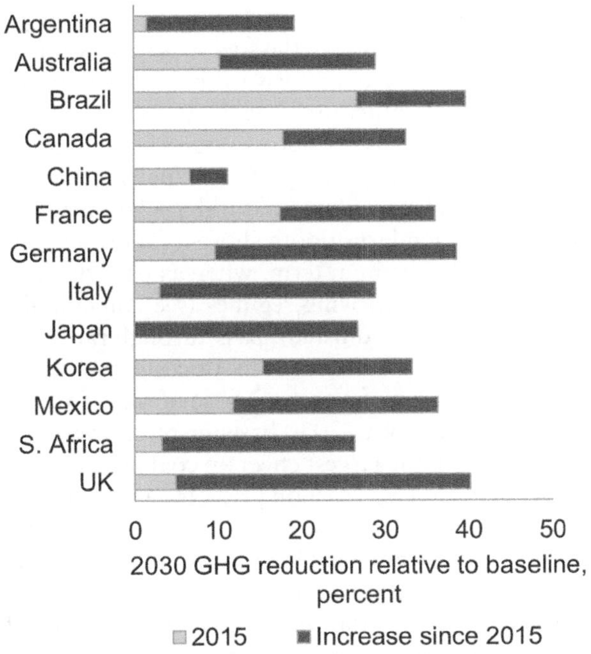

Figure 5.6 GHG Reductions Implied by Mitigation Targets.

Source: Authors using CPAT.

Note: Figure does not show G20 countries with commitments that are non-binding.

- Where pricing is the centerpiece of the mitigation strategy, understanding its effects is critical for policy design (for example, the needed price level, use of revenues);
- For countries using alternative instruments, a carbon pricing reference case indicates the pattern of emissions reductions across responses and sectors that, insofar as possible, would ideally be mimicked by these instruments to contain mitigation costs;
- For countries choosing a balance between pricing and other instruments, understanding the trade-offs across different instruments is important (for example, in terms of emissions, costs, revenues, effects on energy prices).

This subsection therefore discusses how to model economywide carbon pricing and illustrates its various effects across G20 countries.

What Is the Effect of Carbon Pricing on Energy Prices?

The discussion here abstracts from uncertainty over future abatement costs and other factors causing the effects of carbon taxes and ETSs to differ.[6]

Carbon pricing (though either instrument) increases the user price of fuels by the product of (1) the CO_2 price, (2) the fuel's CO_2 emissions factor, and (3) the fraction of the CO_2 price passed forward in higher user prices.

CO_2 emissions factors for fuels are largely given, whereas emissions rates per kWh of power generation vary across countries (Chapter 4, Figure 4.1) and will decline with carbon pricing. Where fuel markets are liberalized, pass-through rates are high for oil and natural gas and when prices are regulated, automatic regimes tend to smooth short-term price volatility but allow full pass-through over the medium term, whereas pass-through rates tend to be lower under discretionary pricing regimes (see Annex 5.4). In the CPAT default settings (which can be adjusted), pass-through rates by fuel/sector are 100 percent, aside from where countries fix prices below supply costs.

Figure 5.7 shows the effect of a carbon price of \$25, \$50, and \$75 per ton on increasing energy prices above 2030 baseline price levels in G20 countries. Carbon pricing has, by far, the largest effect on coal prices, increasing them on average by 100 percent for a \$50 carbon price, intermediate effects on natural gas prices (about 40 percent on average for the \$50 carbon price), and more modest effects on electricity and gasoline prices (about 20 and 15 percent on average, respectively). Proportionate price increases do, however, vary considerably across countries with variation in baseline prices and (for electricity) emissions rates. Carbon pricing also increases the price of general consumer goods produced with energy inputs, though the proportionate price increases are generally small relative to those for energy products (see Chapter 6).

What Determines the Effect of Higher Fuel Prices on Fuel Consumption?

Fuel use effects mostly depend on fuel price elasticities—these parameters summarize the change in demand for energy products per 1 percent increase in their price.[7] Fuel price elasticities reflect two responses:

- *Demand, production, or usage*: for example, reductions in electricity demand, industrial production, vehicle use, or use of heating systems, in response to higher prices for electricity, industrial energy inputs, road fuels, and residential gas.
- *Reductions in fuel intensity*: for example, switching from coal to other fuels in power generation, switching from coal to electric furnaces in steelmaking, adopting more efficient space heating systems or heat pumps, or shifting to more fuel-efficient and EVs.

Based on synthesizing hundreds of empirical studies for different fuels, sectors, and countries, (see Black et al. 2023, 34–38 for details), the average value for fuel price elasticities in CPAT for coal is –0.8, natural gas –0.7, gasoline –0.6, diesel –0.4, other oil products –0.6, and electricity demand

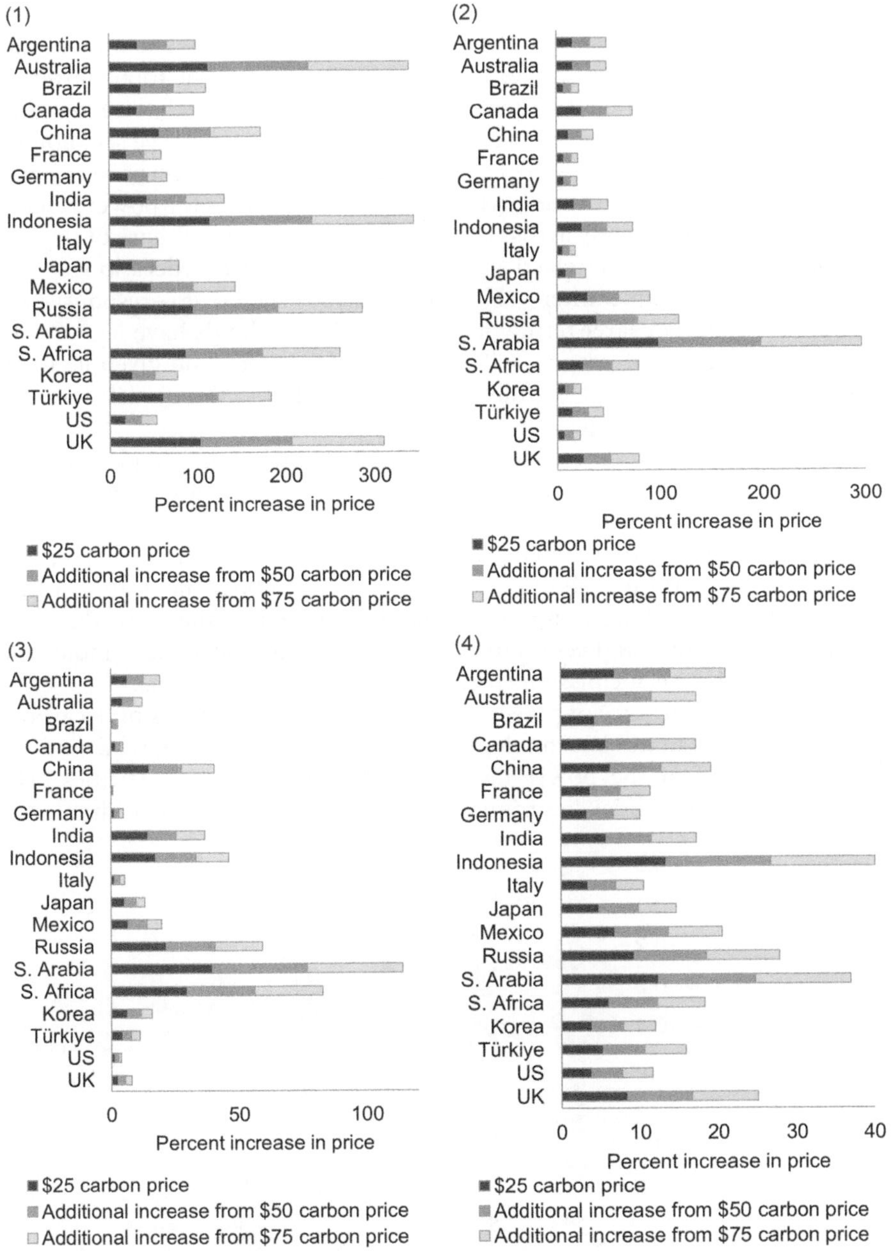

Figure 5.7 Effects of Carbon Pricing on Raising Baseline Energy Prices, G20 Countries, 2030. Panel 1. Coal, Panel 2. Natural Gas, Panel 3. Electricity, Panel 4. Gasoline.

Source: Authors using CPAT.

−0.4 (see Figure 5.8). CPAT also decomposes fuel price elasticities according to the two responses, listed in the previous section, with reductions in fuel intensity typically accounting for about 60–70 percent of the total elasticity.

Within CPAT, average fuel price elasticities are moderately larger in size (by 10 percent) for developing countries than for advanced economies (reflecting slightly higher price responsiveness of vehicle ownership, grid access, and so on in the former case). And price elasticities for power generation fuels vary moderately across countries depending on the share of the fuel in total generation. The elasticity values in Figure 5.8 reflect longer run responses, for example, after vehicle fleets have turned over—responses are more muted in the nearer term when firms and households have less time to adjust. For reasons of keeping CPAT tractable, however, and given its focus on longer-term responses to fully anticipated policies, the model does not distinguish short- and long-term responses.

The fuel price elasticities assumed in CPAT, and what they imply for emissions price responsiveness (see the following section), are also sense checked against the broader energy modeling literature. Typically, these other models either incorporate, for different sectors, detail on currently available, and emerging, low-carbon technologies, or assumptions about the degree of substitution between labor, capital, fuel, and other inputs—either way, the models generate sectoral and economywide mitigation cost schedules, indicating relationships between emissions prices and emissions reductions.[8]

Given the importance of power generation in the early stages of decarbonization, CPAT includes a technology-based model of the sector, which can be selected instead of the power model based on fuel price elasticities. The technology-based model is grounded in observed generation technologies

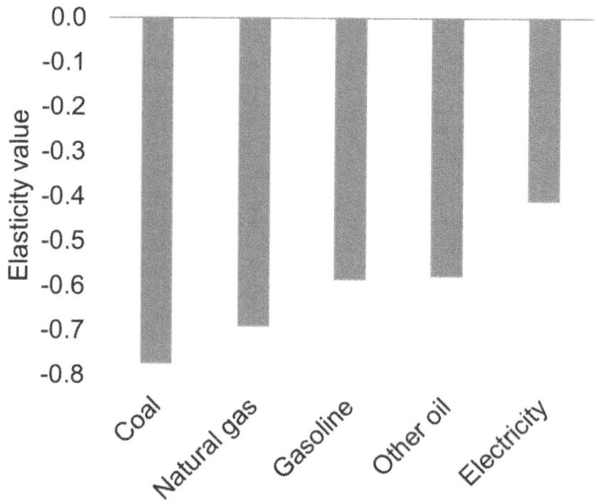

Figure 5.8 Fuel Price Elasticities Used in CPAT.

Source: Black et al. (2023).

Note: Values are a weighted average across those for advanced and developing countries.

and forward-looking investments in new capacity, as well as dispatch from existing technologies, using projections of levelized technology costs, assumptions about capital retirement rates, capacity factors, the increasing need for storing intermittent power, and possible constraints on renewables expansion.[9] The technology-based model provides more accurate baseline projections of the power generation mix, though it tends to be a little less responsive to mitigation policies than implied by empirical evidence on the price responsiveness of generation fuels.

How Does Carbon Pricing Affect Emissions?

The emissions effect of carbon pricing in the energy sector largely boils down to induced changes in fuel prices, the responsiveness of fuel use in different sectors to higher prices, and the emissions intensity of fuels.

Figure 5.9 shows reductions in CO_2 emissions below baseline levels in 2030 for carbon prices of $25, $50, and $75 per ton across G20 countries (imposed on top of any preexisting carbon pricing). Some noteworthy points include:

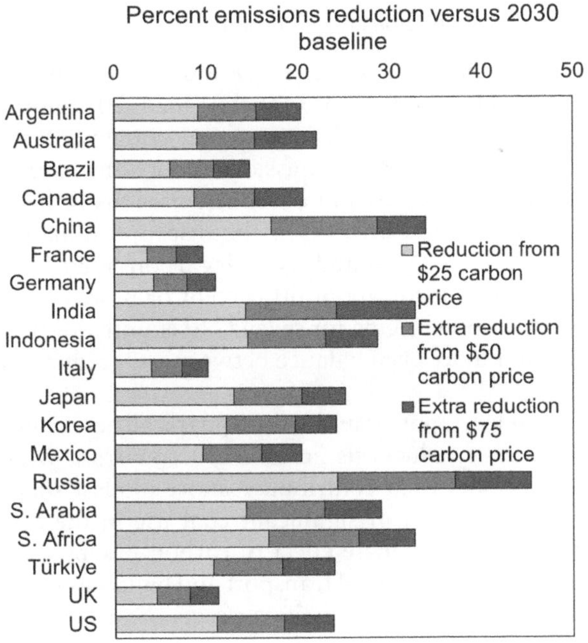

Figure 5.9 Reductions in Energy-Related CO_2 Emissions from Carbon Pricing in 2030, G20 Countries.

Source: Authors using CPAT.

Note: Countries with fossil fuel subsidies are assumed to reduce them by half to 2030.

- Carbon pricing can produce substantial emissions reductions—for example, a $50 carbon price would cut CO_2 emissions by about 10–30 percent below baseline levels in most cases.
- Emissions price responsiveness varies significantly across countries—it is larger in coal-intensive countries like China, India, Indonesia, and South Africa whereas it has more modest effects, for example, in France where power generation has low CO_2 intensity.
- Pricing by itself is likely insufficient to meet the more aggressive mitigation targets (from Figure 5.6), especially in advanced economies.
- Pricing becomes progressively less effective at cutting emissions because the lower cost mitigation opportunities are exhausted—for example, the $25 carbon price cuts emissions in South Africa 17 percent, while raising it to $50 or $75 cuts emissions by an additional 10 and 6 percentage points, respectively.

The last two points underscore the desirability of setting an intermediate (rather than overly ambitious) level of carbon pricing, reinforcing it with sectoral measures (discussed in Chapters 3 and 4), and continued progress on reducing costs for low-carbon technologies (Chapter 7).

Where Do Emissions Reductions Come From?

Figure 5.10 shows the breakdown of CO_2 reductions under carbon pricing in 2030 by fuel (panel 1) and sector (panel 2) for G20 countries (for prices of $75/50/25 per ton in high/middle/low-income countries).

At the fuel level, the share of emissions reductions from reduced coal use is larger than the share of coal in baseline emissions in Figure 5.4 (and vice versa for natural gas and oil), given the disproportionately large effect of carbon pricing on coal prices and its high carbon intensity. Indeed, reduced coal use would account for about 60 percent or more of the fossil fuel CO_2 reductions from carbon pricing for seven G20 countries—in most other cases, however, there is a more even balance between CO_2 reductions from different fossil fuels.

At the sectoral level, power and industry typically account for about 60–90 percent of emissions reductions across G20 countries, while transport and buildings/other sectors each contribute a more modest share. This generally reflects some combination of significant coal use in the former sectors, the relatively modest proportionate effect of carbon pricing on road fuel prices, and the generally smaller share of transport and buildings in baseline emissions.

To an approximation, the emissions effects of fuel- or sector-specific carbon pricing can be inferred from Figure 5.10. For example, in seven G20 countries a tax on coal alone will achieve emissions reductions of 60 percent or more of those from comprehensive carbon pricing, while for all countries an ETS limited to power and industry will typically achieve 60–90 percent of them. Although pricing of emissions for the power and industrial sectors is

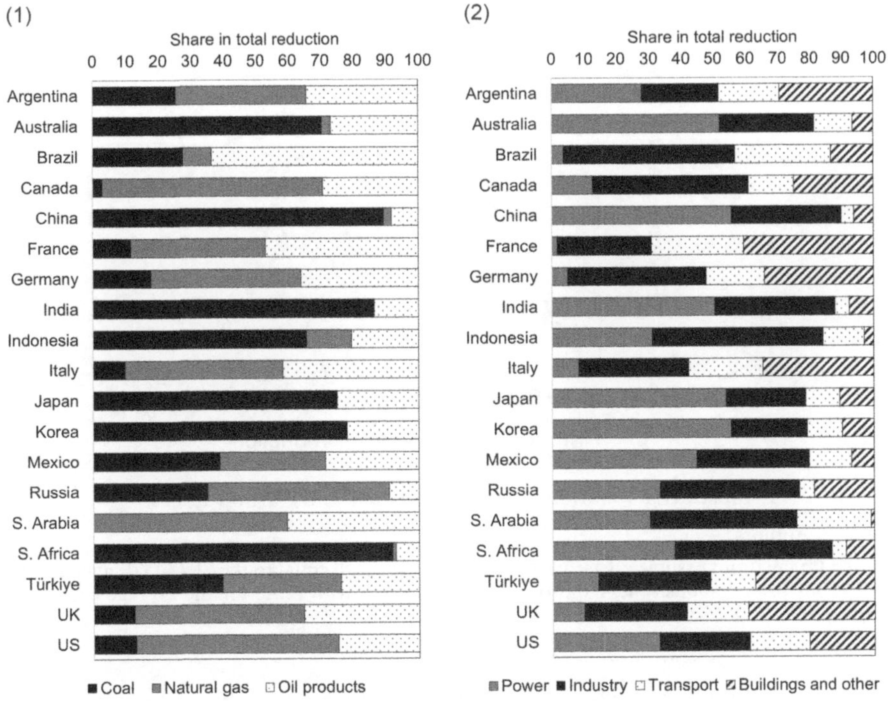

Figure 5.10 Breakdown of Energy-Related CO_2 Reductions under Pricing by Fuel and Sector, G20 Countries, 2030. Panel 1. Fuels, Panel 2. Sectors.

Source: Authors using CPAT.

Note: Estimates are for a $75/50/25 carbon price for high/medium/low-income countries. "Buildings and other" sector includes energy consumption in households, services, food and forestry, and military sectors.

typically most important for the near term (given these sectors account for most low-cost mitigation opportunities), prices will also need to rise steadily for the transport and building sectors if they are to be decarbonized by mid-century (Chapter 7).

How Are Carbon Pricing Revenues Calculated?

It is important to understand the overall fiscal effects of mitigation policies (and to put in place robust governance frameworks to manage these effects). Potential carbon pricing revenues, relative to GDP, can be calculated with reasonable confidence—they are simply the carbon price times the emissions intensity of GDP, where the latter is emissions intensity in the baseline scaled by the proportionate emissions reduction induced by the carbon price. Revenues increase by less than in proportion to the carbon price, because of the erosion of the base for carbon pricing, eventually peaking and converging

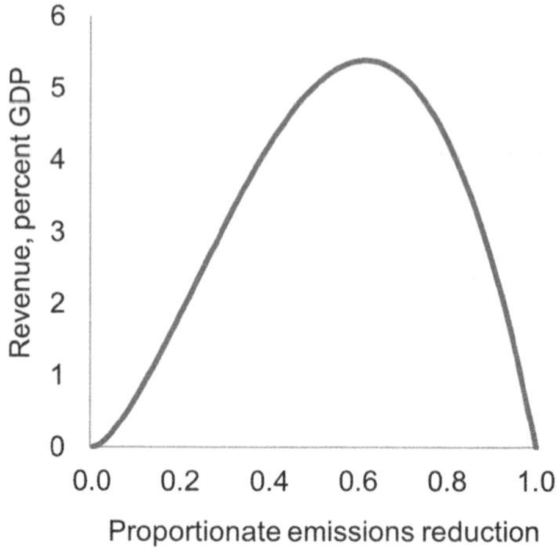

Figure 5.11 Illustrative Relation between Revenues and Carbon Prices.

Source: Authors.

Note: Calculations assume a baseline CO_2 intensity of GDP equal to the 2022 G20 average and emissions price responsiveness approximately consistent with those for the average country in Figure 5.9.

to zero as emissions reductions approach 100 percent. Figure 5.11 shows illustrative calculations for this relationship[10] based on average emissions intensities and emissions price responsiveness across G20 countries. For example, revenues are just under 2 percent of GDP, and just over 4 percent, for emissions reductions of 20 and 40 percent (which require carbon prices of about $50 and $160 per ton, respectively), and peak at just over 5 percent of GDP.

Carbon pricing will cause indirect revenue losses/gains to the extent it reduces base for preexisting energy taxes/subsidies, given by the CO_2 reductions associated with that energy product times the tax/subsidy expressed per ton of CO_2 (revenues will also decline if a subsidized fuel like renewables expands in response to carbon pricing). All these revenue effects are included in CPAT. More generally, carbon pricing may affect the base of economywide taxes on labor, capital, and consumption though the magnitude, and even sign, of this effect depends on how carbon pricing revenues are used (see the following section).

How Does the Revenue Potential from Carbon Pricing Differ Across Countries?

Figure 5.12 shows calculations of revenues from carbon prices of $75, $50, and $25 per ton in 2030 for high-, middle-, and low-income G20 countries, broken down by sector. Gross revenues from carbon pricing in 2030 are mostly between about 0.5 and 1.5 percent of GDP, and about 2 percent or more in China, Saudi Arabia, South Africa, and Russia, with the contribution

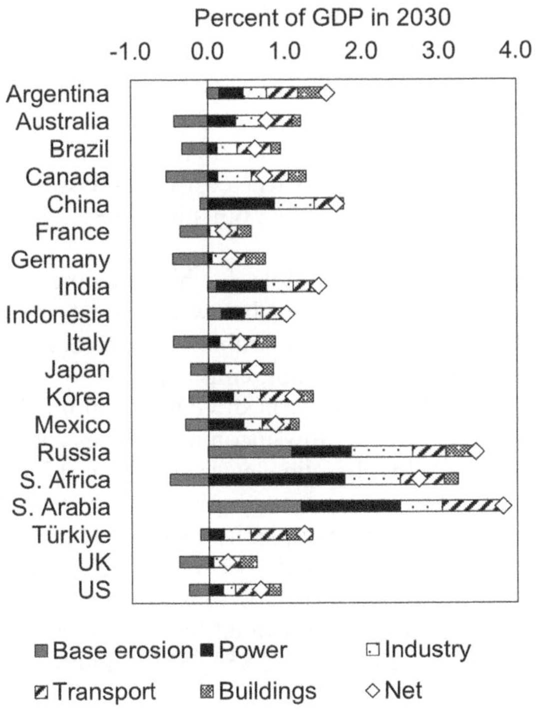

Figure 5.12 Revenues from Carbon Pricing, G20 Countries 2030.

Sources: Authors using CPAT. Estimates are for carbon prices of $75, $50, and $25 per ton of CO_2 in high-, middle-, and low-income countries, respectively.

to revenue from different sectors varying significantly across countries. Erosion of fuel tax bases typically causes revenue losses of about 0.2 percent of GDP or less (though significantly more in Canada), whereas Saudi Arabia and Russia would gain significant revenues from reducing bases for fuel subsidies.

How Do Economists Measure the Costs of Mitigation Policies?

Economists generally measure the costs of environmental and other regulations, government investments, taxes, and other policies using the concept of welfare costs.[11] In the context of climate mitigation, the welfare cost of the CO_2 reductions from reducing a particular fuel with no prior tax or subsidy is just the mitigation cost, or integral under the marginal abatement cost schedule, whereas costs would be larger or smaller if there were a preexisting tax or subsidy on the fuel (see Annex 5.5 for caveats to these measures). The costs from carbon pricing can therefore be approximated by adding up the mitigation costs from the CO_2 reductions for each fuel in each sector, accounting for any preexisting fuel tax or subsidy.

How Do Mitigation Costs from Carbon Pricing Vary by Emissions Reductions and across Countries?

Figure 5.13 shows the mitigation costs in G20 countries from carbon pricing that reduces emissions by 10, 20, 30, or 40 percent below baseline levels in 2030—panels 1 and 2 show total costs from these reductions (expressed relative to GDP) and incremental costs (the cost of the last ton reduced at each percent reduction). Some noteworthy points include:

- Costs are manageable—for example, for high-income countries, the costs of cutting emissions by 40 percent below baseline levels are about 0.4–1 percent of GDP, excluding Saudi Arabia (1.4 percent of GDP); costs for middle-income countries of cutting emissions by 30 percent below baseline levels are about 0.4–0.7 percent of GDP (excluding South Africa with 0.9 percent of GDP); and for low-income countries costs of cutting emissions by 20 percent below baseline levels are about 0.2 percent of GDP.
- Within countries, costs increase disproportionately with the level of mitigation (see Annex 5.5): for example, in the United States, the costs of cutting emissions by 10, 20, 30, and 40 percent are 0.02, 0.1, 0.3, and 0.6 percent of GDP, respectively. This is illustrated most vividly in panel 2 where incremental costs for the United States at emissions reductions of 10, 20, 30, and 40 percent are \$22, \$57, \$113, and \$205, respectively.

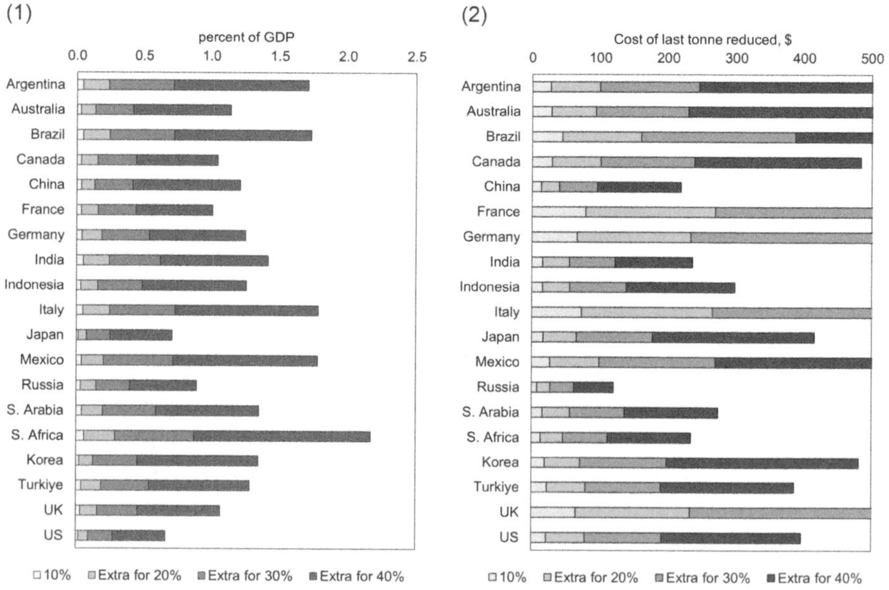

Figure 5.13 Mitigation Costs from Cutting CO_2, G20 Countries 2030. Panel 1. Total Costs, Panel 2. Incremental Costs.

Source: Authors using CPAT.

- Across countries, costs vary significantly for a given emissions reduction, for example, for a 20 percent emissions reduction from 0.1 percent of GDP in China to 0.3 percent of GDP in Brazil. Costs are higher the greater the baseline CO_2 intensity of GDP and the lower the price responsiveness of emissions (the latter implies a higher carbon price is needed to achieve a given percent emissions reduction). These factors tend to be negatively correlated, for example, countries with high baseline emissions intensity of GDP tend to use a lot of coal and there can be ample low-cost opportunities for switching from coal to other fuels (this explains why the costs of achieving a given percent emissions reduction are lower in China than in 15 other countries even though China has one of the highest baseline CO_2 intensities of GDP).

The cost estimates mentioned earlier will likely decline in future, however, with innovation into low-carbon technologies.

How Are the Costs of Mitigation Policies Affected by Interactions with the Broader Fiscal System?

Mitigation policies interact with the broader fiscal system in two opposing respects, with potentially significant implications for their overall net costs.

- *Revenue-recycling benefit.* This is the potential gains in economic efficiency from productive use of carbon pricing revenues. For example, if revenues are used to fund public investments with a benefit-to-cost ratio of 1.3 (or rate of return of 30 percent), each \$1 of revenue recycled generates an economic efficiency benefit of \$0.3. Alternatively, using revenues to reduce labor income taxes—which discourage work effort while promoting informality and excessive spending on tax-favored goods—generates efficiency gains in the order of \$0.3–\$0.4 per \$1 of revenue recycled for advanced economies and \$0.1–\$0.15 for other countries.[12] In contrast, using revenues for lump-sum transfer payments forgoes efficiency benefits.
- *Adverse factor market effects.* However, higher production costs and consumer prices lower the real returns to work effort and investment, which can deter labor supply and investment, thereby exacerbating the distortions from tax wedges in labor and capital markets (and lowering revenue).

As discussed in Annex 5.6, the literature on carbon taxation finds the revenue-recycling benefit can easily exceed the adverse factor market effects at modest abatement levels with productive use of revenues. Figure 5.14 provides illustrative calculations for G20 countries for CO_2 reductions of 10, 20, and 30 percent below 2030 baseline levels in low-, middle-, and high-income countries, respectively, and assuming 70 percent of revenues are used to cut distortionary taxes (in high-income countries) or fund productive investments with benefit–cost ratios of 1.3 (in other countries) while 30 percent of

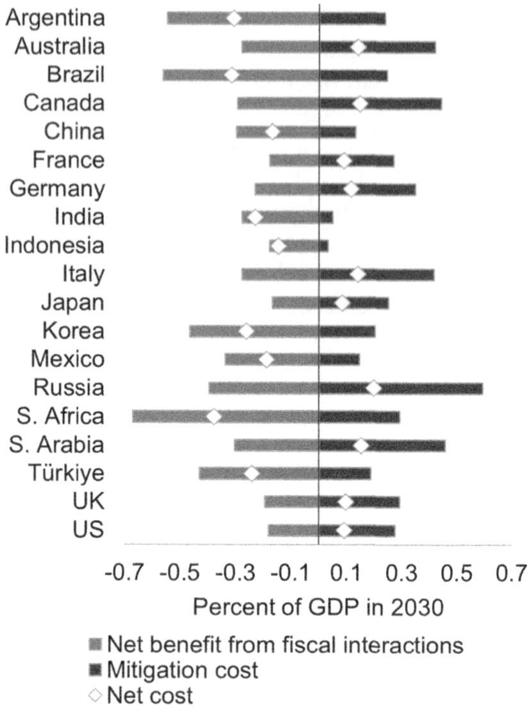

Figure 5.14 Illustrative Net Benefits from Interactions between Carbon Pricing and the Broader Fiscal System, 2030.

Source: Mitigation costs are from Figure 5.13 and fiscal interactions use formulas from Parry and Williams (2010) and standard assumptions about behavioral responses of labor supply and taxable income to tax rates.

Note: Assumes CO_2 reductions in high-, middle-, and low-income countries of 30, 20, and 10 percent below baseline levels in 2030. Seventy percent of carbon pricing revenues are used to cut distortionary taxes (in high-income countries) and public investments with benefit–cost ratio of 1.3 in other countries (the other 30 percent of revenues is used for transfer payments).

revenues are used for transfer payments. In all cases, there is a substantial net benefit from fiscal interactions and for middle- and low-income countries, which is large enough to outweigh the mitigation costs, leaving a net economic gain from carbon pricing, before counting any environmental benefits. This result hinges on the assumption of there being productive investments that currently go unfunded (implicitly from the effect of high informality on constraining revenue mobilization from broader taxes) and most of the extra revenues are spent in productive ways. Moreover, the prospects for negative costs overall diminish at higher abatement levels where the tax base for carbon pricing is narrower.

How Do GDP Costs Differ from Mitigation Costs?

Mitigation costs essentially reflect the annualized value of consumption losses to households, that is, the reduction in purchasing power because of policy-induced increases in prices for energy and consumer goods, as well as any losses in firm profits (which reduce household income), net of any gains in purchasing power from recycling revenues from mitigation policies. Policymakers may, however, be more familiar with GDP, the monetary value of final goods and services produced within a country's borders. Changes in consumption (induced by mitigation policy) are often the main driver of changes in GDP, though GDP effects also depend on:

- *Changes in economywide investment and net exports.* Mitigation policy could reduce GDP to the extent (1) economywide investment falls because the (contracting) fossil fuel energy sector is more capital intensive than other sectors that expand as resources are reallocated across the economy; and (2) net exports fall with migration of industrial production to other countries.
- *Differences across households in the marginal propensity to consume.* Lower income households tend to have a higher propensity to consume out of extra income than wealthier households, so a mitigation policy package that, on net, redistributes income to low-income households could boost aggregate consumption and GDP.
- *Fiscal multipliers and the state-of-the-business cycle.* Fiscal multipliers measure the short-term effect of increases in government spending, or tax changes, on GDP. They tend to be higher (see Batini et al. 2014) in recessions when people spend more out of extra income (which in turn increases income for other households and their spending) than in booms (when a larger share of extra income is saved and there is little slack for expanding production). If the (positive) fiscal multiplier from use of revenues is greater than the (negative) multiplier associated with carbon taxes, on net a revenue-neutral carbon tax could boost short-term GDP.
- *Policy specifics related to revenue recycling and competitiveness.* GDP effects will depend on how productively carbon pricing revenues are used (see the previous section), though there are additional factors—for example, spending programs targeted at low-income households could have a larger short-term effect on GDP (through multiplier effects) than tax reductions benefiting wealthier households. GDP effects will also depend on measures (like free allowance allocations or border carbon adjustments) designed to limit production migration effects of carbon pricing, as well as mitigation policies in trading partners.

Ex ante model simulations and ex post empirical studies have been used to assess the GDP effects of carbon pricing. The former are largely conducted before policy details (like carbon price levels and revenue recycling) are known and typically ignore differences in spending propensities across households and short-term business-cycle effects. Empirical studies (which are emerging given more experiences with carbon pricing) implicitly account for these factors but may lack accuracy because of the difficulty of disentangling the effect of carbon pricing (which often has low prices and limited sectoral coverage) on GDP from other macroeconomic shocks.

Most model-based studies estimate GDP effects of between −1.0 and +0.5 percent for a substantive carbon price, whereas empirical studies show mostly positive, albeit modest, effects (see Figure 5.15).[13] Although these findings suggest carbon pricing has not substantially reduced GDP to date, GDP effects are difficult to accurately pin down (because of the factors mentioned earlier and uncertainties over future low-carbon technology costs), going forward effects could be more severe as countries move to deeper decarbonization.

What Are the Drivers of Changes in GDP?

IMF-ENV can decompose GDP effects by driver—consumption, investment, and net exports, shown in Figure 5.16 for all G20 countries in 2030. These results assume carbon pricing revenues are mostly used for productive purposes (cutting labor taxes in high-income countries and increasing total investment in other cases) and are in line with the conclusions mentioned earlier.

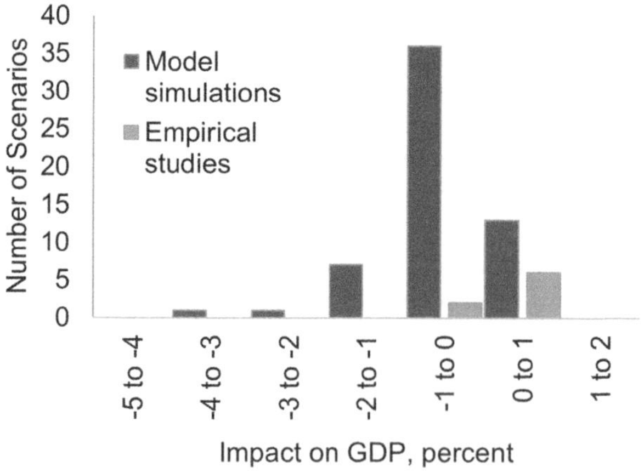

Figure 5.15 GDP Effects (after Five Years) of Carbon Pricing.

Sources: Black, Parry, and Zhunussova (2023) and IMF (2023).

Note: Figure excludes studies that do not include revenue recycling. Endpoints on horizontal axis are included on the left side of each range. Results vary across studies because of different assumptions, for example, about carbon price levels, sectoral coverage of pricing, revenue recycling, and the country under study. Model simulations mainly reflect studies using CGE models.

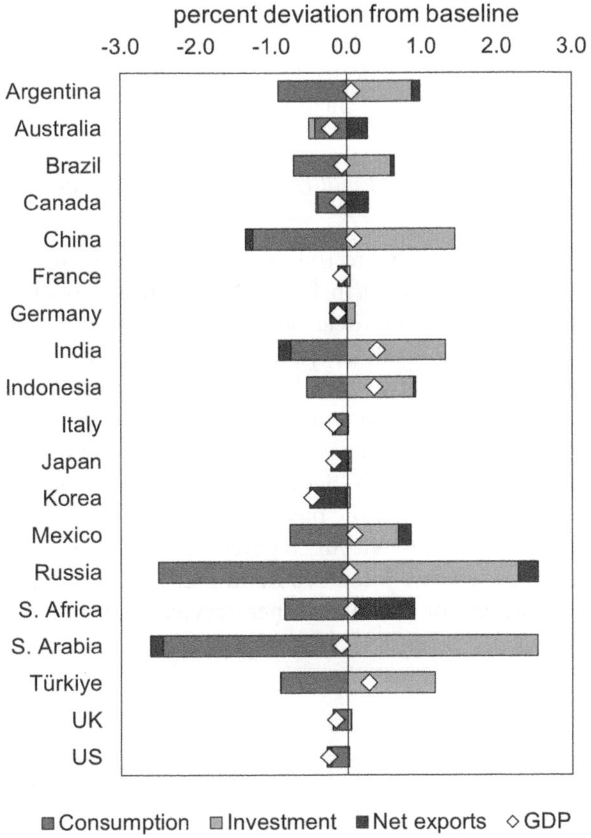

Figure 5.16 GDP Effects of Carbon Pricing by Driver, G20 Countries, 2030.

Source: IMF-ENV.

Note: Carbon prices starting from \$10/\$20/\$30 in 2025 and reaching to \$25/\$50/\$75 in 2030 for lower-middle-income/upper-middle-income/high-income countries. Seventy percent of carbon pricing revenues are used to cut distortionary taxes in high-income countries or on total investments in other countries. The other 30 percent of revenues is used for transfer payments in all countries.

For high-income countries, the average effect of \$75 carbon price on GDP is –0.17 percent (varying from –0.5 to +0.05 percent) relative to baseline GDP. The highest effect comes from reduced consumption (average 0.23 percent), though investments and net exports also change significantly. For upper-middle-income G20 countries, the effect of \$50 carbon price by 2030 on GDP is positive (except for Brazil and Saudi Arabia), leading to an average increase of 0.1 percent relative to baseline levels. For these countries, the reduction in consumption (on average of 1.36 percent) is offset by increased investment and net exports (on average of 1.41 percent). For lower-middle-income countries (India and Indonesia), the effect of \$25 carbon tax on GDP is positive (about 0.4 percent), because investments largely drive this result (+1.1 percent). As discussed in Annex 5.3, however, all GDP effects become negative when all carbon pricing revenues are used for household transfers rather than productive purposes.

How Does Carbon Pricing Affect Employment, Value Added, and Investment in Different Sectors?

These effects are mainly related to the carbon intensity of different sectors, as shown in Figure 5.17, modeled in IMF-ENV. Extraction of fossil fuels and power generation from fossil fuels would face highest negative effects on employment (average 12 and 23 percent reduction against the baseline, respectively, for G20 countries), value added (average 16 and 7 percent below the baseline, respectively), and investment (average 11 and 25 percent reduction from the baseline). Renewable electricity, however, would face an increase in employment, value added, and investments (on average, 10, 14, and 11 percent increase against the baseline, respectively). The effect on other sectors is usually not large (within 5 percent, on average), and might, on average, be negative (energy-intensive manufacturing, transportation), close to neutral (agriculture), or positive (other services and non-energy-intensive manufacturing).

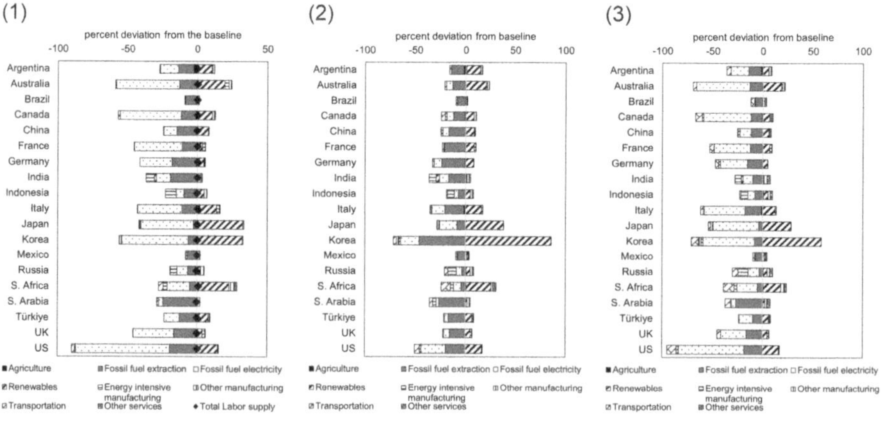

Figure 5.17 Effect of Carbon Pricing on Sectors, 2030. Panel 1. Employment, Panel 2. Value Added, Panel 3. Gross Investment.

Source: IMF-ENV.

Note: Scenarios as specified in Figure 5.16. The percentage deviations are sector specific and not directly comparable between sectors, because absolute deviations depend on the initial values for each sector.

How Do GDP Effects Vary over Time?

In CPAT, GDP effects are estimated for each country using fiscal multipliers extracted for over 100 countries from the World Bank's main macrostructural model (MFMod), in addition to empirically estimated multipliers from a data set on the relationship between changes in taxes and GDP over time (Burns et al. 2019, Burns, Jooste, and Schwerhoff 2021, Schoder 2022). These multipliers implicitly account for differences in spending propensities among households and are updated each year to account for business-cycle effects. They are based on a 1 percentage point of GDP change in taxes (on energy, goods and services, personal income tax, or corporate income tax) or expenditures (public investment, transfers, expenditures on goods and services, or public wages) and are aggregated at the country income-group level, with GDP effects lagged by one year. Fiscal multipliers in CPAT are more reliable for evaluating the effects of moderate carbon pricing—effects from higher pricing (which would induce larger structural changes) might be underestimated.

Using CPAT, Figure 5.18 provides an illustrative sense of GDP transitions over a 10-year horizon in India, China, and the United States, with carbon prices rising progressively from 2025 onward (reaching \$25, \$50, and \$75 per ton in 2030, respectively), and with 30 and 70 percent of revenues used for household transfers and public investment, respectively. India's GDP growth is higher, up to 0.6 percentage points by year 10 of the reform, reflecting the relatively high multipliers on public investment (0.62 in the first year of the reform) and low

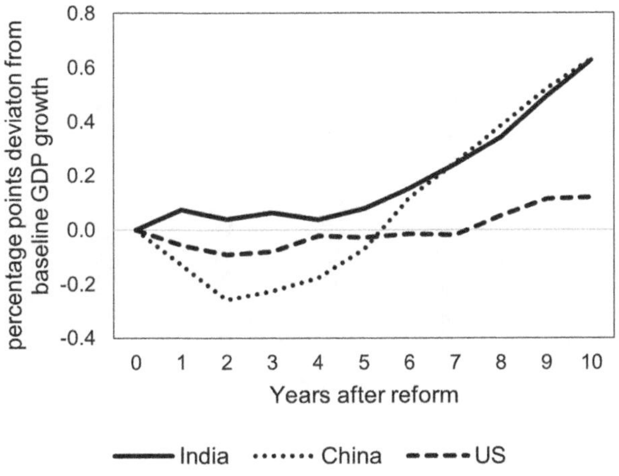

Figure 5.18 Illustrative Time Profile of GDP Effects from (Revenue-Neutral) Carbon Pricing.

Source: Authors using CPAT.

Note: Carbon prices for India, China, and United States start at \$10, \$20, and \$30 per ton in 2025 rising to \$25, \$50, and \$75 by 2030, respectively—thereafter prices rise linearly. Thirty percent of carbon pricing revenue is used for transfers and 70 percent for public investment.

negative multipliers on energy taxes (0.37 in the first year). For the United States, a combination of public investment and cash transfers has a higher multiplier than for energy taxes after year 6 and the reform positively affects GDP growth by year 8. For China, a combination of cash transfers and public investment multipliers becomes higher than the energy taxes multiplier by year 5 of the reform, and the reform starts to positively affect GDP growth by year 6.

How Does Carbon Pricing Affect Inflation?

Carbon pricing affects inflation by both raising production costs and affecting aggregate demand. Taxing emissions increases the cost of fossil fuels and emissions-intensive production processes which are passed to consumer goods prices. Aggregate demand effects are driven by both negative income effects and monetary policy, with the latter—which typically targets a weighted average of headline, core (excluding energy), and wage inflation—playing a more significant role over time. Inflation effects should be generally manageable, however, given that carbon pricing can be phased in progressively over time, while revenues are recycled and are not that large relative to the size of the economy.

Short- and long-term inflation effects from GMMET for China, United States, Euro Area, and rest of the world, from a \$20 carbon price implemented globally in 2025, rising to \$50 in 2030, and flat thereafter, are shown in Figure 5.19. In the first year, inflation increases by about 0.1–0.2 percentage points across countries and regions. Over the medium to longer term, however, inflation increases by less than 0.05 percentage points and is slightly

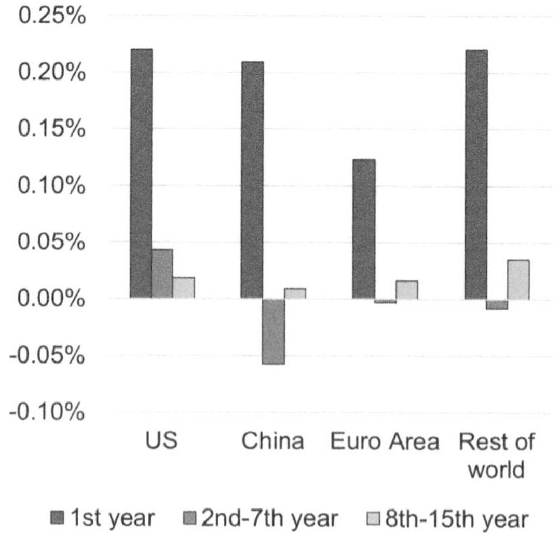

Figure 5.19 Inflation Effects of Carbon Price Rising to \$50 per Ton in 2030.

Source: IMF staff using GMMET.

Note: Carbon price starts at \$20 per ton in 2025, rising to \$50 in 2030, and is flat thereafter. Seventy percent of revenue is used for labor income tax reductions and 30 household transfers.

negative in some cases, because of the deflationary effects of lower aggregate demand from lower household wealth.

Other Policies and Sectors

How Do the Emissions Effects of Other Power Sector Policies Compare with Carbon Pricing?

For power generation, feebates and TPSs can be modeled by a charge (or implicit carbon price) on each generation fuel in proportion to the difference between the emissions rate from that fuel per unit of generation and an exogenous pivot point emissions rate. Subsidies per kWh for renewable generation are straightforward to model in CPAT and a renewable portfolio standard can be modeled by the implicit renewable subsidy that would achieve the same renewable generation share as the standard (but with no revenue loss for the government).

Figure 5.20, panel 1, indicates, for G20 countries in 2030, the CO_2 reductions for the power sector policies mentioned in the previous section,

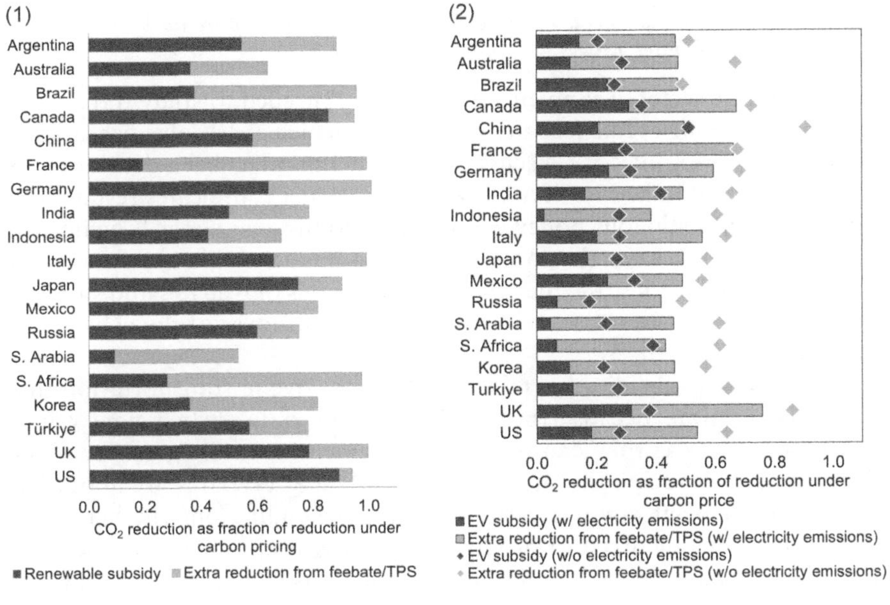

Figure 5.20 Comparing the Effectiveness of Pricing and Non-Pricing Policies for Power in 2030 and Transport in 2035, G20 Countries. Panel 1. Power Generation, Panel 2. Vehicles.

Source: Authors using CPAT.

Note: For the power sector, the subsidy achieves the same share of renewables in generation in 2030 as a \$50 per ton carbon price, whereas the feebate/TPS CO_2 price rises from \$30 per ton in 2025 to \$50 per ton in 2030. For transportation, the carbon tax, feebate, and EV subsidy are all introduced in 2025 and fixed at \$200 per ton. EV = electric vehicle, TPS = tradable performance standard.

expressed relative to CO_2 reductions from pricing power sector emissions, where feebates/TPSs are scaled to have the same explicit or implicit emissions price and renewable policies to have the same effect on renewable generation shares as under carbon pricing. Because feebates and renewables policies have weak effects on electricity demand, and in the latter case do not promote all possibilities for fuel switching (Chapter 4), they are less effective at reducing emissions than carbon pricing. Across G20 countries feebates/TPS on average have effectiveness of about 85 percent of that for carbon pricing, and renewables subsidies about 50 percent.

Results are different for the United States, where there is limited coal use in the 2030 baseline, and the main effect of carbon pricing or feebates is to promote shifting from natural gas to renewables—hence, a renewables subsidy is reasonably effective compared with these policies. Results are also different for Saudi Arabia, where much of the emissions reduction from carbon pricing is from reduced electricity demand, which is not promoted under a feebate/TPS, though the latter instruments are noticeably more effective than renewable subsidies, because they promote shifting from oil to gas and from these fuels to nuclear, as well as shifting to renewables.

How Do the Emissions Effects of Other Vehicle Policies Compare with Carbon Pricing or Fuel Taxes?

For the vehicle sector, a supplementary model is needed to study transitional dynamics for policies like feebates and electric vehicle (EV) subsidies targeted at new capital—Annex 5.7 discusses the model that has been developed for this purpose and linked to CPAT. Figure 5.20, panel 2, indicates results from this model for analogous policy comparisons to those in panel 1, again with policies scaled to have the same explicit or implicit emissions price, and focusing on 2035 (for 2030 the relative effectiveness of feebates and subsidies would be smaller given they rely exclusively on turnover of the vehicle fleet to reduce emissions).

Feebates and subsidies are relatively less effective in transportation than power generation, because these policies apply only to first-time vehicle purchases, whereas they can promote abatement at existing power plants (for example, reducing dispatch from coal plants). Feebates are about half to two-thirds as effective as carbon pricing, depending on whether power sector emissions incurred to produce electricity used by EVs are included. EV subsidies have an even more limited emissions effect, because they promote only switching to EVs, whereas feebates also promote better fuel economy of internal combustion engine vehicles—charging infrastructure constraints and relatively high EV prices further limit the effectiveness of subsidies. EV subsidies achieve 17 percent of the emissions reductions under carbon pricing on average but less than 10 percent in a few cases (Russia, Saudi Arabia, and Indonesia) when including extra power generation emissions.

How Can the Emissions Effect of Mitigation Policy Packages Be Estimated?

In practice, mitigation strategies frequently consist of multiple overlapping policy instruments within sectors—for example, feebates, performance standards, and fuel taxes often apply simultaneously in transportation, and subsidies, mandates, and tax incentives promote renewables in power generation (see Table 3.1, Chapter 3). It can be difficult analytically to decompose the emissions effects of individual measures—from a modeling perspective, in these cases it can make sense to simply assume sectoral targets (for example, for fuel economy, EV sales shares, renewable generation shares) are simply met.

Figure 5.21 shows (as of 2022) illustrative calculations of the emissions effects of current and planned mitigation policies to 2030 for G20 countries,

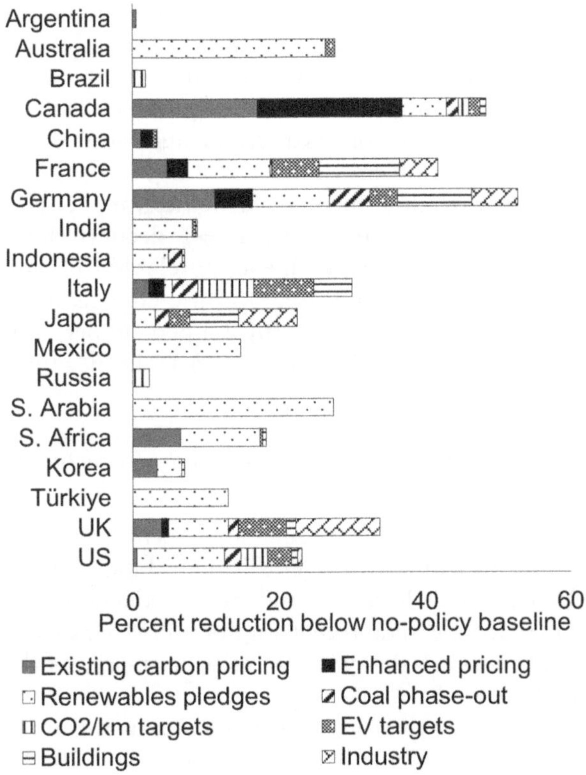

Figure 5.21 Comparing Mitigation Effort: Illustrative Comparisons for G20 Countries, 2030.

Source: Parry et al. (2022).

Note: Baseline removes the effect of any existing carbon pricing. The relative contribution of policies and targets can be ambiguous where they overlap. For example, emissions reductions from carbon pricing are calculated first and then further reductions from renewable targets—if policies were imposed in the reverse order, more emissions reductions would be attributed to renewables targets.

accounting for carbon pricing and targets for renewables, EVs, vehicle emissions rates, coal phaseouts, buildings, and industry emissions. Across G20 countries, the combined effect in 2030 of specified policies and targets varies substantially. CO_2 reductions below a 2030 baseline (with no carbon pricing) are less than 20 percent in eight G20 countries and range from 20 to about 50 percent in the other 11. In addition, countries vary significantly in their choice of instrument and relative contribution of sectoral targets, for example, renewables targets make a significant contribution to emissions reductions in the policy mix for 15 cases and carbon pricing for eight cases.

How Can Non-energy Emissions Be Projected?

In CPAT, data on emissions sources beyond fossil fuel CO_2 are collected, and regularly updated, from the UNFCCC, the Food and Agriculture Organization, national sources, and various other databases. Emissions are then projected forward based on procedures used by the Intergovernmental Panel on Climate Change and other modeling groups (Black et al. 2023). For example, methane emissions from extractives, agriculture, and waste are the product of production and emissions factors—production for the sector scales with GDP growth[14] and income elasticities for the relevant products, although emissions factors (for extractives) decline slowly over time. Industrial process emissions scale with energy-related CO_2 emissions projections in the industry sector. Land use, land-use change, and forestry emissions are assumed to decline gradually (by 2.5 percent per year) for countries with positive emissions and be flat for countries with negative emissions.

What Are the Emissions Effects of Methane Fees in the Extractive and Agricultural Sectors?

An offline model, linked to CPAT, specifies abatement cost schedules for reducing methane emissions from extractives (distinguishing coal, oil, and gas) and agriculture (distinguishing livestock and rice production) parameterized to midrange estimates from several recent studies.[15] Price elasticities of supply for extractives are taken to be –0.4, whereas price elasticities of demand for agricultural products are –0.5.

Figure 5.22 shows, for the top 20 methane emitters from the two sectors combined, the reduction in methane emissions below 2030 baseline levels from a methane fee of $70 per ton of CO_2 equivalent. Across countries, the combined emissions reductions vary from 15 to 55 percent of national methane emissions. Reductions are larger in cases where extractives contribute a large share of baseline emissions (typically extractive emissions decline by about 50 percent and agricultural emissions about 25 percent). Within both sectors, the emissions reduction primarily reflects reductions in emissions intensity (95 percent for extractives, 75 percent for agriculture) rather than reductions in overall production levels for the sector (like meat and non-meat food production combined).

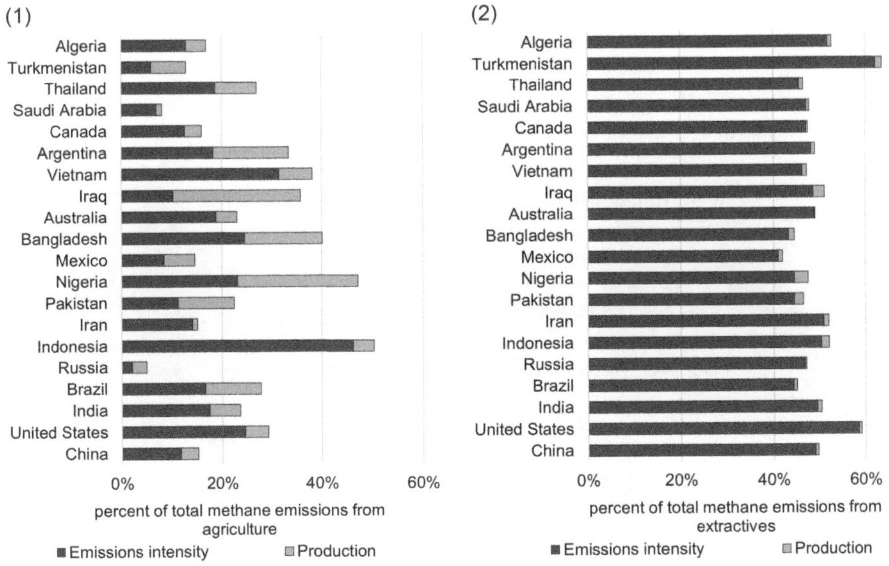

Figure 5.22 Effects of \$70 per Ton CO_2 Equivalent Methane Fee on Methane Emissions Large Emitters, 2030. Panel 1. Agriculture, Panel 2. Extractives.

Source: Updated from Parry et al. (2022).

What Are the Emissions Effects of Pricing in the Forestry Sector?

Figure 5.23 shows emissions effects from pricing in the forestry sector for major forestry emitters, using another offline model parameterized to marginal abatement cost schedules from the literature (Favero and Austin 2024). Brazil, Canada, the Democratic Republic of the Congo, and Indonesia have the largest potential to reduce CO_2 emissions from the sector, ranging from 0.2 to 1.4 billion tons a year by 2035 with options costing less than \$100 per ton of CO_2 reduced. Six other countries—Central African Republic, Peru, Cameroon, Gabon, Papua New Guinea, and Republic of the Congo—each have the potential to cost-effectively reduce emissions by 0.1 or more billion tons a year. The cost-effective balance between different mitigation activities varies by country, however. In 2 of the 10 countries, reduced deforestation/degradation accounts for most of the cost-effective emissions reductions, including Brazil where much deforestation is illegal (Koch et al. 2019). In contrast, in the remaining countries, forest management makes up the bulk of low-cost opportunities.

Suggestions for Further Readings

- *Income elasticities for energy products.* For a discussion on empirical literature on the responsiveness of different energy products to income in different countries, see Burke and Csereklyei (2016).

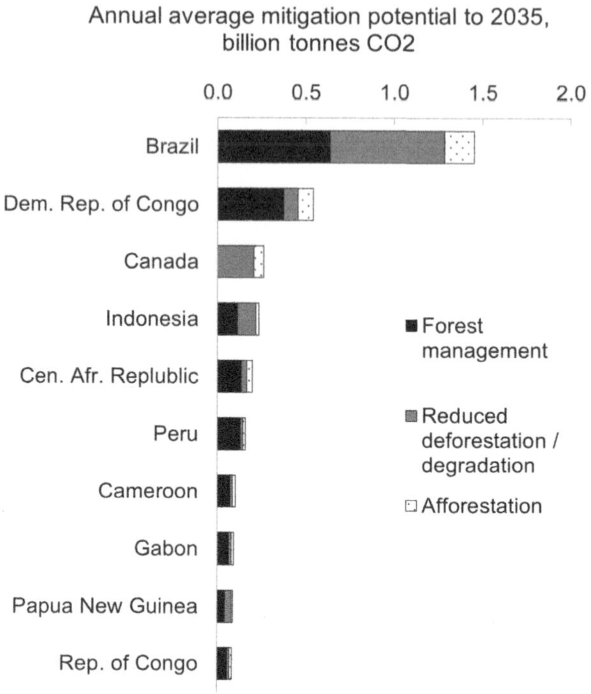

Figure 5.23 Effects of $100 per Ton CO_2 Price on Forestry Emissions, 2035.

Source: Favero and Austin (2024) based on the Global Timber Model.

Note: Cost-effective refers to emissions reductions that can be achieved with costs of up to $100 per ton of CO_2 reduced.

- *Fuel price responsiveness*. For a summary of empirical studies on fuel price elasticities, see Labandeira, Labeaga, and López-Otero (2017).
- *Emissions effects of carbon pricing*. See Metcalf (2019) for a survey of the emissions effects of carbon taxes, and for two recent studies, see Stechemesser et al. (2024) and Xu and Yang (2024).
- *Energy/climate models*. For a discussion of models, see, for example, IPCC (2022) Annex III, Böhringer et al. (2021).
- *Costs of mitigation policies*. For further discussion of the costs of mitigation policies, see, for example, Gillingham and Stock (2018).
- *Macroeconomic effects of mitigation policy*. For some discussion of the GDP effects of carbon pricing from modeling results, see Freire-González (2018), Goulder et al. (2019), and Köppl and Schratzenstaller (2022) and from empirical studies, see Bernard and Kichian (2021) and Metcalf and Stock (2020). Chateau, Jaumotte, and Schwerhoff (2022) also model the GDP effects of regulatory policies. For general discussions of GDP effects, see, for example, Heine and Black (2019), Williams and Wichman (2015). For broader discussions of macroeconomic effects, see IMF (2020, 2022).
- *Other sectors*. For further discussions of mitigation costs for agriculture and extractives, see UNEP (2021) and Parry et al. (2022) and for forestry, see Roe et al. (2021).

Annex 5.1 Recent Applications using CPAT (Table A5.1)

Table A5.1 Selected Reports, Papers, and Other Publications Using CPAT

Coverage		*Year*	*Publication*	*Title*	
Country Analysis					
	Belgium	2023	SIP	Fiscal Policy Options to Accelerate Emissions Reductions in Belgium	Selected Issues Paper
	Chile	2023	TAR	Chile: An Evaluation of Improved Green Tax Options	Technical Assistance Report
	Peru	2023	SR	Peru: 2023 Article IV Consultation	
	Madagascar	2022	TAR	Republic of Madagascar: Climate Macroeconomic Assessment Program (CMAP)	Technical Assistance Report
	Philippines	2022	SIP	Philippines: Selected Issues	Selected Issues Paper
	Thailand	2022	SIP	Thailand: Selected Issues	Selected Issues Paper
	Canada	2021	SIP	Canada: Selected Issues	Selected Issues Paper
	Finland	2021	WP	Fiscal Policies for Achieving Finland's Emission Neutrality Target	Selected Issues Paper
	Germany	2021	WP	Scaling up Climate Mitigation Policy in Germany	Working Paper
	Korea	2021	SIP	Republic of Korea: Selected Issues	Selected Issues Paper
	Mexico	2021	WP	A Comprehensive Climate Mitigation Strategy for Mexico	Working Paper
	Netherlands	2021	WP	A Comprehensive Greenhouse Gas Mitigation Strategy for The Netherlands	Working Paper
	China	2020	BC	Evaluating Policies to Implement the Paris Agreement: Application to China	Book Chapter
	Denmark	2020	WP	Climate Mitigation Policy in Denmark: A Prototype for Other Countries	Book Chapter

(*Continued*)

Table A5.1 (Continued)

Coverage		*Year*	*Publication*	*Title*	
	India	2019	BC	Reforming Energy Policy in India: Assessing the Options	Book Chapter
	Canada	2017	JA	Canada's Carbon Price Floor	Journal Article
	China	2016	WP	Climate Mitigation in China: Which Policies Are Most Effective?	Working Paper
Regional Analysis					
	Middle East	2023	DP	A Low-Carbon Future for the Middle East and Central Asia: What are the Options?	Departmental Paper
	Latin America	2023	REO	Regional Economic Outlook for Latin America and the Caribbean, October 2021	Regional Economic Outlook
	Europe	2022	WP	Targeted, Implementable, and Practical Energy Relief Measures for Households in Europe	
	Europe	2022	WP	Surging Energy Prices in Europe in the Aftermath of the War	Working Paper
Global/Thematic Analysis					
	All countries	2022	SCN	Getting on Track to Net Zero: Accelerating a Global Just Transition in This Decade	IMF Staff Climate Note
	G20	2022	SCN	Carbon Taxes or Emissions Trading Systems?: Instrument Choice and Design	IMF Staff Climate Note
	G20	2022	WP	A Framework for Comparing Climate Mitigation Policies Across Countries	Working Paper
	G20	2022	FM	Fiscal Monitor: Fiscal Policy from Pandemic to War	Fiscal Monitor
	Various	2022	SCN	How to Cut Methane Emissions	IMF Staff Climate Note
	All countries	2021	SCN	Not Yet on Track to Net Zero: The Urgent Need for Greater Ambition and Policy Action	IMF Staff Climate Note

	G20	2021	SCN	Proposal for an International Carbon Price Floor Among Large Emitters	IMF Staff Climate Note
	191 countries	2021	WP	Still Not Getting Energy Prices Right: An Update of Fossil Fuel Subsidies	Working Paper
	G20	2021	JA	Mitigation Policies for the Paris Agreement: An Assessment for G20 Countries	Journal Article
	135 countries	2019	BP	Fiscal Policies for Paris Climate Strategies	Board Paper
	G20	2019	FM	Fiscal Monitor: How to Mitigate Climate Change	Fiscal Monitor
EU + UK		2022	IMF Working Paper	Targeted, Implementable, and Practical Energy Relief Measures for Households in Europe	repetitive (already have Europe paper), barely uses CPAT
G20		2021	IMF Staff Climate Note	Carbon Pricing: What Role for Border Carbon Adjustments?	doesn't use CPAT
G20		2021	IMF Staff Climate Note	Not Yet on Track to Net Zero: The Urgent Need for Greater Ambition and Policy Action to Achieve Paris Temperature Goals	repetitive (old version)
Türkiye		2023	Technical Assistance Report	Climate Mitigation Policy in Türkiye	not yet published

Source: Authors.

Note: BC = Book Chapter; BP = Board Paper; DP = Departmental Paper; FM = Fiscal Monitor; JA = Journal Article; REO = Regional Economic Outlook; SCN = IMF Staff Climate Note; SIP = Selected Issues Paper; SR = Article IV Staff Report; TAR = Technical Assistance Report; WP = Working paper.

Annex 5.2 Caveats to CPAT

Caveats include:

- *Large policy changes.* CPAT, like any other model, is most reliable at predicting the effects of moderate policy changes. The future costs of many low-carbon technologies are uncertain, and this makes it challenging to predict how households and firms will respond to more drastic policy changes, for example, the extent to which industrial firms will accelerate innovation into, and future adoption of, electric furnaces, green hydrogen, and carbon capture.
- *Learning-by-doing spillovers in low-carbon technologies.* Renewables have sharp learning curves, with the costs of solar declining 90 percent between 2010 and 2020, for example. CPAT includes assumptions on learning rates for key technologies, though these are exogenous rather than responding (through faster innovation) to mitigation policy.
- *Feedback from international fuel markets.* The possibility of upward-sloping fuel supply curves and other changes in international fuel prices that might result from simultaneous climate or energy price reform in large countries would affect results. Parameter values are, however, chosen such that the results from CPAT are broadly consistent with those of more detailed energy models that, to varying degrees, account for these types of factors.
- *Effects from policy changes on GDP are simplified.* GDP effects are estimated as described earlier to account for general equilibrium effects of climate policy changes (for example, from changes in employment, balances of payments, monetary factors, and so on) to adjust the forecast growth path. In general, this is a reasonable approach. However, it should be noted that fiscal multipliers are currently aggregated at the region and income-group level, whereas country-specific circumstances (for example, debt distress) are not currently included. Economic effects also do not account for interactions between climate mitigation policies and distortions in the economy created by the broader fiscal system, which can reduce policy costs (for example, through recycling carbon pricing revenues in broader tax reductions). GDP effects from changes in informality, induced technical change, or local air pollution (for example, on productivity) are also not included but could be substantive.
- *Sectors are decoupled at present but will become increasingly integrated into future updates.* Global decarbonization requires cutting emissions in power generation while electrifying the end uses of energy, creating inter-sectoral linkages. For example, EVs will add modestly to electricity demand, whereas hydrogen is likely to become more readily available

for decarbonizing industry (though the share of hydrogen in industry energy consumption is likely to remain small this decade). As a result, future updates will add interactions between electrified sectors and power demand.

- *Price elasticities used may be too high in the short term and too low in the long term.* CPAT assumes the effects of prices on energy use are fully realized within one year. This may somewhat overstate responsiveness in the short term, because firms and households take time to adjust, but it is a reasonable approximation because the focus is on policies that are phased in over several years. Also, there is initial evidence that price elasticities used may be too low in the long term. Empirical elasticity studies tend to examine responses to price changes induced by market fluctuations. However, policy-induced price changes may elicit responses that can be much larger than market-induced changes (for example, because of higher salience and expected permanence of tax-induced changes). Users can, however, adjust price elasticities.
- *Terms of trade effects, which can increase or decrease domestic welfare and GDP effects, are ignored.* It is not clear, however, whether these effects are significant given that: (1) energy-intensive, trade-exposed industries are only a fraction of the traded sector; (2) in some cases carbon pricing only has modest effects on production costs, for example, steel (see Chapter 6); and (3) it is routine for countries to take measures to counteract competitiveness effects (again see Chapter 6). Terms of trade effects are more of an issue for energy exporters, though the primary concern is implications for fiscal revenues (see Chapter 7).

Annex 5.3 Other IMF Climate Models

IMF-ENV

IMF-ENV includes a detailed description of energy production and consumption, and links GHG emissions to specific economic activities. The core components of IMF-ENV—production, demand, trade, factor markets, and inter-temporal linkages—are all relatively standard recursive dynamic multi-sector multi-region CGE model features (Chateau et al. 2025).

The model is built using a neo-classical framework, which optimizes consumption and production decisions by households and firms. It follows the circular flow of the economy based on the activities of its key agents: firms, households, and markets. Firms purchase inputs (from other firms) and primary factors (from households) to produce goods and services. Households receive factor incomes and in turn demand the goods and services produced by firms. Markets determine equilibrium prices for factors, goods, and services. Countries also exchange commodities and capital on international markets. Factors of production are almost perfectly mobile across sectors (capital excluded) but not across countries. New capital stock (that is, net investment) is allocated without friction such that the return to new capital across sectors is the same for all sectors. However, old installed capital is fixed and cannot be reallocated without high costs (this is referred to as a "putty-clay" specification). Labor supply is determined by the working-age population, labor participation, and long-term unemployment rates. Labor adjusts endogenously to changes in real wages after a reduced-form wage supply curve that accounts for decisions on leisure and work (at both the intensive and extensive margin). The model also includes land and natural resources as production factors, which constrain the expansion of agricultural and mining activities. Production follows a series of nested constant-elasticity-of-substitution functions to capture the different substitution possibilities across all inputs and production factors. Household demand is non-homothetic and international trade is modeled using the so-called Armington specification where demand for goods is differentiated by region of origin. This specification uses a full set of bilateral trade flows, prices, transportation, and trade costs by commodity. IMF-ENV is recursive dynamic: it is solved as a sequence of comparative static equilibria where the factors of production are exogenous for each period and linked between time periods with accumulation expressions. Agents, however, are not forward looking and investment levels are driven by savings, which in turn is a combination of household savings, the government budget balance, and the current account balance.

IMF-ENV creates direct linkages between all economic activities and the corresponding source of emissions of the different GHGs. The granularity of the model supports the inclusion of different sources for all major emissions categories: energy, agriculture, transportation, industry, waste management, commercial and residential buildings, and fugitive emissions, among others. As part of the calibration process, specific emissions levels and intensities for all major GHGs are linked to economic activities and hence, emissions are endogenously determined in the model by changes to the activity levels and emissions intensities of each sector. The exception is emissions from land use, land-use change, and forestry which are exogenously assigned to the forestry sector and do not change endogenously in the simulations but can be linked to specific mitigation policies (like afforestation incentives). This level of detail allows the introduction of mitigation policies that can be GHG- and activity-specific.

The model can also simulate changes in energy efficiency and emissions intensity parameters used to capture other types of mitigation policies. Hence, the model allows for broad or very detailed mitigation policies. These include different carbon pricing schemes, such as carbon taxes (on different activities, emissions sources, and GHGs), national and regional ETS, border carbon adjustments, energy policies (that is, subsidies, feebates, direct and indirect regulations), sectoral regulations (for example, overall and sector-specific energy efficiency standards, requirements to install household heat pumps, regulatory policies on land, fisheries, and forestry sectors), and new green technologies, such as carbon capture utilization and storage and EV penetration. Different combinations of these policies can be implemented simultaneously in different countries and regions.

The IMF-ENV model compares a business-as-usual (baseline) scenario without additional future energy and climate policies with a policy counterfactual scenario that includes new policies. The differences between the baseline and the policy scenario are used to assess the effect of the policies on macroeconomic variables. These include the effects on GDP and its components (aggregate consumption, investment, and net trade), sectoral effects on production, employment and investment, bilateral sectoral trade, changes to energy outcomes (electricity generation mix, energy demand), and environmental outcomes (GHG emissions).

IMF-ENV undergoes continuous development. Recently, two model versions with regional focus on sub-Saharan Africa and Middle East and Central Asia regions have been developed. Ongoing model development work focuses on creating an R&D and technology diffusion module and incorporating international capital flows in the model. Moreover, several model extensions are possible, conditional on data availability and relevance for a country. IMF-ENV is routinely soft-linked to specialized country-specific energy models and can also be linked to agricultural or land-use sectoral models. The model can also include damages from climate change, either at a sectoral or factor level (that is, agricultural labor or capital, transportation services, energy supply) or at the aggregate level (real GDP effects, overall labor productivity reductions). This applies to both slow-moving long-term shifts in climate and changes to the intensity and frequency of extreme weather events. In both cases, the model requires country-specific information on the specific damages that need to be modeled. Finally, the model can also be linked to household microsimulation models or use detailed household survey data to provide detailed poverty and inequality effects through both household incomes and expenditures for all the macro policies simulated.

Applications of IMF-ENV (Table A5.2)

Table A5.2 Reports, Papers, and Other Publications Using IMF-ENV

Coverage		*Year*	*Publication*	*Title*
Country Analysis				
	USA	2021	WP	Modeling the U.S. Climate Agenda: Macro-Climate Trade-offs and Considerations
	China	2022	WP	A Comprehensive Package of Macroeconomic Policy Measures for Implementing China's Climate Mitigation Strategy
	Germany	2022	FSAP	Germany: Financial System Stability Assessment
	Italy	2022	SIP	Securing a Smooth Green Transition
	Mexico	2022	FSAP	Mexico: Financial Sector Assessment Program-Financial System Stability Assessment
	Canada	2023	SR	Canada: Staff Report for the 2023 Article IV Consultation (see Box 7)
	India	2023	WP	A Framework for Climate Change Mitigation in India
	Indonesia	2023	SR	Indonesia: Staff Report for the 2023 Article IV Consultation (see Box 2)
	Mexico	2023	SR	Mexico: Staff Report for the 2023 Article IV Consultation (see Annex VI)
	Poland	2023	SIP	Balancing Decarbonization with Energy Security in Poland
	Saudi Arabia	2023	SR	Saudi Arabia: Staff Report for the 2023 Article IV Consultation (see Box 2)
	South Africa	2023	SIP	South Africa Carbon Pricing and Climate Mitigation Policy
	USA	2023	SR	United States: Staff Report for the 2023 Article IV Consultation (see Box 8)
	Kazakhstan	2024	FSAP	Republic of Kazakhstan: Financial Sector Assessment Program-Technical Note on Climate-Related Risks and Financial Stability
	France	2024	WP	Climate Transition Risk and Financial Stability in France.
	France	2024	SIP	Deep Dive on the Climate Transition for France: Macroeconomic Implications, Fiscal Policies, and Financial Risks
	Japan	2024	FSAP	Japan: Financial Sector Assessment Program-Financial System Stability Assessment
	Australia	2024	SIP	Global and domestic energy transition risks: Australia

(*Continued*)

Regional Analysis				
	Europe	2024	DP	The Energy Security Gains from Strengthening Europe's Climate Action
	Europe	2024	WP	Medium-term Macroeconomic Effects of Russia's War in Ukraine and How it Affects Energy Security and Global Emission Targets.
	North America	2024	WP	Cross-border effects of climate policies in North America
	Sub-Saharan Africa	2024	SCN	Harnessing Renewables in Sub-Saharan Africa – Barriers, Reforms, and Economic Prospects
Global/Thematic Analysis				
	Global	2022	SCN	Getting on Track to Net Zero: Accelerating a Global Just Transition in This Decade
	Global	2022	DP	Economic and Environmental Benefits from International Cooperation on Climate Policies
	G7+	2022	WP	Climate Policy Options: A Comparison of Economic Performance
	Global	2023	JA	Global climate policy with differentiated carbon price floors
	G7+	2024	JA	Climate Policy Options: A Comparison of Economic Performance
	Global	2024	WP	Energy Security and the Green Transition

Note: BC = Book Chapter; BP = Board Paper; DP = Departmental Paper; FM = Fiscal Monitor; JA = Journal Article; REO = Regional Economic Outlook; SCN = IMF Staff Climate Note; SIP = Selected Issues Paper; SR = Article IV Staff Report; TAR = Technical Assistance Report; WP = Working paper.

IMF-ENV: Effect of Revenue-Recycling Rule on GDP Effects

GDP effects from carbon pricing are sensitive to recycling assumptions. Using IMF-ENV, Figure A5.1 compares GDP effects from the model's standard recycling rule (all revenues used for transfer payments to households) with mixed recycling (70 percent of revenues go to public investment in the $50 carbon price scenario or reduction of labor taxes in the $75 carbon price scenario with the remaining 30 percent for household transfers). Because IMF-ENV does not distinguish between public and private investment, revenue recycling through public investment was modeled through a reduction of the budget deficit (that is, an increase in government savings), which is then

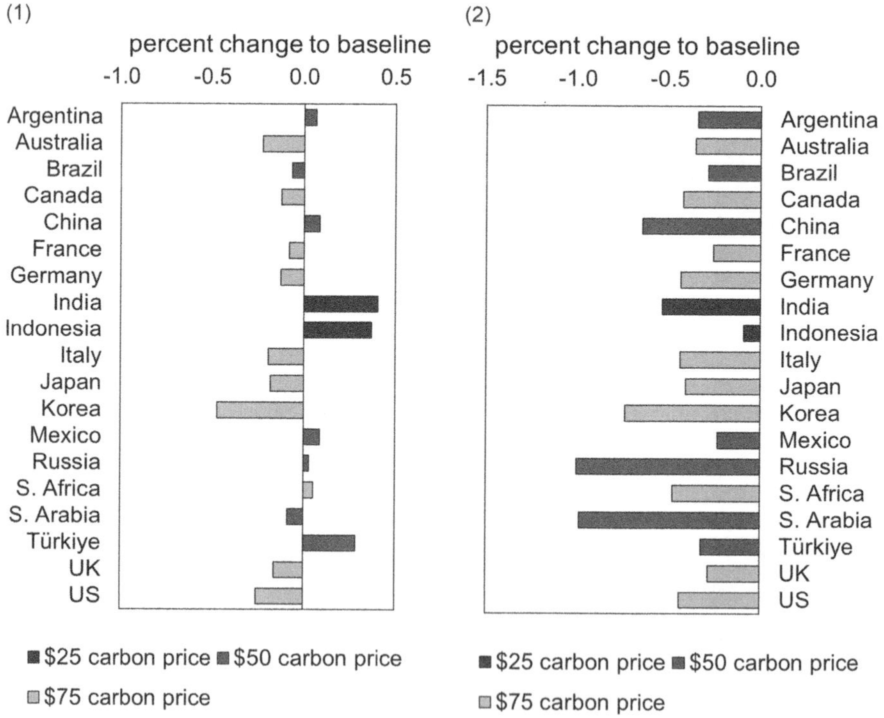

Figure A5.1 GDP Effects Estimated in IMF-ENV under Different Recycling Rules. Panel 1. Mixed Recycling, Panel 2. Household Transfers Only.

Source: IMF-ENV.

Note: Panel 1 assumes 70 percent of carbon pricing revenue is used for public investment ($25 and $50 carbon price) or labor tax reductions ($75 carbon price) and 30 percent for household transfers, whereas panel 2 assumes all revenues are used for household transfers.

directly translated into an increase in total (private and public) investment. Using this indirect mechanism the model is implicitly assuming that private investment is not affected by carbon pricing, the increase in public investment does not crowd out private investment, and public and private investment are equally productive. Given these limitations, using the differentiated recycling rule is likely to provide an upper-bound estimation on the increase in total investment, which in turn will provide larger and positive effects to GDP compared with using alternative recycling rules. This is indicated in the figure, where GDP effects from carbon pricing are all negative and significant (between about 0.3 and 1 percent) when all revenues are used for household transfers, although GDP effects are smaller, and often of opposite sign, under mixed recycling.

GMMET

GMMET is a large-scale, dynamic, nonlinear, micro-founded, multicounty model designed to analyze the short- and medium-term macroeconomic effects of curbing (GHG) emissions (Carton et al. 2023).

GMMET builds on the Global Integrated Monetary and Fiscal model, the IMF's workhorse model for business-cycle and structural macroeconomic analysis. It is an annual, multi-region, large-scale structural New-Keynesian dynamic general equilibrium model with forward-looking households, firms, monetary, and fiscal policy, and a large set of nominal and real rigidities. These models are traditionally used for quantitative short- and medium-term analysis of monetary and fiscal policy. The model has a well-articulated steady state, and therefore also features stock-flow consistency, which is important when assessing investment, government debt, and international flows in general.

The focus of GMMET is on assessing potential costs of different mitigation policies, including the effect on output and employment, inflation, the external sector, and the fiscal accounts. This focus means the model captures various nonlinear sectoral details of energy production, trade, and use by various sectors, and their implications for emissions. The model provides a detailed description of GHG-emitting activities (related to both fossil fuel and non-fossil-fuel processes) and their interaction with the rest of the economy. Fossil fuel mining, especially the implied supply elasticity, is a key determinant for the effectiveness of a GHG price in reducing emissions. As such, the model features resource input factors whose volumes adjust to the price of the fuel output such that their fossil-fuel-specific supply elasticities align with empirical estimates. The model features five electricity generation technologies that differ in their cost structure and emissions intensities: coal, fossil gas, nuclear power, hydroelectric power, and renewables.

GMMET captures a key real-world obstacle to increasing the share of renewables in electricity generation, being weather and solar-driven intermittency. The model has renewable-plus-backup generation, which pairs renewables with a flexible fossil-fuel-based backup. This structure is determined endogenously by a cost-minimization accounting for the variable and fixed costs and the distribution of weather regimes. The model also features a dedicated transportation sector that distinguishes between internal combustion engine and EVs. The sector has stock-flow accounting of vehicle fleets and newly purchased vehicles, an explicit role for charging and fueling stations, and network externalities between EV adoption and the deployment of charging stations. GMMET includes non-fossil fuel GHG emissions and the possibility to abate by sector-specific emissions abatement technologies.

GMMET features a rich treatment of fiscal policy levers. To analyze the macroeconomic effect of mitigation, the model allows for a wide set of GHG mitigation policies, including subsidies, regulatory measures, and GHG taxes that are sector specific according to the respective GHG emissions intensity.

Annex 5.4 The Pass-through of Carbon Prices into Fuel Prices

This annex briefly discusses pass-through mechanisms under alternative fuel pricing regimes and summarizes empirical evidence.

Liberalized pricing. In these regimes, fuel prices are set by private sector distributors purchasing fuel on world markets. Where countries are price takers in international fuel markets—a reasonable approximation for most countries in the case of gasoline—then a carbon price will be fully passed forward into domestic consumer prices (see Chapter 6). For a large country where collectively fuel distributors have some market power, the import supply curve is upward sloping and a (likely minor) portion of the carbon price will be passed back to domestic producers.

Regulated pricing: This includes two broad types of regimes (Coady et al. 2012):

- *Automatic pricing mechanisms*: Here fuel prices are set by the routine application of a pricing formula, with domestic prices determined as the sum of supply costs, domestic margins, and taxation (both ad valorem and specific). Prices are typically adjusted at regular intervals (for example, monthly or quarterly), and adjustments can involve formal smoothing rules to avoid large short-term price changes—but usually the aim is full pass-through over the medium term.
- *Ad hoc pricing*: Fuel prices are adjusted on a discretionary basis at irregular time intervals.
- *Evidence*: For gasoline and diesel, pass-through rates are typically estimated at above 90 percent in liberalized regimes, about 70–80 percent in automatic pricing regimes, and 30–50 percent in ad hoc pricing regimes (Abdallah and Kpodar 2020).

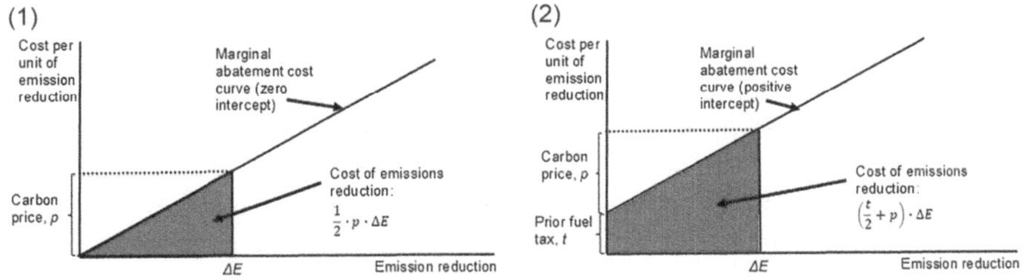

Figure A5.2 Mitigation or Welfare Costs from Reducing CO_2 from a Fuel. Panel 1. Without Fuel Tax, Panel 2. With Fuel Tax.

Source: Authors.

Note: Figure compares mitigation costs from reducing emissions from a fuel tax that is not, and is, subject to a preexisting fuel tax.

Annex 5.5 Measuring the Costs of Carbon Pricing

Following the discussion in Chapter 3, the welfare cost of CO_2 reductions from reducing a fuel with no preexisting tax or subsidy is the area under the marginal abatement cost schedule. With a linear approximation for this curve, the welfare cost is simply a triangle with base equal to the emissions reduction and height equal to the carbon price (see Annex Figure A5.2, panel 1).

If the fuel is subject to a preexisting excise tax, again the mitigation cost is the integral under the marginal abatement cost schedule, but this time takes the form of a trapezoid, or equivalently a triangle with base equal to the emissions reduction and height equal to the carbon price plus a rectangle equal to the emissions reduction times the preexisting fuel tax expressed per ton of CO_2 (see Annex Figure A5.2, panel 2). Where fuel is subsidized, the abatement cost is a triangle with base equal to the emissions reduction and height equal to the carbon price, less a rectangle equal to the emissions reduction times the preexisting fuel subsidy expressed per ton of CO_2—if the latter exceeds the former, on net abatement costs from reducing the fuel are negative. Although preexisting fuel taxes and subsidies affect the costs of carbon pricing, they do not affect the reduction in emissions from current levels (which already reflects the effects of existing fuel taxes/subsidies) needed to meet an emissions target and in this sense do not affect the required level of carbon pricing or other mitigation instruments.

The main caveats are that these cost measures ignore recycling of carbon pricing revenues (see Chapter 3), technology-related market imperfections (see Chapter 7), and domestic environmental co-benefits (see Chapter 8). Some further considerations include the following.

- *Distortions in electricity markets.* To the extent that carbon mitigation policies reduce electricity demand, and electricity is subject to taxation, there is an additional welfare cost given by the product of the reduction in electricity use and the electricity tax per unit—the same applies if electricity is subject to monopoly pricing, which causes similar market distortions to a tax on consumption. Conversely, if electricity is subsidized because of regulated pricing or subsidized tariffs there is a corresponding welfare benefit given by the reduction in electricity use times the per unit subsidy. CPAT takes these distortions into account in measuring welfare costs, though generally they make only a minor difference to overall welfare costs.

- *General consumption taxes*. General consumption taxes, like VAT, raise the price of all household products in the same proportion and, unlike fuel excises, do not penalize the use of fuels relative to other goods, and nor do they tax fuel inputs in the industrial sector. These taxes, therefore, have minimal effect on reducing emissions. Some fuels are subject to preferential treatment under the VAT, which implies some subsidy for fuels relative to other consumption goods—again, CPAT captures this effect by measuring fuel taxes as the gap between retail prices and supply costs.
- *Regulations*. Preexisting regulations, like energy efficiency standards for household appliances and vehicles, also push emissions reductions up marginal abatement cost schedules. It is difficult to measure this effect, however—that is, the extent to which these regulations are binding—because the counterfactual (without regulations) is not observed. To the extent regulations are binding (and remain so after carbon pricing), they will tend to (slightly) reduce the responsiveness of emissions to pricing, rather than increase the costs of pricing.
- *Transfer payments*: These are not included in welfare costs because they are payments from one segment of society to another and cancel out on net, for example, between households and firms, or between them and the government.

Annex 5.6 Do Interactions between Mitigation Policies and the Broader Fiscal System Raise or Lower their Costs?

There has been much discussion in the academic literature about whether carbon pricing can reduce emissions with negative cost. For this to be the case, the economic efficiency benefits from productive recycling of carbon pricing revenues would need to exceed the costs from exacerbating tax distortions in factor markets (because higher production costs increase price levels and reduce real factor returns)—and by enough to more than offset the pure mitigation costs in energy markets. Earlier analysis suggested that, under neutral assumptions, this would not happen because adverse effects in factor markets tend to dominate the revenue-recycling benefit so that, on net, linkages with the broader tax system moderately increase the overall costs of carbon pricing (Goulder 1995).

In the late 1990s, however, it was recognized that the overall costs to the economy caused by the tax system are far more extensive than previously recognized in the literature, when the bias toward the informal sector and for tax-favored consumption (for example, fringe benefits, owner-occupied housing) is considered (Saez, Slemrod, and Giertz 2012). In turn, this meant that the economic efficiency benefits from using carbon pricing revenues to reduce broader taxes are larger. Indeed, up to a point, the overall costs of carbon pricing can be negative, though the prospects for negative costs diminish because deeper decarbonization progressively erodes the base of carbon pricing (see, for example, Bento, Jacobsen, and Liu 2018, Parry and Bento 2000). As for developing countries, the rate of return on investments for Sustainable Development Goals may be quite high, given the severe constraints on funding public investment from general taxes in the presence of pervasive informality. A carbon tax that provides new sources of funding for high-return investment may also have negative costs on net (Black et al. 2022).

The most important point from the literature, however, is the importance of using revenues from carbon taxes or ETSs with allowance auctions productively to contain the overall costs of carbon pricing for the economy. Indeed, well-designed combinations of non-pricing policies (like feebates and TPSs) may impose smaller costs on the economy overall than a carbon tax achieving equivalent emissions reductions, but where revenues are used for lump-sum dividends rather than to increase economic efficiency, reflecting the smaller effect of the former policies on energy prices, the general price level, and overall employment/investment (IMF 2019).

Annex 5.7 Modeling Transitional Dynamics in the Vehicle Sector

CPAT has been extended to include a technology-explicit road transportation model that captures changes in the vehicle stock over time, and how these changes effect emissions, revenue, and driving-related externalities. The model performs separate projections for light-duty vehicles (cars and commercial vehicles with weight below 3.5 tons) and heavy-duty vehicles (HDVs, medium- and heavy-duty freight) because the two vehicle types have different existing fuel pricing policies, economics, and abatement pathways—for example, HDVs have higher depreciation rates, lower fuel efficiency, more vehicle-kilometers traveled, and are more costly to electrify—as well as distinguishing between new and used vehicles given differences in purchase prices and fuel economy and varying reliance on used vehicle markets.

Total cost of ownership (TCO) estimates for each vehicle type are used to allocate new vehicle demand across vehicle types with the following steps. Total vehicle demand is estimated using the Gompertz function (for example, see Dargay, Gately, and Sommer 2007), with population and GDP projections from the IMF WEO, and vehicle additions are equal to the difference between total demand and ownership after depreciation and used cars sold domestically. A logit function based on the relative TCO of internal combustion engine vehicles (ICEVs) and EVs determines the share of vehicle demand met by ICEV versus EV vehicles, separately for new versus used vehicle purchases. The logit function is fitted to minimize the difference between modeled and actual EV sales between 2015 and 2023 for select economies.[16] The availability of used EVs (both those that are previously owned domestically and imports) is constrained based on new vehicles that reach the end of the initial ownership period. Once the vehicle stock is estimated for a given year, driving distances are adjusted according to changes in the posttax marginal cost of driving and driving elasticities and changes in income per capita. The resulting information on size and disaggregation of the vehicle stock and distance driven per vehicle allows for estimation of fuel use, fiscal revenue, and emissions.

This approach allows for the modeling of key policies, including fuel taxes, distance-based taxes, fuel economy standards, feebates, and EV subsidies. Importantly, it captures the turnover of the vehicle stock and key differences in vehicle markets, such as reliance on used vehicles, network effects related to EVs and charging station infrastructure, and the decline in future EV costs.

Notes

1 See https://www.imf.org/cpat. Black et al. (2023) provide an in-depth discussion of the model and its parameterization.

2 Some review exercises, however, seek to explain differences in results across different models (for example, Kuik, Brander, and Tol 2009).

3 IEA (2024) with www.iea.org/data-and-statistics/data-product/world-energy-balances.

4 Emissions by country and sector are also available from https://climatedata.imf.org.

5 For example, with an income elasticity of 0.6, a 25 percent increase in GDP over a period of time will increase emissions by 14 percent—incorrectly assuming a unitary income elasticity would overstate emissions growth by 80 percent.

6 For ETSs, CPAT contains a default assumption that emissions reductions are 10 percent smaller than for the equivalently scaled carbon tax to allow for small-scale emitters being exempted under the former policy for administrative reasons (see Chapter 3).

7 Effects also depend on the responsiveness of fuel use to changes in the prices of other fuels.

8 Many of these models account for feedback effects on fuel demand from broader changes in the economy (like sectoral consumption, production, employment, and GDP), which become more significant at deeper levels of decarbonization. They also consider large policy changes—for example, based on an extensive review of leading energy models, Stern and Stiglitz (2017) put the global carbon price in 2030 consistent with cutting global emissions by 30 percent below baseline levels (to be aligned with a 2°C target) at $50–100 per ton.

9 In default settings, hydroelectric capacity is fixed on the assumption opportunities have already been exploited, while nuclear can gradually ramp up in countries with fission reactors.

10 Sometimes called the Laffer curve in the context of broader tax policy.

11 This approach has been endorsed by governments around the world. In the United States, for example, a series of executive orders since the mid-1970s mandated government agencies to perform regulatory effect analyses using welfare costs. Principles for measuring welfare costs are long established in the economics literature (see, for example, Harberger 1964, Just, Hueth, and Schmitz 2008).

12 Based on formulas in Parry and Williams (2010), assuming labor tax wedges of 40 and 20 percent for advanced and other countries, and typical assumptions about the responsiveness of labor supply and taxable income to changes in taxes.

13 A good example of a model-based study is Goulder et al. (2019) who estimate a carbon tax in the United States starting at $40 per ton and rising at 2 percent annually in real terms reduces GDP by less than 0.3 percent on average from 2016 to 2050. A good example of the empirical approach is Metcalf and Stock (2020) who find no evidence that carbon taxes in European countries reduced GDP.

14 At the global level for oil, gas, and agricultural production (where international markets are well integrated) and domestic level for coal production (where they are not).

15 Summarized in UNEP (2021). The possibility that marginal abatement cost curves have negative intercepts because firms fail to exploit profitable opportunities for capturing and using/selling methane is ignored. See Black et al. (2022) for more discussion of the offline model.

16 The k-parameter for the logic function is 3.25 and increases to 4.75 because EV uptake crosses 50 percent, reflecting patterns in countries with high EV uptake. Used vehicles are split between imported used vehicles and used vehicles that were previously owned domestically. There is assumed to be a limited supply of both imported and second-hand domestic used vehicles, which is determined based on the global and domestic number of EV purchases from 10 years ago (that is, the assumed vehicle ownership period) for passenger vehicles and 4 years ago for freight.

References

Abdallah, Chadi and Kangni Kpodar. 2020. "How Large and Persistent is the Response of Inflation to Changes in Retail Energy Prices?" IMF Working Paper 2020/093, International Monetary Fund, Washington, DC.

Batini, Nicoletta, Luc Eyraud, Lorenzo Forni, and Anke Weber. 2014. "Fiscal Multipliers: Size, Determinants, and Use in Macroeconomic Projections." Technical Notes and Manuals, International Monetary Fund, Washington, DC.

Bento, Antonio M., Mark R. Jacobsen, and Anthony A. Liu. 2018. "Environmental Policy in the Presence of an Informal Sector." *Journal of Environmental Economics and Management* 90: 61–77.

Bernard, Jean-Thomas, and Maral Kichian. 2021. "The Impact of a Revenue-Neutral Carbon Tax on GDP Dynamics: The Case of British Columbia." *Energy Journal* 42: 205–24.

Black, Simon, Jean Chateau, Florence Jaumotte, Ian Parry, Gregor Schwerhoff, Sneha Thube, and Karlygash Zhunussova. 2022. "Getting on Track to Net Zero: Accelerating a Global Just Transition in This Decade." Staff Discussion Note 2022/010, International Monetary Fund, Washington, DC.

Black, Simon, Ian Parry, Victor Mylonas, and Nate Vernon, Karlygash Zhunussova. 2023. "The IMF-World Bank Climate Policy Assessment Tool (CPAT): A Model to Help Countries Mitigate Climate Change." IMF Working Paper 23/128, International Monetary Fund, Washington, DC.

Black, Simon, Ian Parry, and Karlygash Zhunussova. 2023. "Is the Paris Agreement Working? A Stocktake of Global Climate Mitigation." IMF Staff Climate Notes

2023/002, International Monetary Fund, Washington, DC. https://doi.org/10.5089/9798400257889.066

Böhringer, Christoph, Sonja Peterson, Thomas F. Rutherford, Jan Schneider, and Malte Winkler. 2021. "Climate Policies after Paris: Pledge, Trade and Recycle: Insights from the 36th Energy Modeling Forum Study (EMF36)." *Energy Economics* 103: 105471.

Burke, Paul J., and Zsuzsanna Csereklyei. 2016. "Understanding the Energy-GDP Elasticity: A Sectoral Approach." *Energy Economics* 58: 199–210.

Burns, Andrew, Benoit Campagne, Charl Jooste, David Stephan, and Thi Thanh Bui. 2019. "The World Bank Macro-Fiscal Model: Technical Description." Policy Research Working Paper 8965, World Bank, Washington, DC.

Burns, Andrew, Charl Jooste, and Gregor Schwerhoff. 2021. "Climate Modeling for Macroeconomic Policy: A Case Study for Pakistan." Policy Research Working Paper 9780. World Bank, Washington, DC.

Carton, Benjamin, Christopher Evans, Dirk V. Muir, and Simon Voigts. 2023. "Getting to Know GMMET: The Global Macroeconomic Model for the Energy Transition." IMF Working Paper 2023/269, International Monetary Fund, Washington, DC.

Chateau, Jean, Florence Jaumotte, and Gregor Schwerhoff. 2022. "Climate Policy Options: A Comparison of Economic Performance." IMF Working Paper 2022/242, International Monetary Fund, Washington, DC.

Chateau, Jean, Hugo Rojas-Romagosa, Sneha Thube, and Dominique van der Mensbrugghe. 2025. "IMF-ENV: Integrating Climate, Energy, and Trade Policies in a General Equilibrium Framework." No. 2025/077, International Monetary Fund, Washington, DC.

Coady, David, Javier Arze del Granado, Luc Eyraud, Hui Jin, Vimal Thakoor, Anita Tuladhar, and Lilla Nemeth. 2012. "Automatic Fuel Pricing Mechanisms with Price Smoothing: Design, Implementation, and Fiscal Implications." IMF Technical Notes and Manuals, International Monetary Fund, Washington, DC.

Dargay, Joyce, Dermot Gately, and Martin Sommer. 2007. "Vehicle Ownership and Income Growth, Worldwide: 1960–2030." *Energy Journal* 28 (4): 143–70.

Favero, Alice, and Kemen Austin. 2024. *Charting our Forest Future: National Supply Curves for Forest-Based CO_2 Mitigation.* Research Triangle Park, NC: RTI International.

Freire-González, Jaume. 2018. "Environmental Taxation and the Double Dividend Hypothesis in CGE Modelling Literature: A Critical Review." *Journal of Policy Modeling* 40: 194–223.

Gillingham, Kenneth, and James H. Stock. 2018. "The Cost of Reducing Greenhouse Gas Emissions." *Journal of Economic Perspectives* 32: 53–72.

Goulder, Lawrence H. 1995. "Environmental Taxation and the Double Dividend: A Reader's Guide." *International Tax and Public Finance* 2: 157–83.

Goulder, Lawrence H., Marc A. C. Hafstead, GyuRim Kim, and Xianling Long. 2019. "Impacts of a Carbon Tax across US Household Income Groups: What Are the Equity-Efficiency Trade-Offs?" *Journal of Public Economics* 175: 44–64.

Harberger, Arnold C. 1964. "The Measurement of Waste." *American Economic Review* 54: 58–76.

Heine, Dirk, and Simon J. Black. 2019. "Benefits Beyond Climate: Environmental Tax Reform in Developing Countries." In *Fiscal Policies for Development and Climate Action*, edited by Miria A. Pigato, 1–56. Washington, DC: World Bank.

Intergovernmental Panel on Climate Change (IPCC). 2022. "Climate Change 2022: Mitigation and Climate Change." Contribution of Working Group III to the Sixth Assessment Report of the Intergovernmental Panel on Climate Change, Geneva.

International Monetary Fund (IMF). 2019. *Fiscal Monitor: How to Mitigate Climate Change.* Washington, DC: International Monetary Fund.

International Monetary Fund (IMF). 2020. "Mitigating Climate Change." In *World Economic Outlook, October 2020: A Long and Difficult Ascent*. Washington, DC: International Monetary Fund.

International Monetary Fund (IMF). 2022. "Near-Term Macroeconomic Impact of Decarbonization Policies." In *World Economic Outlook, October 2022*. Washington, DC: International Monetary Fund.

International Monetary Fund (IMF). 2023. *Fiscal Monitor: Climate Crossroads: Fiscal Policies in a Warming World*. Washington, DC.

International Monetary Fund (IMF). 2024. *Energy Subsidies Template*. Washington, DC. https://www.imf.org/-/media/Files/Topics/energy-subsidies/EXTERNALfuelsubsidiestemplate2023new.ashx

Just, Richard E., Darrell L. Hueth, and Andrew Schmitz. 2008. *Applied Welfare Economics*. International Library of Critical Writings in Economics 220. Edward Elgar Publishing.

Koch, Nicolas, Erasmus K. H. J. zu Ermgassen, Johanna Wehkamp, Francisco J. B. Oliveira Filho, and Gregor Schwerhoff. 2019. "Agricultural Productivity and Forest Conservation: Evidence from the Brazilian Amazon." *American Journal of Agricultural Economics* 101 (3): 919–40.

Köppl, Angela, and Margit Schratzenstaller. 2022. "Carbon Taxation: A Review of the Empirical Literature." *Journal of Economic Surveys* 37: 1353–88.

Kuik, Onno, Luke Brander, and Richard S. J. Tol. 2009. "Marginal Abatement Costs of Greenhouse Gas Emissions: A Meta-Analysis." *Energy Policy* 37: 1395–403.

Labandeira, Xavier, José Labeaga, and Xiral López-Otero. 2017. "A Meta-Analysis on the Price Elasticity of Energy Demand." *Energy Policy* 102: 549–68.

Metcalf, Gilbert E. 2019. "On the Economics of a Carbon Tax for the United States." *Brookings Papers on Economic Activity* Spring: 405–58.

Metcalf, Gilbert E., and James H. Stock. 2020. "Measuring the Macroeconomic Impact of Carbon Taxes." *American Economic Association Papers and Proceedings* 110 (May): 101–6.

Parry, Ian, and Antonio M. Bento. 2000. "Tax Deductions, Environmental Policy, and the 'Double Dividend' Hypothesis." *Journal of Environmental Economics and Management* 39: 67–96.

Parry, Ian, Simon Black, Danielle Minnett, Victor Mylonas, and Nate Vernon. 2022. "How to Cut Methane Emissions." IMF Staff Climate Note 22-008, International Monetary Fund, Washington, DC.

Parry, Ian, and Roberton Williams. 2010. "What Are the Costs of Meeting Distributional Objectives for Climate Policy?" *B.E. Journal of Economic Analysis & Policy* 10 (Symposium): Article 9.

Roe, Stephanie, Charlotte Streck, Robert Beach, Jonah Busch, Melissa Chapman, Vassilis Daioglou, Andre Deppermann, et al. 2021. "Land-Based Measures to Mitigate Climate Change: Potential and Feasibility by Country." *Global Change Biology* 27 (23): 6025–58.

Saez, Emmanuel, Joel Slemrod, and Seth H. Giertz. 2012. "The Elasticity of Taxable Income with Respect to Marginal Tax Rates: A Critical Review." *Journal of Economic Literature* 50: 3–50.

Schoder, Christian. 2022. "Regime-Dependent Environmental Tax Multipliers: Evidence from 75 Countries." *Journal of Environmental Economics and Policy* 12: 1–44.

Stechemesser, Annika, Nicolas Koch, Ebba Mark, Elina Dilger, Patrick Klösel, Laura Menicacci, Daniel Nachtigall, et al. 2024. "Climate Policies That Achieved Major Emission Reductions: Global Evidence from Two Decades." *Science* 385 (6711): 884–92.

Stern, Nicholas, and Joseph Stiglitz. 2017. "Report of the High-Level Commission on Carbon Pricing." Paper of the Carbon Pricing Leadership Coalition, World Bank, Washington, DC.

United Nations Environment Program (UNEP). 2021. *Global Methane Assessment: Benefits and Costs of Mitigating Methane Emissions*. Nairobi, Kenya: UNEP and Climate and Clean Air Coalition.

Williams, Roberton C., and Casey J. Wichman. 2015. "Macroeconomic Effects of Carbon Taxes." In *Implementing a US Carbon Tax: Challenges and Debates*, edited by Ian Parry, Adele Morris, and Roberton Williams, 83–96. London, UK: Routledge.

Xu, Lan, and Jun Yang. 2024. "Carbon Pricing Policies and Renewable Energy Development: Analysis Based on Cross-Country Panel Data." *Journal of Environmental Management* 366: 121784.

6 Enhancing Acceptability of the Mitigation Strategy

Main Messages

- Ensuring climate mitigation policies are durable and equitable requires ensuring that poorer households are not adversely affected and that communities are not left behind, that is, there is a "just transition."
- Carbon pricing raises energy prices which have an initially negative effect on households directly through their consumption of fuels and electricity and indirectly through the energy embedded in non-energy goods and services. These effects can be, on aggregate, distributionally progressive (disproportionately affecting wealthier households), neutral, or regressive depending on household income and consumption patterns which vary across countries.
- Ideally, poorer households would be compensated for carbon pricing directly through per capita transfers or labor tax reductions. This is preferable to energy price support, because the latter undermines mitigation incentives, only compensates for the direct burden of higher energy prices (not indirect effects), and may be poorly targeted due to administrative difficulties.
- In countries with comprehensive social safety nets or effective cash transfer schemes, only a modest portion of carbon pricing revenues (below 20 percent in most cases) is required to compensate low-income households, leaving the bulk of revenues for other purposes such as investment or tax cuts. Alternatively, using a larger portion of the revenues for compensation can raise the welfare of poor households in aggregate.
- Feebates and tradable performance standards (TPSs) generally impose much smaller upfront burdens on households than carbon pricing but generate no revenue for recycling to households.

DOI: 10.4324/9781003755012-6
This chapter has been made available under a CC-BY-NC-ND license.

- The Climate Policy Assessment Tool (CPAT) provides incidence analyses for an increasing number (about 100) of countries based on matching household expenditure surveys to input–output tables.
- With appropriate recycling schemes, carbon pricing can be progressive overall, making poor households better off on net, while imposing manageable burdens (of 0.5–2 percent of consumption) on top-income households, across different countries.
- Production cost increases under a $50 carbon price in 2030 are typically about 4–8 percent for the steel industry across different countries, 20–30 percent for ammonia, and 25–35 percent for cement. Charges on unabated emissions account for most of the cost increases.
- Effects of these cost increases on domestic and foreign production depend on the slope of domestic demand, domestic supply, and foreign supply curves. Assuming pricing is imposed unilaterally and with no accompanying competitiveness/leakage measures, domestic production losses are mostly about 5–10 percent for steel and 15–20 percent for cement and ammonia, with most of the reductions offset by additional foreign production.
- Emissions leakage rates are mostly about 20–50 percent across industries and countries.
- Nontrade measures like infra-marginal tax exemptions, free allowance allocation, within-sector recycling, or using feebates/tradable performance standards can mostly address competitiveness and leakage effects but are less robust for deeper decarbonization, undermine some mitigation incentives, and forgo revenues.
- Border carbon adjustments are a more robust and fine-tuned instrument for addressing competitiveness and leakage and involve limited cross-country revenue flows, but they require careful design to address administrative, legal, and equity concerns.

Households

Conceptual Issues

Why Are Policymakers Concerned about the Burdens of Climate Mitigation Policy on Households?

Concerns arise for several reasons, including the following:

- *Poverty*—anti-poverty objectives can be undermined if climate mitigation policies make low-income households worse off. Indeed, the protection of lower-income households from the adverse effect of energy price increases is often seen as being essential to making a reform strategy politically acceptable (see, for example, Sterner 2012);

- *Equity*—if the overall burden of mitigation policy is regressive, that is, it imposes a larger burden relative to consumption on lower-income households than higher-income households, this can also undermine distributional objectives; and
- *Acceptability*—politically influential constituencies (perhaps, for example, middle-income households or vulnerable workers) may oppose (through protests or at the ballot box) mitigation policies imposing significant burdens on them or that are viewed as unfair.[1]

Understanding overall burdens on households, and how they might be made distributional neutral or progressive (imposing a smaller burden relative to consumption on lower-income households than higher-income households), is therefore important, both for designing accompanying fairness and acceptability measures and communicating the overall effects to stakeholders and the public.

Although governments may routinely change a wide range of environmental and broader fiscal and regulatory policies without, in each case, accompanying measures to address the distributional implications, raising energy prices can be especially sensitive given their visibility (for example, in monthly energy bills and at the pump) underscoring the potential need for assistance measures in this case. Indeed, many governments took measures to assist households during the energy price surge in the early 2020s, and a long history of experiences has shown these measures are a key ingredient for successful energy price reform more generally (see Anil et al. 2022 and Clements et al. 2013, respectively).

How Does Carbon Pricing Directly Burden Households?

Households are directly burdened to the extent carbon pricing is reflected in higher consumer prices for electricity, natural gas, road fuels, and other oil products (see Chapter 5). For given price increases, direct burdens expressed relative to total household consumption depend primarily on budget shares for energy products—generally speaking, burdens are only moderately sensitive to reductions in energy consumption (because households still pay higher prices on the remaining consumption).[2] As discussed in Annex 6.1, both these effects are captured by (changes in) "consumer surplus," a standard metric used by economists.

Figure 6.1 shows budget shares for energy products for the top, median, and bottom household income deciles for selected G20 countries in 2023. Some noteworthy points include the following:

- Across countries, total budget shares for (fossil fuel) energy products for the average household vary from 8 to 13 percent.
- Within countries, total budget shares for energy among the bottom-income decile are about the same or smaller than for median households in 7 out of 11 cases, though total budget shares for median households are about

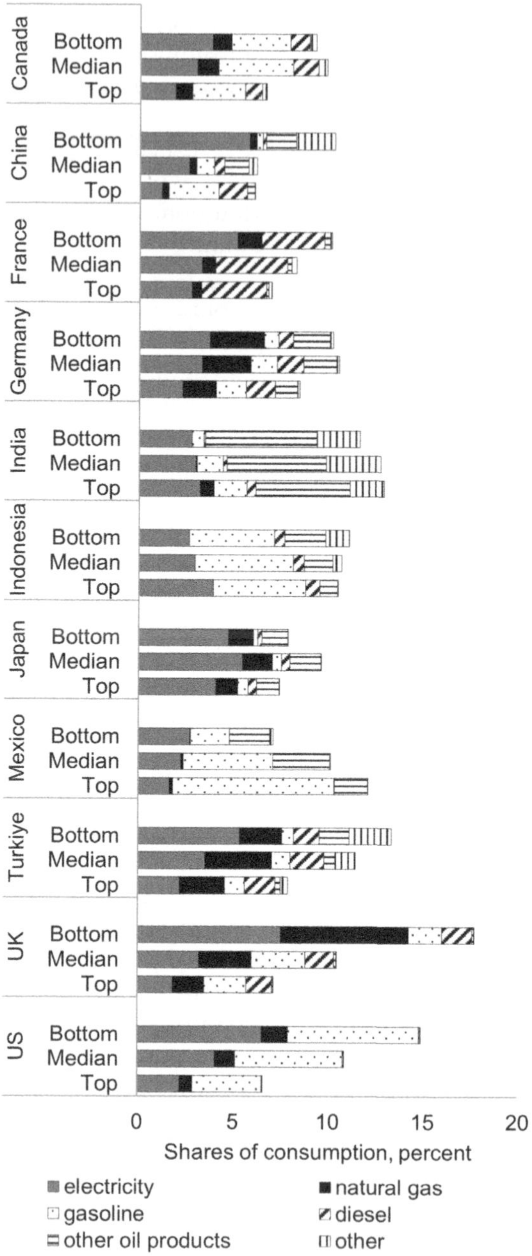

Figure 6.1 Budget Shares by Household Income Deciles for Fossil Fuel Energy Products 2023, Selected Countries.

Source: Authors from CPAT.

Note: Other = coal, charcoal, ethanol, and firewood; other oil products = oil, kerosene, and liquified petroleum gas.

the same or larger than for the top decile. Although wealthier households generally spend more in absolute terms on energy (for example, they use more energy for space heating/cooling and appliances) budget shares for energy tend to decline gradually with higher per capita income for most countries (see Figure 5.3).

- Within energy, budget shares are generally largest for electricity and gasoline, though natural gas also has a high share in Germany and the United Kingdom.

How Else Are Households Affected by Carbon Pricing?

Carbon pricing also affects households through indirectly raising prices for non-energy consumer goods and through lowering income.

- *Indirect price increases.* Prices for general consumer goods and services increase to the extent firms producing these goods pass forward higher energy input costs into higher prices. The price increase for a (non-energy) consumer product, due to carbon pricing, is (approximately) the emissions embodied in the product's supply chain per unit of output (CO_2 from fuel, processes, and embodied in electricity inputs), multiplied by the carbon price and the pass-through fraction. Proportionate price increases for non-energy goods are generally modest—however, because in aggregate budget shares for non-energy consumption are large, indirect burdens on households can still be significant. And indirect burdens are pretty evenly distributed across households relative to their consumption (given relatively small differences in aggregate budget shares for general consumer goods across households), which limits the overall severity of regressive or progressive effects from mitigation policies.
- *Lower income.* To the extent climate mitigation costs, especially in the trade-exposed industrial sector, are passed backward to firms in lower producer prices, this ultimately leads to lower income to households from capital or labor. If lower producer prices reduce the net-of-tax return to capital, the burden is borne by shareholders (who are concentrated among relatively wealthy households) through lower equity values and dividends. But if net-of-tax returns to capital are largely determined in integrated world capital markets, much of the burden of lower producer prices will instead be borne by workers through lower wages—the effects will be roughly proportional to labor income across household groups, unless lower- or higher-skilled workers are significantly more at risk in the affected industries. Burdens from income losses can be difficult to accurately pin down, though they tend to be less important quantitatively than those from higher energy and consumer good prices (especially if countries' trading partners are moving forward simultaneously on mitigation which facilitates pass-through of mitigation costs for trade-exposed sectors in consumer prices).

Assistance Measures

What Are the Trade-offs from Assisting Households through Income and Price Supports?

Table 6.1 compares a range of income and energy price support policies that might be funded from carbon pricing revenues, in terms of their effectiveness at helping low-income households and broader emissions and fiscal/economic efficiency implications. Some noteworthy points include the following:

- *Targeted income support*—such as earned income tax credits or means-tested cash transfers—will be effective at assisting low-income households, while leaving most carbon pricing revenues for general purposes, if benefit systems (1) have high coverage rates for low-income households and (2) avoid significant leakage of benefits to the nonpoor.[3] When cash transfers are not feasible, other programs (for example, food vouchers, school meals, and fee waiver programs) might be expanded, while the capacity to administer cash transfers is developed.
- *Partially targeted income support*—where benefit systems do not cover most poor households and have significant leakage to the nonpoor—will be only partially effective at assisting low-income households and will have larger fiscal costs. Recycling carbon pricing revenues in payroll tax rebates or investments for Sustainable Development Goals raises similar issues in regard to compensating poor households (for example, those not working or not located near investment projects do not benefit), but the recycling does improve economic efficiency (through strengthening work incentives or funding projects with high rates of return).
- *Broad-based income support*—such as proportionate cuts in marginal income tax rates—again increases economic efficiency (through promoting work effort) but is not necessarily effective at helping low-income households (many of whom, because of income tax thresholds, may not face positive marginal income tax rates).
- *Targeted energy price support*—such as rebates on energy bills for low-income households—can effectively compensate them for higher energy prices and leave most carbon pricing revenues for general purposes, but they do not compensate for indirect burdens or income losses, moderately suppress energy demand reductions, and may be administratively complex (because they require matching data on household income and energy expenditure).
- *Broad-based energy price support*—using some carbon pricing revenues to contain increases in electricity prices (for example, through subsidies for local distribution companies)—may be more administratively practical but is worse than targeted energy bill rebates in that it involves a larger fiscal cost and suppression of electricity demand.

Table 6.1 Comparing Income and Price Support Approaches for Compensating Households

Type of Support	*Degree of Targeting*	*Examples*	*Metric*			
			Assistance for Low-Income Households		*Broader Impacts*	
			Coverage across Low-Income Households	*Degree of Compensation*	*Emissions*	*Fiscal/Economic Efficiency*
Income	**Targeted**	Earned income tax credits, means-tested transfers	A: Most receive assistance	A: Can compensate for full burden	A: Does not undermine energy demand reduction	N: Modest fiscal cost leaves most revenue for general purposes
	Partially targeted	Support programs excluding some low income/including some nonpoor	N: Some receive assistance	A: Can compensate for full burden	A: Does not undermine energy demand reduction	D: Larger fiscal cost as many nonpoor receive payments
		Payroll tax rebate, public spending benefiting low/middle income	N: Not all low-income households pay payroll taxes/benefit from public services	A: Can compensate for full burden	A: Does not undermine energy demand reduction	A: Increases efficiency through stronger work incentives/productive investment
	Not targeted	Marginal income tax rate reductions	D: Most low-income households may not face positive marginal tax rates	N: Unlikely to compensate for full burden	A: Does not undermine energy demand reduction	A: Increases efficiency through stronger work incentives
Energy Price	**Targeted**	Energy bill rebate for low income	A: Benefits low-income households with grid access	N: Does not compensate for indirect burdens/income losses	N: Limits energy demand response among low income	A: Modest fiscal cost leaves most revenue for general purposes
	Not targeted	Reduction in electricity/vehicle taxes	A: Benefits most low-income households with grid access/vehicles	N: Does not compensate for indirect burdens/income losses	N: Limits electricity demand response across all households	D: Leaves smaller amount of revenue for general purposes

Source: Authors.

Note: A and D denote an advantage and disadvantage of a compensation scheme, respectively, and N neither a strong advantage nor disadvantage.

In short, ideally some carbon pricing revenue would be used to target low-income households and the remainder recycled to households in equitable tax reductions or public spending that improves economic efficiency, while allowing carbon prices to be reflected in higher energy prices. The acceptability of higher energy prices may be constrained, however, if they are more visible to the public than recycling programs.[4]

How Much Carbon Pricing Revenue Is Needed to Compensate Different Household Income Groups?

Figure 6.2 illustrates, for selected countries, the fraction of carbon pricing revenues needed to compensate households below a certain consumption decile for the burden of carbon pricing, assuming a comprehensive tax and benefit system and carbon prices of $50/$75 per ton for middle-/high-income countries in 2030. The fraction is very similar across countries—about 8 percent for compensating the bottom two consumption deciles and 15 percent for the bottom three deciles. A modest portion of revenues is needed because—in absolute terms—most of the burden of carbon pricing is borne by the

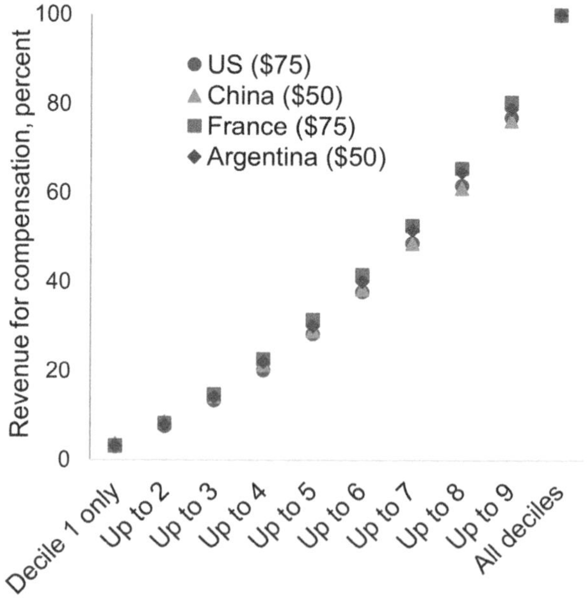

Figure 6.2 Share of Carbon Pricing Revenue Needed to Compensate Household Consumption Deciles, 2030.

Source: Authors using CPAT.

Note: Calculations do not consider erosion in the base of carbon pricing because of mitigation responses. Carbon price for France and the United States is $75 per ton and for Argentina and China $50 per ton.

nonpoor, given their higher (absolute) energy and general consumption. A caveat is that higher levels of carbon pricing erode the revenue base (that is, unabated emissions), which means that a rising share of carbon pricing revenues would be needed to compensate a given household group over time.

How Does the Distributional Burden of Charging and Non-charging Policies Compare?

Where carbon pricing is subject to acceptability constraints, non-charging approaches like feebates and TPSs that can mimic many of the mitigation responses promoted by carbon pricing may be reasonable complements to, or substitutes for, carbon pricing. Although these instruments do not raise revenue, and therefore forgo opportunities to make climate mitigation reforms progressive overall, they likely impose much smaller upfront burdens on all households because of their smaller effects on energy prices (see Chapter 3).

At the economywide level, prior to revenue recycling, the burden from carbon pricing ultimately borne by households (directly, indirectly, and through income losses, combined) is equivalent to the abatement costs and the charge on unabated emissions—the darker shaded triangle and shaded rectangle in Figure 6.3, respectively. Revenue recycling then offsets the shaded rectangle. Under non-charging instruments like feebates and TPSs, there is no charge on unabated emissions, though abatement costs are greater by the lighter shaded triangle in the figure as, to the extent they do not exploit the full range of emissions reductions promoted under carbon pricing, non-charging instruments push along a steeper marginal abatement cost schedule (see Chapter 3). Nonetheless, for illustration, under emissions reductions of 10 and 30 percent, the burden under non-charging approaches is relatively modest—one-tenth or one-third of the burden under carbon pricing prior to recycling, even if the marginal abatement cost schedule for the non-charging instrument is twice as steep as that for carbon pricing (based on simple

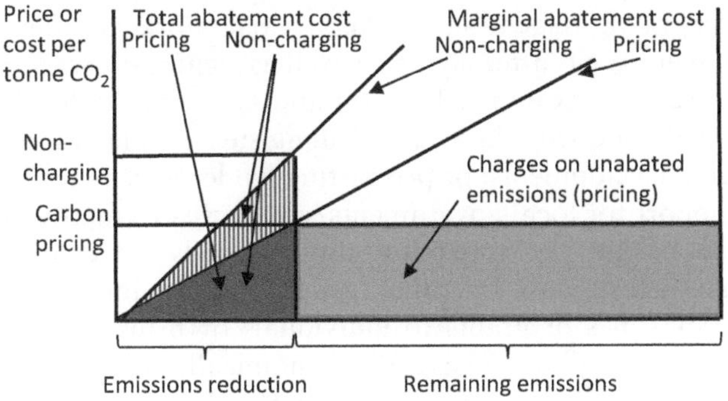

Figure 6.3 Comparing Household Burdens under Carbon Pricing (before Recycling) and Non-Charging Instruments.

Source: Authors.

geometry). Non-charging instruments, however, preclude the possibility of using new revenues to alter the distributional burden of the policy.

Non-charging policies sometimes raise their own distributional concerns. For example, subsidies for electric vehicles (EVs) are often perceived as benefiting the wealthy because current high prices for EVs limit their affordability for the non-wealthy. Vehicle tax systems often, however, also include an ad valorem component, which implies more expensive vehicles pay more taxes. Moreover, the EV subsidy could also be combined with a tax on gas-guzzling (mainly luxury) vehicles purchased by the wealthy or be converted into a feebate. And EV subsidies will phase out over time as these vehicles become more cost competitive, while the availability of used EVs with lower prices will grow over time.

What Measures Might Assist Workers and Regions at Risk from Low-Carbon Energy Transitions?

- *Workers*: Paying compensation to workers losing their jobs equal to their lost wages (substantially) overcompensates them because it does not account for the value of time they can now spend in other jobs or at home (see Annex 6.2). Instead, assistance programs are better focused on helping displaced workers find other employment through training and reemployment services, as well as financial assistance for job search, relocation, extended unemployment, and health care—the appropriateness and details of these programs would depend on existing capacity in different countries. Outreach to increase awareness and take up of the programs, tailoring of job training to the needs of workers, and wage insurance or tax credits, especially for older workers, could also help. Studies suggest the costs of programs providing comprehensive benefits to displaced workers are a modest portion of potential carbon pricing revenues (see, for example, Morris 2016).
- *Regions*: Coal mining is typically concentrated in a few regions of a country, implying sizable job losses in communities with limited alternative employment opportunities—and declining property values can compound the challenges of relocating workers. Coal workers often face longer unemployment spells after layoffs as well as significant wage reductions in new jobs (see, for example, Johnson and Gosselin 2018). Assistance for converting abandoned mining and drilling sites into farms, residential and commercial developments, or preexisting wilderness, as well as temporary budget support for local governments, could create employment opportunities and bridge the transition for adversely affected communities. Additional investments or other geographically targeted policies (for example, subsidies or grants to individuals or firms in affected regions) may also help regions engage in economically viable and sustainable opportunities (see, for example, WBG 2018). Annex 6.3 summarizes measures in Germany, which has especially comprehensive programs to assist workers and regions for the transition away from coal.

Modeling Household Burdens

How Are the Distributional Effects on Households from Carbon Mitigation Policies Measured?

The standard approach (see Fabrizio, Goumilevski, and Kpodar 2016, Heine and Black 2019, and Shang 2023) is to first estimate the effect of carbon pricing or other mitigation policies on energy prices and then prices for non-energy consumption goods, using input–output tables indicating fuel and electricity inputs per unit of output for each production sector. The second step is to map all these price increases into information in household expenditure surveys on budget shares for energy and non-energy consumption goods by household income (or other) groups.

Ideally, the methodology accounts for the following:

- *Forward-looking projections*—of the energy intensity of production (accounting for improvements in energy efficiency) and of household budget shares (accounting for declining shares for energy as per capita income rises);
- *Behavioral responses*—that is, reductions in the energy intensity of production and in household energy demand, in response to mitigation policies;
- *Imperfect pass-through*—of energy price increases for sectors that are trade exposed; and
- *Alternative recycling possibilities*—for carbon pricing revenues.

Again, CPAT accounts for all these factors. It includes, for 120 countries, input–output tables that distinguish 59 non-energy consumption sectors from the Global Trade Analysis Project-10 (GTAP) database. In addition (as of 2024), it also includes household incidence analysis for 100 countries based on household surveys distinguishing 8 energy products and 14 non-energy products.[5] Production sectors from GTAP are aggregated to match those from the household data. CPAT groups households by population-weighted, per capita consumption deciles and by rural versus urban location, and allows the user to choose assumptions about pass-through rates. Revenue recycling possibilities include reductions in personal income taxes (through lower marginal rates or higher tax thresholds); strengthened social protection (assumed to benefit households proportionally to existing country schemes); new transfers (for which the user can decide the targeted deciles, the coverage rate for targeted deciles, and the portion of revenues leaking away to non-targeted deciles); and public investment (assumed to target parts of the income distribution lacking access to water, electricity, sanitation, information technologies, or public transport).

What Is the Distributional Incidence of Carbon Pricing?

Figure 6.4 illustrates the distributional burden on household income groups in selected countries in 2030 from carbon pricing of $75, $50, and $25 per ton for high-, middle-, and low-income countries.

Prior to revenue recycling some noteworthy points include the following:

- *Overall incidence*: for the median household, overall burdens range from 1.2 percent of consumption in Brazil to 3.5 percent in China—burdens are either mildly regressive (in the United States, China, Brazil) or approximately distribution neutral (India).
- *Indirect burdens*: higher prices for non-energy goods account for 30–65 percent of the overall burden and are distributed fairly evenly across household income groups.[6]

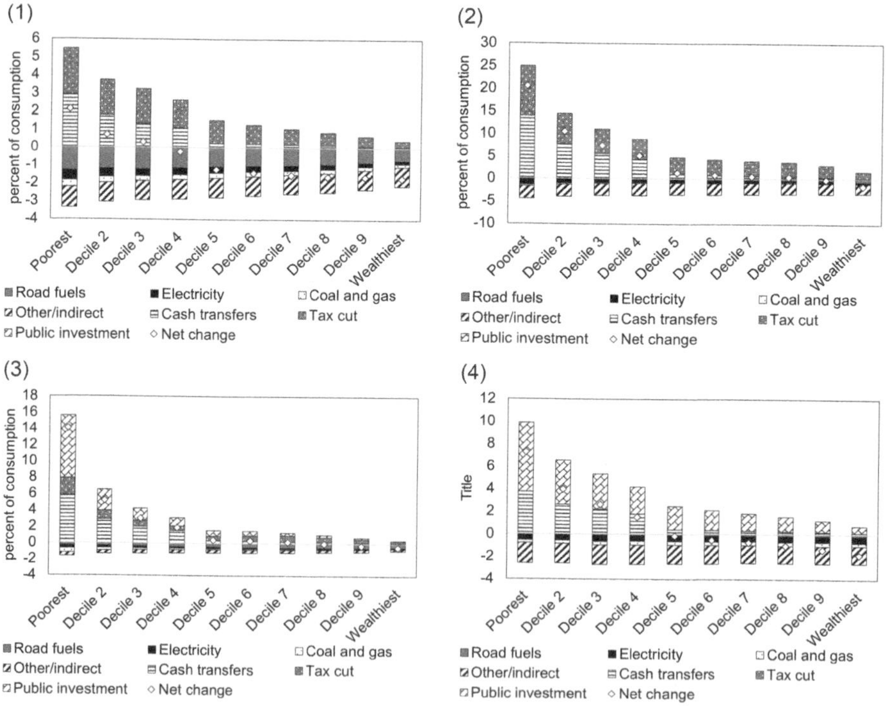

Figure 6.4 Distributional Effect on Households from Carbon Pricing, Selected Countries, 2030. Panel 1. United States ($75), Panel 2. China ($50), Panel 3. Brazil ($50), Panel 4. India ($25).

Source: Authors using CPAT.

Note: Burden is the loss in consumer surplus from higher prices less the benefit from recycling revenue, divided by total consumption. For the United States and China, 70 percent of revenues are used for decreasing labor taxes and 30 percent for cash transfers to bottom four deciles. For Brazil, 35 percent of revenues are used for labor tax reduction, 35 percent for public investment, and 30 percent for cash transfers to bottom four deciles. For India, 70 percent of revenues are used for public investment and 30 percent for cash transfers to bottom four deciles.

- *Composition of direct burdens*: higher electricity prices contribute about 20–50 percent to direct burdens, whereas higher road fuels contribute between 7 percent (India) and 64 percent (the United States) to direct burden. Coal and natural gas contribute remaining 15–20 percent.

Figure 6.4 also illustrates the offsetting benefits to households from recycling carbon pricing revenues, assuming the bottom four income deciles are fully compensated for higher prices through transfers, whereas remaining revenues are used for public investment or proportional income tax cuts (which, respectively, benefit lower- and higher-income households the most). The net effect of higher prices and revenue recycling (shown by the diamonds) is pro-poor (the bottom four deciles are better off) and progressive, with net burdens increasing by income level. And even for the top income decile burdens are not that large—between 0.5 and 2 percent of their consumption across countries. The figure gives a broad-brush sense of the effects of revenue recycling—in practice, broader fiscal adjustments may be more complex (for example, marginal income tax cuts may not be proportional), and it may be difficult to accurately project the distributional effects of specific public investments.

Annex 6.4 provides additional information on 14 G20 countries under the same assumptions as in Figure 6.4. Direct effects for median households range from 0.7 percent in France (because of relatively lower carbon intensity of the economy) to 2.7 percent in South Africa (high carbon intensity), and usually are mildly regressive (except in India, Indonesia, and Mexico). Indirect effects range between 0.3 (France) and 2.9 (South Africa) percent and usually are income neutral. Again, revenue recycling makes the reforms pro-poor and progressive.

The distributional incidence of non-charging policies is not shown here because the results vary with the type of instrument (for example, feebates and performance standards versus incentives for low-carbon technologies), which sectors are covered, and whether instruments are harmonized across sectors. As mentioned earlier, for the same economywide emissions reduction, the burden on the average household under non-charging approaches may be significantly smaller than under carbon pricing prior to revenue recycling but will be larger than the burden from carbon pricing net of revenue recycling.

Are Rural Households Affected Disproportionately from Carbon Pricing?

Figure 6.5 provides the same breakdown of household burdens as in Figure 6.4, and for the same policy scenarios, but this time grouping households into urban and rural categories, and showing results for the bottom, top, and median household decile in each category. The burden from higher gasoline prices is noticeably larger for rural households than their urban counterparts in most cases, and in some cases moderately larger for higher electricity prices. Overall, however, burdens related to consumption (both before and after revenue recycling) are not very different across rural and urban households for a given consumption decile.

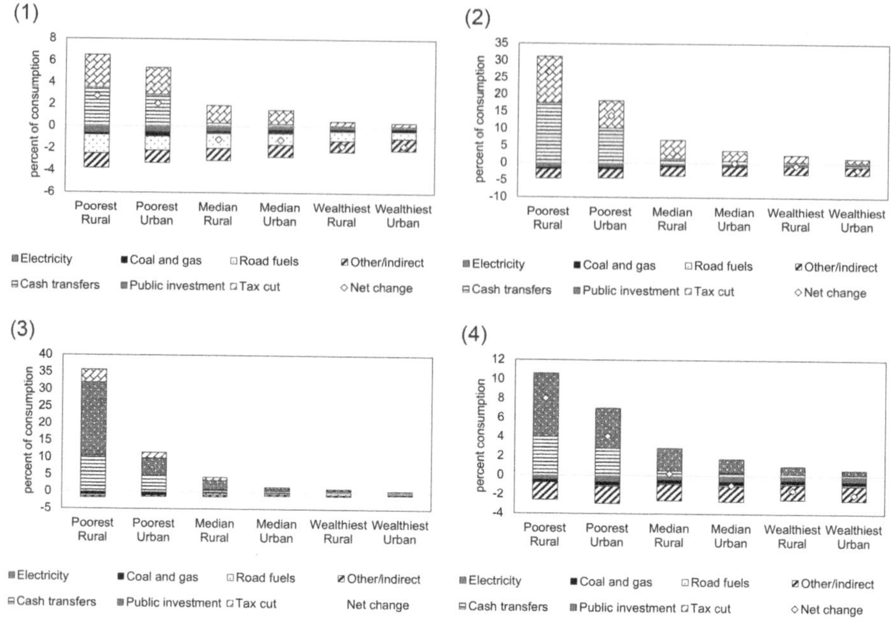

Figure 6.5 Comparing Burdens of Carbon Pricing on Rural and Urban Households, Selected Countries, 2030. Panel 1. United States (\$75), Panel 2. China (\$50), Panel 3. Brazil (\$50), Panel 4. India (\$25).

Source: Authors using CPAT.

Note: Burden is the loss in consumer surplus from higher prices less the benefit from recycling revenue divided by total consumption. For the United States and China, 70 percent of revenues are used for decreasing labor taxes and 30 percent for cash transfers to bottom four deciles. For Brazil, 35 percent of revenues are used for labor tax reduction, 35 percent for public investment, and 30 percent for cash transfers to bottom four deciles. For India, 70 percent of revenues are used for public investment, and 30 percent for cash transfers to bottom four deciles.

Nonetheless, rural households might still be perceived as more vulnerable to carbon pricing given their consumption levels are typically lower than their urban counterparts. Possibilities for assisting them might include extra incentives to purchase heat pumps, solar panels, insulation upgrades, and EVs (in the latter case, along with provision of complementary charging infrastructure).

What Other Strategies Can Enhance the Public Acceptability of Carbon Pricing?

Case studies from episodes of (successful and unsuccessful) energy price reform, and cross-country surveys of public opinion, suggest key ingredients for enhancing the public acceptability of carbon pricing, beyond protecting low-income groups, include (see, for example, Clements et al. 2013, Coady, Parry, and Shang 2018, and Dabla-Norris et al. 2023):

- *Developing a comprehensive reform plan*: One barrier to reform may be the lack of public confidence that the resulting fiscal gains will be used for the benefit of the broader population, which might be addressed by embedding carbon pricing within a more comprehensive strategy clearly specifying the use of fiscal gains. Combining pricing with other measures (like additional incentives for renewables, EVs, and solar panels—see Chapter 4) can enhance the credibility of the program and reduce household and firm vulnerability to higher energy prices.

- *Developing a comprehensive communications strategy.* That is, emphasizing how households benefit from recycling the revenues from reform, as well as the domestic environmental co-benefits (see Chapter 8) and the need to progress on the country's climate commitments. Establishing a reform task force to develop and communicate the strategy and monitor and publicly report on its implementation can also help.
- *Implementing policies progressively and sequentially over time.* A progressive phase in, with the policy and expected price trajectories announced well in advance, allows firms and households time to adjust (for example, by investing in energy efficiency) and starting with a more moderate policy limited to sectors with existing capacity may enhance its credibility. Energy price increases can also be sequenced across energy products (for example, delaying increases in prices for kerosene and liquified petroleum gas (LPG) to reduce the effect on lower-income groups) and sectors (for example, delaying pricing for forestry and agriculture till capacity for emissions and applying policies is in place).
- *Engaging civil society in design consultation.* Getting key stakeholders on board helps build support for the policy early on.
- *Liberalize energy pricing.* This helps to increase the effectiveness of carbon pricing (see Chapter 7) and distance governments from (unpopular) energy price increases.

Trade-Exposed Firms

Understanding the Competitiveness and Leakage Effects of Mitigation Policies

What Is Meant by Competitiveness and Emissions Leakage Effects?

- *Competitiveness*: There is no single accepted definition of competitiveness effects of mitigation policy, but it is generally taken to mean either increases in costs for domestic producers relative to foreign producers, reductions in domestic production, or migration of domestic production to other countries.
- *Emissions leakage*: This is the offsetting emissions increases in other countries from international production migration, divided by domestic emissions reductions to express it as a leakage rate. Domestic emissions reductions are usually measured at the industry level because this is relevant for gauging the need for competitiveness/leakage measures for the industrial sector (leakage rates expressed relative to economywide emissions reductions are much smaller).[7]

The focus has been on energy-intensive, trade-exposed (EITE) industries like iron/steel, aluminum, cement, chemicals, and refined petroleum products because carbon mitigation policy can significantly increase their production costs, potentially causing shifting from domestic to foreign production.[8] Agriculture is also an emissions-intensive, trade-exposed industry, but pricing schemes have not yet been implemented for this sector.

Leakage, and especially competitiveness, risks are a key concern for policymakers given, for example, the employment effects may be larger and more visible for EITE industries (perhaps because of higher unionization rates) than other sectors.

What Determines Production Losses and International Production Migration from Unilateral Mitigation Policy?

For a given increase in domestic production costs (relative to foreign production costs), reductions in domestic production and migration of production to other countries depend on the slope of domestic demand, domestic supply, and foreign supply curves.

Figure 6.6 illustrates the simplest case where domestic producers take international product prices as given—the supply of imports is flat because any quantity of imports can be purchased at an international price. Domestic consumption is met through both domestic and foreign supply (though the

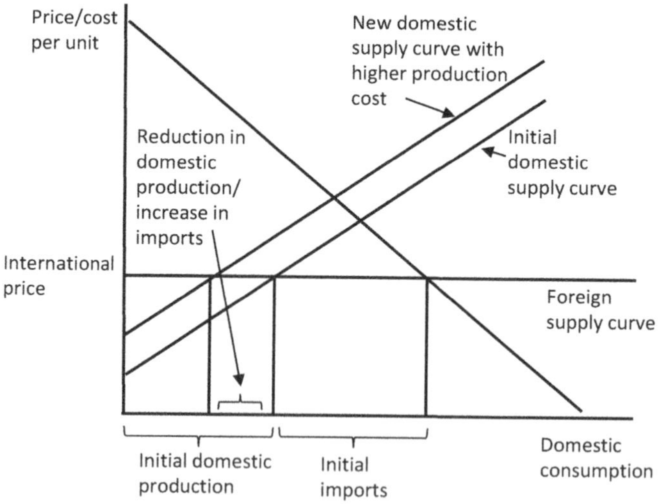

Figure 6.6 Production Impacts of Domestic Carbon Pricing: Fixed International Prices.

Source: Authors.

Note: The analysis is the same for a net exporter, that is, reductions in domestic exports are offset by increased foreign production.

same analysis applies if the domestic industry supplied all domestic as well as some foreign demand). Domestic producers are unable to pass forward any increase in production costs from unilateral mitigation policy into domestic consumer prices, which in turn implies no change in domestic consumption. The reduction in domestic production is larger, the greater the increase in production costs and the flatter the domestic supply curve, that is, the easier it is to shift capital, labor, and other inputs away from the EITE industry to other domestic sectors. All the reduction in domestic production in this case reflects production migration to other countries.

More generally, the foreign supply curve might be upward sloping if domestic producers as a group have some degree of market power in world markets, reflecting product heterogeneity (for example, domestic steel may be stronger than foreign steel), geographical or trade barriers, rising unit costs of transporting bulky imports, or long lead times for foreign firms to ramp up production. Under these conditions, domestic firms can pass forward a portion of domestic production cost increases into higher consumer prices and some of the domestic production reductions reflect reductions in domestic demand. Plausible assumptions about demand and supply elasticities, as well as empirical evidence, suggest, however, that only a minor portion of unilateral mitigation costs for EITE industries is typically passed forward into higher consumer prices (see Parry et al. 2025, Neuhoff and Ritz 2019, and the following section).

What Determines Emissions Leakage Rates?

Carbon leakage is the product of three factors:

- Fraction of the CO_2 reduction induced by mitigation policy because of reduced domestic production (as opposed to reductions in the emissions intensity of production);
- Fraction of the reduction in domestic production because of international production migration abroad (as opposed to reduced domestic demand); and
- The relative carbon intensities of foreign and domestic production.

Leakage rates would tend to be smaller under instruments like feebates and performance standards that do not charge for unabated emissions and where nearly all the emissions reduction comes from reduced emissions intensity rather than reduced production (see Chapter 3). And leakage would not be relevant if a country's trading partners were meeting binding absolute emissions targets—in this case, foreign countries would offset any extra emissions in the industrial sector from inward production migration by reduced emissions in other sectors (Pirlot 2022).

How Can Competitiveness Effects and Emissions Leakage for the Industrial Sector Be Estimated?

The production cost increases from carbon pricing for individual industries are reasonably straightforward to calculate from abatement costs and charges on unabated and indirect emissions (Figure 4.6). The standard GTAP input–output tables do not, however, provide a low-carbon disaggregation of key EITE industries—a supplementary model to CPAT therefore contains a representation of these industries using country-level data on emissions factors, production, producer prices, and abatement cost curves from the literature (see Parry et al. 2025).

The supplementary CPAT model contains a basic representation of trade between a domestic and foreign country, where the latter is a composite of the domestic country's main trading partners for each EITE industry. The model contains industry-specific assumptions about the price responsiveness of domestic demand, domestic supply, and foreign supply, which determine what fraction of a given domestic production cost increase is passed forward in higher consumer prices and what fraction is passed back in lower producer prices—along with production cost increases, these assumptions also determine effects on domestic and foreign production. Foreign supply elasticities are assumed to be larger for more open economies with larger ratios of imports plus exports to domestic production. Emissions leakage is given by the increase in foreign production, weighted by average emissions intensity.

How Does Carbon Pricing Affect Industrial Production Costs in Different Industries and Countries?

Figure 6.7 indicates percentage production cost increases in 2030 for the steel, cement, and chemical industries (globally, some of the largest sources of industrial emissions—see Chapter 4) across selected countries, for unilateral carbon pricing of $50 per ton applied to both industry and power sector emissions. Production cost increases are mostly about 4–8 percent for steel (averaging over production from coal blast and electric arc furnaces), 25–35 percent for cement, and 20–30 percent for ammonia. The larger proportionate cost increases for cement are because of its low baseline prices per ton of output (rather than higher emissions intensity per ton of output). Charges on unabated emissions contribute far more to production cost increases than abatement costs or indirect carbon charges on electricity inputs (abatement costs would play a larger role at higher level of carbon pricing—see Figure 4.6). Across countries, proportionate production cost increases are broadly similar, though with some exceptions. For example, production cost increases for ammonia are larger in China (because its ammonia production is mostly based on coal gasification technologies) and for steel are relatively smaller in the United States (where electric arc furnaces are more common).

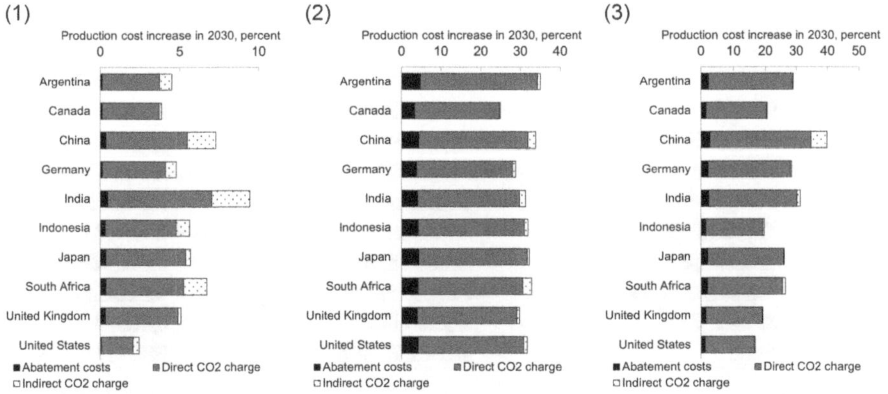

Figure 6.7 Production Cost Increases Relative to Baseline under \$50 Carbon Price, 2030. Panel 1. Steel, Panel 2. Cement, Panel 3. Ammonia.

Source: Parry et al. (2025).

What Are the Production Effects of Unilateral Carbon Pricing (with No Competitiveness Measures) for Different Countries and Industries?

Reductions in domestic production below 2030 baseline levels, assuming pricing is imposed unilaterally and with no accompanying competitiveness/leakage measures, are mostly about 4–8 percent for steel and 15–20 percent for cement and ammonia. For steel and ammonia, typically 75 percent or more of the production cost increases are passed back in lower domestic producer prices and most of the domestic production losses are offset by increased foreign production. Cement is less mobile internationally (because of high transport costs per unit of value) which implies somewhat more scope for mitigation costs to be passed forward, but an offsetting factor is that consumer demand is less responsive (because of limited substitutes for the product) which limits domestic demand effects and again implies that most of the domestic production loss is offset by increased foreign production. See Figure 6.8.

What Are the Domestic Emissions and Leakage Effects?

Emissions for the industries under the \$50 per ton carbon price are reduced about 20–40 percent below 2030 baseline levels across the three industries and across different countries.[9] Emissions fall by more than the reductions in domestic production to the extent that the emissions intensity of production also falls. For steel, typically about 20–30 percent of the emissions reduction is from production losses, whereas for cement and ammonia, the proportion is higher at about 40–55 percent (because of both larger production losses and steeper marginal cost schedules for cutting the emissions intensity of production).

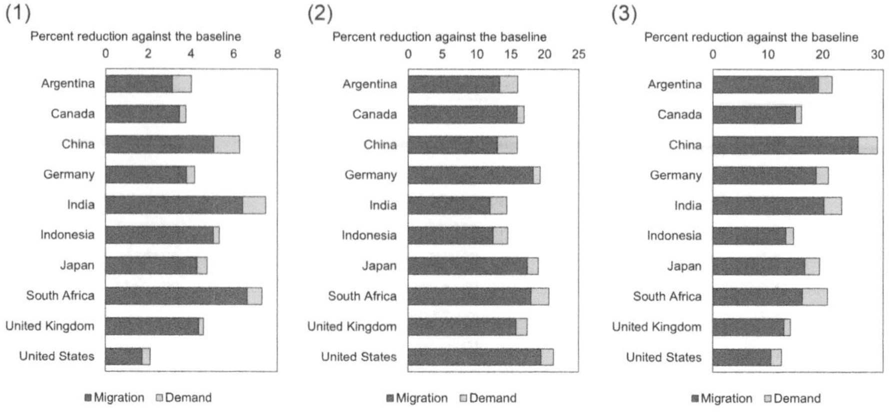

Figure 6.8 Production Effects Relative to Baseline under $50 Carbon Price, 2030. Panel 1. Steel, Panel 2. Cement, Panel 3. Ammonia

Source: Parry et al. (2025).

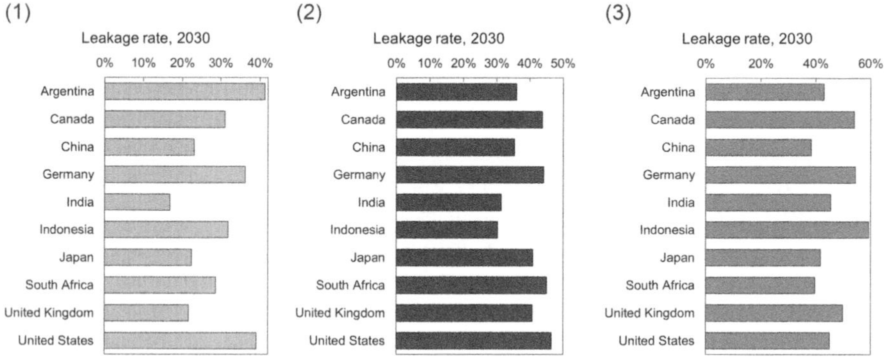

Figure 6.9 Emissions Leakage Rates under Unilateral $50 Carbon Price in 2030 with No Competitiveness Measures. Panel 1. Steel, Panel 2. Cement, Panel 3. Ammonia.

Source: Parry et al. (2025).

Figure 6.9 indicates emissions leakage rates for the industries and countries—these are upper-bound estimates because they assume no accompanying competitiveness/leakage measures nor mitigation policy in countries' trading partners. Leakage rates are mostly about 20–40 percent for steel but are larger for cement (30–45 percent) and ammonia (40–60 percent), given that production losses account for a much larger share of emissions reductions.

What Are the Effects of Unilateral Carbon Pricing (with No Competitiveness Measures) on Market Shares of Different Countries by Industry?

Using IMF-ENV, it is possible to study trade effects in a global context. Figure 6.10 shows changes in market shares for each G20 country by sector from

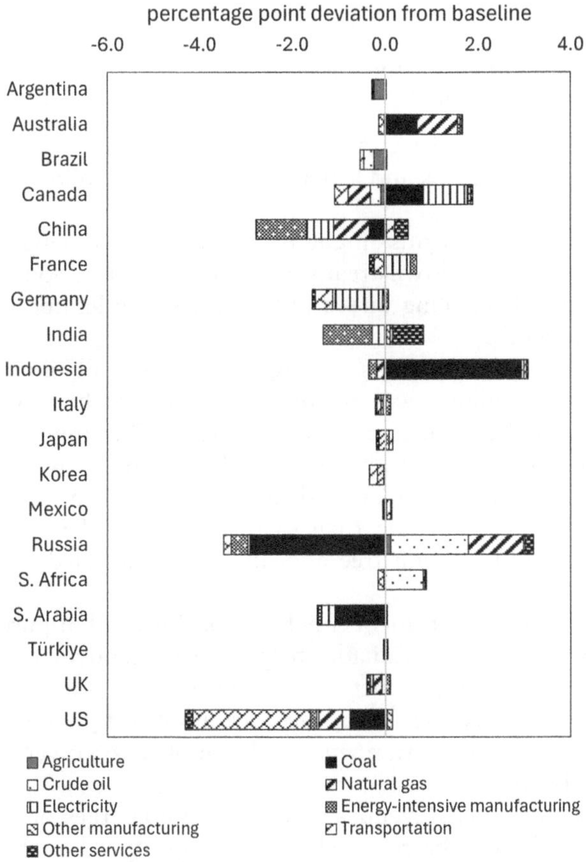

Figure 6.10 Effect of Carbon Pricing on Market Shares of Key Industries, 2030.

Source: IMF staff using IMF-ENV.

carbon pricing ($75 carbon price for high-income countries and $50 carbon price for other countries). In this scenario, although the change in market shares for all industries across countries goes in both directions, the magnitude is not high (within 3 percentage points), with an increase (or decrease) depending on the emissions intensity of a particular sector relative to the other countries and the level of carbon price. The biggest changes in global market shares would be possible for Indonesia (increase in global coal market share because of lower carbon price applied), Russia (decrease in coal market share because of higher price applied), and the United States (decrease in global market share for transportation services).

Policy Responses

What Unilateral, Nontrade Measures Might Help to Address Competitiveness and Leakage?

From a unilateral perspective, there are a variety of nontrade approaches for addressing competitiveness and leakage, including the following:

Tax exemptions. EITE firms might be taxed on their emissions above a threshold level (in a downstream tax system),[10] as in South Africa. This has the effect of reducing direct CO_2 charges (the lighter shaded rectangles) in Figure 6.7.

Free allowances. In an emissions trading system (ETS), EITE industries might be granted free allowances related to exogenous benchmarks, as, for example, in the EU, Korea, and New Zealand. This approach can help to compensate firms for the direct CO_2 charges by providing them with allowances that can either be sold to other firms or used instead of purchasing allowances to cover their own emissions.[11] The compensation is largely lump sum, though free allocations are canceled if firms exit the domestic market.

Feebates/TPSs. These instruments might be used instead of pure carbon pricing, as, for example, in Canada, to preserve incentives for reducing the emissions intensity of production without (on net) collecting government revenues. For the average firm, there are no direct charges on unabated emissions or (if these instruments are also applied to power generation) on indirect emissions.

Within-sector recycling. Revenues collected from charges on EITE industry emissions could also be recycled to firms in output-based rebates—such charging/recycling schemes are operationally like feebates and TPSs because they approximately neutralize, for the average firm, charges on unabated emissions.

All these instruments have similar pros and cons (see Table 6.2). Besides mostly offsetting competitiveness and leakage effects, they are manageable administratively, have little effect on consumer prices (which can be politically difficult), and are generally not subject to risks of legal challenge through the World Trade Organization (WTO). These approaches, however, do not compensate firms for their abatement costs (which become much larger with deeper decarbonization) and do not fully compensate for direct and indirect emissions charges. They also undermine some mitigation incentives—reduced production levels under feebates/performance standards or output-based rebating, slowed exit of polluting firms under free allowances, and reduced incentives to adopt low-carbon technologies when firms are not charged for all their emissions. And these approaches also forgo collecting carbon pricing revenues from the sector.

Table 6.2 Attributes of Unilateral Measures to Address Competitiveness and Leakage

Metric	*Nontrade Measures*				*Trade Measures*
	Exemptions under Carbon Tax	*Free Allowances under ETS*	*Recycling (in Output-Based Rebates)*	*Feebate/Performance Standard*	*Border Adjustments*
Preserve EITE Competitiveness	N: Mostly	N: Mostly	N: Mostly	N: Mostly	A: Yes (if foreign emissions intensity ≥ domestic intensity)
Limit Carbon Leakage	N: Mostly	N: Mostly	N: Mostly	N: Mostly	A: Yes
Mitigation Incentives	N: Reduced incentives for zero-emission investments	N: Can slow exit of polluting firms (as they lose free allowances)	N: Limits production responses	N: Limits production responses	A: Maintains all incentives
Revenue Implications	D: Forgoes carbon pricing revenue	D: Forgoes carbon pricing revenue	D: Forgoes carbon pricing revenue	D: Forgoes carbon pricing revenue	A: Preserves carbon pricing revenue
Political Difficulty from Higher Consumer Prices	N: Minimal price effect	N: Minimal price effect	A: Modest price reduction	A: Modest price reduction	D: Carbon pricing largely passed through
Extra Administrative Burden	A: Modest	A: Modest	A: Modest	A: Modest	D: Significant
Risk of WTO Challenge	A: No	N: Could be challenged as subsidy but has not happened yet	A: No	A: No	D: Significant
Equity Principles of the Paris Agreement	N: na	N: na	N: na	N: na	D: Significant if advanced economies impose measure
Reduction in Global Emissions	D: Not effective	D: Not effective	D: Not effective	D: Not effective	N: May encourage pricing in trading partners

Source: Authors.

Note: A indicates an advantage of an instrument, D a disadvantage, and N neither an advantage nor a disadvantage.

How Do BCAs Work?

Border carbon adjustments (BCAs), sometimes called carbon border adjustment mechanisms (CBAMs), which are being introduced in the EU (see Annex 6.5) and the United Kingdom, impose charges on embodied carbon in products imported into a jurisdiction with carbon pricing, perhaps matched by rebates for embodied carbon in domestic exports.

If a BCA raises the costs of imports by about the same amount as carbon pricing raises domestic production costs—that is, domestic and foreign producers have similar emissions intensities—then the competitiveness effects of domestic carbon pricing are approximately neutralized. If the country is also a price taker in world markets, domestic production would be unaffected—carbon pricing would be fully passed forward in domestic consumer prices and the reduction in domestic demand would come entirely at the expense of imports (Figure 6.11). More generally, if the jurisdiction imposing the BCA has some market power in international markets it faces an upward-sloping supply curve for foreign production and a (likely minor) portion of the burden of carbon pricing will be passed backward in lower producer prices.

What Are the Pros and Cons of BCAs?

On the pro side (see Table 6.2), BCAs are a more robust instrument for addressing competitiveness effects at deeper levels of decarbonization because

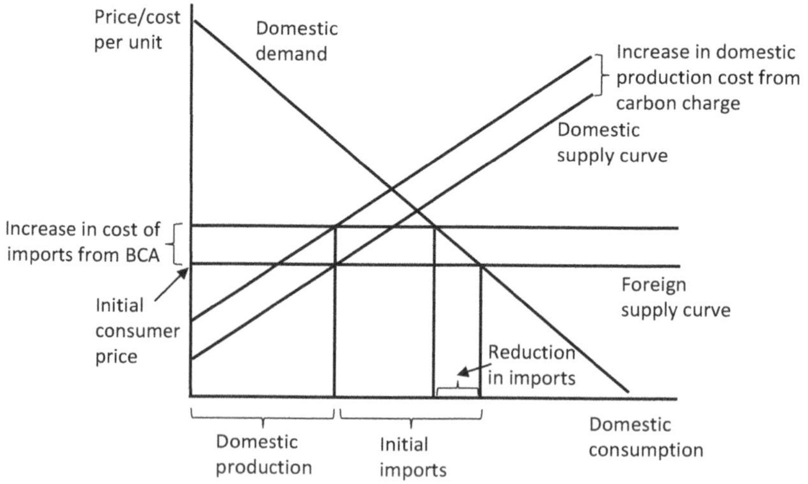

Figure 6.11 Production Impacts of Domestic Carbon Pricing with Border Adjustment: Fixed International Prices.

Source: Authors.

Note: Illustrative case where (1) domestic country is a price taker in the world market for the EITE product; and (2) the BCA raises import costs by the same amount as carbon charging raises domestic production costs. The analysis is essentially the same for a net exporter. BCA = border carbon adjustment.

they progressively raise import prices in line with increases in domestic production costs. They are also a more fine-tuned instrument for addressing emissions leakage than nontrade measures if they vary across foreign suppliers according to their emissions intensity. In addition, BCAs preserve all mitigation responses promoted by carbon pricing—indeed (by addressing competitiveness concerns) they may facilitate a more robust domestic carbon price. BCAs also have a fiscal benefit (if embodied carbon in imports exceeds that for rebated exports), though this revenue is modest relative to that raised from domestic, economywide carbon pricing.

On the con side, BCAs involve significant administrative capacity because they require measurement of embodied carbon for each imported product, supplied by different firms, from different countries (though default emissions factors may be used for foreign countries with limited emissions monitoring capacity). BCAs may also involve legal challenges under WTO rules if they are interpreted as a protectionist rather than environmental measure (see Annex 6.6). Where BCAs are imposed by advanced countries on developing country trading partners they might be viewed as being at odds with the principle of differentiated responsibilities for developing countries under the Paris Agreement (because they impose the same price on emissions from all countries). In addition, by facilitating the pass-through of carbon pricing into domestic consumer prices, BCAs might provoke more opposition from domestic households than nontrade measures.

BCAs might encourage trading partners to adopt or scale up carbon pricing. BCAs price the fraction of nationwide emissions embodied in traded products, but this is modest—only 9 and 12 percent of India and China's nationwide greenhouse gas emissions are embodied in their exports, respectively, and only 1 percent in their exports to the EU (see Figure 6.12). Nonetheless, perhaps from indirect peer pressure, or highlighting the critical role of carbon pricing, the EU's BCA appears to be galvanizing interest in carbon pricing in other countries (see Clausing et al. 2024). International coordination could provide more comprehensive emissions pricing (see Chapter 9) though is more challenging to implement than unilateral BCAs, given the need for agreement across diverse countries.

What Are the Key Design Issues for BCAs?

Key design issues include the following (see, for example, Cosbey et al. 2019 and Parry et al. 2021 for further discussion):

- *Coverage.* Limiting the BCA to EITE industries focuses it on sectors most vulnerable to carbon pricing and foreign competition and would contain administrative costs by limiting the range of products subject to charges—the narrow focus may also limit risks of WTO challenges because the motivation for the BCA based on leakage is more credible for EITE products than for products with low embodied carbon.

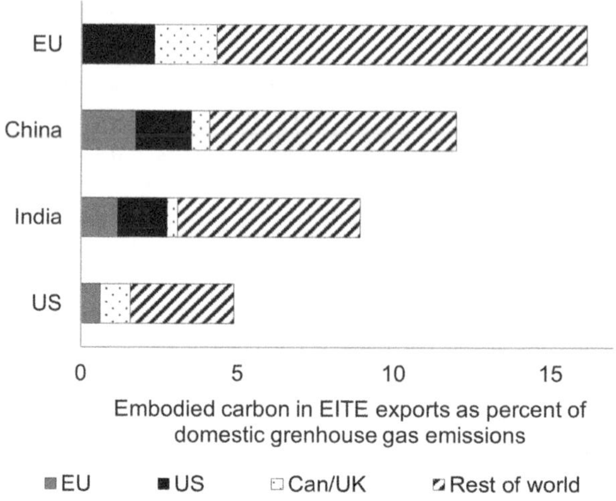

Figure 6.12 Fraction of Domestic Greenhouse Gas Emissions Embodied in Industry Exports to Trading Partners, 2020.

Source: Authors' estimates using OECD (2024) and IMF (2024).

Note: EITE industries include all manufacturing industries and the industry of electricity, gas, steam, and air conditioning supply.

- *Measuring carbon embodied in imports.* Emissions intensity benchmarks might be the following:
  - ✓ *Industry level/country specific*: this approach would impose higher charges on emissions-intensive trading partners for whom leakage risks are greater (though cross-country differences in emissions intensity are often limited).
  - ✓ *Firm or product level/country specific*: in this case, foreign suppliers would be required (because they are under the EU CBAM) to report and validate their embodied emissions in exports and domestic importers would then be required to remit charges, or purchase allowances based, on the reported emissions. This would provide incentives for foreign exporters to reduce their emissions intensity and for foreign governments to price industrial emissions. If reporting is at the plant level, there could, however, be some risk of gaming if the BCA induces firms to switch production from their cleaner plants for export to the BCA-imposing jurisdiction while it redirects products from their dirtier plants to other countries.[12]
  - ✓ *Industry level/domestic*: basing the BCA on domestic industry emissions rates would preserve competitiveness and is administratively simplest but lacks incentives for foreign exporters to reduce emissions and would imply that because domestic industries lower emissions in response to carbon pricing, this would lower charges on imports even though the embodied emissions on these products may not have changed.

- *Rebates for exporters*. Rebates for carbon charges on embodied carbon in exports are, in principle, warranted on competitiveness grounds but they should be based on industry (rather than firm level) emissions rates to avoid undermining individual firm incentives to cut emissions rates. Legal constraints may preclude export rebates under an ETS, however (which is viewed as a regulation rather than a tax—see Annex 6.6).
- *Revenue use*. There are many options for use of BCA revenues but remitting them for international climate finance, or to governments of developing country exporters (without undercutting their incentives for carbon pricing), might help ameliorate opposition from developing country trading partners (even though the incidence of the BCA is largely borne by domestic consumers). It should also reduce legal risks by increasing the likelihood of the BCA being considered an environmental (rather than protectionist or domestic revenue raising) measure.
- *Adjusting import charges for mitigation policies abroad*. Charges on imports should in principle be net of any carbon pricing on embodied emissions imposed by foreign governments, but this is less clear if the foreign government compensates domestic exporters for competitiveness effects (for example, through free allowance allocations). Adjustments for non-charging policies, like performance standards, do not seem warranted from a narrow competitive perspective because they do not charge for unabated emissions.
- *Exemptions for least-developed countries* (LDCs). Applying a lower BCA rate for exporters in LDCs would ease competitiveness concerns for LDC exporters with little at stake for BCA-implementing countries (given the small trade shares of LDCs) and could be broadly consistent with equity principles of both the Paris Agreement and trade rules (Annex 6.6). Exemptions would, however, need to be designed to deter the trans-shipment of goods from countries fully covered by the BCA through partially exempted countries.

What Are the Cross-Country Revenue Implications of BCAs?

Figure 6.12 shows projected revenues that would be collected by China, EU, and the United States from their top 10 trading partners from a \$50 BCA imposed on embodied carbon in all manufacturing imports in 2030, as well as revenue losses if domestic manufacturing exporters were rebated for the carbon price. For simplicity, Figure 6.13 assumes the BCA is imposed unilaterally and ignores carbon pricing programs in trading partners that potentially lower charges on imports.

The EU and the United States would collect, by far, most revenues on imports from China, whereas for China collections would be more evenly distributed across major trading partners. If exports were rebated, the United States would still on net collect significant revenues from its top trading partners, and for the most part the same applies for the EU. In contrast for China, export rebates would imply net revenues losses from most of its trading partners, particularly the EU and United States.

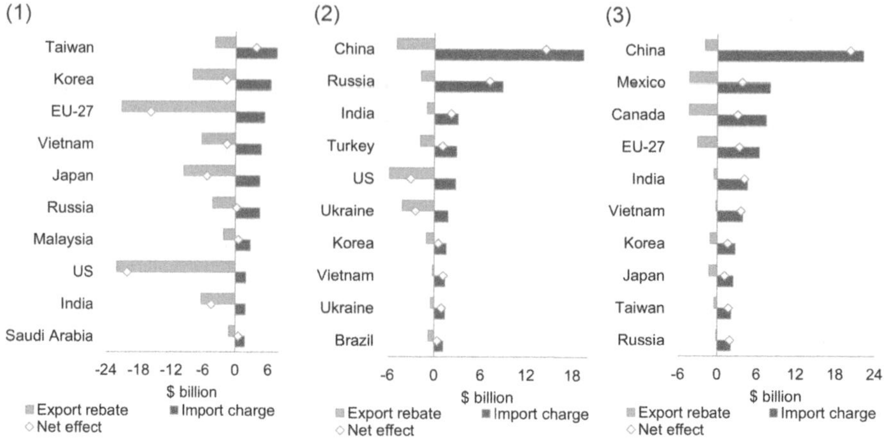

Figure 6.13 Cross-Country Revenue Flows from BCAs for $50 Carbon Price, 2030. Panel 1. China, Panel 2. EU, Panel 3. United States.

Source: Authors using 2020 trade flow data from OECD (2024).

Note: 2030 data are based on projected 2030 GDP relative to 2020 GDP. Revenues are the carbon price, times the embodied carbon across all manufacturing imports or exports between countries and their top 10 trading partners.

What Policies Might Address Competitiveness and Emissions Leakage for Agriculture?

Competitiveness and leakage concerns from emissions pricing would be acute for the agricultural sector (see Nordin et al. 2019) where food products can be mobile internationally and a significant portion of domestic emissions reductions may come from reducing production levels (for example, for beef) rather than reducing the emissions intensity of production (see Chapter 4). One way to address these concerns under an emissions fee for the livestock sector would be to recycle revenues to the sector, for example, in the form of a subsidy per kg of farm output—on net, ruminant farmers would be worse off whereas non-ruminant and crop farmers would be better off. Competitiveness and leakage concerns might alternatively be addressed through using a feebate rather than a (revenue-neutral) emissions tax. Combining an emissions fee with border adjustments for imported farm products is another possibility, though measuring embodied emissions for livestock products (which depend on a range of characteristics at the farm level—see Chapter 4) is more administratively challenging than for industrial products.

Taxes on the supply of livestock products (perhaps at the processor level and scaled by default emissions factors) are another possibility for the sector (see Chapter 4). Where domestic producers take international food prices as given, the production tax would be passed backward in lower producer prices, with no effect on consumer prices and domestic demand—the reduction in domestic production would be fully offset by increased foreign production (as in Figure 6.6). Competitiveness effects might be moderated, however, by lowering the overall level of production taxes—the tax rate could be proportional to the difference between a default emissions rate per kg of output and a pivot point emissions rate per kg common across livestock products.

Taxes on meat consumption (scaled by default emissions factors) address competitiveness concerns by imposing the same charge on imported, as domestically produced, consumption, whereas domestic exports are excluded. In terms of competitiveness, they are similar to emissions pricing combined with a BCA—if domestic producers are price takers in international markets, a consumption tax is fully passed forward to domestic consumers, thereby reducing domestic demand and net imports, without affecting domestic production (as in Figure 6.11). Consumption taxes can make sense for countries whose trading partners have relatively high emissions per unit of production, but they may do little to reduce domestic emissions.

Suggestions for Further Reading

- *Public perceptions of climate mitigation policies.* Based on extensive cross-country surveys, Dabla-Norris et al. (2023) discuss factors that can affect the public acceptability of mitigation policies, noting the growing support for carbon pricing, the importance of communicating the fiscal and environmental benefits of carbon pricing, linking relief to carbon price revenue, and engaging civil society in design consultation.
- *Reactions to the energy price surge of 2020–21.* Anil et al. (2022) describe how European country governments introduced measures to assist households in response to the energy price shock after the pandemic and the Russian invasion of Ukraine.
- *Methodology for assessing household burdens.* See Fabrizio, Goumilevski, and Kpodar (2016) for further discussion of the standard approach for measuring the burden on households from higher energy prices based on matching household surveys to results from input–output tables.
- *Household incidence of carbon mitigation policies.* For some examples of modeling studies, see Goulder et al. (2019), García-Muros, Morris, and Paltsev (2022), Hassett, Mathur, and Metcalf (2009), and Williams et al. (2015). For literature reviews on household incidence, see, for example, Flues and Thomas (2015) and Pizer and Sexton (2019). Dabla-Norris et al. (2021) discuss distributional issues for Asia-Pacific countries. Levinson (2019) compares the incidence of energy efficiency standards and energy taxes. On the distributional effects of road fuel taxes, see Sterner (2012).
- *Worker assistance programs.* Morris (2016) provides a discussion of policies for displaced coal miners in a US context. See IMF (2022) for further discussion of labor market policies.

- *Competitiveness and leakage effects.* For reviews of literature on competitiveness effects of mitigation policies, see Peñasco, Díaz Anadón, and Verdolini (2021) and for individual studies, see, for example, Aldy and Pizer (2015), Carbone and Rivers (2017), Dechezleprêtre and Sato (2017), Joltreau and Sommerfeld (2019), and Venmans, Ellis, and Nachtigall (2020). For further discussion of emissions leakage, see, for example, Ellis, Nachtigall, and Venmans (2019), Verde (2020), and Misch and Wingender (2021). Some studies suggest leakage may be *negative* if mitigation policy in one country catalyzes similar policies in other countries (for example, Aydemir and Zeren 2017).
- *Policies to address competitiveness and leakage.* For discussions of measures to address competitiveness and leakage effects of carbon mitigation policies, see Aldy (2017), Fischer and Fox (2012), and Fischer, Morgenstern, and Richardson (2015).
- *BCAs.* For a general discussion of the rationale for BCAs, design issues, and their effects, see Keen, Parry, and Roaf (2022), Kopp, Pizer, and Rennert (2023), and Parry et al. (2021). For more on design issues for BCAs, see Flannery et al. (2020), Kortum and Weisbach (2017), and Mehling et al. (2019). On legal aspects, see Holzer (2014), OECD (2020), and Pauwelyn Kleimann (2020), and on trade effects, see Condon and Ignaciuk (2013). For modeling results on border adjustments, see, for example, Böhringer, Rosendahl, and Storrøsten (2017), Branger and Quirion (2014), and Burniaux, Chateau, and Duval (2013).

Annex 6.1 Using Consumer Surplus to Measure Household Burdens from Mitigation Policies

Economists usually estimate the distributional burden of climate (and broader public) policies across household income groups using the concept of "consumer surplus." For an individual product, consumer surplus is the benefit to households from their consumption of the product, less what they pay for it.

Figure A6.1 depicts the demand for an individual energy or general consumer good for a household income group. The height of the demand curve at a point is the benefit to households from consuming an extra unit, or their willingness to pay for an extra unit. The integral under the demand curve between the origin and a given consumption level is the total benefits to households from that consumption. Given an initial price p_0 and consumption X_0, the initial consumer surplus is the trapezoid under the demand curve between the origin and X_0 less p_0X_0 (spending on consumption). Suppose (because of carbon mitigation policy) the price increases to p_1 and consumption falls to X_1. The reduction in consumer surplus (or the burden of the price increase on households) has two components. First, the increase in the

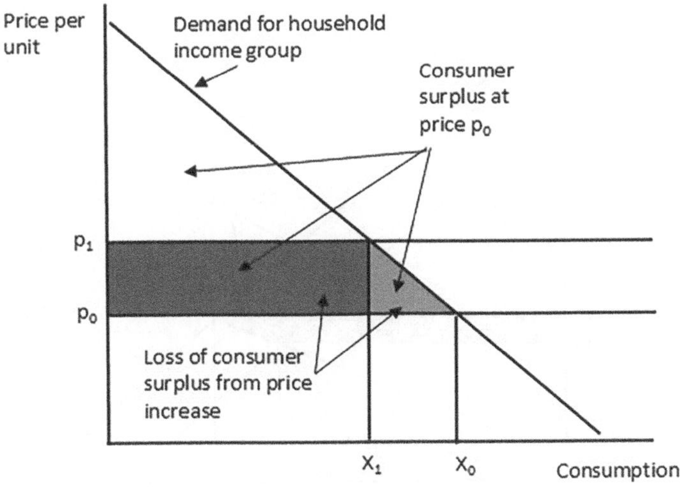

Figure A6.1 Household Burden from an Increase in Product Price.

Source: Authors.

amount households now spend to purchase the new level of consumption $(p_1-p_0)X_1$, and second is the loss of consumption benefits (the trapezoid under the demand curve between X_1 and X_0) less avoided spending $p_0(X_0-X_1)$. Measuring the household burden by the increase in spending at the initial level of consumption would overstate the loss of consumer surplus, whereas measuring it by the increase in spending at the new level of consumption understate it, but, from simple geometry, the over or understatement is relatively modest.

The direct and indirect burden on a household group from the increase in price of energy and general consumption goods induced by carbon mitigation policies is the sum of losses in consumer surplus across all the relevant markets.

Annex 6.2 The Burdens on Workers from Reduced Labor Demand

Analogous to consumer surplus, the economic burden of climate policies on workers in domestic industries that contract in response to mitigation policy can be measured using the concept of "worker surplus." This refers to wages they currently earn, less the costs of supplying labor for their job—the wages they could earn in their next best occupation or the value of time at the home that they give up (for example, in childrearing).

Consider Figure A6.2 that depicts the demand and supply for workers in a particular industry (leaving aside taxes paid on labor earnings). The height

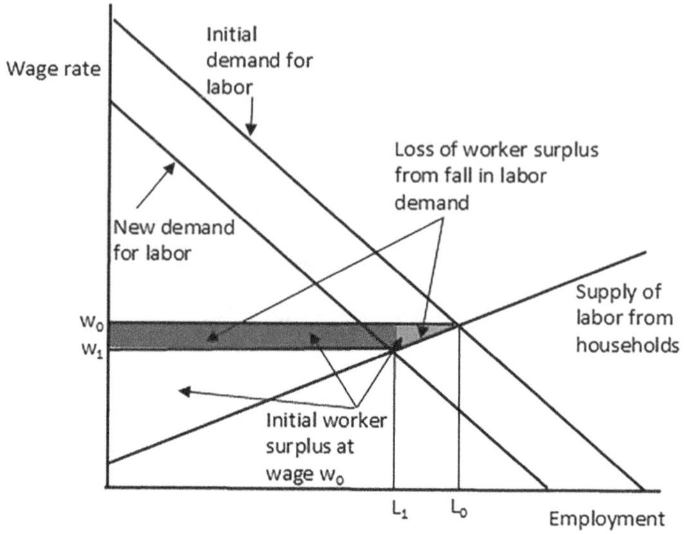

Figure A6.2 Reduction in Worker Surplus from a Reduction in Labor Demand.

Source: Authors.

of the supply curve at any point reflects the cost to workers from supplying an extra unit of labor. In the initial market equilibrium, where the demand for labor from firms equals the supply of labor from households, the wage rate is w_0 and employment is L_0. The initial worker surplus is given by w_0L_0 (wages received), less the trapezoid under the supply curve integrated between the origin and L_0 (the costs of supplying that amount of effort to the industry).

Suppose that in response to carbon mitigation policy, the demand for labor from firms shifts in leading to a new equilibrium with lower wage w_1 and employment L_1. The reduction in worker surplus has two components. First, the reduction in the wages workers receive at the new level of employment $(w_0-w_1)L_1$, and second is the wages forgone from the reduction in labor supply, $w_0(L_0-L_1)$, less avoided costs from working in the industry (the trapezoid under the labor supply curve between L_1 and L_0).

Annex 6.3 Policies to Assist German Coal Miners and Communities

Table A6.1 provides a summary of measures to assist coal miners and mining communities in the transition away from coal in Germany.

Table A6.1 Examples of Ongoing Measures to Assist Displaced Coal Workers and Coal Mining Regions in Germany

Goals		*Examples of Mechanisms*						
Overarching	*Specific*	*Financial Support (from National Government, EU, Banks)*			*Service and Assistance*			*Infrastructure Investment*
		Public/ Nonprofit Organizations	*Firms*	*Workers*	*Public/ Nonprofit Organizations*	*Firms*	*Workers*	
Economic Reorientation and Diversification	Support new/ existing small/ medium (non-coal) firms	Land acquisition, local infrastructure construction, office conversions	Loans, tax cuts, debt repayment schemes		Assistance in creating strategies and networks	Network building, country counseling for exporting companies		
	Expand educational activities	Implementation/ extension of universities/ training centers			Creation/ support of networks between firms/ research institutions			
	Technology development	Clean technology R&D support for universities	Clean technology R&D support for universities			Innovation transfer between research institutions/ firms		
	Preserve energy role beyond coal	Clean technology R&D support for universities				Network between universities/ firms		

(*Continued*)

Table A6.1 (Continued)

Goals		*Examples of Mechanisms*						
Overarching	*Specific*	*Financial Support (from National Government, EU, Banks)*			*Service and Assistance*			*Infrastructure Investment*
		Public/ Nonprofit Organizations	*Firms*	*Workers*	*Public/ Nonprofit Organizations*	*Firms*	*Workers*	
Workforce Support	Allowances		Subsidies for employers paying share of allowances	Wage subsidies, unemployment allowances, transitional aid			Help with application for allowances	
	Training programs	Support for creating/ extending training facilities	Subsidies for employers paying share of training				Counseling workers on training programs	
	Job-seeking assistance	Payments to firms for employing the unemployed					Counseling to find jobs	
	Job creation		Financial support for firms creating jobs					Jobs in environmental remediation
Social Well-being and Quality of Life	Urban development	Upgrading municipalities (e.g., buildings, parks)		Modernization of houses				
	Culture and leisure	Creation/ operation of cultural/ leisure facilities						

Environmental Remediation and Protection	Decommissioning/ environmental rehabilitation	Construction of sewage plants	Incentives for air quality measured/ decommissioning mining sites
	Water management	Safeguarding nature, water monitoring/ cleaning in mines	
	Other	Restoration/ extension of forest areas	

Source: Furnaro et al. (2021).

Annex 6.4 Distributional Effect on Households from Carbon Pricing: Further Country Studies

Table A6.2 Components of Burden, Percent of Consumption

Country	*Component of Burden*	*Poorest*			*Household Consumption Decile*						*Wealthiest*
		1	*2*	*3*	*4*	*5*	*6*	*7*	*8*	*9*	*10*
Brazil	Electricity	−0.34	−0.26	−0.22	−0.19	−0.17	−0.15	−0.13	−0.11	−0.09	−0.07
	Natural gas	−0.54	−0.31	−0.24	−0.19	−0.15	−0.12	−0.10	−0.08	−0.06	−0.04
	Road fuels	−0.30	−0.33	−0.39	−0.44	−0.47	−0.53	−0.55	−0.56	−0.54	−0.47
	Other/indirect	−0.40	−0.42	−0.40	−0.39	−0.38	−0.36	−0.35	−0.33	−0.31	−0.27
	Cash transfers	5.83	2.90	2.02	1.52	0.34	0.27	0.21	0.16	0.12	0.06
	Tax cut	2.07	1.03	0.72	0.57	0.54	0.68	0.72	0.58	0.42	0.23
	Public investment	7.74	2.58	1.50	1.00	0.69	0.54	0.38	0.29	0.19	0.09
	Net change	14.06	5.20	2.99	1.88	0.41	0.33	0.18	−0.05	−0.27	−0.46
Canada	Electricity	−0.15	−0.14	−0.14	−0.13	−0.12	−0.11	−0.11	−0.10	−0.10	−0.08
	Natural gas	−0.35	−0.35	−0.45	−0.43	−0.41	−0.39	−0.40	−0.35	−0.35	−0.32
	Road fuels	−0.64	−0.77	−0.78	−0.75	−0.81	−0.78	−0.77	−0.67	−0.66	−0.56
	Other/indirect	−1.02	−0.93	−0.92	−0.91	−0.89	−0.89	−0.88	−0.89	−0.88	−0.87
	Cash transfers	2.40	1.71	1.42	1.24	0.32	0.28	0.25	0.22	0.18	0.12
	Tax cut	1.34	2.41	2.02	1.77	1.58	1.40	1.24	1.07	0.88	0.61
	Public investment	0.00	0.00	0.00	0.00	0.00	0.00	0.00	0.00	0.00	0.00
	Net change	1.57	1.92	1.14	0.78	−0.34	−0.49	−0.66	−0.73	−0.92	−1.10
China	Electricity	−1.29	−0.90	−0.75	−0.67	−0.58	−0.55	−0.48	−0.43	−0.38	−0.27
	Natural gas	−0.09	−0.10	−0.08	−0.11	−0.09	−0.08	−0.09	−0.11	−0.10	−0.08
	Road fuels	−0.07	−0.15	−0.16	−0.18	−0.21	−0.27	−0.30	−0.32	−0.39	−0.58
	Other/indirect	−2.94	−2.77	−2.71	−2.73	−2.64	−2.59	−2.55	−2.49	−2.41	−2.26
	Cash transfers	13.98	7.74	5.68	4.40	1.00	0.81	0.65	0.51	0.38	0.20
	Tax cut	10.94	6.71	5.38	4.49	3.84	3.54	3.30	3.25	2.72	1.44
	Public investment	0.00	0.00	0.00	0.00	0.00	0.00	0.00	0.00	0.00	0.00
	Net change	20.52	10.54	7.36	5.19	1.31	0.85	0.54	0.41	−0.18	−1.55

France	Electricity	−0.03	−0.03	−0.02	−0.02	−0.02	−0.02	−0.02	−0.02	−0.02	−0.02
	Natural gas	−0.21	−0.13	−0.10	−0.11	−0.12	−0.11	−0.09	−0.10	−0.10	−0.08
	Road fuels	−0.42	−0.41	−0.49	−0.54	−0.49	−0.50	−0.51	−0.50	−0.49	−0.44
	Other/indirect	−0.37	−0.38	−0.37	−0.37	−0.38	−0.38	−0.37	−0.37	−0.35	−0.35
	Cash transfers	1.39	0.84	0.67	0.58	0.15	0.13	0.11	0.10	0.08	0.06
	Tax cut	1.85	1.12	0.90	0.77	0.68	0.59	0.52	0.45	0.38	0.27
	Public investment	0.00	0.00	0.00	0.00	0.00	0.00	0.00	0.00	0.00	0.00
	Net change	2.20	1.01	0.58	0.31	−0.18	−0.29	−0.35	−0.44	−0.50	−0.56
Germany	Electricity	−0.03	−0.03	−0.03	−0.03	−0.03	−0.03	−0.03	−0.03	−0.02	−0.02
	Natural gas	−0.35	−0.33	−0.32	−0.32	−0.32	−0.31	−0.30	−0.26	−0.24	−0.22
	Road fuels	−0.18	−0.25	−0.29	−0.31	−0.33	−0.37	−0.39	−0.38	−0.38	−0.37
	Other/indirect	−0.92	−0.91	−0.91	−0.92	−0.92	−0.91	−0.90	−0.88	−0.86	−0.84
	Cash transfers	1.19	0.99	0.84	0.77	0.20	0.19	0.18	0.15	0.14	0.12
	Tax cut	1.58	1.31	1.12	1.03	0.94	0.88	0.83	0.72	0.64	0.56
	Public investment	0.00	0.00	0.00	0.00	0.00	0.00	0.00	0.00	0.00	0.00
	Net change	1.28	0.78	0.42	0.22	−0.46	−0.54	−0.62	−0.68	−0.73	−0.76
India	Electricity	−0.47	−0.50	−0.55	−0.50	−0.51	−0.52	−0.51	−0.51	−0.53	−0.55
	Natural gas	0.00	0.00	0.00	−0.01	−0.01	−0.01	−0.01	−0.03	−0.03	−0.07
	Road fuels	−0.05	−0.06	−0.08	−0.09	−0.11	−0.12	−0.12	−0.15	−0.14	−0.15
	Other/indirect	−2.07	−2.02	−2.07	−2.08	−2.01	−1.98	−1.92	−1.88	−1.89	−1.80
	Cash transfers	3.76	2.64	2.21	1.80	0.43	0.38	0.34	0.29	0.24	0.16
	Tax cut	0.00	0.00	0.00	0.00	0.00	0.00	0.00	0.00	0.00	0.00
	Public investment	6.12	3.93	3.13	2.41	2.06	1.75	1.50	1.28	1.00	0.59
	Net change	7.29	3.99	2.63	1.52	−0.15	−0.49	−0.72	−0.99	−1.35	−1.82

(*Continued*)

Table A6.2 (Continued)

Country	Component of Burden	Poorest 1	2	3	Household Consumption Decile 4	5	6	7	8	9	Wealthiest 10
Indonesia	Electricity	−0.28	−0.27	−0.28	−0.30	−0.31	−0.33	−0.34	−0.36	−0.38	−0.41
	Natural gas	0.00	0.00	0.00	0.00	0.00	0.00	0.00	0.00	0.00	0.00
	Road fuels	−0.50	−0.54	−0.57	−0.57	−0.57	−0.56	−0.56	−0.56	−0.56	−0.56
	Other/indirect	−0.74	−0.72	−0.71	−0.70	−0.69	−0.69	−0.68	−0.68	−0.67	−0.67
	Cash transfers	2.42	1.74	1.43	1.23	0.30	0.26	0.22	0.19	0.15	0.11
	Tax cut	0.00	0.00	0.00	0.00	0.00	0.00	0.00	0.00	0.00	0.00
	Public investment	3.63	2.46	1.97	1.67	1.41	1.18	0.99	0.83	0.68	0.46
	Net change	4.53	2.66	1.84	1.33	0.14	−0.14	−0.37	−0.58	−0.78	−1.08
Italy	Electricity	−0.15	−0.11	−0.10	−0.09	−0.09	−0.08	−0.08	−0.07	−0.07	−0.06
	Natural gas	−0.43	−0.34	−0.32	−0.34	−0.31	−0.33	−0.31	−0.34	−0.32	−0.29
	Road fuels	−0.65	−0.73	−0.68	−0.68	−0.60	−0.60	−0.56	−0.51	−0.44	−0.43
	Other/indirect	−0.57	−0.55	−0.54	−0.53	−0.53	−0.52	−0.51	−0.49	−0.48	−0.45
	Cash transfers	1.91	1.26	1.03	0.89	0.22	0.19	0.17	0.15	0.12	0.08
	Tax cut	2.55	1.68	1.38	1.19	1.03	0.91	0.79	0.68	0.55	0.36
	Public investment	0.00	0.00	0.00	0.00	0.00	0.00	0.00	0.00	0.00	0.00
	Net change	2.65	1.20	0.76	0.43	−0.29	−0.43	−0.51	−0.59	−0.65	−0.79
Japan	Electricity	−0.42	−0.68	−0.58	−0.52	−0.49	−0.45	−0.49	−0.45	−0.41	−0.36
	Natural gas	−0.22	−0.36	−0.30	−0.27	−0.26	−0.24	−0.25	−0.23	−0.22	−0.19
	Road fuels	−0.09	−0.15	−0.16	−0.21	−0.20	−0.16	−0.21	−0.25	−0.17	−0.20
	Other/indirect	−0.88	−1.45	−1.41	−1.41	−1.39	−1.35	−1.37	−1.36	−1.32	−1.26
	Cash transfers	4.32	1.46	1.24	1.05	0.26	0.23	0.20	0.18	0.15	0.09
	Tax cut	2.73	2.10	1.72	1.49	1.29	1.15	1.01	0.89	0.74	0.46
	Public investment	0.00	0.00	0.00	0.00	0.00	0.00	0.00	0.00	0.00	0.00
	Net change	5.43	0.91	0.49	0.13	−0.79	−0.82	−1.11	−1.22	−1.23	−1.46

Mexico	Electricity	−0.40	−0.39	−0.36	−0.35	−0.33	−0.33	−0.30	−0.30	−0.28	−0.25
	Natural gas	−0.01	−0.01	−0.02	−0.02	−0.02	−0.02	−0.02	−0.02	−0.03	−0.03
	Road fuels	−0.23	−0.37	−0.43	−0.51	−0.53	−0.63	−0.68	−0.77	−0.89	−0.96
	Other/indirect	−1.39	−1.53	−1.52	−1.48	−1.48	−1.44	−1.37	−1.32	−1.21	−1.08
	Cash transfers	3.54	2.17	1.71	1.42	0.35	0.30	0.25	0.21	0.16	0.10
	Tax cut	0.56	0.67	1.28	1.10	0.94	0.81	0.68	0.57	0.45	0.27
	Public investment	4.84	1.98	1.24	0.93	0.72	0.58	0.44	0.33	0.26	0.15
	Net change	6.91	2.52	1.91	1.08	−0.35	−0.74	−1.00	−1.30	−1.54	−1.79
South Africa	Electricity	−3.28	−2.69	−2.48	−2.43	−2.31	−2.27	−2.13	−1.96	−1.78	−1.47
	Natural gas	0.00	0.00	0.00	0.00	0.00	0.00	0.00	0.00	0.00	0.00
	Road fuels	−0.05	−0.12	−0.18	−0.27	−0.33	−0.42	−0.60	−0.75	−1.00	−1.11
	Other/indirect	−3.30	−3.26	−3.31	−3.24	−3.16	−3.12	−2.96	−2.75	−2.43	−2.13
	Cash transfers	19.11	11.04	8.04	6.26	1.39	1.06	0.80	0.57	0.38	0.19
	Tax cut	7.17	4.14	3.02	2.37	2.05	2.12	2.92	2.09	1.37	0.70
	Public investment	20.91	8.96	5.15	3.75	2.41	1.61	1.11	0.91	0.86	0.72
	Net change	40.57	18.06	10.23	6.43	0.05	−1.02	−0.86	−1.90	−2.61	−3.10
Türkiye	Electricity	−0.28	−0.23	−0.21	−0.20	−0.19	−0.17	−0.17	−0.16	−0.14	−0.12
	Natural gas	−0.83	−0.90	−1.09	−1.20	−1.30	−1.27	−1.24	−1.09	−1.00	−0.88
	Road fuels	−0.27	−0.26	−0.31	−0.34	−0.38	−0.38	−0.43	−0.42	−0.41	−0.36
	Other/indirect	−0.86	−0.79	−0.71	−0.69	−0.60	−0.57	−0.56	−0.55	−0.51	−0.46
	Cash transfers	5.04	3.28	2.55	2.10	0.51	0.44	0.37	0.31	0.25	0.15
	Tax cut	0.81	1.70	1.91	1.57	1.33	1.16	0.98	0.82	0.65	0.39
	Public investment	6.69	2.88	1.70	1.28	0.91	0.85	0.72	0.56	0.46	0.27
	Net change	10.30	5.69	3.85	2.53	0.29	0.06	−0.33	−0.53	−0.71	−1.00

(Continued)

Table A6.2 (Continued)

Country	*Component of Burden*	*Poorest*			*Household Consumption Decile*						*Wealthiest*
		1	*2*	*3*	*4*	*5*	*6*	*7*	*8*	*9*	*10*
UK	Electricity	−0.12	−0.09	−0.06	−0.06	−0.05	−0.05	−0.04	−0.04	−0.04	−0.03
	Natural gas	−0.91	−0.65	−0.48	−0.47	−0.37	−0.35	−0.31	−0.31	−0.29	−0.22
	Road fuels	−0.41	−0.45	−0.54	−0.51	−0.53	−0.56	−0.56	−0.58	−0.46	−0.43
	Other/indirect	−0.45	−0.45	−0.46	−0.48	−0.49	−0.46	−0.47	−0.45	−0.46	−0.45
	Cash transfers	1.29	0.82	0.66	0.56	0.14	0.12	0.10	0.09	0.07	0.05
	Tax cut	1.73	1.09	0.88	0.75	0.65	0.56	0.49	0.42	0.34	0.24
	Public investment	0.00	0.00	0.00	0.00	0.00	0.00	0.00	0.00	0.00	0.00
	Net change	1.13	0.27	0.00	−0.21	−0.66	−0.73	−0.79	−0.87	−0.82	−0.84
US	Electricity	−0.54	−0.45	−0.38	−0.36	−0.34	−0.30	−0.28	−0.26	−0.23	−0.19
	Natural gas	−0.36	−0.32	−0.26	−0.27	−0.28	−0.27	−0.23	−0.22	−0.21	−0.17
	Road fuels	−1.30	−1.19	−1.22	−1.16	−1.09	−1.04	−1.01	−0.94	−0.81	−0.69
	Other/indirect	−1.14	−1.06	−1.06	−1.08	−1.08	−1.07	−1.07	−1.06	−1.06	−1.06
	Cash transfers	2.93	1.79	1.34	1.09	0.26	0.21	0.17	0.14	0.11	0.07
	Tax cut	2.54	1.94	1.90	1.55	1.27	1.05	0.87	0.71	0.55	0.33
	Public investment	0.00	0.00	0.00	0.00	0.00	0.00	0.00	0.00	0.00	0.00
	Net change	2.13	0.71	0.31	−0.23	−1.25	−1.41	−1.53	−1.63	−1.65	−1.71

Source: Authors using CPAT.

Note: Carbon taxes are \$25, \$50, and \$75 for low-, middle-, and high-income countries. Revenue recycling: all countries use 30 percent of revenues on cash transfers to bottom four deciles. Remaining revenue use by income group: 70 percent of revenues to labor tax cuts in high-income countries and China; 35 percent for decreasing labor taxes and 35 percent for public investment in middle-income countries; 70 percent on public investment in low-income countries.

Annex 6.5 EU CBAM

The EU is gradually phasing in a CBAM, through a pilot phase from 2023 to 2025 to set up emissions reporting procedures, followed by a 10-year transition period. The CBAM focuses initially on sectors deemed most at risk of carbon leakage, including iron/steel, aluminum, electricity, cement, and fertilizers (sectoral coverage may be expanded later). The CBAM applies at the product level—approximately 50,000 (mostly small) importers will be required to buy emissions certificates at the prevailing ETS price to cover the embedded emissions in products being imported into the EU. This will impose emissions monitoring requirements on exporters to the EU, though in the absence of reporting default emissions factors will be applied.

The CBAM will run in parallel to the current ETS and be operationally equivalent to an import tariff, though the price would be linked to market conditions in the ETS rather than set exogenously. During the 2026–35 transition period, the free ETS allocations would be progressively phased out for the sectors included in the CBAM[13]—for the interim, the CBAM payment is reduced proportionally to the quantity of free allowances in each sector. Importers can deduct, based on verified information from third-country producers, the amount of any carbon price that has already been paid during the production of the imported goods. There is no proposal to grant rebates for ETS payments embodied in EU exports reflecting WTO rules that such rebates are not permissible for regulations like ETSs (see Annex 6.6). Revenue collected from the CBAM will be a source of own resources, initially to pay down debt incurred during the COVID-19 pandemic.[14]

Annex 6.6 Uncertainties Surrounding the Compatibility of BCAs with Trade Law

Legal risks associated with BCAs are difficult to gauge, not least because trade rules were written before the recent attention to them. In principle, WTO rules allow countries to adopt harmonizing measures like BCAs for indirect taxes but whether carbon pricing counts as an indirect tax is unclear, and even more so for ETSs than carbon taxes. There is also uncertainty about whether a charge varying by the exporting country's carbon intensity would violate the most favored nation (MFN) principle, which precludes differentiation based on the country of origin of the imports. If a BCA does not meet these rules, it might still qualify as an exception under Article XX if it is viewed as addressing environmental issues, though strict legal tests must be met in this case.

Possible channels for compatibility of BCAs with WTO rules include (for further discussion, see, for example, Cosbey et al. 2019 and OECD 2020) the following:

- *BCAs with carbon taxes.* Charges on imports accompanying a domestic carbon tax might be characterized as a "customs duty" or a "charge imposed on or in connection with importation" under the General Agreement on Tariffs and Trade (GATT) Article II:2(a) which allows import charges equivalent to domestic taxes. The BCA must, however, be imposed on a specific product or input to that product—it is not clear whether this allows for the taxing of embodied carbon, which might be interpreted as a by-product rather than an input. Moreover, according to Article III:2, the BCA could not exceed the tax rate on "like" domestic products, raising some uncertainty about applying higher charges to imports with higher embodied carbon, unless the latter are interpreted as "unlike" domestic products. Export rebates for carbon taxes might be allowable under the WTO Agreement on Subsidies and Countervailing Measures, footnote 1, which specifies that rebates of domestic indirect taxes (in principle including energy taxes) should not be deemed export subsidies. Again however, the rebate would have to be offered on the same terms to all domestic firms covered by the carbon tax—if "like" products are interpreted by characteristics other than embodied carbon, the no-greater-than requirement would imply the rebate could not exceed the lowest tax rate levied on domestic producers, that is, the rate assessed on the cleanest producer.

- *BCAs with ETSs.* If a BCA requires importers to purchase allowances from a domestic ETS or separate allowance pool, this would likely be considered a form of domestic regulation under GATT Article III:4, which requires that the imported product receive regulatory treatment no less favorable than the like domestic product. Again, if imports are viewed as "like" domestic products requiring allowance purchases according to the carbon content of imports (rather than the carbon content of domestic products), this might breach WTO rules. However, a BCA on exports, taking the form of a rebate for the costs of an ETS, could be considered a prohibited export subsidy if rebates were not available for like products sold domestically—there is no provision in WTO law for border rebates of regulatory costs.

Irrespective of whether the BCA accompanies a carbon tax or an ETS, Article I prohibits discrimination among imports based on their country of origin. If a BCA regime differentiates imports based on country-specific estimates of embodied carbon, rather than applying the same embodied carbon to all countries, it could violate the MFN principle if measures of embodied carbon were viewed as arbitrary—though allowing relatively low-carbon foreign suppliers to request lower BCAs might lower the risks of measurement procedures being viewed as arbitrary. Special treatment for some countries (for example, those meeting ambitious Paris mitigation targets) might also violate the MFN principle, in the absence of an objective test applicable to all. Exemptions for LDCs might be allowed under the WTO's Enabling Clause, if the exemption criteria are based on development indicators, and countries in similar conditions are treated the same way.

Even if a BCA is found to violate other Articles, it may still be allowable under GATT Article XX (General Exceptions). This would apply if, according to subparagraph (a), it is necessary to protect human, animal, or plant life or health or, according to subparagraph (g), it relates to the conservation of exhaustible natural resources. Most analysts see subparagraph (g) as easier to comply with given the requirement to prove necessity in paragraph (a). In effect, any BCA must demonstrate that it is effectively addressing climate change, for example, through containing emissions leakage. The BCA would also need to satisfy the introductory paragraph or "chapeau" of Article XX, which requires that it not be applied in a manner that would constitute "a means of arbitrary or unjustifiable discrimination between countries where the same conditions prevail" and is not "a disguised restriction on international trade." Historically, very few measures have survived scrutiny under the chapeau, underscoring the importance of designing BCAs in a WTO compliant fashion, with the need to rely on the exceptions only as a fallback.

A BCA may fail to satisfy Article XX if it

- *Requires specific policy changes as a basis for exemption from the BCA*. This might constitute arbitrary discrimination under GATT's exceptions provisions because measures tied to country-level policies will punish all producers from targeted countries, regardless of their individual environmental performance. Instead, the BCA should offset the differential between foreign and domestic carbon pricing.
- *Assesses adjustments based on the country of origin, rather than based on objective criteria applicable to all countries.*
- *Implements the BCA without having tried to negotiate in good faith to reach some multilateral solution to the problem of carbon leakage.* Negotiations under the Paris process could arguably be considered steps in this direction.
- *Allows exemptions from the BCA that are not based on the objective of mitigating climate change by preventing leakage.*

Notes

1 Prominent examples include the suspension of large carbon tax increases in France in 2018 following opposition from the "yellow vest" movement and the Ecuador government's reversal of (unanticipated) fuel subsidy reforms in 2019 following widespread protests.

2 Burdens are usually measured relative to household consumption because (1) consumption is more stable over the lifecycle than income (and therefore, viewed as a better measure of household well-being); (2) survey data on cross-household differences in consumption is more reliable than for income, and (3) consumption accounts for differences in local price levels faced by different household groups.

3 Digitalization is helping countries to improve the targeting of social safety nets through better identification of recipients and electronic payments (to bank accounts and mobile phones). See Bird and Hanedar (2023).

4 In cases where benefit systems are indexed to the general price level, there will be some automatic compensation to low-income households for carbon pricing, but it will fall short of the amount needed for full compensation to the extent, for example, that their consumption is financed through non-benefit income.

5 The energy sectors are coal, electricity, natural gas, oil, gasoline, diesel, kerosene, and liquified petroleum gas (LPG), whereas the non-energy sectors are appliances, chemicals, clothing, communications, education, food, health services, housing, paper, pharmaceuticals, recreation/tourism, transportation equipment, public transportation, and other. Aggregate household consumption (which tends to be underreported in surveys) is scaled to be consistent with (more reliable) consumption data in national accounts.

6 Roughly speaking, the share of the indirect burden in the overall burden equals the share of nationwide emissions from the industrial sector, including industrial buildings, embodied carbon in electricity inputs, and goods transportation.

7 Emissions leakage might also result from increased fossil fuel demand in other countries in response to downward pressure on international fuel prices from a group of large emitting countries taking mitigation action. However, because this form of leakage depends on the reduction in aggregate consumption of fossil fuels in mitigating countries, it is not affected by either the type of mitigation instrument or accompanying competitiveness measures.

8 In the EU ETS, for example, industries are classified as EITE if the ETS increases their production costs by at least 5 percent and their trade share with non-EU countries (imports plus exports relative to domestic production) exceeds 10 percent. For other industries, factors like labor costs, availability of resources, and the rule of law likely play a much bigger role than carbon pricing in determining the location of production.

9 Figures from this paragraph are from Parry et al. (2025).

10 The threshold might be based on a portion of a firm's historical emissions.

11 If, for example, allocations are based on past production and emissions rates of relatively low-carbon firms, they will fall short of fully compensating firms with average emissions rates.

12 This perverse incentive is avoided under a firm-level scheme where embodied emissions are based on an average across all their plants, though this approach is more burdensome administratively.

13 2.5 percent of free allowances will be phased out in 2025, rising to 10 percent by 2028, 48.5 percent by 2030, and 100 percent by 2034.

14 For more details on the CBAM, see https://taxation-customs.ec.europa.eu/carbon-border-adjustment-mechanism_en.

References

Aldy, Joseph E. 2017. "Frameworks for Evaluating Policy Approaches to Address the Competitiveness Concerns of Mitigating Greenhouse Gas Emissions." *National Tax Journal* 70 (2): 395–420.

Aldy, Joseph E., and William A. Pizer. 2015. "The Competitiveness Impacts of Climate Change Mitigation Policies." *Journal of the Association of Environmental and Resource Economists* 2: 565–95.

Anil, Ari, Nicolas Arregui, Simon Black, Oya Celasun, Dora Iakova, Aiko Mineshima, Victor Mylonas, et al. 2022. "Surging Energy Prices in Europe in the Aftermath of the War: How to Support the Vulnerable and Speed Up the Transition Away from Fossil Fuels." IMF Working Paper 22/152, International Monetary Fund, Washington, DC.

Aydemir, Oguzhan, and Feyyaz Zeren. 2017. "The Impact of Foreign Direct Investment on CO_2 Emission: Evidence from Selected G-20 Countries." In *Handbook of Research on Global Enterprise Operations and Opportunities*, edited by Mehdi Khosrow-Pour, 81–92. IGI Global. https://www.igi-global.com/chapter/the-impact-of-foreign-direct-investment-on-co2-emission/180761

Bird, Nicolò, and Emine Hanedar. 2023. "Expanding and Improving Social Safety Nets through Digitalization: Conceptual Framework and Review of Country Experiences." IMF Note 2023/007, International Monetary Fund, Washington, DC.

Böhringer, Christoph, Knut Einar Rosendahl, and Halvor Briseid Storrøsten. 2017. "Robust Policies to Mitigate Carbon Leakage." *Journal of Public Economics* 149: 35–46.

Branger, Frédéric, and Philippe Quirion. 2014. "Would Border Carbon Adjustments Prevent Carbon Leakage and Heavy Industry Competitiveness Losses? Insights from a Meta-Analysis of Recent Economic Studies." *Ecological Economics* 99: 29–39.

Burniaux, Jean-Marc, Jean Chateau, and Romain Duval. 2013. "Is There a Case for Carbon-Based Border Tax Adjustment? An applied General Equilibrium Analysis." *Applied Economics* 45: 2231–40.

Carbone, Jared, and Nicholas Rivers. 2017. "The Impacts of Unilateral Climate Policy on Competitiveness: Evidence from Computable General Equilibrium Models." *Review of Environmental Economics and Policy* 1 (1): 24–42.

Clausing, Kimberly, Milan Elkerbout, Katarina Nehrkorn, and Catherine Wolfram. 2024. "How Carbon Border Adjustments Might Drive Global Climate Policy Momentum." Report 24-20, Resources for the Future, Washington, DC.

Clements, Benedict, David Coady, Stefania Fabrizio, Sanjeev Gupta, Trevor Serge Coleridge Alleyne, and Carlo A. Sdralevich, eds. 2013. *Energy Subsidy Reform: Lessons and Implications*. Washington, DC: IMF.

Coady, David, Ian Parry, and Baoping Shang. 2018. "Energy Price Reform: Lessons for Policymakers." *Review of Environmental Economics and Policy* 12: 197–219.

Condon, Madison, and Ada Ignaciuk. 2013. "Border Carbon Adjustment and International Trade: A Literature Review." Working Paper 2013/6, OECD Trade and Environment, Organisation for Economic Cooperation and Development, Paris.

Cosbey, Aaron, Susanne Droege, Carolyn Fischer, and Clayton Munnings. 2019. "Developing Guidance for Implementing Border Carbon Adjustments: Lessons, Cautions, and Research Needs from the Literature." *Review of Environmental Economics and Policy* 13: 3–22.

Dabla-Norris, Era, James Daniel, Masahiro Nozaki, Cristian Alonso, Vybhavi Balasundharam, Matthieu Bellon, Chuling Chen, et al. 2021. "Fiscal Policies to Address Climate Change in Asia and the Pacific." IMF Department Paper 21/07, International Monetary Fund, Washington, DC.

Dabla-Norris, Era, Thomas Helbling, Salma Khalid, Hibah Khan, Giacomo Magistretti, Alexandre Sollaci, and Krishna Srinivasan. 2023. "Public Perceptions of Climate Mitigation Policies: Evidence from Cross-Country Surveys." Staff Discussion Note 2023/002, International Monetary Fund, Washington, DC.

Dechezleprêtre, Antoine, and Misato Sato. 2017. "The Impacts of Environmental Regulations on Competitiveness." *Review of Environmental Economics and Policy* 11 (2): 183–206.

Ellis, Jane, Daniel Nachtigall, and Frank Venmans. 2019. "Carbon Pricing and Competitiveness: Are They at Odds?" OECD Environment Working Paper 152, Organisation for Economic Co-operation and Development, Paris.

Fabrizio, Stefania, Alexei Goumilevski, and Kangni Kpodar. 2016. "A New Tool for Distributional Incidence Analysis: An Application to Fuel Subsidy Reform." Technical Notes and Manuals 16/07, International Monetary Fund, Washington, DC.

Fischer, Carolyn, and Alan K. Fox. 2012. "Comparing Policies to Combat Emissions Leakage: Border Carbon Adjustments versus Rebates." *Journal of Environmental Economics and Management* 64: 199–216.

Fischer, Carolyn, Richard Morgenstern, and Nathan Richardson. 2015. "Carbon Taxes and Energy-Intensive Trade-Exposed Industries: Impacts and Options," In *Implementing a U.S. Carbon Tax: Challenges and Debates*, edited by Ian Parry, Adele Morris, and Roberton Williams. New York, NY: Routledge.

Flannery, Brian, Jennifer A. Hillman, Jan Mares, and Matthew C. Porterfield. 2020. "Framework Proposal for a US Upstream GHG Tax with WTO-Compliant Border Adjustments: 2020 Update." Report 20-14, Resources for the Future, Washington, DC.

Flues, Florens, and Alastair Thomas. 2015. *The Distributional Effects of Energy Taxes*. Paris: Organization for Economic Cooperation and Development.

Furnaro, Andrea, Philipp Herpich, Hanna Brauers, Pao-Yu Oei, Claudia Kemfert, and Wesley Look. 2021. "German Just Transition: A Review of Public Policies to Assist German Coal Communities in Transition." Report 21-13, Resources for the Future and Environmental Defense Fund, Washington, DC.

García-Muros, Xaquín, Jennifer Morris, and Sergey Paltsev. 2022. "Toward a Just Energy Transition: A Distributional Analysis of Low-Carbon Policies in the USA." *Energy Economics* 105: 105769.

Goulder, Lawrence H., Marc A. C. Hafstead, GyuRim Kim, and Xianling Long. 2019. "Impacts of a US Carbon Tax across Household Income Groups: What Are the Equity-Efficiency Trade-Offs?" *Journal of Public Economics* 175: 44–64.

Hassett, Kevin A., Aparna Mathur, and Gilbert E. Metcalf. 2009. "The Incidence of a US Carbon Tax: A Lifetime and Regional Analysis." *Energy Journal* 30: 155–77.

Heine, Dirk, and Simon J. Black. 2019. "Benefits Beyond Climate: Environmental Tax Reform in Developing Countries." In *Fiscal Policies for Development and Climate Action*, edited by Miria A. Pigato, 1–56. Washington, DC: World Bank.

Holzer, Kateryna. 2014. *Carbon-Related Border Adjustment and WTO Law*. Bern: World Trade Institute.

International Monetary Fund (IMF). 2022. "A Greener Labor Market: Employment, Policies, and Economic Transformation." In *World Economic Outlook: War Sets Back the Global Recovery* (April). Washington, DC.

International Monetary Fund (IMF). 2024. *Climate Change Indicator Dashboard*. Washington, DC. https://climatedata.IMF.org

Johnson, Richard W., and Peter Gosselin. 2018. *How Secure Is Employment at Older Ages?* Washington, DC: Urban Institute.

Joltreau, Eugénie, and Katrin Sommerfeld. 2019. "Why Does Emissions Trading under the EU Emissions Trading System (ETS) Not Affect Firms' Competitiveness? Empirical Findings from the Literature." *Climate Policy* 19 (4): 453–71.

Keen, Michael, Ian Parry, and James Roaf. 2022. "Border Carbon Adjustments: Rationale, Design and Impact." *Fiscal Studies* 43: 209–34.

Kopp, Raymond, William A. Pizer, and Kevin Rennert. 2023. "Carbon Border Adjustments: Design Elements, Options, and Policy Decisions." Working Paper, Resources for the Future, Washington, DC.

Kortum, Samuel, and David Weisbach. 2017. "Border Adjustments for Carbon Prices." *National Tax Journal* 70: 421–46.

Levinson, Arik. 2019. "Energy Efficiency Standards are More Regressive than Energy Taxes: Theory and Evidence." *Journal of the Association of Environmental and Resource Economists* 6: S7–S36.

Mehling, Michael A., Harro van Asselt, Kasturi Das, Susanne Droege, and Cleo Verkuijl. 2019. "Designing Border Carbon Adjustments for Enhanced Climate Action." *American Journal of International Law* 113 (3): 433–81.

Misch, Florian, and Philippe Wingender. 2021. "Revisiting Carbon Leakage." IMF Working Paper 21/207, International Monetary Fund, Washington, DC.

Morris, Adele. 2016. "Build a Better Future for Coal Workers and Their Communities." Climate and Energy Economics Discussion Paper, Brookings Institution, Washington, DC.

Neuhoff, Karsten, and Robert A. Ritz. 2019. "Carbon Cost Pass-Through in Industrial Sectors." Working Paper 1935, Energy Policy Research Group, Cambridge Judge Business School, University of Cambridge.

Nordin, Ida, Frederik Wilhelmsson, Torbjörn Jansson, Thomas Fellmann, Jesús Barreiro-Hurle, and Mihaly Himics. 2019. "Impact of Border Carbon Adjustments on Agricultural Emissions–Can Tariffs Reduce Carbon Leakage?.". Selected paper prepared for presentation at the 2019 Summer Symposium: Trading for Good–Agricultural Trade in the Context of Climate Change Adaptation and Mitigation: Synergies, Obstacles and Possible Solutions, co-organized by the International Agricultural Trade Research Consortium (IATRC) and the European Commission Joint Research Center (EU-JRC), June 23–25, 2019 in Seville, Spain.

Organisation for Economic Co-operation and Development (OECD). 2020. *Climate Policy Leadership in an Interconnected World: What Role for Border Carbon Adjustments?* Paris: OECD.

Organisation for Economic Co-operation and Development (OECD). 2024. *Greenhouse Gas Footprint Indicators*. Paris. https://www.oecd.org/en/data/datasets/greenhouse-gas-footprint-indicators.html

Parry, Ian, Simon Black, Danielle Minnett, and Karlygash Zhunussova. 2025. "Policies to Decarbonize Industry while Addressing Competitiveness and Carbon Leakage." CESifo Working Paper 12272, Munich, Germany.

Parry, Ian, Peter Dohlman, Cory Hillier, Martin Kaufman, Kyung Kwak, Florian Misch, James Roaf, et al. 2021. "Carbon Pricing: What Role for Border Carbon Adjustments?" IMF Staff Climate Note 2021/004, International Monetary Fund, Washington, DC.

Pauwelyn, Joost, and David Kleimann. 2020. "Trade Related Aspects of a Carbon Border Adjustment Mechanism. A Legal Assessment." European Parliament, Policy Department for External Relations, Directorate General for External Policies of the Union, Brussels, Belgium.

Peñasco, Cristina, Laura Díaz Anadón, and Elena Verdolini. 2021. "Systematic Review of the Outcomes and Trade-Offs of Ten Types of Decarbonization Policy Instruments." *Nature Climate Change, Nature* 11 (3): 257–65.

Pirlot, Alice. 2022. "Carbon Leakage under International Climate Change Law: Myth, Environmental Risk, or Economic Problem?" Unpublished manuscript, Centre for Business Taxation, Saïd Business School, Oxford.

Pizer, William A., and Steven Sexton. 2019. "The Distributional Impacts of Energy Taxes." *Review of Environmental Economics and Policy* 13 (1): 104–22.

Shang, Baoping. 2023. "The Poverty and Distributional Impacts of Carbon Pricing: Channels and Policy Implications." *Review of Environmental Economics and Policy* 17: 64–85.

Sterner, Tomas, ed. 2012. *Fuel Taxes and the Poor: The Distributional Effects of Gasoline Taxation and Their Implications for Climate Policy*. Washington, DC: Resources for the Future.

Venmans, Frank, Jane Ellis, and Daniel Nachtigall. 2020. "Carbon Pricing and Competitiveness: Are They at Odds?" *Climate Policy* 20 (9): 1070–91.

Verde, Stefano F. 2020. "The Impact of the EU Emissions Trading System on Competitiveness and Carbon Leakage: The Econometric Evidence." *Journal of Economic Surveys* 34: 320–43.

Williams, Roberton C., III, Hal Gordon, Dallas Burtraw, Jared C. Carbone, and Richard Morgenstern. 2015. "The Initial Incidence of a Carbon Tax Across Income Groups." *National Tax Journal* 68: 195–213.

World Bank Group (WBG). 2018. *Groundswell: Preparing for Internal Climate Migration*. Washington, DC.

7 Supporting Policies

Main Messages

- Decarbonizing the global economy requires significant investments across sectors. Projected global investment needs aligned with achieving net zero emissions by mid-century are about $5 trillion annually in 2030 (4 percent of GDP) compared with recent levels of under $1 trillion. Much of the needed investment is redirected (rather than additional) and most should be mobilized privately through appropriate price signals.
- Public investment needs are generally modest relative to potential revenues from carbon pricing. Indeed, a mitigation strategy with carbon pricing can substantially improve fiscal balances on net for emerging market economies. Moreover, much of the public investment can be financed through user fees at the sectoral level (rather than general budgets), whereas various energy conservation measures (for example, peak period electricity pricing) can reduce infrastructure needs.
- Even with aggressive carbon pricing, the advancement of low-carbon technologies may be hindered by various market impediments at different stages, including basic research, applied R&D by firms, demonstration, and deployment.
- A package of complementary technology policies is needed, comprising:
  For advanced and large emerging market economies, funding for basic energy research; (well designed) demonstration projects; and a mix of patents, (general) R&D subsidies, and technology prizes.

DOI: 10.4324/9781003755012-7
This chapter has been made available under a CC-BY-NC-ND license.

For countries in general, a mix of transitory/technology-specific incentives (where there is significant scope for moving down learning curves for critical technologies like direct air capture), and permanent/technology-neutral deployment incentives; energy efficiency awareness programs; and financing instruments (for example, to amortize investment costs in household energy bills).

- Governments may wish to promote domestic production of low-carbon sectors (for example on national security grounds) through green industrial policies. But the domestic demand, fiscal, and potential trade retaliation implications of different policy designs need to be carefully weighed.
- Additional measures may be needed where state-owned enterprises produce electricity. Besides governance and market reform, these might include performance standards (to force abatement where price signals have limited effects) and internal carbon pricing within these enterprises (to guide cost-effective mitigation investments).
- Financial sector policies are not a substitute for, but can reinforce the effectiveness of, pricing carbon emissions. Examples include information on firms' climate risks (to help investors efficiently allocate capital), market frameworks for financial instruments like green bonds, and, especially for developing countries, carefully targeted instruments like loan guarantees to leverage private investments.
- Energy producers face substantial revenue declines under aggressive global decarbonization scenarios and need broad economic and revenue diversification strategies. A coordinated carbon tax on exports from energy producers would help but is challenging to maintain.

Public Investment

How Large Are Total (Public and Private) Investment Needs for Mitigation?

Investment needs for getting on track with a global transition to net zero emissions are subject to much uncertainty (because of uncertainty over future cost of low-carbon technologies) but broadly speaking (see Figure 7.1) public and private investment combined needs to be scaled up from $0.9 trillion in 2020 (4 percent of total investment) to about $5 trillion annually by 2030 (5 percent of global GDP). About two-thirds of the needed investment is in the energy sector, notably power generation/distribution (about half of energy sector investment) and energy efficiency (about a quarter). Investment needs for developing countries, where external support is important, are an estimated $2 trillion in 2030, or $1.2 trillion excluding China, a fivefold increase from 2020 levels.

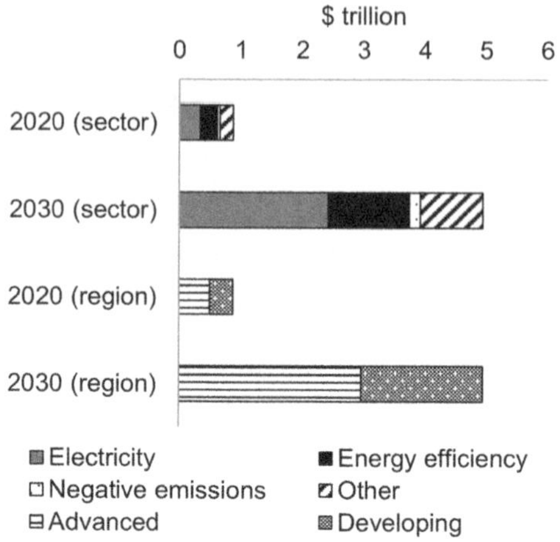

Figure 7.1 Gross Investment for Mitigation Needed for Net Zero Emissions.
Source: Black et al. (2024) complied from International Energy Agency and other sources.
Note: Investment needs are consistent with a pathway to net zero emissions by 2050.

There are some important caveats to these projections:

- Especially for advanced economies with mature energy systems, much of the needed investment is from redirecting existing investment, for example, generators expanding renewable rather than fossil capacity, steel producers investing in an electric arc rather than a coal furnace, or from households purchasing an electric rather than gasoline vehicle.[1] A substantial overall increase in investment is required, however, for example: because of the need for accelerating retirement of existing, emissions-intensive, or low energy efficiency capital before it would be retired on pure economic grounds; to make retrofits (like building insulation, heat pumps, and possibly carbon capture technologies); to provide enabling infrastructure (see the following section); and (especially for some developing countries) to meet rising energy demands.
- Estimates for public investments feature a hump-shaped pattern over time (IMF 2021) with the increase concentrated over the next two decades (for example, with construction of power grid infrastructure for renewables) and declining thereafter to mid-century.
- For energy efficiency investments, investment costs exclude offsetting future energy savings.

How Much Investment Is Needed from the Public Sector?

Ideally, most of the investment for mitigation would be privately financed (from firms, households, and the financial sector) given: the dominant scale and scope of global private capital markets; with the right price signals, the private sector can allocate most investments cost-effectively (see Chapter 3); and the macro context of limited fiscal space and historically high public debt. There is, however, a potentially important role for the public sector in several regards.

- *Network externalities*: These refer to infrastructure investments by one firm that potentially benefit other firms and households where the investing firm may lack incentives to consider these benefits—as a result, these investments may be undersupplied by the private sector, even with a robust carbon price. For example, a generator making the initial investments in a network of high-voltage transmission lines to link up renewable sites to the grid may not be able to entirely capture (through charging user fees) all the benefits to subsequent renewables investors that use the network. Similarly, a firm constructing a pipeline to supply it with hydrogen, or dispose of its captured CO_2 emissions, may be unable to capture the full benefits to other firms establishing new pipeline investments that tap into the original pipeline. And an electric vehicle (EV) seller might invest in public charging stations for reducing range anxiety, because this can increase demand for its own vehicles, but the seller may not account for benefits to other EV sellers whose customers might also use the charging facilities.
- *State-owned capital*: The public sector also has a role where it has some ownership and influence over investment decisions for capital in the energy sector. State-owned enterprises (SOEs)—companies that are either wholly or majority-owned by a government—currently make about 50 percent of global investments in fossil fuel generation and electricity networks (IEA 2020) (SOEs are discussed in the following section). Less importantly, governments are responsible for (emissions-saving) investments in publicly owned buildings and vehicle fleets.
- *Financing low-carbon technology subsidies*: For political acceptability reasons, governments may prefer to use subsidies financed centrally (rather than sectoral user fees) to promote private investments (for example, in the building sector).

Leaving aside the past rationale, studies suggest that, globally, the public share of climate investment should in 2030 be about 10–20 percent—realistically, in developing countries, the share will likely be much higher, given the public share (excluding China) was more than 50 percent in 2021 (see Figure 7.2). Public infrastructure investments will need to be carefully coordinated and sequenced with private investments where there are important synergies (for example, public investments in batteries to store power from intermittent sources and enhance grid reliability).

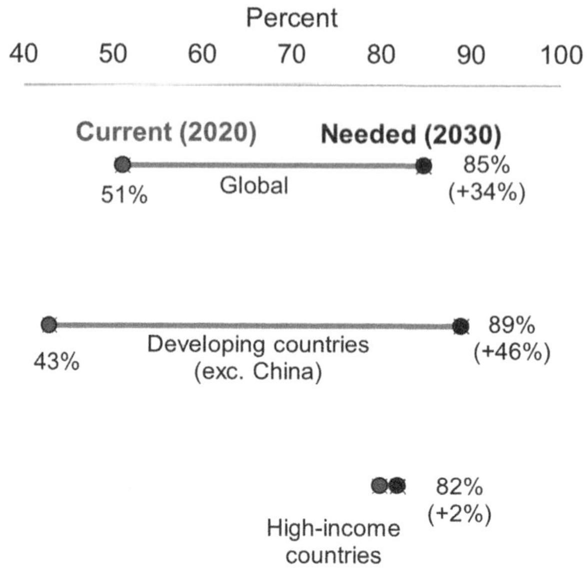

Figure 7.2 Private Sector Share in Investment Needs.

Source: Black et al. (2024) based on various sources.

How Do Investment Needs Affect Fiscal Balances?

In advanced economies, public investment costs are put at about 0.2 percent of GDP a year in coming decades (IEA 2022). In developing countries where SOEs are more common in the energy sector, a larger share of low-carbon technology investments may be reflected in government accounts, though future shares will depend on the pace of energy sector liberalization—assumptions in Figures 7.1 and 7.2 imply public investment needs for these countries of about 0.3 percent of GDP in 2030.[2]

These public investment figures are small relative to potential revenues from carbon pricing and (in most cases) are less than revenue losses due to erosion of preexisting fuel taxes—they are about the same size as transfers needed to compensate low-income households for carbon pricing (see Figure 7.3). Concerns about the budgetary implications of public investment should therefore not hold up an aggressive mitigation strategy, at least one that is not top-heavy with subsidies.

Moreover, it is more efficient to finance public investments (and low-carbon technology subsidies) through sectoral user fees rather than subsidize them from public budgets (see Chapter 3). This would help promote the efficient allocation of capital and other resources across different sectors of the economy (rather than favoring one sector with public subsidies). For example, investments in supportive infrastructure for renewables could be recouped in charges for renewable energy or in higher electricity tariffs, whereas costs for EV charging station infrastructure could be reflected in charges for using the stations.

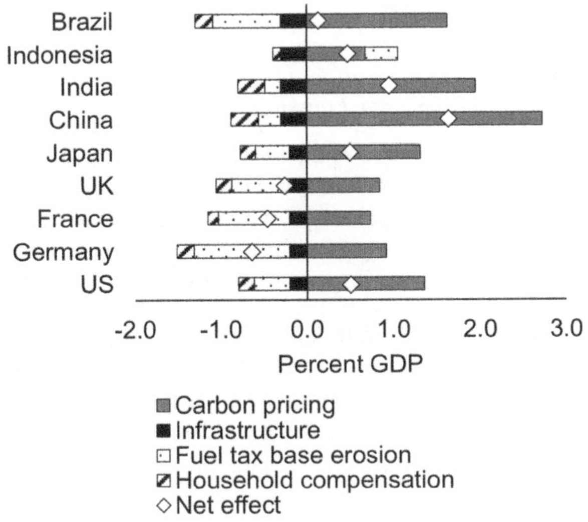

Figure 7.3 Effect of Public Investment on Fiscal Balances, 2030.

Source: Black et al. (2024) and authors.

Note: Estimates are for carbon prices of $75, $50, and $25 in high-, middle-, and low-income countries, respectively.

How Can Governments Reduce the Need for Infrastructure Investments?

Complementary measures might also reduce infrastructure spending needs. For example, in the power sector, there are a diverse range of measures that can reduce needs for on-grid generation capacity such as:

- *Incentives for rooftop solar*—encouraging households to install off-grid renewable energy systems reduces on-grid capacity requirements.
- *Time-of-day pricing*—smooths demand over the course of the day thereby reducing the need for extra capacity to meet peak demand.
- *Permitting reforms*—can ensure the availability of renewables sites with least need for complementary infrastructure to integrate them into the grid.
- *Energy storage*—batteries and pumped hydro can facilitate integration of intermittent renewable power into the grid reducing overall capacity needs.
- *Improving transmission efficiency*—reducing resistance of power lines through higher transmission voltages or larger size wires can reduce efficiency losses thereby reducing capacity needs for a given delivered electricity demand.
- *Limiting electricity use in EVs*—electricity demand for these vehicles can be moderated by including them in (future) systems to charge motorists per km driven and by applying user fees at public charging stations.
- *Limiting electricity use in heat pumps*—electricity demand for heat pumps can be reduced through accompanying incentives for insulation upgrades to buildings.

Technology and Industrial Policies

What Obstacles Hinder Development and Deployment of Low-Carbon Technologies (Even with Aggressive Emissions Pricing)?

Innovation is needed to improve scalability and affordability of existing technologies and fill remaining technology gaps. The development and deployment of low-carbon technologies may involve four main stages with potential impediments at each stage—even with an aggressive carbon price—which implies a need for supplementary policy instruments.[3]

- *Basic research*: This research (conducted by universities, other nonprofits, government laboratories, and firms) develops knowledge laying the groundwork for future advances in unproven or currently costly technologies that may ultimately be essential for low-carbon transitions. Firms underinvest in this basic knowledge because of its high risks and the inability to capture spillover benefits of new knowledge to other firms.
- *Applied research and development (R&D)*: Applied R&D (by firms) seeks to develop (major or incremental) technologies, products, or processes to meet a specific, identifiable need. Again, even with a robust carbon price, firms tend to underinvest in low-carbon technology R&D because they cannot capture all the (potentially substantial) spillover benefits to other firms who might copy new technologies or use knowledge embodied in them to further their own R&D efforts (IMF 2016b).
- *Demonstration*: Demonstration projects seek to prove the viability of newly developed technologies at commercial scale. Particularly for major technologies (like a large coal plant with carbon capture and storage), firms might underinvest in demonstration projects because of their inability to capture the rewards to other firms from knowledge generated during design and construction of these first-of-a-kind facilities.
- *Technology deployment*: Even after demonstrations have validated the commercial viability of new technologies, their deployment may be hindered by a variety of further impediments, including:

  1. *Learning-by-doing spillovers*—early adopters of a new technology may be unable to appropriate the benefits to latter adopters of the technology because the former learn how to produce or use the technology more efficiently.[4]
  2. *Economies of scale*—with demand for new technologies initially limited, firms may be reluctant to produce them if large-scale production is required to minimize unit production costs (for example, unit costs may not be minimized at car factories until production levels reach about 20,000 vehicles a year).
  3. *Consumer undervaluation of lifetime energy savings*—some analysts suggest that consumers excessively discount future energy savings from

energy-efficient investments, though the issue is unsettled in the literature (see Annex 7.1).

4 *Uncertainty over long-range emissions prices*—even if carbon taxes or emissions trading systems (ETSs) with price floors are in place, long-range emissions prices may be uncertain (for example, perhaps a government less committed to climate mitigation may come to power) which can deter long-lived, low-carbon investments.
5 *Uncertainty over future electricity prices*—may deter investments in low-carbon generation plants.
6 *Other impediments to energy-efficient investments*—these might include mismatches between those who pay for investments and those benefiting from them (for example, landlords versus tenants), and constraints on the ability of households and firms to finance investment costs through borrowing.

Table 7.1 summarizes the impediments along with policy responses, which are discussed in the following section, whereas Chapter 9 discusses barriers to international technology diffusion.

Should Governments in High-Income or Large-Emerging Market Economies Ramp Up Basic Research and Demonstration Projects?

Fiscal outlays for basic research into low-carbon energy technologies are about $30 billion per year globally, mostly in high-income countries and China (IEA 2020). In principle, governments might compare current spending with estimates of efficient levels of basic research using detailed evaluations of technical opportunities, costs of research efforts, likelihood of success, and the ultimate climate and economic benefits—but this can be unrealistic in practice, given how far technologies are from the market. Nonetheless, governments could still act like a venture capitalist in taking risk-weighted bets on different technologies, supporting those that are working out but abandoning those that are failing. Based on potential opportunities for technological advance and plausible assumptions about the rate of return on such spending, some analysts recommend a significant expansion of well-directed basic energy research, at least for the EU and the United States (for example, Newell 2015, Dechezleprêtre and Popp 2017, Armitage et al. 2023, Cervantes et al. 2023). A gradual and sustained ramp-up is preferable to a large, once-and-for all increase, to allow time for training of new scientists and engineers and to lower risks of diverting this specialized labor away from important research for non-energy sectors.

As for public funding of large-scale demonstration projects, caution is needed given some prominent failures in the past[5] and limited R&D budgets. Nonetheless, there may be a rationale for public support of a limited number of well-designed, first-of-a-kind projects, where the purpose is for generating substantial new knowledge.

Table 7.1 Market Impediments to Clean Technology Development and Deployment and Policy Responses

Stage of Technology Development		*Market Impediment*	*Recommended Policy Instruments*	*Country Relevance*
Far from Market ↑	Basic research	Firms do not capture spillover benefit to other firms from new knowledge	Gradual ramping up of government funding for basic research into clean energy	↑ Advanced/large emerging market
	Applied R&D at firms	Innovators do not capture spillover benefits to other firms that might copy new technologies or use knowledge embedded in them	Combination of (i) patents and subsidies/tax credits for general R&D and (ii) prizes for breakthrough low-carbon technologies	
	Demonstration (large projects)	Demonstrators do not capture spillover benefits to other firms from knowledge generated in developing first-of-a-kind facilities	Public support for limited number of projects with potential to generate substantial new knowledge	
	Deployment	Learning-by-doing spillovers, scale economies	Temporary, technology-specific subsidies, preferably financed by higher user fees	
		Consumer undervaluation of energy efficiency	Consumer awareness campaigns; permanent, technology-neutral feebates/performance standards	
		Uncertainty over long-range emissions prices	Carbon contracts for difference	
		Uncertainty over future electricity prices	Ensuring investor revenue (e.g., power purchase agreements)	
Close to Market ↓		Mismatch between investor/ energy user, borrowing constraints	Novel financing mechanisms (e.g., allowing amortization in energy bills)	↓ All countries

Source: Authors.

What Instruments Can Promote Applied R&D into Low-Carbon Technologies?

R&D policies are also most relevant for high-income and large emerging market economies. There are three main instruments, including:

- *Intellectual property rights.* Almost all countries have patent systems granting exclusive rights (typically for 20 years) for products or processes providing a new way of doing something, or a new technical solution to a problem. The patent holder can either preclude other firms from using the technology for the duration of the patent or license the technology to other firms for a fee. Patent systems are best suited for new technologies that are (1) difficult to anticipate in advance (at least for governments) and (2) difficult for other firms to legally imitate about the scope of the original patent. And patents are relatively straightforward for governments to administer because granting of patent rights is determined by legal processes. Diffusion of technologies under patent may, however, be severely limited (though knowledge disclosed in patent applications can be used by other firms).
- *R&D subsidies.* These instruments are commonly applied, for example, in the form of tax credits for general R&D expenditures against corporate taxes—the fiscal outlays are on average about 0.2 percent of GDP per year for advanced economies (OECD 2024). R&D subsidies can encourage firms to develop technologies whose benefits might be large but are subject to substantial uncertainty (which could deter incentives to develop these technologies under patents). Targeting subsidies to low-carbon energy R&D may not be practical if governments cannot easily monitor whether scientists and engineers at individual firms are engaged in R&D efforts for low-carbon technologies as opposed to other technologies and products (with mainly commercial rather than environmental benefits). And even if targeting were practical, it may not be desirable if the severity of knowledge spillovers is similar across energy and non-energy technologies.
- *Technology prizes.* These instruments (which are less common) would provide prizes for developers of specific new technologies (or more basic advances). They can work well for technologies that are identifiable in advance, which is the case for many critical mitigation technologies (like battery storage, carbon capture, direct air capture, hydrogen). And prizes can attract a diverse and potentially effective range of innovators from the private sector (including industry or individual entrepreneurs, universities, and other research institutions), whereas R&D tax credits are limited to corporations. Prizes can be administratively complex, however, because a different prize must be specified for each potential technology, related to its expected benefits, which in turn depends on how many firms or households might adopt it and its benefit per adoption (in terms of cutting emissions or lowering the costs of cutting emissions). Prizes are best limited to a few key breakthrough technologies, perhaps (where it is difficult for governments to project future use of the technology) with a subsidy paid each time the technology is adopted.

In short, a mix of the three instruments is likely needed, given that no one instrument is effective at mobilizing the full diverse range of potential low-emissions technologies.

What Instruments Can Promote Deployment of Low-Carbon Technologies?

Deployment policies are potentially applicable for any country implementing a mitigation strategy. The different market impediments at this stage, however, call for different responses, both in terms of instruments and their design:

- *Technology-specific incentives, progressively phasing out over time*—are needed to address learning-by-doing spillovers and scale economies, given the severity of the market impediments varies by technology and decline as the technology penetrates the market. A possibility is technology-specific adoption subsidies, preferably financed through higher user fees for the sector (see the discussion regarding Table 3.12)—adoption subsidies are more flexible than production or sales mandates which force adoption of the new technology, even if future costs are higher than expected.
- *Awareness campaigns*—such as labeling requirements for appliances and vehicles, can inform households (and firms) of the benefits from more energy-efficient products and technologies.
- *Permanent instruments, neutral with respect to low-carbon technologies*—these can reinforce awareness campaigns where policymakers believe energy savings from general energy efficiency improvements are being undervalued. Options include feebates and performance standards (again see Chapter 3).
- *Carbon contracts for difference (CCfDs)*—these contracts associated with low-carbon investments seek to address uncertainty over long-range emissions prices by either the government paying the investor for the difference during periods when the prevailing market price is below a "strike price" or requiring payments from them if the carbon price is above the strike price. In this way, CCfDs transfer risks from uncertain emissions prices from the investor to the government.[6]
- *Ensuring investor revenue*—measures might include purchasing power agreements where a third party invests in and operates a (clean) generation plant in return for a guaranteed price per kWh over the length of the contract, typically 6–30 years (ideally, these agreements are specified in a stable currency, accounting for fiscal risks and grid capacity). Other measures to encourage low-carbon generation could include setting prices using a competitive process like an auction, connecting markets to increase market access, or anything else that signals a government commitment to investors to ensure that large initial investments will pay off over extended project lifetimes (Jaumotte et al. 2024).

- *Financial instruments to ease borrowing constraints*—in the context of buildings, these might include (fiscal incentives to promote) instruments that amortize investment costs over time, for example, on-bill financing and energy-as-a-service models (where investment costs are paid over time in monthly energy bills or out of energy savings), or green mortgages offering lower monthly payments for buildings achieving higher energy performance ratings.[7]

What Is the Appropriate Scale of Deployment Policies?

As regards deployment subsidies to address learning-by-doing, one way to automatically reduce them over time as technologies mature is to base them on gaps between current production costs and estimated production costs over the longer run, once learning opportunities have been fully exploited. Based on a simple analytical model described in Annex 7.2, meant to roughly span plausible scenarios for the pace of learning-by-doing and the long-run potential for diffusing a new, low-carbon technology across a market, Figure 7.4 illustrates the effect of different levels of per unit production subsidies (as a percent of the cost gap) on diffusion of the technology after 10 years

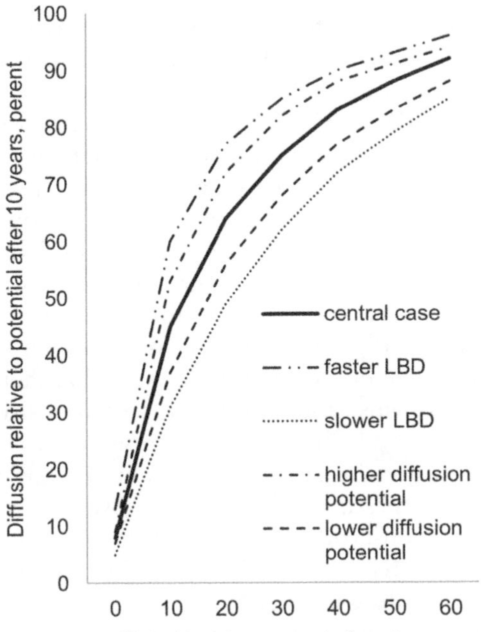

Figure 7.4 Effect of Deployment Subsidies on Speeding Up Technology Diffusion.

Source: See Annex 7.2 for explanation of underlying model and different scenarios.

Note: Cost gap is the difference between the prevailing production cost and the (estimated) production cost when learning opportunities have been fully exploited. LBD = learning-by-doing.

relative to its deployment potential over the longer run. With no subsidy, diffusion rates after 10 years are modest, typically about 5–15 percent of long-run diffusion potential. But even with modest subsidies, diffusion rates are substantially increased under all scenarios, to about 30–60 percent of long-run potential with a 10 percent subsidy and 50–75 percent with a 20 percent subsidy. In short, there appears to be strong case for such transitory subsidies to speed up diffusion rates of technologies (like direct air capture) with potential to move down learning curves.

As regards feebates and performance standards to address possible undervaluation of energy efficiency benefits, the efficient policy incentive is simply the consumer price for the energy product, multiplied by the fraction of energy-saving benefits from higher efficiency that consumers do not consider. For example, this incentive would be equivalent to an additional CO_2 price of $100–150 per ton for policies targeted at vehicle sales for gasoline prices of between $0.7 and 1.1 per liter and an illustrative assumption that consumers fail to consider one-third of lifetime fuel-saving benefits from more efficient vehicles.[8]

Should Governments Foster Domestic Production of Low-Carbon Technologies through Green Industrial Policy?

Green industrial policies refer to government strategies to promote domestic production of low-carbon technologies—recent examples include the US Inflation Reduction Act and the EU Green Deal (see Annex 7.3). Economists generally favor free trade over industrial policies to promote domestic industries because this allows firms and households to purchase products from the lowest-cost suppliers, but there are exceptions to this. For example, governments may wish to promote domestic production of low-carbon technologies, products, product components, or raw materials (like solar panels, EVs, batteries, lithium) on national security grounds to avoid becoming overly dependent on other countries (who might then leverage that dependence for other purposes)—especially where trading partners explicitly or implicitly (through lax environmental/labor standards) subsidize their own production. This makes more sense when the country has a natural advantage (for example, Argentina, Bolivia, and Chile have large reserves of lithium).[9]

A variety of alternative instruments (see Table 7.2 for a summary) might be used to promote domestic production of a low-carbon technology/product, including tariffs, non-tariff barriers,[10] subsidies for domestic production that may or may not have domestic content requirements, and feebates (domestic production subsidies financed by taxes on domestic production of emissions-intensive substitutes for the low-carbon technology/product). Most of these instruments aside, for example, from domestic consumption subsidies applying to domestic and foreign supply alike, risk similar retaliatory measures being adopted in trading partners. Some instruments may strongly increase domestic consumption of the low-carbon technology/product (consumer subsidies with no domestic content requirements) or increase it

Table 7.2 Comparing Instruments for Green Industrial Policy

Metric	*Policy Instrument*					
	Tariff	*Non-tariff Barrier*	*Domestic Production Subsidy*	*Consumer Subsidy: No Domestic Content Requirement*	*Consumer Subsidy: Domestic Content Requirement*	*Feebate for Domestic Producers*
Promotes domestic production of clean product/ technology	A: Incentivizes domestic production	A: Incentivizes domestic production	A: Incentivizes domestic production	N: Incentivizes domestic and foreign production	A: Incentivizes domestic production	A: Incentivizes domestic production
Promotes domestic consumption of clean product/ technology	D: Raises domestic prices	D: Raises domestic prices	N: Moderately lowers domestic prices	A: Strong consumption effect	N: Moderately lowers domestic prices	N: Little effect
Revenue	A: Raises revenue	N: No impact	D: Loses revenue	D: Loses revenue	D: Loses revenue	N: Little impact
Reaction of foreign governments	D: Likely increases risk of retaliation	D: Likely increases risk of retaliation	D: Likely increases risk of retaliation	N: No risk as it does not discriminate against foreign production	D: Likely increases risk of retaliation	N: Unclear

Source: Authors.

Note: A indicates an advantage of an instrument, D a disadvantage, and N neither an advantage nor a disadvantage.

moderately (production subsidies, consumer subsidies with domestic content requirements, feebates) through lowering consumer prices. Tariff and non-tariff barriers, by contrast, have the opposite effect by reducing demand. Tariffs raise revenue however, whereas other instruments can be revenue neutral or lose revenue. Whichever instrument is employed, it should be designed to phase out over time as domestic production matures.[11]

Scaling up production and operation of low-carbon technologies will also require adequate scientific, engineering, information technology, or other expertise among the labor force. Although to some extent growth in demand for specialized labor will lead to wage adjustments that encourage greater supply (through more people acquiring the necessary college degrees or training), some government coordination will likely be needed (for example, through educational and training programs, immigration policy, and promotion of female labor force participation).[12]

Energy and Financial Market Reforms

Energy Market Frictions

How Common Are Energy Market Frictions from SOEs?

SOEs are the most common element of government control in energy markets and account for about one-sixth of global greenhouse gases (GHGs) (Clark and Benoit 2022). By country, China by far accounted for the largest share of SOE emissions (70 percent), followed by Russia (4 percent) and India, Indonesia, South Africa, and Korea (3 percent each). And by sector, power generation by far accounted for the largest share of SOE emissions (85 percent), followed by oil and gas extractors (10 percent, mostly methane leaks), and transport (2 percent, for example, national air companies). See Figure 7.5.[13]

How Does the Operation of SOEs Differ from That of Private Companies and How Does This Affect Their Response to Mitigation Policies?

Especially for the power sector, where SOEs may be involved at both the generation and transmission/distribution stage, the operation of SOEs may differ from that of private sector firms, for example (see also Benoit 2019):

- *Objectives*: private firms have incentives to minimize production costs and maximize profits, whereas SOEs may instead have social objectives like holding down electricity prices for households and firms or meeting production and employment targets.
- *Funding*: private firms raise funds from capital markets and are free to allocate it cost-effectively across investment opportunities, whereas financial assistance for SOEs may come from budgetary transfers, government equity injections, targeted credit lines, and preferential lending, all with more restrictions on what investments can be made.

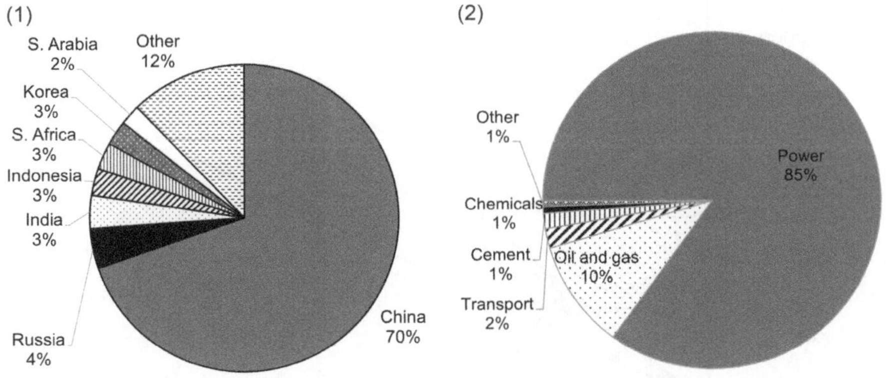

Figure 7.5 Sources of Global GHG Emissions from State-Owned Enterprises, 2017. Panel 1. By Country, Panel 2. By Sector.

Source: Clark and Benoit (2022).

Note: Data are for enterprises where governments have majority ownership and exclude private production in energy markets subject to price regulation.

- *Price setting*: in liberalized power sectors, carbon tax revenues/allowance rents and the costs of cutting emissions tend to be passed forward in higher electricity prices, whereas in SOEs these costs might at least in part be reflected in losses covered by government budgets (at least for ad hoc, rather than automatic, pricing regimes—see Annex 5.4).

These features lead to two potential inefficiencies in the response of SOEs to mitigation instruments.

- *Excessive mitigation costs*: if there is no automatic mechanism for prioritizing cost-effective investment and other efficient behavioral responses to cut emissions, SOEs may face a steeper, inefficient marginal abatement cost schedule for cutting emissions, resulting in excessive costs for a given emissions reduction.
- *Inadequate incentives to cut emissions*: under mitigation instruments that put a price on emissions, including carbon taxes, (cross-sectional) ETSs, and feebates, SOEs may lack incentives to cut emissions up to the point where incremental mitigation costs equal the emissions price. For example, an SOE whose principal mandate is power production may be reluctant to switch to intermittent renewable fuels because this may reduce certainty over production levels.

For both reasons (excessive costs and inadequate mitigation incentives), there may be a large shortfall between efficient and actual emissions reductions (see Figure 7.6).

The extent of excessive costs and abatement shortfalls will vary considerably with the specific characteristics of the SOE and the type of market. For

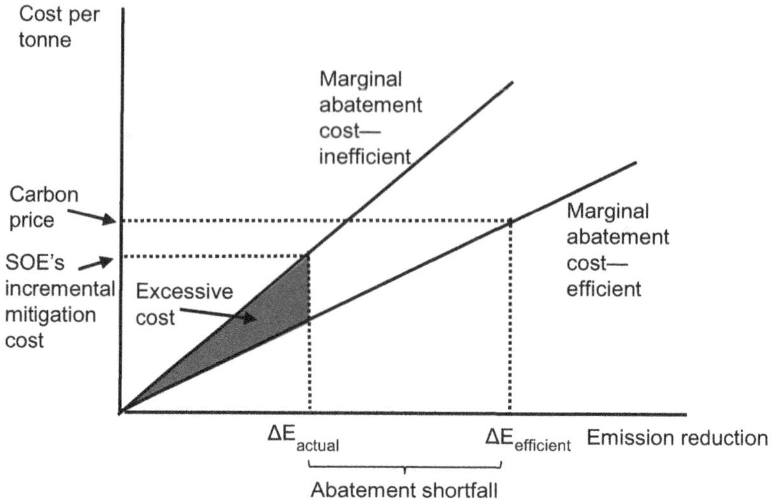

Figure 7.6 Excessive Costs and Abatement Shortfalls under State-Owned Enterprise.
Source: Authors.

example, some SOEs are protected from competition and are subject to substantial government control, whereas others operate in market-based systems with other competitors and have more latitude to make cost-effective investment decisions—carbon pricing may work reasonably well in the latter case.

What Complementary Measures Might Be Needed for Energy Markets Dominated by SOEs?

Complementary measures might include:

- *Governance and market reform*: one possibility is to combine carbon pricing with changes to the governance of SOEs (for example, allowing them to behave more like cost minimizing/profit maximizing firms) and market liberalization (allowing more competition in energy production and market-determined prices). Realistically, however, although both reforms can promote more efficient allocation of resources, they may be more gradual, rather than on the time frame needed for effective mitigation policy—and they may be limited anyway, for example, if governments wish to retain control over electricity pricing.[14]
- *Regulatory approaches*: another possibility is to complement carbon pricing with regulatory instruments that force emissions reductions, regardless of how SOEs are operating.[15] Of the instruments in Table 3.2, the preferred option would be a performance standard to reduce the emissions intensity of the SOE (this provides more flexibility in cutting emissions than a specific technology mandate).[16] The SOE should not be allowed to

purchase credits from other sectors in lieu of meeting the standard because this will likely lead to too little abatement in the SOE and excessive abatement elsewhere—moreover, the performance standard by itself does not provide mechanisms for cost-effective emissions reductions.

- *Shadow pricing investments*: this involves internal assessments within SOEs of emissions reductions from alternative investment options and the costs per ton of CO_2 reduced, which can help guide more cost-effective mitigation decisions.[17] International support could also help SOEs develop marginal abatement cost schedules for different investment possibilities.

In short, some combination of the last two measures may help largely address the two inefficiencies highlighted in Figure 7.6, even if there is limited progress on the first measure (insufficient access to capital for SOEs is discussed in the following section).[18]

Financial Markets

What Is the Importance of Climate Information Architecture?

A fundamental function of financial markets is to price risks associated with investing in different organizations to support informed and efficient capital-allocation decisions by investors, lenders, and insurance underwriters. By providing high-quality, reliable, and comparable data, climate information architecture can provide critical information about how climate risks on both the effects and mitigation side may affect asset values and the profitability of investment opportunities—conversely, weak climate information architecture reduces market transparency and increases risks of greenwashing (where firms or investments are less environmentally friendly than they appear). Climate information architecture has a key role in enhancing the effectiveness and efficiency of emissions pricing policies, but not substituting for them (IMF 2023)—information can be included in annual financial reports that companies are routinely required to make public.

Ideally, these reports should discuss board and management oversight and assessment of climate risks and opportunities; how these risks factor into the business and financial planning strategy; the process for identifying climate-related risks and how they are incorporated in the overall risk management; and targets and metrics used to assess risks (see Table 7.3).

One key metric is a firm's direct and indirect emissions, which encompass:

- *Scope 1 emissions*—direct emissions from on-site fuel combustion in company-owned vehicles, furnaces, diesel generators, and so on, as well as process emissions, for example, for cement and chemical producers.
- *Scope 2 emissions*—indirect emissions from electricity, steam, heat, and cooling purchased from utilities or other suppliers.

Table 7.3 Recommended Climate Information Architecture

	Recommended Information
Governance	Board and management assessment and oversight of climate-related risks and opportunities.
Strategy	Impacts of short-/long-term climate-related risks and opportunities on business strategy/financial planning under different climate change and mitigation policy scenarios.
Risk Management	Process for identifying, assessing, and managing climate-related risks and how they are integrated into the organization's overall risk management strategy.
Metrics and Targets	Metrics and targets for assessing and managing climate-related risks and opportunities, including scope 1, scope 2, and perhaps scope 3 emissions, and risks from current and future policies affecting these emissions.

Source: Adapted from TCFD (2017).

- *Scope 3 emissions*—all other indirect emissions associated with assets or activities that may affect a firm's value chain, but that are not owned or controlled by the firm, such as emissions embodied in material inputs purchased from other firms (like metals and chemicals), transportation for products and employees, and end-of-life disposal of the firm's products.

Investors need to know what companies might be doing to cut their scope 1 emissions, the costs of these strategies, and how future government policies affecting scope 1, 2, and 3 emissions might affect firm profits. A starting point is common standards, such as those in the GHG Protocol methodology (see https://ghgprotocol.org/tools-resources), for measuring these carbon footprints across different organizations.

Should Governments Promote Low-Carbon Financial Instruments Like Green Bonds?

Green bonds are the most prominent financial instrument on the climate mitigation side (and are also used for adaptation).[19] Green bonds differ from conventional bonds in that the funds are earmarked for purposes like climate mitigation (for example, renewable energy, solar panels, sustainable transportation, eco-friendly buildings) or broader environmental projects (like climate adaptation and biodiversity conservation). Green bond issuances by corporations, local and central governments, and financial institutions have exceeded $500 billion a year globally since 2021, compared with about $50 billion in 2014 with most issues from Europe, Asia-Pacific (mainly China), and North America (see Figure 7.7).

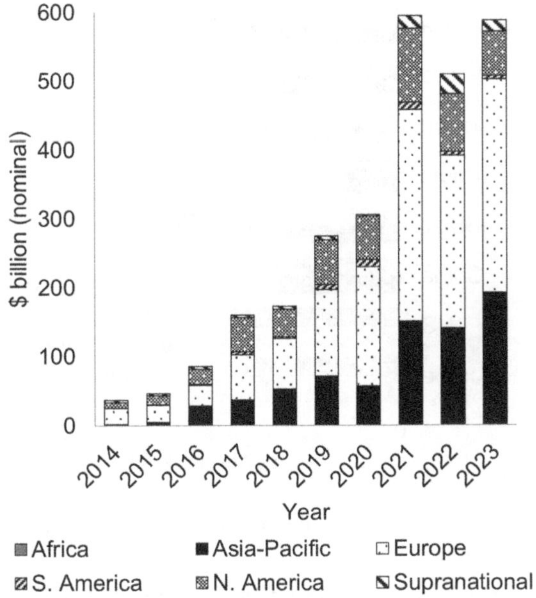

Figure 7.7 Value of Green Bonds Issued by Region, 2014 to 2023.

Source: https://www.climatebonds.net/market/data

Green bonds can mobilize funding for mitigation projects by matching them to investors with a preference for environmental investments and can facilitate bond issues with longer maturities (for low-carbon investments with long horizons), potentially lowering borrowing costs relative to conventional bonds.[20] However, green bonds involve greater administrative burdens as emissions savings (or other environmental benefits), and use of proceeds, need to be verified.

In general, governments should be cautious about promoting green bonds through fiscal incentives, because this can distort the allocation of investment, for example, creating a bias in favor of bond- rather than equity-financed investments (the former tend to have lower risk but lower expected returns). Instead, government policy might focus on green bond frameworks, describing how the sovereign will govern its green bond process, third-party validation of emissions reductions, and legal or contractual protection for investors against risks of fund mismanagement.[21]

How Can Capital Costs for Developing Countries Be Reduced?

High borrowing costs can be a major barrier to adoption of low-carbon technologies with high upfront costs. The problem is especially pervasive in developing countries where macroeconomic, currency, political, and other risks yield significantly higher interest rates.[22] For example, the levelized cost (capital and operating costs averaged over the lifecycle) of renewables

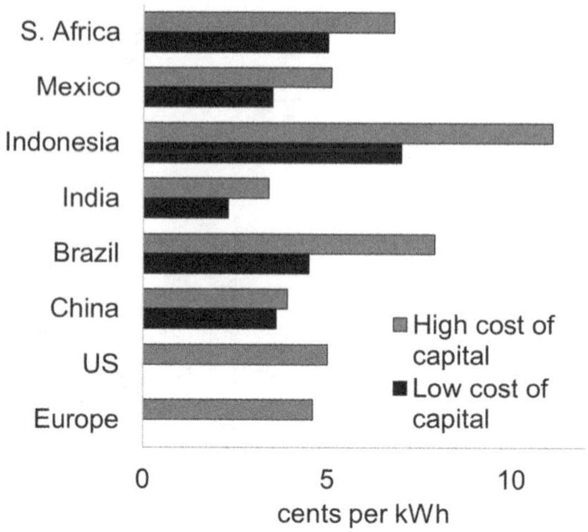

Figure 7.8 Levelized Costs of Renewable Generation with Lower Capital Costs.

Source: Black et al. (2024).

Note: High and low capital costs are those reflective of current capital costs in developing and advanced economies, respectively, for a stylized 100-megawatt solar plant. Estimates are prior to the rise in interest rates that started in 2022.

generation in developing countries (excluding China) could be reduced by about a quarter to a third if they had access to capital at the same rate as advanced economies (Figure 7.8).

Capital costs for developing countries might be reduced through structural policies to strengthen macroeconomic fundamentals (like reducing inflation and currency risks), deepen financial and capital markets, improve policy predictability, foster institutional and governance frameworks, promote flexible labor markets, streamline business regulations, promote free trade, improve tax capacity, and credit ratings, and so on. These reforms can both lower the emissions intensity of GDP (by enabling faster growth of services and other low-carbon sectors) and increase the responsiveness of emissions to mitigation policies (by strengthening policy credibility and enabling firms to respond more dynamically to price signals) (see Budina et al. 2023, Cai et al. 2024).

A shorter-term possibility is blended finance where national governments or international financial institutions fund instruments that leverage private investment (in SOEs and other organizations) by improving its risk-return profile. A common example of such de-risking tools is loan guarantees providing legally binding commitments to pay (some or all) the debt if a borrower defaults.[23] Such guarantees, however, result in contingent liabilities, which cause fiscal risks if the central government is the guarantor. Again, international support could help countries assess the cost-effectiveness of, and therefore prioritize funding across, potential investment projects.

What Makes Financing Needs for Power Generation Unique in Developing Countries?

Additional economic- and policy-related risks can further increase financing costs for the power sector in developing countries. Renewable energy investments often take a decade to become profitable, and electricity can rarely be traded across borders, which exposes investors to the host country's macroeconomic conditions (like foreign exchange risks)—these issues are further exacerbated when the primary electricity purchaser is an SOE with low credit rating.[24] Other sector-specific risks include, for example, whether the grid is flexible enough to incorporate more intermittent renewables and reaches areas with high renewables potential, land availability and tenure, the general financial solvency of the sector across the value chain, information on resource quality (mostly wind strength), uncertainty over whether the fixed cost of entering a market can be spread over several investments.

In addition to blended finance (on a project-by-project basis), a comprehensive, long-term strategy to provide the scale and integrated planning needed to meet energy access and decarbonization goals in many low-income countries might include:[25]

- A plan for least-cost transmission and generation investments, accounting for the grid's ability to accommodate intermittent renewables, shadow pricing for carbon and local air emissions, and fiscal risks.[26]
- Adjusting regulations to allow private sector investment in generation and competitive tenders with model contracts, both of which can promote transparent procurement at a low cost.
- Location- or substation-specific competitive tenders, where the government identifies the site based on least-cost planning, grid connections and flexibility, and availability of land rights, can help address land tenure or resource certainty issues.
- Improving the financial solvency of the power sector, through progressively aligning tariffs with supply costs and reducing transmission/distribution losses, to reduce investment costs and risks related to uncreditworthy off takers.

Issues for Energy-Producing Countries

What Are the Potential Revenue Losses to Fossil Fuel Exporters from Global Mitigation?

Fossil fuel-exporting countries face additional challenges because of the vulnerability of their fiscal positions and economic structure to the global energy transition.[27] Potentially affected countries are highly concentrated in Africa, the Middle East and Central Asia, and South America—indeed in more than half of fossil fuel-exporting countries, commodity tax revenues contribute more than 50 percent of total fiscal revenues and a quarter of these countries have fossil fuel exports greater than 25 percent of GDP (IMF 2023b). In contrast, some of the largest producers (for example, Canada, China, and the United States) have more diversified economies.

Figure 7.9 illustrates effects on revenues to selected fossil fuel producers under a net zero (1.5°C aligned) scenario with falling prices. All countries face large revenue declines by 2030—and 10 countries could face revenue reductions upward of 80 percent by 2040 (for example, Equatorial Guinea, Iraq, and Oman).

Should Energy Exporters Levy Carbon Taxes?

At first glance, levying a carbon tax on fossil fuel production appears to make sense for exporters because this would factor climate costs into exploration/development decisions, while potentially appropriating some revenues from energy importers (who might otherwise tax the fuel imports). Administratively, a carbon tax would be a straightforward modification of existing fiscal regimes for extractives, which commonly include a royalty component based on the value of production. On closer inspection, however, implementing an effective carbon tax on fuel production is quite challenging.

Applying the tax retroactively to existing projects may not be feasible, because stability clauses in contracts often preclude subsequent adjustments to fiscal regimes. Moreover, if exporters act unilaterally, and take prices in international fuel markets as given, the carbon tax would be fully borne by domestic producers (rather than passed forward to foreign consumers in higher prices). And if (as seems a reasonable approximation) existing fiscal regimes are optimally designed to trade extra fiscal revenues against the costs of deterring exploration and development, adding a new carbon tax will cause excessive taxation overall for the extractive sector.

If, however, major energy exporters collude over a carbon tax to exploit their joint market power, some of the tax will be reflected in higher international fuel prices, and exporters can be better off on net. The relative stability of Organization of the Petroleum Exporting Countries (which accounts for about 40 percent of global oil production) and its existing institutional structure could reduce the initial setup cost of such a system. Maintaining the agreement could be challenging, however, given incentives for individual exporters to "free ride" and not levy the tax (to avoid deterring domestic production), whereas they still benefit from higher international prices.

This free-rider problem might be avoided if energy-importing countries with carbon pricing were also part of the agreement and charged a lower carbon price on imports previously subject to a carbon tax in the extracting country (and a full carbon price on imports from other countries). Besides the difficulty of coordinating a large group of (exporting and importing) countries, however, individual exporters may have an incentive to undercut the agreement by offsetting the agreed carbon tax through subtle adjustments to

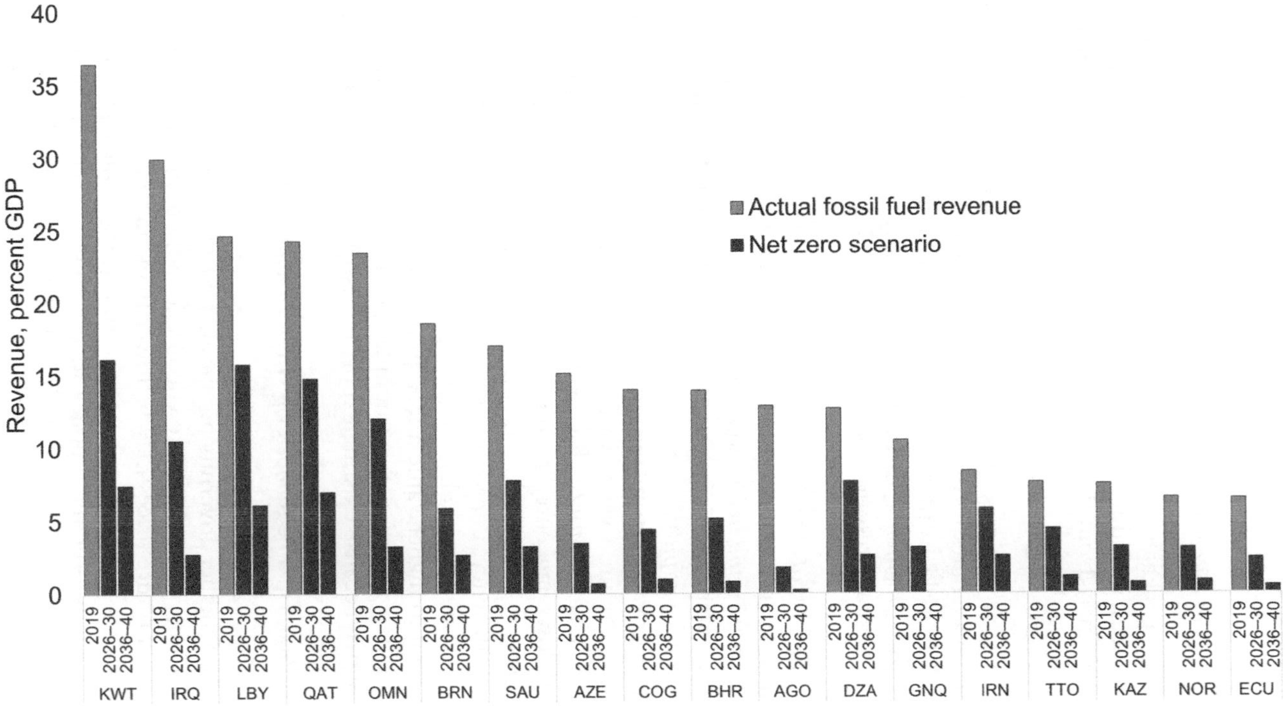

Figure 7.9 Fiscal Revenues for Selected Fossil Fuel Producers under a Net Zero Transition Scenario.

Source: Updated from IMF (2023b).

Note: Figure uses country-level data on fossil fuel production, prices, and costs under the International Energy Agency's net zero scenario to estimate net cash flows. These flows are then split between the government and investor according to a country's fiscal regime (such as royalties and production sharing arrangements between national and private companies). The framework uses the Fiscal Analysis of Resource Industries library of fiscal regime parameters and project-level financial models. See IMF (2023b), Annex 1 for details.

other elements of the fiscal regime (which may be difficult to monitor)—again, the country would then benefit from higher international prices without the deterrent effect of higher domestic taxation.

What Are the Elements of a Revenue Diversification Strategy?

Appropriate policy packages and sequencing of reforms will vary with national circumstances, including which main fuel a country exports and current diversification away from the extractive sector. Elements might include (see IMF 2016a):

- *Adjustments to fiscal regimes* such as shifting the mix from production-based to profit-based taxes if countries wish to extend the life of fossil fuel reserves (this shifts risks from investors to the government).
- *Strengthening fiscal resilience* through building fiscal buffers and frameworks to better manage resource wealth (for example, through sovereign wealth funds).
- *Enhancing resilience of the financial sector to energy price volatility* through strong regulatory, supervisory, and macroprudential frameworks.
- *Pro-growth regulatory and institutional frameworks* such as removing regulatory barriers to competition, trade integration, and labor market flexibility.
- *Promoting an enabling public sector* through, for example, infrastructure investments for growth sectors and limiting the size of the public sector workforce and premiums over private sector wages.
- *Promoting a diverse economy*, for example, through streamlining tax structures and lowering entry requirements to mobilize foreign direct investment; deepening integration in global value chains through enhancing production efficiency, improving technological capacity, and ensuring wage competitiveness; and enhancing vertical diversification in existing sectors by shifting to higher value-added products.
- *Targeting green technologies*, for example, green hydrogen production might be attractive because existing export infrastructure could be used.

Should Fossil Fuel Production Be Ramped Up Given Downward Pressure on Future Prices?

One further issue is whether governments should take measures, like relaxing permitting and leasing requirements, to encourage more mining and drilling for fossil fuels, given future prices may be lower than current prices. Private investors will, however, consider future price projections in their investment and extraction decisions—the main policy focus should instead be on maintaining optimal fiscal regimes, supported by other environmental and safety measures. For example, for shale gas extraction, regulations are needed to prevent drilling in environmentally sensitive areas and to ensure proper procedures and technologies are used to limit risks of water pollution, seismic activity, and harm to wildlife from ongoing operations—ex post liability can also play a role in penalizing non-compliance with regulations or unanticipated environmental hazards.[28] Also, the project design phase should ensure proper management of methane and other emissions related to extraction, partly to protect competitiveness because importers increasingly consider the emissions intensity of fossil fuel production.

Suggestions for Further Reading

- *Investment needs.* On total investment needs for net zero transitions, see IEA (2023) and IRENA (2023) and on public sector needs, see IMF (2021).
- *Effects of fiscal balances of comprehensive mitigation strategies.* See Black et al. (2024) for a discussion of how mitigation strategies with carbon pricing, public investment, compensation for low-income households, and international transfers on net affect fiscal balances in different countries.
- *Technology policies.* See Dechezleprêtre and Popp (2017) and Newell (2015) for overviews of technology policy for climate mitigation in the EU and the United States, respectively. Fischer and Newell (2008) compare the efficiency of mitigation and technology policies at reducing emissions. Barwick et al. (2025) discuss the role of government incentives in driving down EV battery costs by 90 percent.
- *Energy paradox.* For more discussion of the energy paradox and how households value energy savings, see Allcott and Greenstone (2012), Allcott and Wozny (2014), Gerarden et al. (2017), and Leard et al. (2023). On the design of subsidies for low-carbon technology deployment, see Newell et al. (2019).
- *Industrial policies.* For a discussion of recent trends in industrial policies more generally (not just green policies), see Ilynia et al. (2024).
- *Mitigation policies and regulated energy markets.* For further discussion of how ETSs work in regulated energy markets, see Acworth et al. (2020).
- *Financial market measures.* See Jaumotte et al. (2024) and Prasad et al. (2022) for broad discussions of mobilizing private finance for climate action in emerging market and developing countries. On climate information architectures, see IMF (2023a), NGFS (2021, 2022), Greenstone et al. (2023), TCFD (2017), and WBG, IMF, and OECD (2023). For guidance on climate disclosures specifically for central banks, see NGFS (2021). Ando et al. (2022) discuss green bond markets. Lim et al. (2024) discuss strategies to mobilize climate finance in the Asia-Pacific region. Budina et al. (2023) and IMF (2023a) discuss structural reforms to promote low-carbon transitions in developing countries.
- *Energy exporters.* See Baunsgaard and Vernon (2023) on modeling fiscal implications of global decarbonization for energy producers. IMF (2016a) and Puyo et al. (2024) discuss revenue diversification strategies for fossil fuel exporters.

Annex 7.1 Do Households Undervalue Energy Efficiency?[29]

The "energy paradox" refers to the observation that many energy efficiency investments that are seemingly cost-effective, that is, the discounted lifecycle energy savings from them exceed their upfront costs, are not adopted by the private sector, especially households. Put another way, households discount future energy savings at excessive rates.

Various explanations have been proposed to explain the energy paradox. Most of them do indeed suggest a market impediment warranting policy intervention, though there is a need for more definitive evidence about the extent and exact nature of any energy paradox.

For example, consumers may have short horizons (and not consider energy savings over the full lifetime of the investment), limited information about energy-saving benefits, or limited ability to calculate future energy savings costs from the information they have. On the latter, there is some evidence, for example, of the incorrect belief that increasing fuel economy from say 15 to 16 km per liter provides the same future fuel savings as increasing it from 10 to 11 km per liter. Consumers may also omit energy efficiency when buying vehicles because they have too many other attributes to process (acceleration, cabin space, payload, navigation systems, color, and so on). Or they may be mistrustful of claimed energy savings, doubtful about future prices, or uncertain they are able to fully recoup energy efficiency improvements when they sell vehicles, properties, and other energy capital.

Other potential explanations for the energy paradox, however, do not imply a market imperfection. For example, assessments of the cost-effectiveness of energy efficiency investments in engineering studies might miss "hidden costs," such as reduced acceleration in more fuel-efficient vehicles. Other hidden costs might include those associated with implementing new technologies, such as marketing, maintenance, and retraining mechanics. And hidden costs might arise if consumers discount energy-saving benefits at above market rates because of uncertainty over future energy prices or energy savings.

Research on the energy paradox remains inconclusive. In the context of vehicles, laboratory experiments suggest that consumers are confused by the fact that cost savings are linear in liters per km—not km per liter, which is often the way vehicle efficiency is reported—whereas surveys suggest that many consumers have limited knowledge about the fuel economy of their current vehicles, their future driving pattern, and how to discount fuel savings. Although these findings suggest that consumers may inaccurately assess energy-saving benefits, the direction of any bias is unclear. Tests of market behavior in the United States provide an even murkier picture. Implicit discount rates for new vehicle fuel economy have been estimated at up to about 20 percent, which is broadly consistent with estimated implicit discount rates for other energy durables. However, the rate of a private automobile loan was about 10–15 percent during their sample period in the studies, suggesting that high implicit discount rates may largely reflect borrowing costs. Given that credit markets for automobile loans are extensive and competitive, these high rates may simply reflect default risks, rather than market impediments. Another branch of the literature uses fuel price variation to test whether vehicle prices adjust by as much as predicted when consumers fully value fuel economy, but again the findings are mixed.

Annex 7.2 Illustrative Model of Learning-by-Doing

This annex develops a simple dynamic model of learning-by-doing associated with use of a new, low-carbon technology to illustrate the effects of deployment subsidies under alternative scenarios. The model consists of the following four equations:

$$c_t = (c_0 - \bar{c}) \cdot (1 - \eta)^{Q_{t-1}} + \bar{c} \tag{7.1}$$

$$Q_t = Q_{t-1} + q_{t-1}, Q_0 = 0 \tag{7.2}$$

$$q_t = (q_0 - \bar{q}) \cdot \left(\frac{c_t - s_t - \bar{c}}{c_0 - \bar{c}} \right) + \bar{q} \tag{7.3}$$

$$s_t = \beta \cdot (c_t - \bar{c}) \tag{7.4}$$

where t denotes a time period with $t = 0$ the initial period. c_t is the per unit cost from producing with the low-carbon technology before any government subsidy. q_t is the fraction of industry output that is produced with the new low-carbon technology (for example, the share of power generation produced with renewable power). Q_t is cumulative production with the low-carbon technology. And s_t is a government subsidy for the low-carbon technology per unit of production. c_0, $\bar{c}$, η, Q_0, q_0, $\bar{q}$, and β are parameters.

According to equation 7.1, the unit production cost for the new technology declines over time from its initial level c_0 and converges to a least-cost achievable level $\bar{c}$ because cumulative use of the technology, or learning-by-doing, increases. η determines the rate at which costs decline in response to cumulative production or learning-by-doing. Equation 7.2 simply shows that cumulative production with the new technology increases with use of the technology in each period. In equation 7.3, production levels for the low-carbon technology converge over time from an initial level q_0 to a maximum level $\bar{q}$ because production costs, net of any subsidy, decline over time toward $\bar{c}$. A larger $\bar{q}$ implies production levels are more responsive to reductions in production costs. In equation 7.4, the production subsidy in a period is a fixed fraction β of the difference between current production costs and the minimum production cost so the subsidy phases out over time because the technology moves down the learning curve.

Diffusion of the technology in the initial period q_0 is set at 1 percent of the market (implicitly because of policy and economic factors). Three other assumptions determine the effect of deployment subsidies:

- The ratio of $\bar{c}$ to c_0, that is, the scope for learning-by-doing over the long term to lower production costs from their initial level ($\bar{c}$ is necessarily positive because of construction and operating costs that cannot be reduced through learning). In the central case, $\bar{c}$ is taken to be 25 percent of c_0, with lower and higher cost scenarios of 10 and 50 percent. For comparison, the costs of solar panels declined nearly 90 percent between 2010 and 2020, whereas the costs of on- and off-shore wind declined about 60–70 percent (Black et al. 2024, Annex G).
- The maximum potential for diffusing the technology when learning-by-doing has been fully exploited. In the central case, $\bar{q}$ is taken to be 75 percent of the market with lower and higher diffusion scenarios of 60 and 90 percent.
- The speed with which costs fall in response to learning-by-doing. In low, central, and high-value cases η is set at 0.002, 0.003, and 0.004, respectively, implying that each 1 percent increase in cumulative output reduces the cost gap by 0.2, 0.3, and 0.4 percent, respectively—this is consistent with estimates of learning curves for solar, wind, and electric batteries, respectively (Way et al. 2022). The central case implies, with other central case assumptions and a 50 percent subsidy for the cost gap ($\beta = 0.5$), that least costs are fully achieved within 33 years. The lower and higher values for η imply (for the same assumptions about other parameters) least costs are achieved within 49 and 25 years, respectively.

Given the previous scenarios, different values for β are chosen to explore how different levels of subsidy affect how quickly technology costs fall, and the technology diffuses, over time.

Annex 7.3 Recent Examples of Green Industrial Policy

The 2022 Inflation Reduction Act (IRA)[30] formed the centerpiece of the US climate mitigation strategy under the Biden Administration. The law directed federal funding over a 10-year period to low-carbon energy (especially for low-carbon electricity and transmission, followed by low-carbon transportation), mostly through tax credits.

- Fifty-five percent of the funding was for corporations, including \$30 per megawatt-hour (MWh) for new zero-carbon generation (progressively reducing to \$15 per MWH in 2035); \$15 per megawatt-hour (MWh) for new nuclear; \$1.75 per gallon for sustainable aviation fuel; and \$3 per kg for low-carbon hydrogen.

- Consumer incentives included tax credits of up to: $7,500 and $4,000 for new and used EVs and 30 percent of the costs of emissions- and energy-saving upgrades in homes.

Many tax incentives contained domestic production or procurement requirements—for example, 80 percent of the critical minerals for EV batteries must have been recycled in the United States (or a country with a free trade agreement with the United States) for the vehicle to qualify for the full credit and the battery must have been manufactured in the United States.

The EU argued the IRA's tax credit for EVs and manufacturing subsidies for battery and wind turbine producers violate World Trade Organization rules. In response, the EU has proposed the Green Deal Investment Plan (see https://commission.europa.eu/strategy-and-policy/priorities-2019-2024/european-green-deal_en), containing €250 billion in tax breaks to further boost private sector renewable investment, along with loosening of the bloc's state aid rules.

Notes

1 Currently these investments are about $2 trillion globally (IEA 2022).

2 In practice, even within country groupings, public investment needs will vary, for example, with the carbon intensity of GDP and the share of power generation in economywide emissions—the numbers used in the previous section are illustrative.

3 For further discussion of these impediments, see, for example, Armitage et al. (2023), Newell (2015), Oman and Svartzman (2021), Pigato et al. (2020), Stern and Stiglitz (2021).

4 For many low-carbon technologies, unit production costs decline over time with greater experience using the technology—for example, solar costs declined by about 90 percent in 2010s (Way et al. 2022).

5 US examples include the Synthetic Fuels Corporation (a federally funded operation lasting only six years in the 1980s that failed to develop any synthetic fuel manufacturing projects); the Clinch River Breeder Reactor (in the early 1980s, the largest public-works project in the United States, which was eventually abandoned); and FutureGen (a federally subsidized project to demonstrate coal generation with carbon capture that was suspended in 2015).

6 CCfDs are drawn up as follows: firms assess the costs of alternative low-carbon investments per ton of CO_2 reduced; the government auctions carbon contracts for projects (for example, 10 years for hydrogen-based steel), with firms bidding down the strike price based on expected project costs; CCfD-winning projects are bankable and face lower market and political risk; and after investment, governments and CCfD-holding firms remunerate each other (for example, on an annual basis) for differences between the strike and prevailing emissions price. CCfDs are gaining in popularity, for example, the EU and Norway plan to implement them to support the rollout of hydrogen in steel and other industries.

7 See Arregui et al. (2020) and Burke et al. (2019) for more discussion of these instruments.

8 Formula is from Parry et al. (2014), illustrative gasoline prices are from Chapter 5, Figure 5.2, divided by the gasoline emissions factor from Chapter 2, Table 2.2.

9 Evidence suggests green industrial policies can also have larger competitiveness and innovation benefits than similar policies targeting non-green products (Baquie et al. 2025, Box 2).
10 For example, regulations that penalize foreign supply, such as restrictions on allowable sockets for charging EVs.
11 See IMF (2024a) for a broader discussion of principles for designing green industrial policy.
12 See Alexander et al. (2024) for further discussion.
13 Besides presence of SOEs, government intervention in energy markets through price regulation is also common, including in markets dominated by private firms. A common pricing regime is to allow private firms to reflect average production costs per unit in higher prices, including explicit charges on unabated emissions from carbon taxes or allowance purchases, but not the rents from feely allocated allowances—this provides a further rationale for auctioning allowances in ETSs.
14 Another possibility (that might be implemented in the short term) is to link executive compensation to progress on (ideally cost-effective) emissions reduction.
15 Governments can also leverage their ownership rights to convey to executives the importance they attach to complying with such regulations.
16 A further possibility is an absolute emissions quota allowing the SOE to both reduce production levels as well as the emissions intensity of production to meet the regulation, though reducing production may contradict the SOE mandate.
17 Various energy SOEs around the world are now using shadow carbon pricing (Benoit 2019).
18 Even where power generation is privately supplied, governments may regulate electricity prices to limit market power by, for example, restricting firms to charge for their average production cost. An implication for mitigation policy is that generators may be able to pass forward carbon tax payments or ETS allowance purchases in higher prices but not the market value of freely allocated allowances, implying ETSs with free allocation are less efficient because they do not exploit reductions in electricity demand (see Burtraw et al. 2001).
19 Other instruments include green loans, equity finance, and debt for climate swaps (see WWF 2018; Rose 2021; CBI 2023). Sustainable bonds are broader than green bonds because the proceeds can also be used for social projects like supporting vulnerable groups (see IMF 2024b).
20 These cost differentials appear modest, however (Ando et al. 2022).
21 Many countries have issued green bond frameworks (see CBI 2019; Ferreira et al. 2021). ICMA (2021) provides standards for issuers of green bonds (such as transparency on use and management of proceeds, process for project evaluation and selection, and reporting) that are commonly used.
22 Recent interest rates on external borrowing have on average been three times more for developing countries than for developed countries (UN 2022).
23 According to Yahmed et al. (2024), loan guarantees can lower private investors' cost of capital from 25 to 15 percent for a high-risk country.
24 WBG (2024) find that about three-quarters of utilities in sub-Saharan Africa and half in Asia have below investment grade credit ratings (see also IRENA 2023).
25 See IMF (2023a) and WBG (2024). Given changing costs of technology and economic conditions, it is important to revisit the strategy at a pre-defined frequency, so that it adapts to structural changes and provides certainty to investors.
26 Either explicitly through formal guarantees or implicitly because the utility's beneficial owner—these risks are elevated when state-backed utilities sign long-term power purchase agreements to pay for electricity in a stable foreign currency.

27 Meeting global temperature goals implies most of the currently proven coal, oil, and gas reserves will need to remain unexploited (IEA 2021).
28 See Daniel et al. (2017) for a comprehensive discussion of environmental measures for shale gas extraction.
29 This annex, and the literature discussed, which mostly focuses on vehicles, is based on the review in Parry and Small (2015).
30 For further discussion of the IRA, see Bistline et al. (2023).

References

Acworth, William, Mariza Montes Anatole de Oca Carlotta Piantieri Boute, and Felix Christian Matthes. 2020. "Emissions Trading in Regulated Electricity Markets." *Climate Policy* 20 (1): 60–70. https://doi.org/10.1080/14693062.2019.1682491

Alexander, Naomi-Rose, Florence Jaumotte, Longji Li, Jorge Mondragon, Sahar Priano, and Marina Mendes Tavares. 2024. "The Green Future: Labor Market Implications for Men and Women." Working Paper 2024/156, International Monetary Fund, Washington, DC.

Allcott, Hunt, and Michael Greenstone. 2012. "Is There an Energy Efficiency Gap?" *Journal of Economic Perspectives* 26: 3–28. https://doi.org/10.1257/jep.26.1.3

Allcott, Hunt, and Nathan Wozny. 2014. "Gasoline Prices, Fuel Economy, and the Energy Paradox." *Review of Economics and Statistics* 96 (5): 779–95. https://doi.org/10.1162/REST_a_00419

Ando, Sakai, Chenxu Fu, Francisco Roch, and Ursula Wiriadinata. 2022. "Sovereign Climate Debt Instruments: An Overview of the Green and Catastrophe Bond Markets." IMF Staff Climate Note 2022/004, International Monetary Fund, Washington, DC.

Armitage, Sarah C., Noël Bakhtian, and Adam B. Jaffe 2023. "Innovation Market Failures and the Design of New Climate Policy Instruments." Working Paper 31622, National Bureau of Economic Research, Cambridge, MA.

Arregui, Nicolas, Ruo Chen, Christian H. Ebeke, Jan-Martin Frie, Daniel Garcia Macia, Dora M. Iakova, Andreas Jobst, et al. 2020. *Sectoral Policies for Climate Change Mitigation in the EU*. Washington, DC: International Monetary Fund.

Baquie, Sandra, Yueling Huang, Florence Jaumotte, Jaden Kim, Rafael Machado Parente, and Samuel Pienknagura. 2025. "Industrial Policies: Handle with Care." Staff Discussion Note 2025/002, International Monetary Fund, Washington, DC.

Barwick, Panle Jia, Hyuk-Soo Kwon, Shanjun Li, and Nahim B. Zahur. 2025. "Drive Down the Cost: Learning by Doing and Government Policies in the Global EV Battery Industry." Working Paper 33378, National Bureau of Economic Research, Cambridge, MA.

Baunsgaard, Thomas, and Nate Vernon. 2023. "Climate Change Mitigation and Extractive Industries: Scenario Analysis of Revenue Implications." Unpublished, International Monetary Fund, Washington, DC.

Benoit, Philippe. 2019. *Engaging State-Owned Enterprises in Climate Action*. New York, NY: Center on Global Energy Policy, School of International and Public Affairs, Columbia University.

Bistline, John E.T., Neil R. Mehrotra, and Catherine Wolfram. 2023. "Strategic Climate Cooperation and Greenhouse Gas Price Coordination." *Brookings Papers on Economic Activity* 1: 77–182.

Black, Simon, Ruud de Mooij, Vitor Gaspar, Ian Parry, and Karlygash Zhunussova. 2024. "Fiscal Implications of Global Decarbonization." Working Paper 24/45, International Monetary Fund, Washington, DC.

Budina, Nina, Christian Ebeke, Florence Jaumotte, Andrea Medici, Augustus J. Panton, Marina M. Tavares, and Bella Yao. 2023. "Structural Reforms to

Accelerate Growth, Ease Policy Trade-Offs, and Support the Green Transition in Emerging Market and Developing Economies." Staff Discussion Note 2023/007, International Monetary Fund, Washington, DC.

Burke, Josh, Rebecca Byrnes, and Sam Fankhauser. 2019. "How to Price Carbon to Reach Net-Zero Emissions in the UK." Policy Report, London School of Economics, London.

Burtraw, Dallas, Karen Palmer, Ranjit Bharvirkar, and Anthony Paul. 2001. "The Effect of Allowance Allocation on the Cost of Carbon Emission Trading." Discussion Paper 01-30, Resources for the Future, Washington, DC.

Cai, Kaihao, Thibault Lemaire, Andrea Medici, Giovanni Melina, Gregor Schwerhoff, and Sneha Thube, 2024. "Harnessing Renewables in Sub-Saharan Africa: Barriers, Reforms, and Economic Prospects." Staff Climate Note 2024/005, IMF, Washington, DC.

Cervantes, Mario, Chiara Criscuolo, Antoine Dechezleprêtre, and Dirk Pilat. 2023. "Driving Low-Carbon Innovations for Climate Neutrality." OECD Science, Technology and Industry Policy Papers No. 143, Organization for Economic Cooperation and Development, Paris.

Clark, Alex, and Philippe Benoit. 2022. *Greenhouse Gas Emissions from State-Owned Enterprises: A Preliminary Inventory*. New York, NY: Center on Global Energy Policy, School of International and Public Affairs, Columbia University.

Climate Bonds Initiative (CBI). 2019. *Climate Bonds Standard Version 3.0*. https://www.climatebonds.net/files/files/climate-bonds-standard-v3-20191210.pdf

Climate Bonds Initiative (CBI). 2023. *Sustainable Debt: Global State of the Market 2023*. https://www.climatebonds.net/files/reports/cbi_sotm23_02h.pdf

Daniel, Philip, Alan Krupnick, Thornton Matheson, Peter Mullins, Ian Parry, and Artur Swistak. 2017. "How Should Shale Gas Extraction Be Taxed?" Working Paper 17/254, International Monetary Fund, Washington, DC.

Dechezleprêtre, Antoine, and David Popp, 2017. "Fiscal and Regulatory Instruments for Clean Technology Development in the European Union." In *Energy Tax and Regulatory Policy in Europe: Reform Priorities*, edited by Ian Parry, Karen Pittel, and Herman Vollebergh, 167–214. Cambridge, MA: MIT Press.

Ferreira, Caio, David Lukas Rozumek, Ranjit Singh, and Felix Suntheim. 2021. "Strengthening the Climate Information Architecture." IMF Staff Climate Note 2021/003, International Monetary Fund, Washington, DC.

Fischer, Carolyn, and Richard G. Newell. 2008. "Environmental and Technology Policies for Climate Mitigation." *Journal of Environmental Economics and Management* 55: 142–62. https://doi.org/10.1016/j.jeem.2007.11.001

Gerarden, Todd D., Richard G. Newell, and Robert N. Stavins. 2017. "Assessing the Energy-Efficiency Gap." *Journal of Economic Literature* 55: 1486–525. https://doi.org/10.1257/jel.20161360

Greenstone, Michael, Christian Leuz, and Patricia Breuer. 2023. "Mandatory Disclosure would Reveal Corporate Carbon Damages: Accurate Reporting Is Critical for Markets and Climate Policies." *Science* 381 (6660): 837–40.

Ilynia, Anna, Celya Pazarbasioglu, and Michele Ruta. 2024. "Industrial Policy Is Back: Is that a Good Thing?" Econofact, International Monetary Fund, Washington, DC.

International Capital Market Association (ICMA). 2021. *Green Bond Principles: Voluntary Process Guidelines for Issuing Green Bonds*. Zürich.

International Energy Agency (IEA). 2020. *Clean Energy Innovation*. Paris.

International Energy Agency (IEA). 2021. *Net Zero by 2050: A Roadmap for the Global Energy Sector*. Paris.

International Energy Agency (IEA). 2022. *World Energy Outlook 2022*. Paris.

International Energy Agency (IEA). 2023. *World Energy Investment 2023*. Paris.

International Monetary Fund (IMF). 2016a. "Economic Diversification in Oil-Exporting Arab Countries." Paper prepared for the Annual Meeting of Arab Ministers of Finance, IMF, Washington, DC.

International Monetary Fund (IMF). 2016b. *Fiscal Monitor: Acting Now, Acting Together*. Washington, DC.

International Monetary Fund (IMF). 2021. *Reaching Net Zero Emissions*. G20 Note. Washington, DC.

International Monetary Fund (IMF). 2023a. "Financial Sector Policies to Unlock Private Climate Finance in Emerging Market and Developing Economies." In *Global Financial Stability Report*. Washington, DC.

International Monetary Fund (IMF). 2023b. *Fiscal Monitor: Climate Crossroads: Fiscal Policies in a Warming World*. Washington, DC.

International Monetary Fund (IMF). 2024a. "Industrial Policy Coverage in IMF Surveillance—Broad Considerations." Policy Paper No. 2024-008, IMF, Washington, DC.

International Monetary Fund (IMF). 2024b. "Ecuador: Selected Issues." Country Report 24/358, IMF, Washington, DC.

International Renewable Energy Agency (IRENA). 2023. *World Energy Transition Outlook*. Masdar City: International Renewable Energy Agency.

Jaumotte, Florence, Jaden Kim, Samuel Pienknagura, and Gregor Schwerhof. 2024. "Policies to Foster Green FDI: Best Practices for Emerging Market and Developing Economies." Staff Climate Note 2024/004, International Monetary Fund, Washington, DC.

Leard, Benjamin, Joshua Linn, and Yichen Christy Zhou. 2023. "How Much Do Consumers Value Fuel Economy and Performance? Evidence from Technology Adoption." *The Review of Economics and Statistics* 105: 158–74. https://doi.org/10.1162/rest_a_01045

Lim, Cheng Hoon, Ritu Basu, Yan Carriere-Swallow, Kenichiro Kashiwase, Mahmut Kutlukaya, Mike Li, Ehraz Refayet, Dulani Seneviratne, Mouhamadou Sy, and Ruihua Yang. 2024. "Unlocking Climate Finance in Asia-Pacific: Transitioning to a Sustainable Future." Departmental Paper 2024/01, International Monetary Fund, Washington, DC.

Network for Greening the Financial System (NGFS). 2021. *Guide on Climate-Related Disclosure for Central Banks*. Network for Greening the Financial System. https://www.ngfs.net/sites/default/files/medias/documents/guide_on_climate-related_disclosure_for_central_banks.pdf

Network for Greening the Financial System (NGFS). 2022. *Final Report on Bridging Data Gaps*. Paris.

Newell, Richard. 2015. "The Role of Energy Technology Policy Alongside Carbon Pricing." In *Implementing a U.S. Carbon Tax: Challenges and Debates*, edited by Ian Parry, Adele Morris, and Roberton C. Williams. New York, NY: Routledge.

Newell, Richard G., William A. Pizer, and Daniel Raimi. 2019. "US Federal Government Subsidies for Clean Energy: Design Choices and Implications." *Energy Economics* 80: 831–41. https://doi.org/10.1016/j.eneco.2019.02.018

Oman, William, and Romain Svartzman. 2021. "Sustainable Finance: Current Needs, Measures, and Impact." *CESifo Forum* 22 (3): 3–11.

Organisation for Economic Co-operation and Development (OECD). 2024. *Tax Incentives for R&D and Innovation*. Paris.

Parry, Ian, David Evans, and Wallace E. Oates, 2014. "Are Energy Efficiency Standards Justified?" *Journal of Environmental Economics and Management* 67: 104–25. https://doi.org/10.1016/j.jeem.2013.11.003

Parry, Ian, and Kenneth A. Small. 2015. "Implications of Carbon Taxes for Transportation Policies." In *Implementing a US Carbon Tax: Challenges and Debates*, edited by Ian Parry, Adele Morris, and Roberton C. Williams, 211–32. London: Routledge.

Pigato, Miria A., Simon J. Black, Damien Dussaux, Zhimin Mao, Miles McKenna, Ryan Rafaty, and Simon Touboul. 2020. "Using Patents to Measure the International Transfer of Low-Carbon Technologies and Its Determinants." In *Technology Transfer and Innovation for Low-Carbon Development*, edited by M. Pigato et al., 61–87. Washington, DC: World Bank.

Prasad, Ananthakrishnan, Elena Loukoianova, Alan Xiaochen Feng, and William Oman. 2022. "Mobilizing Private Climate Financing in Emerging Market and Developing Economies." IMF Staff Climate Note 2022-007, International Monetary Fund, Washington, DC.

Puyo, Diego Mesa, Augustus J. Panton, Tarun Sridhar, Martin Stuermer, Christoph Ungerer, and Alice Tianbo Zhang. 2024. "Key Challenges Faced by Fossil Fuel Exporters during the Energy Transition." Staff Climate Note 2024/001, International Monetary Fund, Washington, DC.

Rose, Paul. 2021. "Debt for Climate: Green Bonds and Other Instruments." In *Research Handbook on Climate Finance and Investment Law*. Ohio State Legal Studies Research Paper No. 595.

Stern, Nicholas, and Joseph Stiglitz. 2021. "The Social Cost of Carbon, Risk, Distribution, Market Failures: An Alternative Approach." Working Paper 28472, National Bureau of Economic Research, Cambridge, MA.

Task Force on Climate-related Financial Disclosures (TCFD). 2017. *Recommendations of the Task Force on Climate-related Financial Disclosures*. https://assets.bbhub.io/company/sites/60/2021/10/FINAL-2017-TCFD-Report.pdf

United Nations (UN). 2022. *Financing for Sustainable Development Report 2022: Bridging the Finance Divide*. New York, NY: Inter-agency Task Force on Financing for Development.

Way, Rupert, Matthew C. Ives, Penny Mealy, and Doyne Farmer. 2022. "Empirically Grounded Technology Forecasts and the Energy Transition." *Joule* 6 (9): 2057–82. https://doi.org/10.1016/j.joule.2022.08.009

World Bank Group (WBG). 2024. "How to Unlock Pipelines of Bankable Renewable Energy Projects in Emerging Markets and Developing Countries?" Position Paper, WBG, Washington, DC.

World Bank Group (WBG), International Monetary Fund (IMF), and Organisation for Economic Co-operation and Development (OECD). 2023. *Activating Alignment: Applying the G20 Principles for Sustainable Finance Alignment with a Focus on Climate Change Mitigation*. Washington, DC: World Bank Group.

World Wildlife Fund (WWF). 2018. *Annual Report 2018*. Washington, DC.

Yahmed, Zeineb Ben, Nicole Pinko, Chris Grant, and Jonathan First. 2024. *Landscape of Guarantees for Climate Finance in EMDEs*. Cape Town: Climate Policy Initiative.

8 Other Environmental Impacts

Implications for Fuel Pricing and Climate Mitigation

Main Messages

- Local (outdoor) air pollution from fossil fuel combustion kills about 2.7 million people prematurely a year (mostly from coal and diesel fuel) with costs valued at about 3 percent of global GDP in 2023.
- The most efficient policy for reducing local air pollution from large stationary sources is emissions fees—for example, fees of about $15,000 per ton can be warranted for sulfur dioxide emissions.
- Across G20 countries, automobile drivers impose congestion and accident costs on other road users of about $0.05–0.20 and $0.02–0.10 per vehicle km, respectively, while truck drivers also impose road damage costs of about $0.12 per km on average.
- Given transportation infrastructure, fine-tuned policies to address congestion and road damage include per km charges varying by region and time of day and charges on truck km driven scaled by axle weight, whereas accident risk can be reduced through shifting to pay-as-you-drive auto insurance plans.
- For the interim (until fine-tuned policies are widespread), the next best policy is to reflect domestic environmental costs in fuel prices along with carbon damages.
- For many countries, there is ample scope for reforming coal, gas, gasoline, and diesel prices to fully reflect supply costs, carbon damages, and domestic environmental costs.
- Across G20 countries, full energy price reform would reduce CO_2 emissions by 25–60 percent below baseline levels in 2030, reduce annual global fossil fuel air pollution deaths by 15–50 percent, raise revenues of 2–10 percent of GDP, and generate net economic benefits of up to 10 percent of GDP.

DOI: 10.4324/9781003755012-8
This chapter has been made available under a CC-BY-NC-ND license.

- In the absence of comprehensive fine-tuned policies or fuel price reform, the domestic environmental co-benefits of carbon mitigation policies are large and can easily exceed mitigation costs—indeed CO_2 reductions of over 20 percent are in countries' own domestic interests before even counting climate benefits.
- Where fine-tuned policies or fuel price reforms are constrained, local air emissions might be integrated into feebates or tradable performance standards for CO_2 mitigation.

Local Air Pollution and Efficient Responses

What Are the Sources of Local (Outdoor) Air Pollution?

Long-term exposure to concentrations of fine particulate matter $PM_{2.5}$ (with a diameter less than 2.5 micrometers) is associated with elevated risks of various heart and lung diseases and strokes. As of 2019, nationwide average concentrations of fine particulates exceeded safe levels of 5 micrograms per cubic meter (WHO 2021) in all G20 countries and were at least four times this level in seven cases (see Figure 8.1). Local air pollutants have relatively short atmospheric lifetimes, so reducing their emissions has immediate effects on pollution concentrations and health risks.

Coal combustion produces fine particulates not only directly but also indirectly through atmospheric reactions involving (most importantly) sulfur dioxide (SO_2) and (less importantly) nitrogen oxide (NO_x). Emissions rates of these pollutants vary depending on use of control technologies and fuel quality (for example, bituminous coal has a higher sulfur content than lignite and anthracite). In contrast, natural gas produces only NO_x and in moderate amounts. Gasoline and diesel produce NO_x and other pollutants, though emissions rates vary by country with vehicle regulations and can be much higher for diesel than gasoline.

What Are the Mortality and Monetary Costs of Local Air Pollution?

Local outdoor air pollution caused an estimated 4.5 million premature deaths in 2019 broken down by:[1]

- 60 percent from fossil fuels as opposed to other emissions sources (like dust and burning crop residues);
- 92 percent from (direct and indirect) $PM_{2.5}$ and 8 percent (low-lying) ozone (formed from NO_x and other pollutants); and
- Two-thirds of people aged 65 and over (who are more vulnerable because of preexisting conditions like asthma).

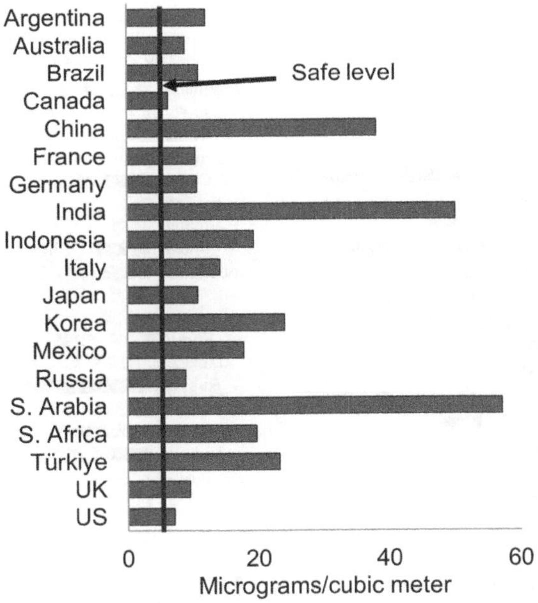

Figure 8.1 Fine Particulate Air Pollution Concentrations 2019, G20 Countries.

Source: WHO (2024).

Note: Figure shows nationwide averages based on population-weighted averages of regional concentrations.

Among G20 countries, local air pollution death rates from fossil fuels exceeded 60 per 100,000 population in three cases (China, India, and Russia), were between 40 and 60 in six cases, and were between 20 and 40 in ten cases, with heart disease usually the most important fatal illness. See Figure 8.2, panel 1. In absolute terms, deaths were highest in China (1,163 million) and India (883 million).

Estimates of local air pollution damages by fuel type have been compiled (see Annex 8.2) from country-specific data on baseline mortality rates, population exposure to pollution, the sensitivity of mortality rates to pollution exposure, local air emissions rates per unit of fuel use, and how much people in different countries are willing to pay for lower mortality risks.[2] Damages from fossil fuel air pollution were on average 4 percent of GDP across G20 countries in 2024, varying between about 1 and 5 percent (though substantially higher in China and Russia because of high population exposure and emissions rates), with most of the damages from coal and diesel. Underpinning these estimates is an assumption that the value per fatality is between about $2 and $7 million across most countries. See Figure 8.2, panel 2.

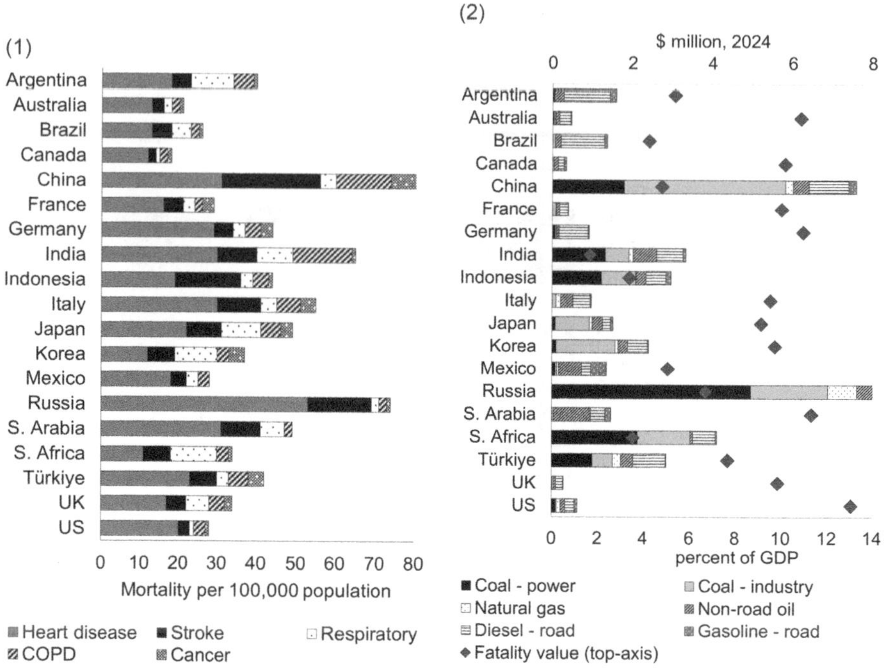

Figure 8.2 Mortality and Monetary Costs of Local Air Pollution, G20 Countries. Panel 1. Mortality (from Fossil and Non-fossil Emissions) by Disease, 2019, Panel 2. Total Monetary Costs (from Fossil Emissions) Relative to GDP by Fuel, 2024.

Sources: WHO (2024); authors using Climate Policy Assessment Tool (CPAT).

Note: Besides strokes, illnesses refer to ischemic heart disease, lower respiratory infections, chronic obstructive pulmonary disease, and trachea/bronchitis/lung cancers.

Why Are Emissions Fees the Most Efficient Policy to Reduce Local Air Pollution from Stationary Sources?

Potential behavioral responses for reducing air pollutants like SO_2 from (large) stationary sources include installing SO_2 scrubbers in smokestacks, shifting to coal with lower sulfur content, shifting from coal to cleaner fuels like natural gas and renewables, processing coal to lower sulfur content, and reducing electricity demand. Local air emissions fees promote all these responses because the first four lower generators' tax liabilities, whereas the pass-through of emissions fees and abatement costs in higher electricity prices promotes the last response. In contrast, for example, mandating SO_2 scrubbing technologies promotes only the first response (and limiting the standard to new plants only, as common in practice, is less effective still), whereas a coal tax promotes only the third and fifth response.

An emissions fee equal to the environmental damage per ton of emissions will maximize the domestic environmental benefits from reducing emissions net of mitigation costs because it equates the environmental benefit and cost from the last ton reduced (see Figure 8.3). Fees should be applied to smokestack emissions which, for high-capacity countries, can be monitored by requiring firms have continuous emissions monitoring systems (subject to third-party verification). Where it is impractical for governments to monitor all emissions sources, another option is to impose upfront taxes on fuel inputs in proportion to default emissions rates but allow firms to petition for rebates if they demonstrate (through their own metering) their emissions rate is below the default (these administrative options are similar to those for methane fees discussed in Chapter 4).

How Large Are Efficient Fees on Local Air Emissions?

Figure 8.4 shows, for G20 countries with significant coal use, estimates of efficient fees on coal plant SO_2 emissions in 2022 and deaths per ton of SO_2. Based on a simple average, efficient fees are \$30,000 per ton but vary from above \$60,000 per ton in two cases (China and Russia) to below \$20,000 in six others (for example, Australia, Canada, and South Africa). Deaths per ton of SO_2 vary from close to zero (in Australia) to 0.04 (in China). Although the damages per ton of SO_2 may sound large, SO_2 is emitted in much smaller quantities than CO_2.[3]

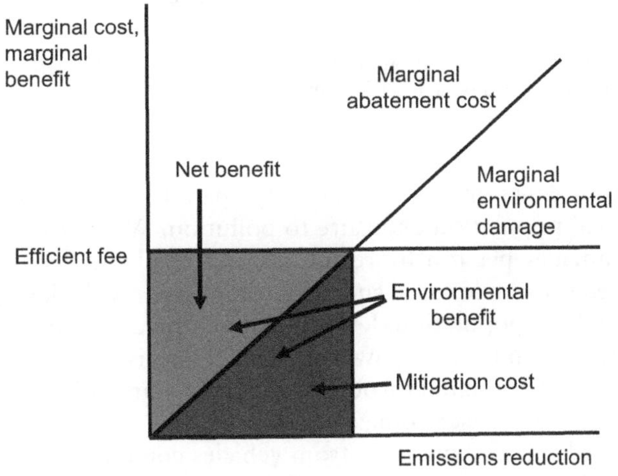

Figure 8.3 Efficient Air Pollution Fee: Graphical Representation.

Source: Authors.

Note: Marginal damage is equivalent to the marginal environmental benefit from reducing emissions. The assumption of a flat marginal benefit curve for local air pollution seems reasonable (see Annex 8.2).

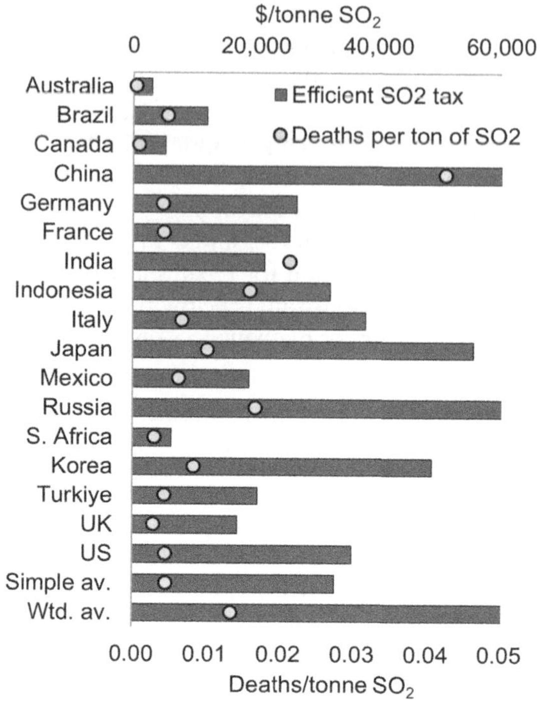

Figure 8.4 Efficient Fees on Coal Plant SO_2, Selected G20 Countries, 2022.

Source: Black et al. (2023).

Note: Figure excludes Argentina and Saudi Arabia which have minimal or zero coal use in power generation. Estimates are available for 170 countries from CPAT.

Ideally, local emissions fees would vary spatially across urban and rural areas with local population exposure to pollution. Where estimates of environmental damages per ton by region are not available, fee differentiation might be based on simple rules, such as scaling nationwide damage estimates per ton by regional population density relative to nationwide average population density. By and large, however, local air emissions from power and industry have been regulated through technology standards though there are some examples of fees—see Annex 8.3.

In principle, local air emissions from vehicles could be subject to a proxy tax based on the amount vehicles are driven, their emissions rate, and local population exposure—this tax would promote less driving and switching to cleaner vehicles, especially for urban motorists. But administrative burdens (to fine-tune kilometer charges to emissions rates and population exposure) would be significant—and may not be worthwhile if local air emissions are being progressively reduced through tighter new vehicle emissions standards and shifting to electric vehicles. As for buildings, where they are heated by natural gas, local air emissions are modest and can be reflected in fuel prices.

In some countries (for example, China), coal provides district heating for buildings, but the heat generation plant (which typically produces electricity as well) could be subject to emissions fees.

Additional Side Effects of Transportation and Efficient Responses

What Are the Costs of Traffic Congestion?

A major side effect of transport systems is the cost of lost time from traffic congestion. This cost can be estimated using data on average travel delays per km driven and studies measuring how people value an hour of travel time relative to wage rates (see Annex 8.4). Across G20 countries, the value of travel time is put at about \$2 to \$20 per hour, whereas the total costs of travel delays are about 0.2 to 1 percent of GDP. See Figure 8.5, panel 1.

According to economic theory, motorists should consider average (vehicle operating and time) costs per km in their driving decisions. From society's perspective, however, congestion is excessive and warrants policy intervention, because motorists do not consider external costs—their effect on adding to road congestion, slowing speeds, and increasing travel times for other road users. External costs per vehicle km can be calculated from average travel

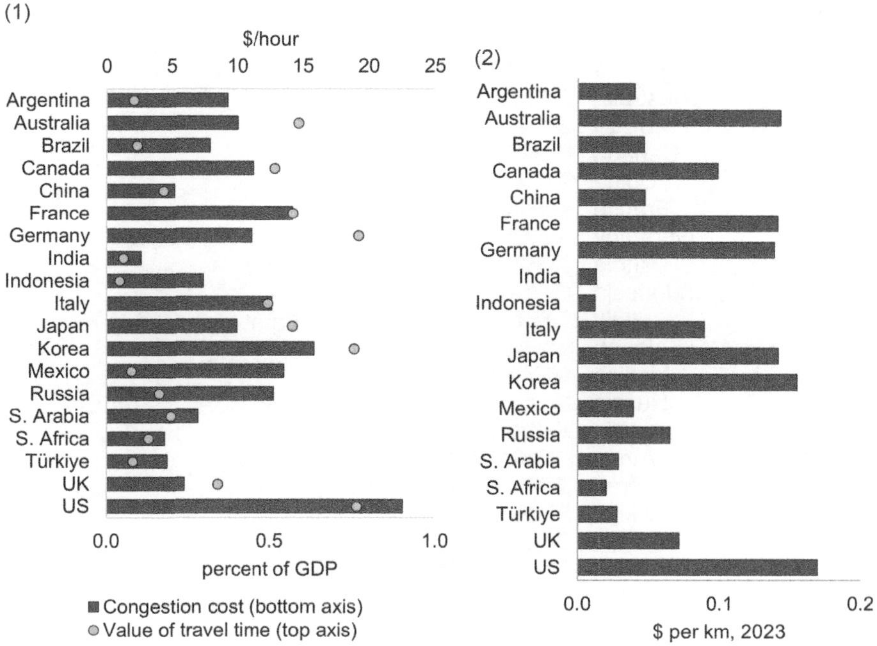

Figure 8.5 Costs of Traffic Congestion, G20 Countries, 2024. Panel 1. Total Costs Relative to GDP, Panel 2. External Cost per Vehicle km.

Source: Updated from Black et al. (2023).

Note: Estimates are available for 170 countries in CPAT.

time costs per km driven and functional relationships between travel speeds and traffic flows (again see Annex 8.4). Averaged nationwide (across urban and rural driving, and peak and off-peak periods) external costs are between about \$0.05 and \$0.20 per vehicle km for most G20 countries. See Figure 8.5, panel 2.

What Are the Other Main Side Effects of Road Transport?

Another side effect of road transportation is traffic accidents, which killed 1.2 million people worldwide in 2019 (WHO 2024). Traffic accidents are excessive from society's perspective because, although some risks are internal to drivers (such as injury risks to themselves in single-vehicle collisions), other risks are external or not considered (such as injury risks their driving poses for pedestrians). Despite some analytical challenges (such as apportioning injuries in multivehicle collisions, medical burdens, and property damages to internal versus external risks), reasonable first-pass estimates of external accident costs per vehicle km are available (see Annex 8.5).

Estimated external costs in 2024 varied from about \$0.01 to \$0.05 per vehicle km across most G20 countries, with nonfatal costs accounting for about 20 to 50 percent of the external cost (see Figure 8.6). Compared with Figure 8.5, panel 2, for high-income countries, external costs from accidents are well below those for congestion (in part reflecting high values of travel

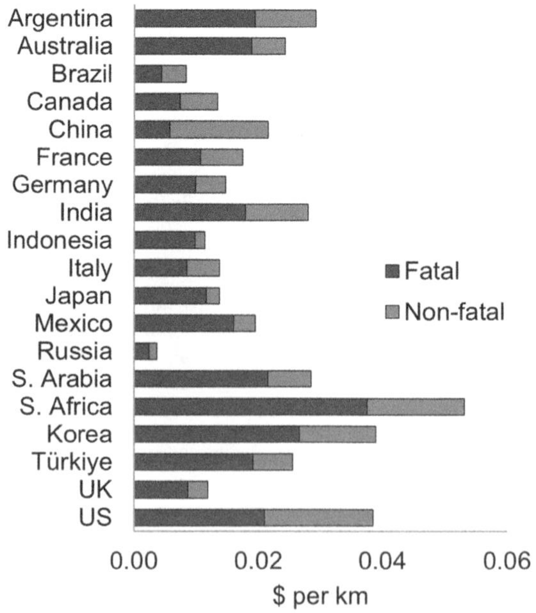

Figure 8.6 External Costs per Vehicle km from Traffic Accidents, G20 Countries, 2024.
Source: Updated from Black et al. (2023).

time, stringent road/vehicle/driver safety policies, and low incidence of pedestrian deaths), whereas the opposite applies in some emerging market economies.

Vehicle use also results in wear and tear on the road network, which is another external cost. Given that road damage is a rapidly rising function of a vehicle's axle weight, nearly all of the vehicle damage is caused by heavy-duty trucks.[4] In principle, this cost can be proxied by government spending on road maintenance (see IRF 2022) after apportioning a fraction (typically assumed to be 50 percent) to vehicle traffic and the remainder to physical deterioration exacerbated by weather (such as ice creating and expanding pavement cracks). On average across G20 countries, external costs from road damage in 2024 were $0.12 per truck km (this figure is used for all countries in the analysis discussed in the following section).[5]

Why Are Peak Period Fees the Most Efficient Policy for Managing Road Congestion?

Road congestion depends on infrastructure policies (the size of the road and transit network, parking facilities, positioning of traffic lights, and so on) but efficiently managing use of the infrastructure requires pricing policies to charge motorists for the congestion costs they impose on others. Charging all motorists per km driven on busy roads, with the tax progressively rising and falling during the course of the peak period, will exploit all behavioral responses for alleviating congestion, such as using other transport modes (transit, cycling, walking), switching to less congested routes, departing earlier/later to avoid the rush-hour peak, shifting from peak to off-peak driving, reducing trip frequency (remote working or combining trips), carpooling, and changing residences/workplaces to reduce commutes. Other policies promote fewer responses: for example, a transit fare subsidy only exploits part of the first response, whereas a toll per km driven on busy roads that does not vary with time of day does not promote shifting of trips within the peak or to off-peak period.

To maximize the net economic benefits to road users, traffic flows should be limited to where the benefit to motorists of an extra km driven equals the average (operating and time cost) plus the external cost (the added travel costs imposed on other road users)—this is indicated by traffic flow T^* in Figure 8.7, whereas traffic flow will be T_0 when motorists only consider average travel costs. The external cost schedule is zero under free-flowing traffic conditions but rises sharply once the number of vehicles per km (per hour) is large enough to slow travel speeds for other road users—only a modest reduction in traffic flows on congested roads below the level with no toll is needed to achieve the efficient flow (most drivers can still use the road).

At a top-down level, the most comprehensive tolling approach would be monitoring driving behavior by satellite with toll bills remitted periodically to households based on their km driven and per km charges varying according to congestion levels on the road. Concerns about abuse of data on individuals' driving behavior might be addressed through third-party data

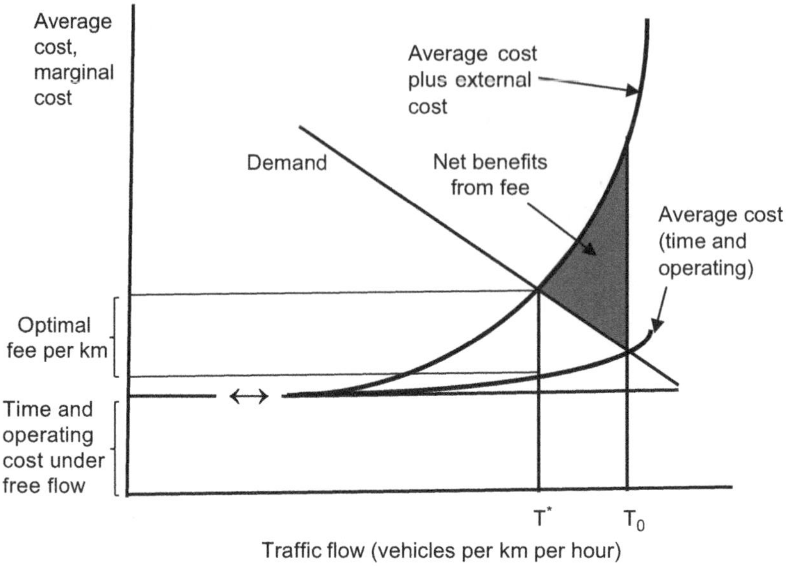

Figure 8.7 Efficient Peak-Period Congestion Fee: Graphical Representation.

Source: Authors.

Note: The efficient fee is given by the external cost at the efficient level of driving—implementing it yields net benefits given by the reduction in travel costs (the integral under the average plus external cost curve) less the value of trips foregone (the area under the travel demand curve).

collection with strict legal requirements to prevent information disclosure. The progressive transition from fuel taxes to comprehensive km-based taxing might be promoted on a voluntary basis (allowing drivers of vehicles with low fuel economy to opt into the new charging system in exchange for rebating their fuel tax payments) along with subsidies/taxes for vehicles with/without satellite tracking capacity. A bottom-up possibility is electronic debiting from prepaid, onboard smart cards as vehicles pass transponder points for urban road networks (tag plates of noncompliant vehicles could be recorded and bills sent to the vehicle owners).

No country has yet implemented nationwide km-based pricing for cars, but these schemes seem likely to emerge eventually as decarbonization of vehicle fleets erodes fuel tax revenues. Meanwhile, some European countries have implemented nationwide km tolling for trucks and congestion pricing is emerging at the local level (see Annex 8.6).

What Are Efficient Pricing Instruments for Reducing Traffic Accidents and Road Damage?

Accidents. Driving will also be excessive if motorists are not charged for costs posed to other road users and third parties from their contribution to accident risk. The case for pricing reform is generally less pressing than for congestion as (1) congestion externalities often exceed those for accidents (see the previous section); (2) there is a broader range of alternative measures for improving road safety than for congestion;[6] and (3) the range of behavioral responses to pricing accident risk is more limited than for congestion (for example, reallocating trips across time of day or routes does not necessarily lower accident risks).

In principle, per km charges to address accident externalities might be scaled according to driver risks (higher for those with prior crash records or limited experience) and perhaps higher for larger vehicles posing greater injury risk to others. A differentiated tax system would be complicated to administer, however. A promising alternative is to encourage (through fiscal incentives) a transition from lump-sum to pay-as-you-drive (PAYD) auto insurance where payments are proportional to how much people drive and their risk factors (as determined by insurance companies). PAYD insurance (which is now offered by insurance companies in many countries) encourages people to drive less (because it raises the marginal costs of driving), especially for riskier drivers, without a politically sensitive increase in tax burden for the average motorist or new capacity for the government.[7]

Road damage. Although road surfaces can be strengthened to enhance resilience to climatic factors and vehicle use, wear and tear on the road system will still be excessive if truck drivers are not charged for their contribution to road damage. The most efficient policy is a per km toll on heavy trucks, scaled by their axle weight. These charges would encourage truckers to seek vehicle fleets that carry goods efficiently over more axles. In the Netherlands, for example, truck drivers register their tag plates and pay these fees, with enforcement through random satellite checking of tag plates.

Implications for Fuel Pricing

Conceptually, What Are Efficient Fuel Prices and the Benefits from Price Reform?

Countries may ultimately gravitate toward the fine-tuned policies discussed in the previous section, but at present, they have yet to be comprehensively implemented in any country, and in the meantime, it is appropriate to reflect the full range of climate and domestic environmental costs (as defined in the following section) in fuel prices (see Parry and Small 2005). Indeed, there can be large environmental, fiscal, and economic benefits from raising fuel prices from their current to their efficient levels, where the efficient price reflects both supply and environmental costs (and any general consumer taxes for fuels consumed at the household level).

Figure 8.8, panels 1 and 2 illustrate, schematically, the benefits from fuel price reform for cases when a fuel is subject to a preexisting tax and subsidy, respectively. In these panels, the height of the fuel demand curve at any point reflects the benefit from an extra unit of consumption, whereas the height of

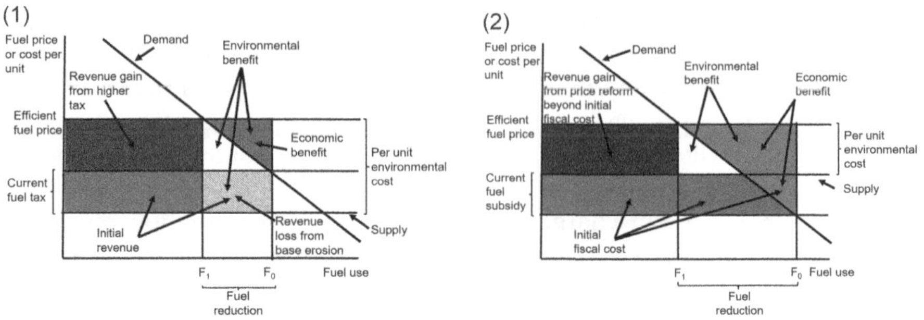

Figure 8.8 Benefits from Raising Fuel Prices to Efficient Levels: Graphical Representation. Panel 1. Preexisting Fuel Tax, Panel 2. Preexisting Fuel Subsidy.

Source: Authors.

the supply curve reflects the cost of producing (or importing) an extra unit of fuel. As fuel prices increase from current levels (the supply cost plus the current fuel tax or minus the current fuel subsidy) to the efficient level, environmental benefits will be proportional to the reduction in fuel use. Fiscal benefits, in panel 1, are the extra revenues from increasing the fuel tax, less revenue losses from eroding the base of the initial fuel tax. In panel 2, fiscal benefits are initial subsidy outlays plus new revenues from imposing a fuel tax. And in either case, the net economic benefit from price reform is the reduction in environmental and supply costs from less fuel use, less the loss of consumer benefits (the area under the fuel demand curve integrated over the fuel reduction).

How Do Currently Projected Prices for Coal and Natural Gas Compare with Efficient Prices Across Countries?

Figure 8.9, panels 1 and 2 show estimates of economywide supply costs and retail prices, and efficient prices for coal and natural gas, averaging over sectoral prices paid by households and firms and focusing on 2030 projections (which are more relevant for price reform than historical prices). Besides the supply cost, the efficient fuel price includes carbon damages—the emissions factor times an illustrative CO_2 price of \$80 per ton for all countries consistent with a 2°C target (see Chapter 9)—and domestic environmental costs. The efficient price also includes general consumption taxes where the fuel is consumed at the household level. For coal, the domestic environmental cost is the sum of tons of direct $PM_{2.5}$, SO_2, and NO_x per unit of energy, with each multiplied by their respective damages per ton of emissions, whereas for natural gas, domestic environmental costs include only NO_x. Fuel taxes, or subsidies, are the difference between baseline prices and supply costs and implicitly include excises and VAT as well as any carbon pricing. The discussion here mainly focuses on environmental costs, given that Chapter 5 discusses supply costs and baseline prices.

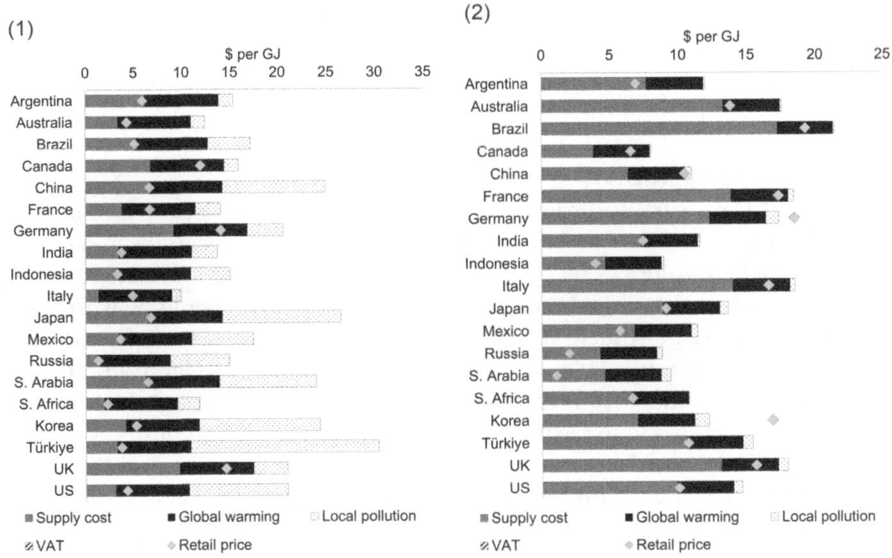

Figure 8.9 Current and Efficient Coal and Gas Prices for G20 Countries, 2030 Projections. Panel 1. Coal, Panel 2. Natural Gas.

Source: Authors using CPAT.

Note: Prices and externalities are shown for fuel used in the weighted average of power, industrial, and residential sectors.

Climate change damages from coal are quite large—equivalent to nearly $9 per gigajoule (GJ) or about 100–700 percent of supply costs. Local air pollution damages can also be large, but these costs vary widely across countries—local air pollution damages are at least as large as climate damages in eight cases in Figure 8.9 (for example, China, Russia) but are less than 50 percent of climate damages in five cases (for example, Australia, Canada, South Africa). Carbon damages are mostly about 15–60 percent of supply costs for natural gas, a much lower proportion than for coal, because of both the much higher supply costs per GJ for gas and lower CO_2 emissions rates per GJ. Local air pollution damages from natural gas are typically modest (below $1 per GJ) because of the relatively low emissions rates. The VAT component of efficient natural gas prices would contribute 5–20 percent of the efficient price for household consumption alone (Figure 8.9 shows an average across sectors). Summing up, there is substantial and pervasive underpricing for the environmental costs of coal use, and to a lesser extent, natural gas.

How Do Currently Projected Prices for Gasoline and Diesel Compare with Efficient Prices Across Countries?

If fuel taxes were the only fiscal instrument available for the road vehicle sector, again they should be set to reflect environmental costs. One complication is that driving-related costs (congestion, accidents, road damage) are only reduced by fuel taxes to the extent they reduce driving, but not to the extent they improve fuel economy or cause shifting to electric vehicles. These costs are therefore multiplied by the fraction of the tax-induced reduction in fuel use because of reduced driving (typically assumed to be about 0.3) in computing efficient fuel taxes, after multiplying them by fuel economy to express them in per liter terms.[8]

Efficient taxes vary according to whether fuels are used by cars (gasoline) or by both cars and trucks (diesel). Given administrative complications in differentiating diesel pump prices by car or truck, efficient diesel tax estimates average over cars and trucks, though not much tax differentiation would be warranted anyway. However, a (much) lower tax rate would be appropriate for off-road diesel uses (for example, farm vehicles do not contribute to congestion), though differentiation in this case is more feasible (for example, through fuel dyes or allowing farmers to claim partial fuel tax rebates when paying business tax).

Figure 8.10 provides analogous information, for gasoline and diesel, to that in Figure 8.9, accounting for the broader range of environmental costs. Carbon damages are equivalent to \$0.23 and \$0.26 per liter for gasoline and diesel, respectively, about one-fourth of supply costs. Local air pollution damages are generally small relative to carbon damages for gasoline. In contrast, for diesel, local air pollution damages are typically 1–4 times as large as carbon damages. Congestion and accident externalities combined are relatively large for gasoline, contributing about \$0.1–\$0.7 per liter to

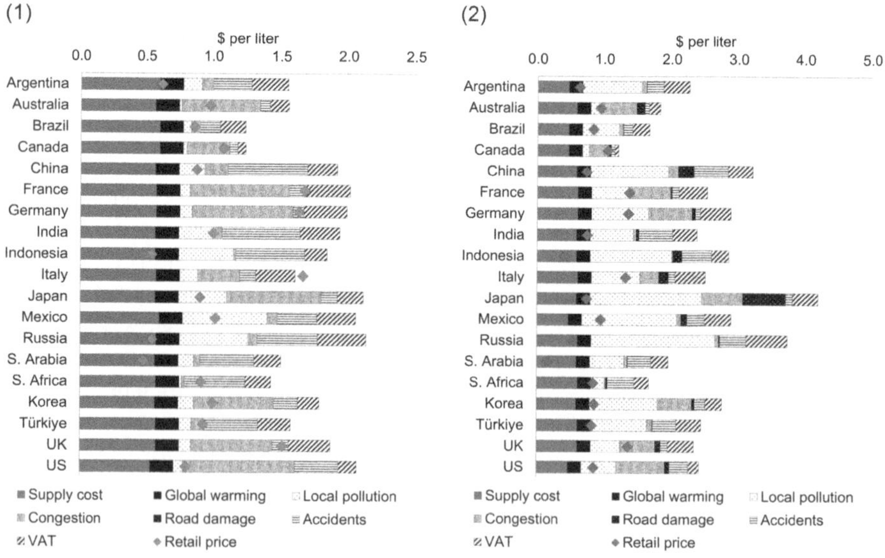

Figure 8.10 Current and Efficient Road Fuel Prices for G20 Countries, 2030 Projections. Panel 1. Gasoline, Panel 2. Diesel.

Source: Updated from Black et al. (2023).

Note: For diesel, estimates average overuse in light- and heavy-duty vehicles.

efficient fuel taxes. For diesel, combined congestion and accident externalities per liter are smaller, given the significant portion of diesel fuel used in heavy-duty vehicles with much lower km driven per liter of fuel (a partially offsetting factor is the higher congestion costs per km for these vehicles because they take up more road space). The VAT component of the efficient fuel price is significant for gasoline (about \$0.10–\$0.35 per liter) but less so for road diesel (where typically 50 percent or more of consumption is an intermediate product). In short, underpricing of road fuels is also pervasive.

What Are the Benefits of Fuel Price Reforms?

The previous discussion suggests ample scope for reforming prices of many fuel products in many countries. Figure 8.11 indicates the CO_2, local air pollution mortality, fiscal, and economic benefits if countries were to raise fuel prices to reach their efficient levels by 2035.

- *CO_2*: Projected fossil fuel CO_2 emissions for most G20 countries would fall by 25–60 percent below baseline levels in 2035. Countries with small subsidies, primarily in Europe, see smaller reductions.
- *Local air pollution*: Full fuel price reform would reduce G20 air pollution deaths from fossil fuel combustion by 10–50 percent relative to baseline levels in 2035 across G20 countries, or by 1 million a year in total. The reduction is dominated by coal (at about 70 percent) reflecting, in part, the disproportionately large reduction in coal consumption.[9] The differences in proportionate mortality reductions are broadly similar to those for CO_2.
- *Fiscal*: Raising fuel prices to efficient levels would raise revenues of about 3.2 percent of GDP on average across G20 countries in 2035 relative to baseline levels (accounting for revenue losses because of erosion of preexisting fuel tax bases). Revenue gains vary substantially across countries, however, from about 1 to 10 percent of GDP.
- *Economic*: For the G20 as a whole, full fuel price reform would generate net economic benefits of 3.4 percent of GDP, equal to environmental benefits (including CO_2 reductions valued at \$80 per ton) of 5.2 percent of GDP less economic costs of 1.8 percent of GDP. Across countries, net benefits range from just above 0 to 10 percent of GDP.

Implications for Climate Mitigation Policy

How Much CO_2 Mitigation Is in Countries' Own Interests because of Domestic Environmental Benefits?

Ideally, the domestic environmental costs of fossil fuel use would be addressed through fine-tuned policies, or failing that, they would be fully reflected in fuel prices. But in the absence of either reform, it is appropriate to consider (unpriced) domestic environmental co-benefits when evaluating the economic

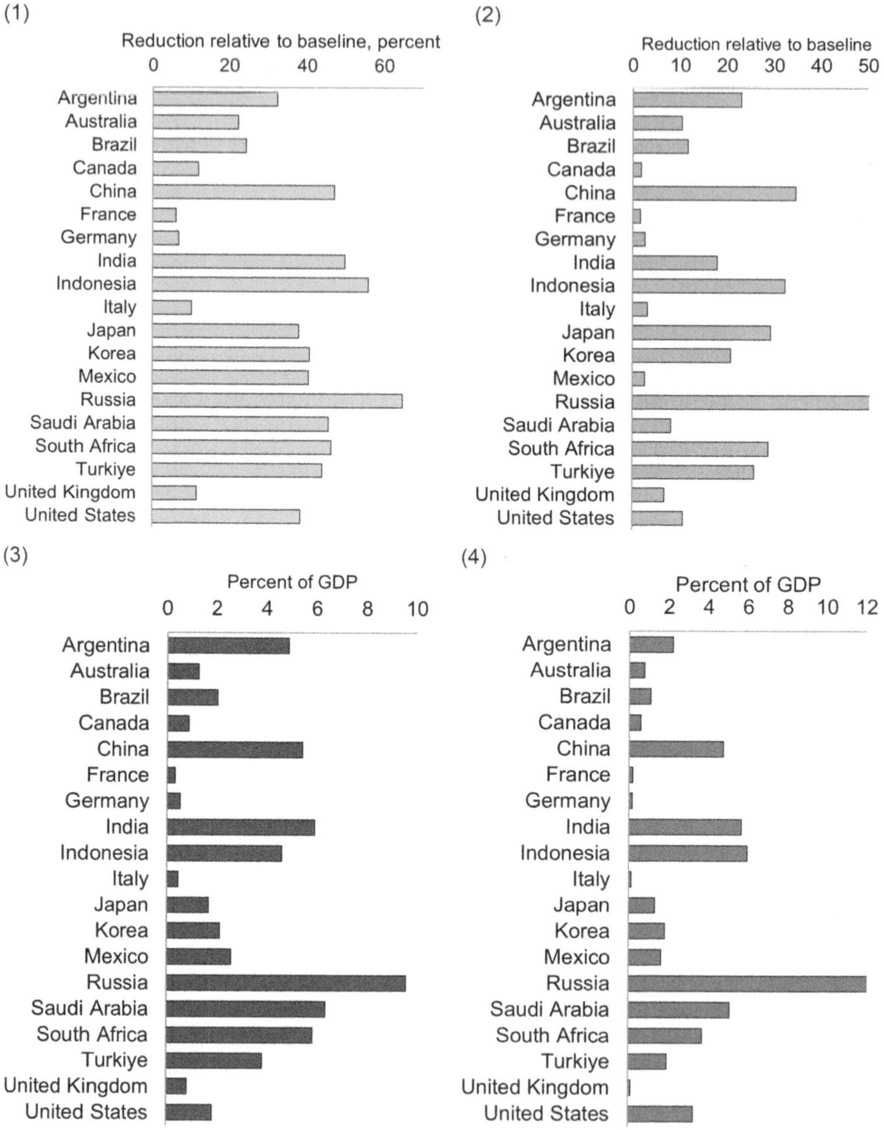

Figure 8.11 Benefits of Fuel Price Reform, G20 Countries, 2030. Panel 1. CO_2 Reductions, Panel 2. Air Pollution Deaths Avoided, Panel 3. Fiscal Revenues, Panel 4. Net Economic Benefits.

Source: Updated from Black et al. (2023).

Note: Results are available from CPAT in 170 countries.

effects of carbon mitigation policies. Indeed, up to a point, countries can make themselves better off by fossil fuel use to reduce CO_2 emissions if the domestic environmental co-benefits outweigh CO_2 mitigation costs—before even counting the global climate benefits.

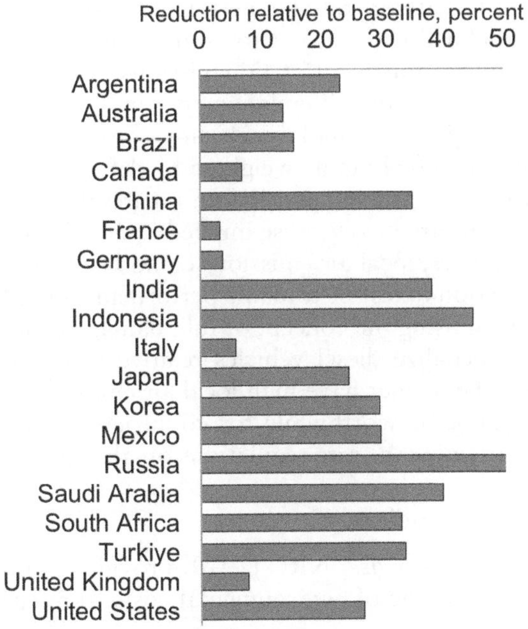

Figure 8.12 CO_2 Reductions in G20 Countries' Own Domestic Interest, 2030.

Source: Authors' calculations from CPAT.

Figure 8.12 shows, for G20 countries, estimates of economywide CO_2 reductions in 2030 that maximize domestic net benefits, that is, where the incremental domestic environmental co-benefit from an additional ton of CO_2 reduction equals the incremental mitigation cost.[10] These CO_2 reductions, which are in countries' own domestic interests, are very large—25 percent below 2035 baseline levels based on a simple average across countries. There is substantial cross-country variation, however—reductions exceed 25 percent in 10 cases (for example, China, Türkiye) but are less than 20 percent in seven other cases where local air pollution mortality is less severe and existing fuel taxes and carbon pricing are relatively high (for example, Canada and European G20 countries). At the G20 level, carbon mitigation in countries' own interests would save 0.9 million premature deaths from local air pollution, with 300,000 and 120,000 lives saved in China and India, respectively.

How Could Climate Mitigation Policies Be Modified to Account for Local Air Pollution?

If fine-tuned policies and fuel price reform are subject to acceptability or other constraints, local air pollution damages might be accounted for by modifying non-charging instruments for climate mitigation.

For example, a feebate or tradable performance standard for power generators might be defined with respect to "full" emissions and SO_2 emissions converted to "damage-equivalent" CO_2 emissions,[11] with the pivot point or standard defined in terms of full emissions per unit of output. Again, these policies could be applied to smokestack emissions if there is capacity for monitoring them, or to fuel inputs weighted by default factors for full emissions (but allowing generators to petition for rebates if they can validate their smokestack emissions are below those implied by the default rates).

Similarly for vehicles, local air emissions could be integrated into feebates (applied to registration taxes) or tradable performance standards (applied to vehicle sellers) again using the concept of full, damage-equivalent CO_2 emissions. This could penalize diesel vehicles relative to gasoline vehicles and electric vehicles if the former have high local air emissions rates, though the modification may not be worthwhile for countries enforcing progressively tightening local air emissions rate regulations on all vehicles.

Suggestions for Further Reading

- *Broader costs of energy use.* NRC (2010) provides a comprehensive discussion of the full range of environmental costs from energy use in a US context.
- *Valuing income/mortality risk trade-offs.* OECD (2012) provides a comprehensive synthesis of hundreds of studies in different countries that infer peoples' willingness to pay to lower mortality risks based on questionnaires.
- *Methodologies for and studies on quantifying environmental costs of fuel use.* For details on methodologies, see, for example, European Commission et al. (2020), EEA (2023), NRC (2010), Parry et al. (2014). Kim and Chaeyoung (2024) provide a survey of individual country studies on the external costs of transportation.
- *Traffic congestion.* For background on traffic congestion and policies to address it, see, for example, Parry (2009), Santos (2004), and Small, Verhoef, and Lindsey (2024) and for transportation policies more generally, see Lindsey and Santos (2020).
- *PAYD car insurance.* For more discussion, see, for example, Tselentis, Yannis, and Vlahogianni (2016).
- *Co-benefits of climate mitigation.* Parry, Veung, and Heine (2015) describe a methodology to estimate the domestic environmental co-benefits from carbon mitigation, whereas Black et al. (2023) provide more recent estimates.
- *Experiences with energy pricing reforms.* Clements et al. (2013) provide numerous case studies of successful and unsuccessful attempts to reform energy prices in different countries and draw lessons on how to design reforms to enhance the likelihood for successful policy reform. See Coady, Parry, and Shang (2018). For more discussion of the political economy of energy price reform, see Inchauste and Victor (2017).

Annex 8.1 Broader Side Effects of Fossil Fuel Production and Use

Fossil fuel production and use are associated with additional side effects, but they do not have strong implications for the policy reforms discussed in the previous section because these effects may be considered by households and firms, be modest in quantitative terms, be too difficult to quantify, or call for other measures. Examples include the following:

- *Additional local air pollutants.* Carbon monoxide (a by-product of incomplete fuel combustion) can reduce oxygen in the bloodstream and increase risks of heart and lung disease, but when released outdoors, its concentration is usually insufficient to cause health effects. Lead emissions from combusting oil products cause neurological effects (especially for children) but lead has been, or is being, phased out from petroleum products in most countries. Various other toxins (like benzene) cause health effects but on a much smaller scale than those for more pervasive air pollutants.
- *Upstream environmental effects.* Leaving aside methane (see Chapter 4), fuel extraction and production cause a variety of other environmental effects. For example, despoiling of the natural environment (perhaps from mountaintop removal for coal, accidental spills from oil wells); waste from fuel processing (such as slurry caused by the "washing" of raw coal); emissions leaks during fuel storage (perhaps from corrosion or evaporation at underground tanks at refineries and gasoline stations); and further leakage during transportation (such as spills from oil tankers). When expressed per unit of fuel use, however, the damage from these effects appears modest in relative terms (for example, NRC 2010, Chapter 2). Moreover, these problems call for interventions other than fuel taxes, like requirements that mined areas be returned to their original vegetative state and double hulls for tankers.
- *Occupational hazards.* For fossil fuel extraction industries, occupational hazards include, for example, lung disease from long-term exposure to coal dust, coal mine collapses, and explosions at oil rigs. Individuals may account for these risks, however, when choosing among different occupations.[12] And to the extent policy intervention is warranted (perhaps because individuals are misinformed about risks), targeted measures, like workplace health and safety regulations, would be warranted.
- *Indoor air pollution.* Indoor air pollution causes an estimated 3.2 million deaths worldwide each year, mainly in low-income countries, because of health effects from burning fuel in poorly ventilated stoves or open fires (see Ezzati 2005, WHO 2024). From a conceptual perspective, the externality and need for policy intervention are not clear-cut because households burning fuels are the ones affected by it, and often the fuel is biomass rather than fossil fuels. The main policy priority is to ensure availability of cleaner energy sources (like charcoal, natural gas, electricity, or even processed coal that burns more cleanly) and better technologies (such as better ventilated stoves).

Annex 8.2 Methodology for Estimating Local Air Pollution Damages in CPAT

The CPAT model is unique in providing estimates of local air pollution damages by emissions, fuel product, and country for over 170 countries. These estimates are based on compiling data from several sources (see Black et al. 2023, Parry et al. 2014).

Baseline mortality rates—for illnesses affected by local air pollution in different countries—are from the World Health Organization (WHO 2024). These mortality rates are relatively high in countries with high rates of preexisting heart and lung disease (such as from high alcohol and cigarette consumption) and low in countries with low life expectancy (where people are less likely to survive long enough to be at risk from pollution-related illness).

Population exposure to air pollution—here CPAT averages across two different modeling approaches.

The first approach is based on "intake fractions," which measure the fraction of $PM_{2.5}$ (equivalent) emissions inhaled by exposed populations. For coal and gas plants which have tall smokestacks—implying emissions can be transported long distances through the atmosphere including across borders—intake fractions are calculated by

- Mapping geographical data on the location of individual plants in different countries to very granular data on population density at different distance classifications from each plant (up to 2,000 km away, within, and across borders);
- Statistically estimated coefficients indicating how intake fractions (for given population size) decline at greater distances from the emissions source; and
- Averaging over plants within each country.

For vehicle and building emissions (which tend to stay close to the ground rather than be transported through the atmosphere), intake fractions are extrapolated to the nationwide level from an international database of intake fractions for over 3,000 urban areas.

The second approach is computational modeling of how emissions released from one location affect air quality (from $PM_{2.5}$ and ozone) and mortality risk in that and other locations based on TM5-Fast Scenario Screening Tool, a downscaled "source-receptor" model applied at the country level. This air quality modeling approach is more sophisticated than the intake fraction approach in that it accounts for local meteorological and topographical factors influencing ambient pollution concentrations. However, air quality modeling is less granular than the intake fraction approach, implying less precision in measuring population sizes potentially exposed to fossil fuel-related pollution.

Overall exposure is higher in densely populated countries and where emissions sources are inland, whereas exposure is lower in coastal areas (where much of the pollution disperses over the oceans).

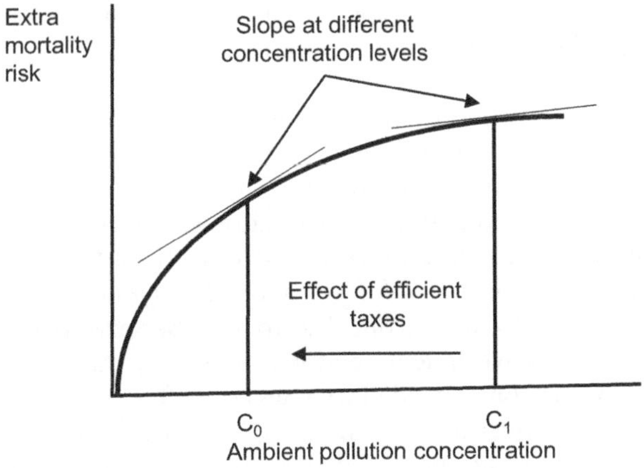

Figure A8.1 Shape of the Concentration Response Function.

Source: Authors.

Concentration response functions—these functions, which are estimated in the epidemiological literature, indicate how relative mortality risks for different illnesses vary with local $PM_{2.5}$ concentrations.

Some evidence suggests that the relationship between relative mortality risk and air pollution concentrations begins to flatten out at high levels of pollution concentration, because people's ability to absorb more pollution becomes saturated (see Figure A8.1). Somewhat paradoxically, additional pollution emissions do less harm in this case at concentration C_1 than at C_0 in the figure. This function might suggest that the efficient tax on emissions or fuels should be lower (given other factors) in countries with high pollution concentrations. If, however, emissions or fuel taxes of the scale typically needed to reflect local air emissions damages in high-pollution countries were implemented, emissions would fall considerably, most likely lowering pollution concentrations below levels at which the response function might flatten out. In turn, this implies it is reasonable to assume the environmental damage function is flat when assessing efficient emissions fees.

Mortality risk values—these are from studies measuring peoples' willingness to pay for mortality risk reductions in different countries. One approach is "stated preference" studies using responses to questionnaires, where people are asked direct questions about their money and risk trade-offs. These studies can target a sample that is representative of the at-risk populations and specific hazards, such as cancer, posed by air pollution. The studies are, however, hypothetical—whether survey respondents would actually behave the way they say they would when confronted with risk-money trade-offs in practice is unclear, leaving open the question of how accurately they describe people's actual trade-offs. Other studies infer mortality/income trade-offs from market data, such as wage premiums paid to jobs with higher occupational hazards, though studies are only available for a limited number of countries.[13]

The estimates in CPAT start with a synthesis of 700 stated preference studies (see OECD 2012). After updating for inflation and real per capita income, the analysis implies a value of about $5.2 million per death avoided for 2022 for the average advanced country. This figure is extrapolated to other countries based on their per capita income relative to the advanced country average and an assumed elasticity for the mortality value with respect to per capita income that declines from 1.2 to 0.8 because per capita income increases.[14] Not all governments endorse monetary valuation of mortality risk, but some valuation is needed to assess the efficient policy response and is implicit in actual government policies affecting health outcomes.

Local air emissions factors—local air emissions rates for fossil fuels in different sectors (and projections out to 2030) in CPAT are taken from an international database.[15] The emissions factors represent an average over newer emissions sources (that may have advanced emissions control technologies) and older sources—the average therefore tends to decline over time because capital stocks turn over.[16] The cross-country data are more extensive for the power and transport sectors—for the industrial and building sectors, data gaps in CPAT are filled using power sector emissions rates (this tends to give conservative estimates to the extent abatement technologies are more common in power).

Annex 8.3 Examples of Local Air Pollution Fees[17]

Chile. Chile is a pioneer in applying taxes to local air pollutants, including $PM_{2.5}$, NO_x, and SO_2, where fees vary across municipalities. The tax rate for a given pollutant in a municipality is the product of three factors:

- *An air quality coefficient*: equal to 1.2 if the municipality has "saturated" pollution concentrations exceeding national standards, 1.1 if concentrations are "latent" or 80–100 percent of the standard, and 1.0 otherwise;
- *Per capita environmental cost of the pollutant*: set at $0.9 for $PM_{2.5}$, $0.01 for SO_2, and $0.025 for NO_x; and
- *Population in the municipality*.

Under this formula, a hypothetical coal plant in Puente Alto, a municipality with population of 625,500 and defined as saturated will be subject to a tax of $67,560 per ton of $PM_{2.5}$. In contrast, if the same plant is located in Contulmo, an area with 5,500 inhabitants, which is neither saturated nor latent, it would face a tax of $495 per ton of $PM_{2.5}$.

Sweden. In 1992, Sweden introduced a tax on NO_x emissions from electricity and heat-producing boilers, stationary combustion engines, and gas turbines producing at least 25 gigawatt hours of energy per year. At the time,

Sweden was facing a serious soil acidification and water eutrophication problem caused partly by NO_x emissions. Revenues from the tax are rebated in proportion to energy generation—sources with high emissions relative to their energy output are net payers to the program, whereas sources with low emissions intensity are net recipients. The charge was raised in 2008 to $4,600 per ton of NO_x. Continuous monitoring of emissions was also made mandatory—every plant submits a tax return once a year stating NO_x emitted and energy produced with all sites subject to on-site inspection every 7–10 years.

Annex 8.4 Measuring the Costs of Traffic Congestion

CPAT provides estimates for 170 countries of the average and external costs of traffic congestion (for urban centers or average nationwide) using the following assumptions and data sources.

The starting point is average travel delay per vehicle km collected by TomTom (see https://www.tomtom.com) through navigation devices, in-dashboard systems, and smartphones in 400 cities across 54 countries. TomTom establishes a baseline of travel times during uncongested, free-flow conditions across each road segment in each city—observed travel times are then compared with free-flow times to infer average delays per vehicle km. Delays are weighted by the amount of driving on road segments to calculate average delays across different cities, and these are then averaged across cities to obtain nationwide average delays.

Statistical methods are used to infer, for countries in the TomTom database, relationships between travel delays and various country-level characteristics like per capita income growth rate, portion of vehicle travel on highways, and energy use per capita.[18] The relationships are then combined with country-level characteristics for countries outside the TomTom database to extrapolate congestion costs per km to these countries. Where data are unavailable for doing extrapolations (for example, some African countries) average travel delays are inferred from an average of countries with a similar per capita income in the same region.

Regarding the value of travel time (VOT), according to economic theory, at the margin, people should organize their time such that they are indifferent between an extra hour at work and at home. This means that an extra hour of time (whether spent at home or at work) can be valued by the benefit to individuals from an extra hour of work, namely, the net-of-tax wage. More generally, the VOT could be somewhat lower than the net-of-tax wage (if people enjoy driving, for example, because they can listen to music) or higher (if people enjoy the workplace, for example, because of social interactions).

A large empirical literature estimates the VOT for personal travel using questionnaires (for example, asking people what tolls they might pay for a faster commute) and studies of market behavior (for example, inferring people's willingness to pay extra auto fuel and parking costs to save time compared with a slower travel mode). These studies suggest that the VOT is about half the market wage for general automobile travel, moderately higher for commuting (for example, because of penalties for late arrival at work), and rises approximately in proportion to income.[19] In CPAT, the VOT is assumed to be 60 percent of the market wage, given that most delays occur during the commuter-dominated peak period. Market wage data are taken from the International Labor Organization's Global Wage Database (see https://www.ilo.org/resource/global-wage-report).

Another data source—on the functional relationship between travel speed or time and traffic volume—can be used to convert average time costs per vehicle km driven to external time costs imposed on other vehicles on the road. A commonly used relation specifies travel delay as a simple power function of traffic volume relative to road capacity:

$$T = T_f \cdot \left\{1 + \alpha \cdot \left(V / V_K\right)^{\beta}\right\} \tag{A8.1}$$

where α and β are parameters, T denotes travel time per km, T_f is travel time under free-flow conditions, V is traffic volume, and V_K is the maximum traffic volume (typically about 2,000 vehicles per hour). In this function, the extra delay one vehicle imposes on other vehicles is simply β times the average delay per kilometer. Empirical studies suggest that β is roughly in the range of 2.5–5.0, with higher values in this range applicable to larger urban centers.[20] In CPAT, β is taken as 0.4.

Costs need to be scaled by average vehicle occupancy rates to infer the costs that one vehicle imposes on other road users. For advanced economies, average car occupancy rates in urban centers are about 1.4—average occupancy rates for buses are higher (about 10–20) but buses account for a tiny share (1 percent or less) of vehicle km traveled.[21] In CPAT, occupancy rates averaged across all vehicles are taken to be 1.6 for all countries.[22] Finally, an extra vehicle km by a truck is assumed to contribute twice as much to congestion as an extra car km—although trucks take up more road space and are driven more slowly, a partially offsetting factor is that they tend to be driven on less congested roads.

Annex 8.5 Measuring the Costs of Traffic Accidents

Again, CPAT provides data for 170 countries on external accident costs per vehicle km, based on various data and assumptions (estimates are only moderately sensitive to alternative assumptions).

Following economic theory, motorists are assumed to consider risks posed to themselves (or other vehicle occupants) from single-vehicle collisions in their driving decisions but not injury risks they pose to pedestrians and cyclists. For injury risks to occupants in multivehicle collisions, the delineation between those considered by drivers and external costs is murkier. In an extreme case with no change in driving behavior, an extra km driven by one vehicle increases risks to others (because vehicles have less road space and are more likely to collide). In this case, injury risks to other vehicle occupants increase in proportion with the amount of traffic and on average half the injuries in multivehicle collisions are external (assuming one driver is at fault who considers risks to occupants of their, but not other, vehicles). In practice, with more vehicles on the road, motorists may drive more slowly and carefully, leading to a reduction in accident frequency and severity—in an extreme case, with no change in the severity-adjusted injury risk to other vehicle occupants. An intermediate assumption is used in CPAT, splitting the difference between the two extreme cases, with one-quarter of multivehicle collision injuries treated as external (see also Parry 2004).

Data on road fatalities in CPAT, and their breakdown by pedestrian/cyclists and single and multivehicle accidents, are pooled from various sources (IRF 2022, OECD 2023, WHO 2024) using an assumption (based on several country case studies) that approximately 60 percent of vehicle occupant deaths occur in single-vehicle collisions. Fatalities are monetized using the same mortality value as used for pollution deaths.

Data are not available for most countries for other components of external accident costs—nonfatal injuries and third-party medical costs/property damages. However, CPAT extrapolates these costs using a functional relationship, estimated using several country case studies, between (1) the ratio of these external costs to the external costs of fatalities and (2) the share of external fatalities in total fatalities (see Parry et al. 2014, Chapter 5). In countries with a low incidence of pedestrian deaths, the relative size of other external costs tends to be higher (because injuries to vehicle occupants are less likely to be fatal than to pedestrians). In the case studies, most of the medical costs associated with all traffic-related injuries are assumed to be external to drivers (borne by the government and insurance companies), though individuals bear a minor portion of these costs through co-payments and deductibles. Similarly, some of the property damage costs are borne by individuals (in co-payments, elevated future premiums after a crash) and some by third-party insurance companies.

At first glance, given their much greater weight, it might appear that trucks would impose greater accident risks to other road users than cars, but a counteracting factor is that trucks are driven at slower speeds than cars and by professionals. In CPAT, accident costs per km for heavy vehicles are assumed to be the same as for cars (see also Parry and Small 2009).

Annex 8.6 Local Congestion Pricing

Congestion pricing emerges at the local level, often in the form of cordon tolls, where drivers pay as they pass points connecting a cordon about a city center—these programs have appeal for older cities with higgledy-piggledy streets that would be impractical to price individually. A close relation is the area license program, where drivers also pay for trips starting and ending within the pricing area.

Cordon-pricing type programs are inefficient in that they impose the same fee regardless of trip distance and can exacerbate congestion elsewhere because people change routes to bypass the pricing region. Nonetheless, well-designed cordon tolls (including appropriate placement of the pricing boundary, varying the toll with driving direction and time of day, and possibly using multiple pricing rings) may still capture a large portion of the benefits from more comprehensive pricing of the road network (see, for example, Safirova et al. 2005). Other local programs (more common in the United States) price individual highway lanes, leaving drivers with the option to use a free, but more congested, lane—sometimes these take the form of opening lanes previously restricted to high-occupancy vehicles to single-occupancy vehicles in exchange for a fee, or they are applied to newly constructed lanes.

Ideally, congestion fees would be more fine-tuned, varying by road class within urban networks and with congestion levels at different times within the peak period to reduce driving more where and when congestion is most severe. However, there is a trade-off between effectiveness and practicality. It may be computationally challenging to estimate external costs for every road segment in an urban road network (particularly given that pricing at one point diverts traffic, affecting congestion elsewhere within the network), and elaborate pricing systems would also impose substantial information-processing costs on drivers (though satellite navigation systems might provide toll calculations).

Congestion tolls may also impose a disproportionately large burden relative to income on low-income households because they have higher driving-to-income ratios than wealthier households, and they value the travel time savings less than high-wage earners (see, for example, Parry 2009). This may warrant targeting some of the toll revenues to low-income households (for example, through subsidized fares for transit services patronized by poor households or lump-sum annual rebates to low-income vehicle owners residing in urban centers with tolls).

Examples of congestion fees include:[23]

- *Singapore.* An area license (or day-pass) program was introduced in 1975 that dramatically raised travel speeds within the restricted zone, though also initially increased congestion outside of the zone (Santos 2005). In 1998, area licensing was replaced with an electronically debited toll on certain links, with the objective of maintaining average speeds of 30–40 miles per hour on expressways and 12–18 miles per hour on major roads. Charges rise and fall in 30-minute steps during peak periods, based on congestion levels observed in the previous quarter.
- *London.* An area licensing program was introduced in 2003. The current charge is equivalent to $19, which applies to all driving between 7 AM and 6 PM on weekdays and 12 PM and 6 PM on weekends. Collection is

enabled by video cameras at checkpoints into and within the priced area that record each vehicle's license plate, with penalties mailed to drivers who have not prepaid.

- *Milan.* A similar program to the London charge operates in Milan, with a fixed daily charge equivalent to $8.
- *Stockholm.* A cordon toll was implemented in 2007 covering an area of about 36 square kilometers (again, enforcement is based on license plate recognition, with exemptions for emergency and low emissions vehicles, buses, and motorcycles). Fees vary between the equivalent of $1.6 and $3.8 over the course of the weekday.

Notes

1 See WHO (2024). Indoor air pollution also poses mortality risks but with less relevance for fossil fuel pricing (see Annex 8.1).

2 Broader costs of local air pollution include morbidity, impaired visibility, building corrosion, and reduced agricultural yields (from acid rain), though studies suggest these cost effects are modest relative to those from mortality (see NRC 2010).

3 For example, in China tons of power plant CO_2 emissions in 2022 were about 10,000 times higher than SO_2 emissions (authors' calculation from CPAT).

4 On average, road damage increases approximately in proportion to the third power of a vehicle's axle weight (Small, Winston, and Evans 1989).

5 This estimate is updated from Black et al. (2023).

6 Including measures targeted at vehicles (for example, requirements for seat belts, airbags, infant seats, sensors); drivers (for example, penalties for drunk driving, cell phone use, speeding); and infrastructure (for example, crash barriers, speed limits, medians, traffic lights).

7 The transition to PAYD can occur on a voluntary basis: drivers with below-average annual km would have the strongest incentives to take up PAYD, and because they switched, premiums would rise (to maintain insurance company profits) for the remaining pool of drivers with lump-sum insurance, encouraging further shifting to PAYD.

8 Parry and Small (2005). Local air emissions can also be proportional to driving, rather than fuel use, in countries where new vehicle emissions are regulated on a grams per km basis and are largely maintained during vehicle lifetimes through inspection maintenance programs.

9 The calculations assume local air emissions rates (averaged over all firms) would decline to those of the cleanest firms in the country in response to fuel price reform because of implicit rebating for downstream mitigation technologies.

10 Accounting for preexisting fuel taxes (see Chapter 5). The emissions reductions are computed assuming emissions are reduced in a least-cost way through economywide carbon pricing.

11 This would be given by the estimated damages per ton of SO_2 divided by a price per ton of CO_2.

12 At least in competitive labor markets, higher-risk jobs tend to compensate workers through higher wages (for example, Rosen 1986).

13 See, for example, Alberini (2019) for more discussion of methodologies for mortality risk valuation.

14 Based on Robinson, Hammitt, and O'Keeffe (2019). The extrapolations use purchasing power parity income per capita, which accounts for local price levels and more accurately reflects people's willingness to pay for risk reductions out of their

own income (Masterman and Viscusi 2018; Robinson, Hammitt, and O'Keeffe 2019). The approach in CPAT is conservative in that studies using market data tend to yield somewhat higher values for mortality risks than those from stated preference studies. Mortality valuations may also differ across countries with differences in life expectancy, health, religion, culture, economic and social support, and so on; however, the quantitative implications of these factors are not well established.

15 Wagner et al. (2020). The database is based on various estimation techniques, assumptions (for example that emissions rates conform to regulations), and extrapolations.

16 An exception is diesel vehicles where emissions rate estimates were revised upward after evidence (in the Volkswagen case) that on-road emissions rates exceeded new vehicle standards.

17 This Annex is based on IEA (2017) and Mesa-Puyo and Zhunussova (2023).

18 Compiled from IRF (2022), OECD (2023), and the World Bank's World Development Indicators.

19 See Small, Verhoef, and Lindsey (2024), Ch 2, for a recent summary of the literature.

20 With $\alpha = 0.15$ and $\beta = 4$, the formula is known as the Bureau of Public Roads function, which is used widely in US transportation planning. For more discussion, see Small, Verhoef, and Lindsey (2024), Ch 3.

21 All figures are from Parry and Small (2009), Table 2.

22 Buses may account for a higher portion of road traffic in developing countries (which would raise average occupancy rates across all vehicles), but scooters and other motorized two wheelers may have high modal shares (which lowers average occupancy rates).

23 Examples are compiled from various websites.

References

Alberini, Anna. 2019. "Revealed versus Stated Preferences: What Have We Learned about Valuation and Behavior?" *Review of Environmental Economics and Policy* 13: 283–98.

Black, Simon, Antung A. Liu, Ian Parry, and Nate Vernon. 2023. "IMF Fossil Fuel Subsidies Data: 2023 Update." IMF Working Paper 23/169, International Monetary Fund, Washington, DC.

Clements, Benedict, David Coady, Stefania Fabrizio, Sanjeev Gupta, Trevor Serge Coleridge Alleyne, and Carlo A Sdralevich, eds. 2013. *Energy Subsidy Reform: Lessons and Implications.* Washington, DC: IMF.

Coady, David, Ian Parry, and Baoping Shang. 2018. "Energy Price Reform: Lessons for Policymakers." *Review of Environmental Economics and Policy* 12: 197–219.

European Commission: CE Delft, Directorate-General for Mobility and Transport, Huib van Essen, Davide Fiorello, Kareen El Beyrouty, Cuno Bieler, Lisanne van Wijngaarden, Arno Schroten, Riccardo Parolin, Marco Brambilla, Daniel Sutter, MaffiiSilvia, & Francesca Fermi. (2020). Handbook on the external costs of transport: version 2019 – 1.1, Publications Office. https://doi.org/10.2832/51388

European Environment Agency (EEA). 2023. *Harm to Human Health from Air Pollution in Europe: Burden of Disease 2023.* Copenhagen.

Ezzati, Majid. 2005. "Indoor Air Pollution and Health in Developing Countries." *Lancet* 366: 104–106.

Inchauste, Gabriela, and David G. Victor. 2017. *The Political Economy of Energy Subsidy Reform.* Washington, DC: World Bank.

International Energy Agency (IEA). 2017. *Nitrogen Oxides (NOx) Charge.* Paris. https://www.iea.org/policies/1198-nitrogen-oxides-nox-charge

International Road Federation (IRF). 2022. *World Road Statistics 2022*. Geneva.
Kim, He, and He Chaeyoung. 2024. "Vehicle and Fuel Taxation for Transport Demand Management: Learnings from the Literature through a Development Lens." Policy Research Working Paper 10647, World Bank, Washington, DC.
Lindsey, Robin, and Georgina Santos. 2020. "Addressing Transportation and Environmental Externalities with Economics: Are Policy Makers Listening?" *Research in Transportation Economics* 82: 100872.
Masterman, Clayton, and Kip W. Viscusi. 2018. "The Income Elasticity of Global Values of a Statistical Life: Stated Preference Evidence." *Journal of Benefit-Cost Analysis* 9: 407–34.
Mesa-Puyo, Diego, and Karlygash Zhunussova. 2023. "Chile: Technical Assistance Report-An Evaluation of Improved Tax Options." IMF Country Report 23/35, International Monetary Fund, Washington, DC. https://www.imf.org/en/Publications/CR/Issues/2023/01/19/Chile-Technical-Assistance-Report-An-Evaluation-of-Improved-Tax-Options-528348
National Research Council (NRC). 2010. *Hidden Costs of Energy: Unpriced Consequences of Energy Production and Use*. Washington, DC: NRC, National Academies Press.
Organization for Economic Co-operation and Development (OECD). 2012. *Mortality Risk Valuation in Environment, Health and Transport Policies*. Paris.
Organization for Economic Co-operation and Development (OECD). 2023. *International Transport Forum Statistics*. Paris.
Parry, Ian. 2004. "Comparing Alternative Policies to Reduce Traffic Accidents." *Journal of Urban Economics* 56: 346–68.
Parry, Ian. 2009. "Pricing Urban Congestion." *Annual Review of Resource Economics* 1: 461–84.
Parry, Ian, Dirk Heine, Shanjun Li, and Eliza Lis. 2014. *Getting Energy Prices Right: from Principle to Practice*. Washington, DC: International Monetary Fund.
Parry, Ian, and Kenneth A. Small. 2005. "Does Britain or The United States Have the Right Gasoline Tax?" *American Economic Review* 95: 1276–89.
Parry, Ian, and Kenneth A. Small. 2009. "Should Urban Transit Subsidies Be Reduced?" *American Economic Review* 99: 700–24.
Parry, Ian, Chandara Veung, and Dirk Heine. 2015. "How Much Carbon Pricing is in Countries Own Interests? The Critical Role of Co-Benefits." *Climate Change Economics* 6 (4): 1–26.
Robinson, Lisa A., James K. Hammitt, and Lucy O'Keeffe. 2019. "Valuing Mortality Risk Reductions in Global Benefit-Cost Analysis." *Journal of Benefit Cost Analysis* 10 (Supplement 1): 15–50.
Rosen, Sherwin. 1986. "The Theory of Equalizing Differences." *Handbook of Labor Economics*, vol. 1, edited by In Orley C. Ashenfelter and Richard Layard, 641–92. New York, NY: Elsevier.
Safirova, Elena, Kenneth Gillingham, Winston Harrington, Peter Nelson, and Abram Lipman. 2005. "Choosing Congestion Pricing Policy: Cordon Tolls Versus Link-Based Tolls." *Transportation Research Record* 1932: 169–177.
Santos, Georgina, ed. 2004. *Road Pricing: Theory and Practice*. Research in Transportation Economics 9. Amsterdam: Elsevier.
Santos, Georgina. 2005. "Urban Congestion Charging: A Comparison between London and Singapore." *Transport Reviews* 25: 511–34.
Small, Kenneth A., Erik T. Verhoef, and Robin Lindsey. 2024. *The Economics of Urban Transportation*. 3rd ed. New York, NY: Routledge.
Small, Kenneth A., Clifford Winston, and Carol A. Evans. 1989. *Road Work*. Washington, DC: Brookings Institution.

Tselentis, Dimitrios, George Yannis, and Eleni I. Vlahogianni. 2016. “Innovative Insurance Schemes: Pay as/how You Drive.” *Transportation Research Procedia* 14: 362–71.

Wagner, Fabian, Jens Borken-Kleefeld, Gregor Kiesewetter, Zbigniew Klimont, Wolfgang Schoepp, and Markus Amann. 2020. *Implied Emission Factors in the World Bank’s Climate Policy Assessment Tool (CPAT)*. Laxenburg: Institute for Applied Systems Analysis.

World Health Organization (WHO). 2021. *WHO Global Air Quality Guidelines: Particulate Matter (PM2.5 and PM10), Ozone, Nitrogen Dioxide, Sulfur Dioxide and Carbon Monoxide*. Geneva.

World Health Organization (WHO). 2024. *The Global Health Observatory*. Geneva. https://www.who.int/data/gho/data/indicators

9 The Role of International Coordination

Main Messages

- A dramatic scaling up of mitigation ambition and policy at the global level is urgently needed if temperature goals are to be achieved. Getting global GHG emissions on track with limiting warming to below 2°C requires new measures equivalent to a global CO_2 price upward of $80 per ton by 2030.
- The global annual mitigation costs of aligning emissions in 2030 with 2°C are manageable (about 0.5 percent of global GDP), can be progressively distributed across country groups, and for many countries (especially developing ones) could be offset by (non-climate) domestic environmental co-benefits.
- Scaling up ambition and policy action under the Paris Agreement is hampered by obstacles to stronger negotiation (too many parties and parameters) and to unilateral mitigation (concerns about competitiveness and policy uncertainties in other countries).
- Additional international policy coordination mechanisms could also complement and reinforce the Paris Agreement—core elements include a limited number of negotiators/parameters, concrete and monitorable policy actions, and differential requirements/financing mechanisms to address equity concerns.
- Coordination mechanisms might include agreement over carbon price floors—perhaps starting with regional coordination regimes—or over enhanced emissions targets among large emitters.
- Supplementary global coordination regimes over carbon pricing and feebates could progressively decarbonize international transportation and reduce methane emissions from extractives.

DOI: 10.4324/9781003755012-9
This chapter has been made available under a CC-BY-NC-ND license.

- Private and public sources of climate finance from advanced to developing countries can be scaled up through bilateral and multilateral donations, robust carbon price signals in developing countries, and public sources like carbon pricing or charges on international aviation and maritime.
- International cooperation over critical technologies could focus on scaling up public and private research and demonstration, robust cross-border patenting, lowering tariff and non-tariff barriers, preventing market fragmentation for critical minerals, and appropriate governance for geoengineering.
- Emissions offsets can promote more cost-effective mitigation from a global perspective and direct finance to developing countries but, for multiple reasons, they may on net increase emissions. Focusing offsets on nationwide emissions may help with these risks.

Coordination Mechanisms for Aligning Global Emissions with Temperature Goals

Implementation and Ambition Gaps—A Closer Look

What Policies at the Global Level Are Needed to Get on Track with Warming Goals?

As noted in Chapter 1, without new or tightening of existing mitigation policies, global greenhouse gases (GHGs) are projected to continue rising gradually to 2030, whereas reductions of 25 or 50 percent below 2019 levels are needed to be on track with keeping warming to 2°C or 1.5°C, respectively. Achieving these emissions reductions is extremely challenging—it would require new measures (on top of already implemented mitigation policies) that have the equivalent effect on global emissions as an additional global carbon price rising to over $80 per ton by 2030 for 2°C, and dramatically higher for 1.5°C. See Figure 9.1, though uncertainties over needed prices escalate rapidly with more ambitious temperature goals.

How Does Delayed Action on Cutting Global Emissions Put Temperature Goals at Risk?

To avoid an "emissions cliff edge" in the 2030s, it is critical that global emissions are cut rapidly this decade. For example, if current targets for 2030 remain (and are achieved on linear emissions reduction trajectories), keeping 1.5°C alive would require (improbably): (1) cutting 2035 emissions by 75 percent; (2) achieving net zero emissions in 2040; and (3) net removals of CO_2 from the atmosphere after 2040 (see Figure 9.2). The last requirement

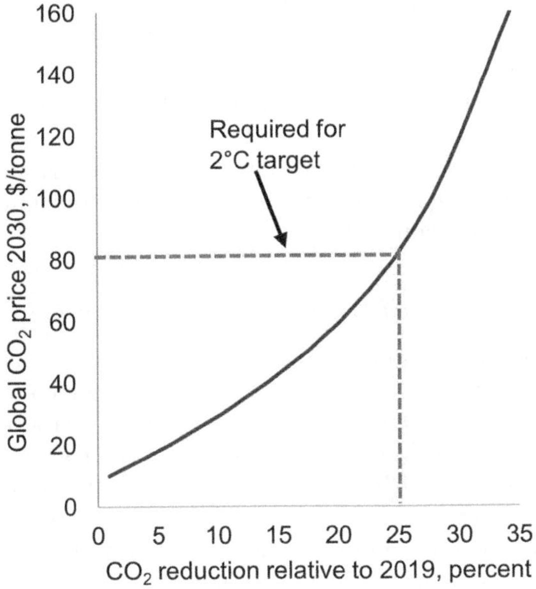

Figure 9.1 2030 Global CO_2 Price Implied by Alternative Temperature Goals.

Source: Authors using CPAT.

Note: Calculations are based on energy-related CO_2 but the functional relationship in the figure would be similar for total greenhouse gases.

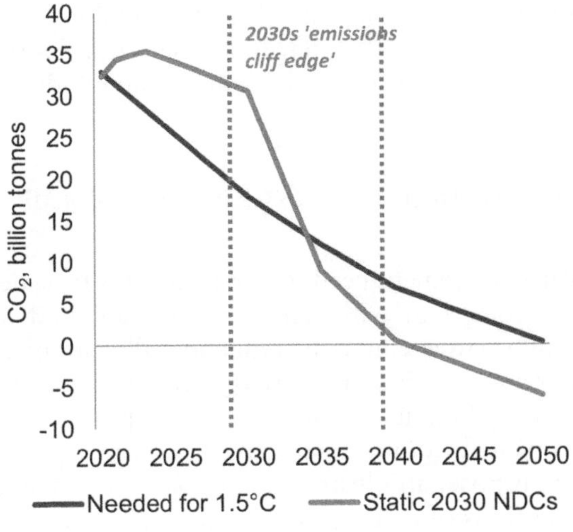

Figure 9.2 Emissions Pathways for 1.5°C with and without Delayed Emissions Reductions.

Source: Black et al. (2024) based on IPCC (2022).

Note: NDCs = Nationally Determined Contributions.

implies widescale use of very costly technologies—for example, direct air capture currently costs about $100–600 per ton CO_2 removed,[1] or 1–6 percent of global GDP for removing 10 billion tons a year.

The rate of decarbonization under this cliff edge scenario is dramatic—global CO_2 emissions would need to decline over 7 percent each year from 2030 to 2040. For comparison, the once-in-a-generation annual fall in global CO_2 emissions in 2020, because of the coronavirus pandemic, was just under 6 percent (after which emissions rebounded).[2]

How Does Current Mitigation Ambition Vary across Country Groups?

For informing dialogue over enhanced global mitigation action, it is important to start with a clear understanding of where key country groups, and large emitters, are in terms of current ambition in Nationally Determined Contributions (NDCs). High-income countries as a group have the most aggressive mitigation ambition—relative to 2030 baseline levels, they increased their ambition from 10 to 32 percent between 2015 and 2024. By contrast, middle-income countries increased their ambition by 6 percentage points, to 14 percent in 2024, while ambition in low-income countries is largely unchanged at 8 percent (see Figure 9.3, panel 1). Realistically, the global ambition gap cannot be closed without more action in middle- and low-income countries, given (from Chapter 2, Figure 2.7) they account for 68 percent of global baseline CO_2 emissions in 2030 (and 55 percent of cumulative emissions). Under current NDCs, per capita emissions in the EU, Japan, and other advanced economies would drop below those of major middle-income countries such as China and Russia. Emissions per capita in most low-income countries, such as India, Indonesia, and South Africa, would, however, remain much lower than in both high- and middle-income countries (see Figure 9.3, panel 2).

What Might Be an Equitable Approach to Closing the Global Mitigation Ambition Gap?

Parties to the Paris Agreement need to agree on ways to scale up global mitigation ambition, consistent with temperature goals, and informed by the trade-offs from alternative emissions reduction allocations in terms of their burdens on different countries and country groups. Central to this dialogue will be some notion of equity—although there is presently no consensus on how this should be defined, it is instructive to consider possibilities to frame debate. For this purpose, an illustrative approach, which averages over several alternative notions of equity from a recent, large study involving developed and developing country analysts, is used here.[3]

For a 2°C scenario, the illustrative approach implies reducing high-, middle-, and low-income country CO_2 emissions by 40, 27, and 11 percent, respectively, below baseline levels in 2030 and global emissions by 25

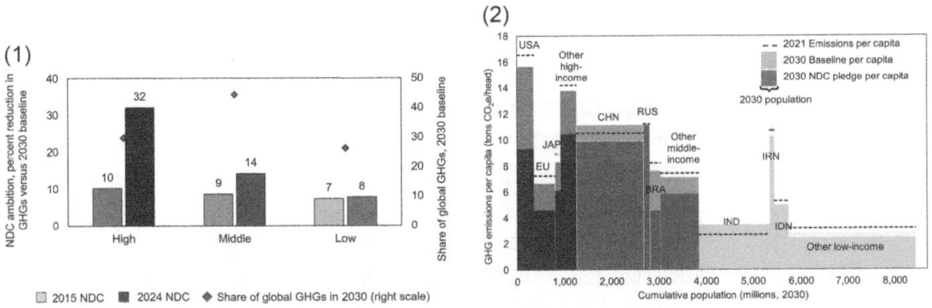

Figure 9.3 Distribution of Ambition in NDCs. Panel 1. By Country Income Group, Panel 2. By Per Capita Income.

Source: Black et al. (2024) using CPAT.

Note: Panel 1 is for 150 countries with quantifiable NDCs and (for developing countries) averaging over unconditional and conditional NDCs (as of writing some countries are updating NDCs but only modestly). Panel 2 shows the top three emitters in 2030 in the baseline scenario in each country grouping, with the areas on chart representing total country emissions (emissions per capita times population). Income groups follow the World Bank classification, with low income including upper-lower-income and low-income countries and middle income including upper-middle-income countries. US NDC is from 2024. GHGs = global greenhouse gases; NDCs = Nationally Determined Contributions.

percent—this could still accommodate absolute emissions growth (above current levels) in some low-income countries like India. For a 1.5°C scenario, the approach implies reducing high-, middle-, and low-income country CO_2 emissions by 64, 52, and 35 percent, respectively, below baseline levels in 2030 and global emissions by 50 percent. Under the 2°C scenario, for example, ambition increases above current NDCs by 8, 16, and 4 percentage points for high-, middle-, and low-income country groups, respectively, though with significant differences across individual countries (see Figure 9.4).

What Are the Costs of Achieving (Illustrative) Temperature-Aligned Emissions Reductions?

Figure 9.5 provides estimates of the annualized mitigation costs in 2030 for G20 countries and globally from meeting the above emissions reductions. The figure focuses on the 2°C scenario (given uncertainties over costs for 1.5°C), energy-related CO_2 emissions, and assumes countries achieve their reductions at least cost (implicitly through carbon pricing but leaving aside recycling benefits). Globally mitigation costs, expressed relative to GDP, are a manageable 0.5 percent and, for the most part, are progressively distributed across G20 countries, with costs typically higher in advanced economies and smaller in low-income countries. These cost estimates largely build off standard mitigation cost curves in the literature (see Chapter 5), though they may miss some transitional costs (like temporarily idled labor and capital) and they would rise disproportionately with deeper abatement levels.

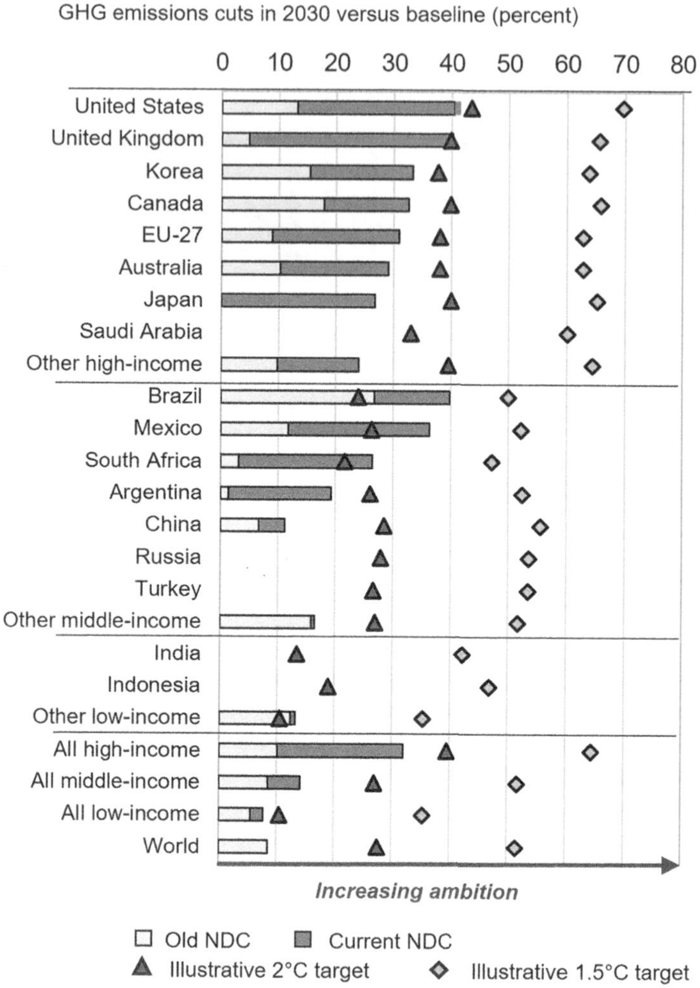

Figure 9.4 Ambition Gaps between Illustrative Equitable Emissions Reductions and NDCs.

Source: Black et al. (2024).

Note: If no NDC is shown, the target is either already met in the baseline or is not possible to quantify. See Figure 9.3 for the definition of income groups. US NDC is for 2024. GHGs = global greenhouse gases; NDCs = Nationally Determined Contributions.

Figure 9.5 also indicates the domestic environmental co-benefits from reduced fossil fuel use in response to carbon mitigation, such as reduced local air pollution mortality (see Chapter 8) but excluding global climate benefits. For many, especially developing, countries such as China and India, these co-benefits exceed mitigation costs, underscoring again that mitigation (up to a point) can be in many countries' own interests before even counting climate benefits.

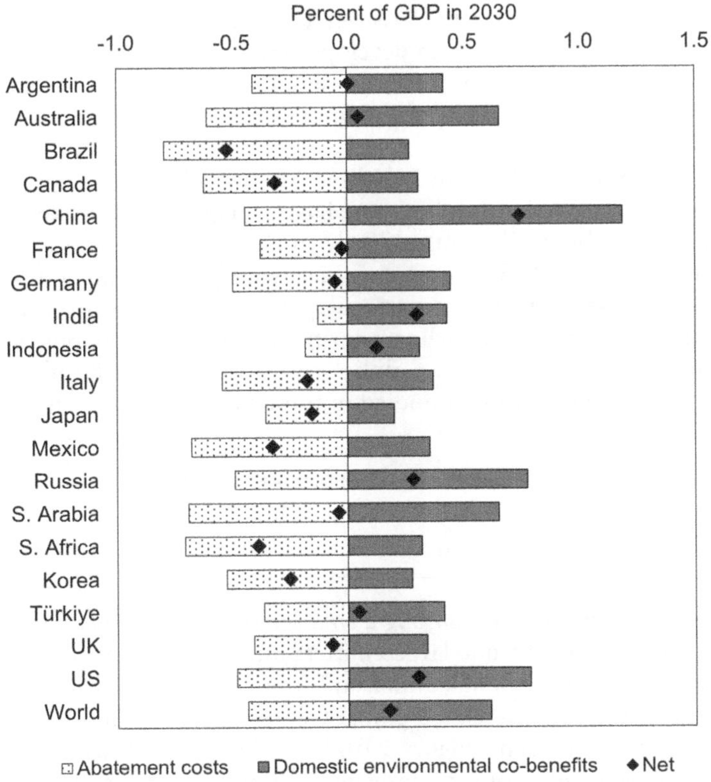

Figure 9.5 Mitigation Costs and Domestic Environmental Co-benefits from Illustrative Scenario for Aligning CO_2 Emissions with 2°C Goal, 2030.

Source: Authors using CPAT.

Note: Assumes countries meet emissions goals at least cost through carbon pricing (benefits from recycling revenues are ignored). Costs would be moderately larger if broader GHGs (mainly methane and forestry) were included. See Figure 9.3 for the definition of income groups.

Policy Coordination Mechanisms for Cutting Global Emissions

Are Supplementary International Policy Coordination Mechanisms Needed?

Key obstacles hinder the scaling up of global mitigation action under the Paris framework, including:

- *Negotiating ambition.* Negotiating enhanced mitigation ambition is difficult given the large number of parties to the Agreement (195) and the considerable heterogeneity in mitigation targets which hinders cross-country comparisons (see Chapter 2).
- *Unilateral action.* It is difficult to aggressively scale up mitigation policy when countries act unilaterally because of concerns about competitiveness and policy uncertainties in other countries.

- *Addressing equity*. Under the Paris Agreement there are no automatic mechanisms for ensuring policies in developed countries are more stringent than in developing countries, or for ensuring an accessible, transparent amount of climate finance for low-income countries (see the following section).

Enhanced ambition and action by China, the world's largest emitter, could galvanize other countries to follow and have a major effect. Nonetheless, the Paris Agreement by itself seems unlikely to achieve the reductions in global emissions needed by 2030 to get on track with global temperature goals.[4] Without a supplementary international policy coordination mechanism, a unilateral regime of border carbon adjustments may emerge, but this would have limited effects on scaling up global mitigation because it only prices the minor portion of emissions embodied in traded products (see Chapter 6).

What Core Elements Are Needed for a Complementary Policy Coordination Mechanism?

Ideally, the mechanism should:

- *Ensure core participation among a small number of key players*. Potential participants might include large emitters and (representatives of) country blocs. For example, China, India, and the EU alone account for almost half of baseline energy-related global CO_2 emissions in 2030 and the G20 accounts for 82 percent (Figure 9.6). Procedures for allowing other countries to subsequently join the agreement should also be established.
- *Specify concrete, coordinated, and monitorable policy actions*. This will facilitate stronger domestic policy action.
- *Address international equity*. This could be achieved through (1) mitigation requirements differentiated by development level;[5] and (2) transparent mechanisms providing financial and technological support to developing countries (conditional on their meeting mitigation requirements).

How Might Coordination over Carbon Pricing Work?

Under a price coordination mechanism, such as an international carbon price floor (ICPF),[6] participants would agree to implement minimum carbon prices (rising over time) and also meet their NDC pledge if this is more stringent than the floor price. A carbon tax is the most natural instrument for implementing a price floor requirement, but emissions trading systems (ETSs) can be accommodated by combining them with price floors or setting allowance caps to align expected emissions prices with the international floor price. An ICPF offers focused negotiation because it targets a shared price floor, and if one country pushes for a higher price floor, this raises mitigation action for all participants (see Weitzman 2016).

At first, an ICPF might apply to CO_2 emissions from power and industry, given they are generally the most responsive emissions to pricing (see Chapter 5),

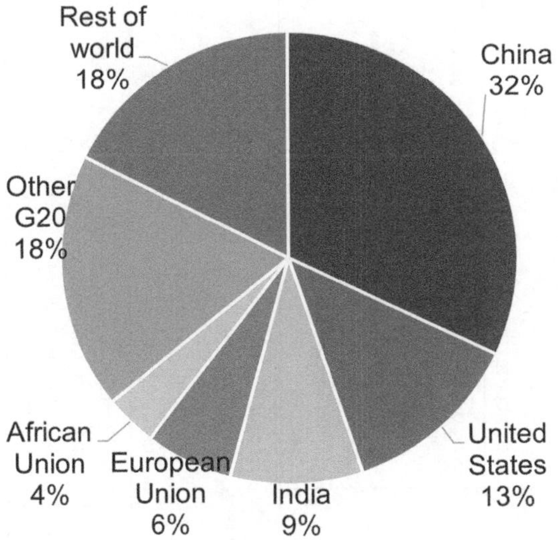

Figure 9.6 Shares of Global CO_2 Emissions in 2030 Business-as-Usual.

Source: Authors using CPAT.

The arrangement should work in conjunction with the Paris Agreement, meaning that participants should reduce their emissions by at least the amount implied by current NDC commitments and increase their climate finance donations.

most existing ETSs (operating nationally in about 35 countries) already cover these sectors (see Chapter 3), and fuels in these sectors are generally subject to light taxation (see Chapter 8), limiting the scope for undercutting a carbon price through lowering prior energy taxes. The price floor might be subsequently extended to all energy-related CO_2 emissions (separate agreements might cover other emissions—see the following section). Participants in a price floor agreement might impose border carbon adjustments on imports from non-participants to encourage broader participation, though this complicates negotiation and administration, especially when existing participants are subject to differing pricing requirements.

What Other Forms Might International Coordination Mechanisms Take?

Alternative coordination mechanisms among key countries might include (see Table 9.1 for a summary):

- *Country-level emissions targets.* Under this regime, participants would agree annual country-level emissions targets (progressively tightening over time), with flexibility in choosing mitigation instruments to implement the targets. This approach, however, involves a larger number of parameters (one per participant), leaves uncertainties over the policies that will be enacted in other countries, and if one member proposes a more stringent target this does not automatically raise action for other participants.

Table 9.1 Comparing International Regimes to Address Limitations of the Paris Agreement

Metric		*Paris Process by Itself (All Parties)*	*Supplementary Arrangement (Large Emitters)*		
			Carbon Price Floor	*Country-Level Emissions Targets*	*Global ETS*
Negotiating Greater Ambition	**Number of Parties**	D: Large	A: Small	A: Small	A: Small
	Number of Parameters	D. Large	A: One parameter per country grouping	N: One parameter per country	N: One parameter per country
	Type of Parameters	D: Heterogeneous pledges difficult to compare	A: Concrete global targets; higher prices → greater collective action	N: Concrete targets but more commitment by one country does not raise commitments in others	N: Concrete targets but more commitment by one country does not raise commitments in others
Scaling up Mitigation policy	**Policy uncertainty**	D: Aggressive unilateral policies deterred by uncertainty over others' policies	A: Concrete policies for all participants	N: Small group → pressure for ambitious targets but policies unspecified	A: Concrete policies for all participants
	Competitiveness	D: Deters aggressive unilateral policies	A: Largely addressed through coordinated policies	N: Partially addressed through targets but policies not specified	A: Largely addressed through coordinated policies
International Equity		D: Differentiated responsibilities difficult to compare, finance unclear	A: Allows differentiated floors and transparent transfers	A: Allows differentiated targets and transparent transfers	A: Allows permit trading ratios and transparent transfers

Source: Authors.

Note: A and D indicate an advantage or disadvantage of a regime, respectively, whereas N indicates neither a strong advantage nor disadvantage.

- *Global ETS*. This approach builds up a global emissions trading market through linking domestic ETSs. In its pure form, a global ETS would be cost-effective across participants and would eliminate country-specific volatility in emissions prices (due, for example, to country-level shifts in energy demand and supply). To help address international equity issues, permit trading ratios could be incorporated (specifying a permit from a low-income country is, say, worth three permits from an advanced country) though with some loss of global cost-effectiveness. Again, country-specific parameters (emissions caps) need to be agreed and a stricter target in one country does not affect commitments in others.

How Might International Coordination Regimes Be Monitored?

- *Pricing agreements*. Monitoring a carbon price floor agreement is straightforward in the sense that data on sectoral coverage and prices in carbon pricing programs are publicly available (see Chapter 3). Countries might also be allowed to meet the agreement through increases in their "emissions equivalent carbon price" (EECP) which adds up carbon pricing programs, accounting for their sectoral coverage, and fuel taxes, weighting each by their effectiveness at cutting economywide CO_2 emissions (relative to an economywide CO_2 price). Countries might, for example, meet a price floor requirement through increasing preexisting fuel taxes, or extending coverage of carbon pricing, rather than raising their formal carbon price, so long as the increase in their EECP is the same as that from meeting the formal requirements over carbon prices and sectoral coverage.[7]
- *Emissions agreements*. Monitoring an agreement over future emissions targets likely means assessing whether actual or envisioned policies are likely to achieve these targets. This requires operational methodologies for consistently measuring emissions baselines across countries and the emissions effects of different mitigation policies—in some cases, it might be simpler to monitor whether sectoral targets (for example, for renewables, electric vehicles) are being met rather than to disentangle the effects of granular policy measures (see Chapter 5).

What Are the Prospects for International Policy Coordination?

Predicting when an international policy coordination mechanism might emerge, who will participate in it, and what form it will take is highly speculative (not least given rising trade and security tensions) but there are some grounds for cautious optimism:

- *Collective benefits*: Countries may participate in an international coordination regime, and support robust mitigation requirements, because of the collective benefits of much larger emissions reductions if all participants meet these requirements.

- *National interests*: A coordination regime that successfully scaled up global mitigation is in the interests of key large emitters like China and India (which are especially vulnerable to climate change given their long and densely populated coastlines and large agricultural sectors).
- *Climate finance*: For low-income countries, a complementary agreement among a small number of advanced economies could provide robust and transparent financial and technological assistance in return for concrete mitigation actions.
- *Ring-fencing*: Separating a climate mitigation agreement from broader trade and security issues might be possible given the agreement would confer collective benefits on all participants.
- *Emerging regional programs may catalyze global action*: As most countries implement mitigation strategies over coming decades, it seems quite plausible that regional coordination mechanisms will emerge (for example, in Asia where carbon pricing programs are evolving, or between the EU and some of its trading partners), which could be stepping stones to a broader global agreement.
- *Precedents*: There is a diverse range of climate-specific and broader precedents for coordinated CO_2 mitigation regimes, such as the 1987 Montreal Protocol and 2016 Kigali Agreement to phase out ozone-depleting substances and hydrofluorocarbons, respectively, and agreements on minimal energy and corporate income taxes. In addition, there are a variety of international fora where coordination regimes for CO_2 mitigation might be discussed (see Annex 9.1).

Coordination Regimes for Specific Sectors, Gases, and Producers

What Are Current Targets and Policies for Decarbonizing International Maritime and Aviation?

Emissions from international aviation and maritime are about 1.5 and 2 percent of global CO_2 emissions, respectively (Black et al. 2024). The UN supervisory agencies for the industries, the International Civil Aviation Organization (ICAO) and International Maritime Organization (IMO), have adopted net zero emissions targets by mid-century and the IMO has set intermediate targets for emissions and zero-emissions fuels. The centerpiece of ICAO's strategy is the Carbon Offsetting and Reduction Scheme for International Aviation (CORSIA), requiring flight operators (from 2027 onward) to purchase international offsets for emissions exceeding 85 percent of 2019 levels. This plan, however, is not aligned with (a linear path to) net zero emissions by mid-century; offsets may not be fully additional (see the following section); and CORSIA does not raise revenue. IMO promulgates new ship fuel efficiency standards, has ruled out offsets, and is considering options for a global emissions pricing plan (see Table 9.2).

Table 9.2 Emissions Targets and Policies for International Transport Emissions

		Aviation	*Maritime*
Targets	Emissions: long term	Aspirational goal of net zero CO_2 emissions by 2050	Net zero CO_2 emissions close to 2050
	Emissions: Intermediate	none	Reduce net CO_2 emissions 20–30 percent by 2030 and 70–80 percent by 2040, relative to 2008
	Zero emissions planes/ships	none	These ships to account for 5–10 percent of energy used by 2030
Policies	Implemented	International offsets required for emissions above 85 percent of 2019 levels (becoming mandatory after 2027)	Fuel efficiency standards for new ships
	Under consideration	none	Emissions pricing

Sources: ICAO (2022) and IMO (2023).

Note: Net emissions refer to lifecycle emissions, including those from any fossil fuels used in the production of ammonia (or other low-carbon fuels) through electrolysis. For aviation, international offsets can count toward reducing net emissions but not for maritime.

What Is the Rationale for Applying Global Carbon Pricing Schemes to International Aviation and Maritime?

A robust carbon price is needed to close the cost gap for zero-emissions fuels (mainly biofuels for aviation and hydrogen-based fuels for ships) as they come closer to market. It would also raise substantial revenues, which could be a game-changer if some were used for climate finance—pricing consistent with net zero goals would raise about $200 billion a year in 2035 (Figure 9.7).

Additional environmental and fiscal considerations strengthen the case for global carbon pricing plans. Without mitigation actions, emissions from the sectors are set to expand rapidly with growth in the global economy; the high mobility of the tax base (especially for maritime where ships can refuel at ports with low fuel prices) provides a strong rationale for a globally imposed price; and a carbon price would, to some degree, counteract the uniquely favorable treatment of both industries from a broader tax perspective (see Annex 9.2 for details).

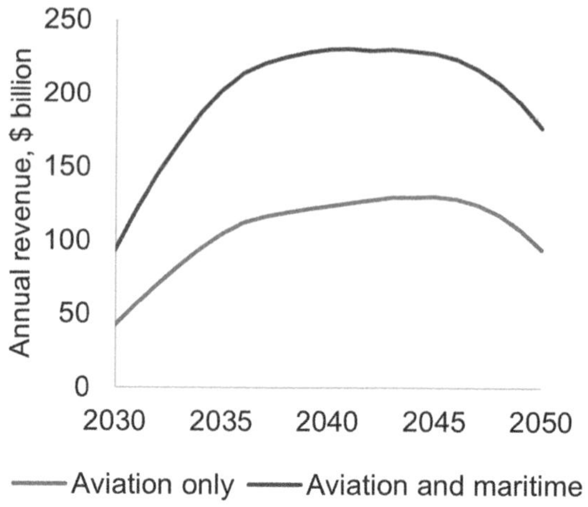

Figure 9.7 Projected Revenue from Charges on International Transportation Fuels.

Source: Black et al. (2024).

Note: CO_2 price increases linearly from $20 per ton in 2028 to $500 per ton by 2050 in line with achieving net zero emissions targets.

ICAO and IMO have established the necessary data collection procedures from plane and ship operators for applying pricing systems, though actual enforcement could be delegated to national tax authorities or newly created global entities. Either way, tax administration should be manageable, given large planes and ships are continuously tracked by satellite, operators could remit the carbon tax digitally, and the number of tax collection points (for example, 25,000 ships initially) is modest. If all major airport or port states were party to the plan, it could be enforced through the denial of airport or port access to operators lacking invoices verifying upfront tax payments. Administration is a bit more involved for a global ETS than a carbon tax, given the need to monitor trading markets, but the inclusion of international aviation and maritime in the EU ETS demonstrates the workability of ETSs for these sectors.

There are, however, tensions which could create a role for other instruments. One is the difficulty of agreeing allocation of revenue among ICAO and IMO member states. Another is that pure carbon pricing may need to be accompanied by compensation schemes for small island and other vulnerable states (again see Annex 9.2). Feebates, applying a sliding scale of fees/rebates on (plane or ship) operators with emissions rates above/below a pivot point emissions rate, are a possible alternative, or complement, to pure carbon pricing. The feebate price can be set to mobilize adoption of zero-emissions fuels, and the pivot point can be set separately to meet a (lower) revenue target, with smaller effects on production costs and less need for compensating vulnerable states.

How Feasible Is an International Coordination Regime for Methane Mitigation?

Several factors are favorable to establishing an international policy coordination mechanism to cut methane emissions:

- *Participants*: Signatories to the Global Methane Pledge, or representatives from blocs of signatories, would be a natural group to negotiate an agreement.[8]
- *Initial coverage*: An initial agreement could focus on extractives which account for most low-cost opportunities for cutting methane and are already covered administratively through business tax regimes.
- *Parameters*: The agreement could focus on simple parameters like a minimum methane price or emissions rate standards.
- *Competitiveness*: Concerns might be addressed through implementing revenue-neutral fees for industries, or other policies like feebates that avoid new tax burdens on the average producer, though competitiveness effects are modest anyway (see Chapter 4).
- *International equity*: Equity issues are less challenging than for CO_2 because methane mitigation costs are much smaller (Parry et al. 2022). Again, equity issues might be dealt with through stricter requirements for advanced economies and transfer of know-how on monitoring and mitigation technologies to developing countries.
- *Flexibility*: The choice of mitigation instrument could be left with national governments because countries should be able to agree on methodologies for mapping instruments to emissions reductions.

The arrangement would need to encompass mutually agreed procedures for measuring methane emissions. Again, a tricky issue is whether the agreement should be supported by a border methane adjustment, charging for embodied methane in fuel imports from non-participants (see Clausing, Garicano, and Wolfram 2023). This adjustment would, however, complicate the agreement's initial setup and may not be needed if competitiveness concerns are addressed through other measures (like revenue-neutral fees or regulations).

Climate Finance, Technology, and Offsets

Finance

How Much Climate Finance Has Been, and Might in Future Be, Flowing to Developing Countries?

Climate finance flows from developed to developing countries (see Figure 9.8) have increased from $50 billion in 2013 to $83 billion in 2020 and $115 billion in 2022—in the latter case, about a quarter of total mitigation investment of $400 billion in developing countries.

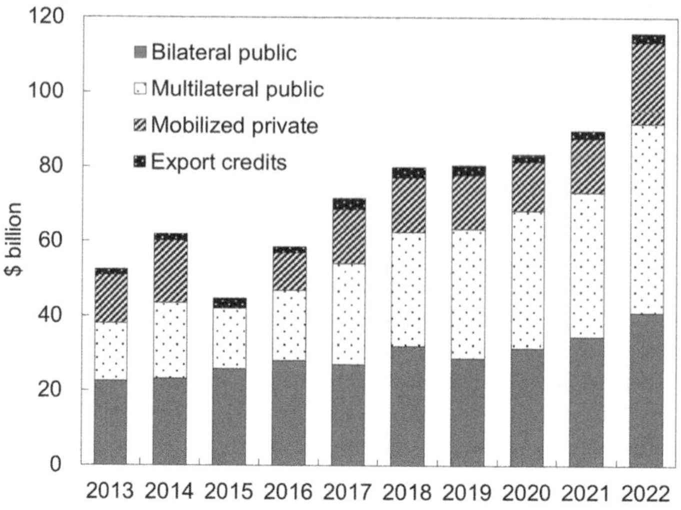

Figure 9.8 Previous Climate Finance Flows from Advanced to Developing Countries.
Source: OECD (2024).
Note: The gap for mobilized private in 2015 reflects measurement changes so totals before and after 2015 are slightly inconsistent.

Of climate finance flows in 2023, bilateral (government-to-government), multilateral, and private finance from international capital markets accounted for about 35, 45, and 20 percent, respectively, whereas mitigation accounted for 75 percent (and adaptation 25 percent).[9] Of the multilateral sources, 86 percent was for projects and 14 percent for policy initiatives (UNEP 2023).

At COP29 in Azerbaijan it was agreed to triple the climate finance goal to $300 billion annually by 2035. This target should be implemented jointly, by developed and developing countries, with the former mainly responsible for public funding and the latter for attracting private flows. And the portion of finance allocated to mitigation and adaptation should be based on relative needs at different points in time. For mitigation, investment needs should be defined net of avoided investments in fossil fuel technologies and lifecycle energy savings (see Chapter 7), whereas adaptation needs should be over and above investment for normal development (see Aligishiev, Massetti, and Bellon 2022).

How Might Enhanced Climate Finance Goals Be Met?

Scaling up bilateral public sources is currently challenging given tight budgetary pressures. Multilateral development banks recently announced a goal to raise annual climate finance for low- and middle-income countries to $120 billion, including $42 billion for adaptation, and $65 billion leveraged from the private sector (for example, through loan guarantees—see Chapter 7).

Private flows for mitigation could also be scaled up through robust carbon price signals in developing countries and improving financing mechanisms through climate information architecture (again see Chapter 7).

Traditional and more novel sources of public finance, involving common deployment of a tax instrument with (partial or full) earmarking of revenues, might include:

- *Carbon pricing*: A $5 charge per ton on advanced country CO_2 emissions could raise about $50 billion in 2030.[10]
- *Reducing fossil fuel subsidies*: Removing explicit fossil fuel subsidies (that is, closing any positive gaps between supply costs and prices because of price regulations) in advanced economies could raise about $200 billion in revenue in 2030 with 17, 27, and 55 percent coming from subsidies for oil, gas, and electricity use, respectively (from Black et al. 2023).
- *International aviation and maritime*: See the previous section.
- *Financial sector taxes*: Options discussed here include taxes on a wide range of financial transactions or on financial activities (the sum of wages and profits from financial institutions)—the former has acquired greater political momentum, whereas the latter has more economic appeal.[11]

Are There More Efficient Possibilities for Allocating Finance for Mitigation?

To date, most public sources of finance have focused on specific projects (like afforestation or renewable plants) or, to a lesser extent, mitigation policy initiatives, both of which can also leverage private finance. These approaches, however, do not account for reductions (or increases) in emissions from other policies or sectors beyond those targeted with climate finance, and they may lack automatic mechanisms for promoting cost-effective emissions reductions within recipient countries.

Another possibility is to focus finance on nationwide emissions to provide more comprehensive incentives to cut emissions cost-effectively across the economy. Addressing additionality concerns suggests a need to reward emissions reductions below future emissions baselines implied by countries' unconditional commitments (without finance) in their NDCs. Future baselines, however, would need to be exogenous to country actions going forward (to avoid perverse incentives for the country to inflate future baseline emissions or avoid tightening emissions commitments)—they might, for example, be based on previously stated unconditional targets for 2030, with baseline emissions beyond that declining linearly over time in line with the country's net zero emissions target.

Maximizing global emissions reductions across countries from a given international financial budget would require a fine-tuned mechanism to skew finance toward countries with lower costs for cutting emissions. This could, for example, involve countries submitting bids for contracts to cut nationwide emissions below unconditional baselines, with the bid specifying a payment per ton of emissions reduced, and finance prioritized to countries with the lowest bids per ton. The bids could be based on concrete and monitorable policy actions over a multiyear period (to accommodate year-to-year variability in emissions from market forces and lags in the response of emissions to new policies).

Technology

Is the Development and Transfer of Low-Carbon Technologies Aligned with Warming Goals?

About 85 percent of global CO_2 reductions out to 2030 (relative to 2020 levels) on a pathway to net zero emissions by mid-century might be achieved from proven technologies, though many of them need further development to bring them closer to market. By 2050, however, almost half of the required emissions reductions will need to come from technologies that are currently unproven or not yet discovered. Only a handful of countries have clear plans for advancing near- and long-term technologies (see IEA 2021, Powis et al. 2023).

Overall, the current global pace of development and transfer of low-carbon technologies needs scaling up:

- *Development*: There have been some notable success stories;[12] however, other critical technologies need accelerating down the learning curve, such as green cement, steel, hydrogen, shipping, aviation; direct air capture; battery storage; and technologies for addressing agriculture emissions.
- *Transfer*: At the global level (Figure 9.9, panel 1), trade in low-carbon technologies (like solar panels, electric vehicles, wind turbines) has expanded rapidly, from $200 billion (3.5 percent of total trade) in 1999 to $1.1 trillion (5 percent) in 2020. However, although developing countries have long called for "technology transfer" in terms of both physical movement in trade and transfer of knowledge (in foreign direct investment, patents, and training of specialized labor) for using and producing technologies, in the former case at least, the share of developing countries in global exports and imports of low-carbon technologies has stagnated (or fallen slightly for imports) since 2015 (Figure 9.9, panel 2).

Are International Agreements on Technology Development/Transfer Needed?

At each of the four main stages in technology development and adoption (discussed in Chapter 7), there are potential opportunities for international coordination through pooling and scaling up funding for research and to improve its productivity by avoiding duplication of effort. For example, given the cross-border knowledge and learning-by-doing spillovers there is a case for countries to coordinate over basic research, technology prizes, demonstration

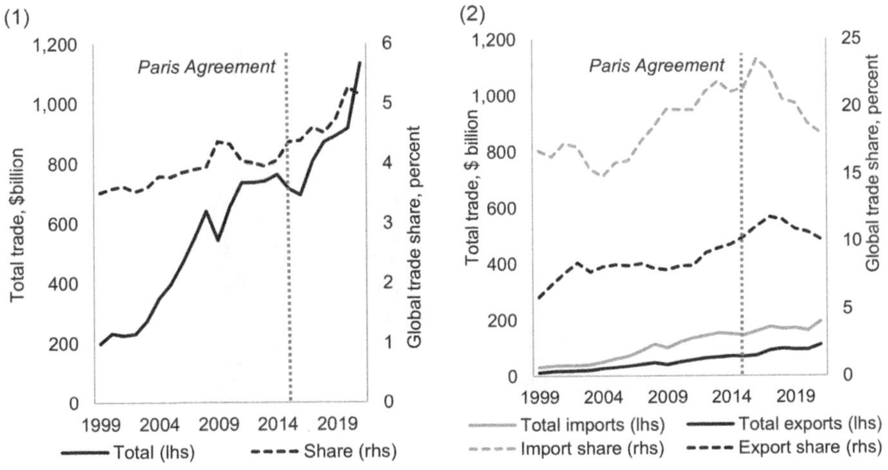

Figure 9.9 Growth in Low-Carbon Technologies. Panel 1. Global Exports, Panel 2. Developing Country Exports/Imports (excluding China).

Source: Black et al. (2023).

Note: rhs = right-hand side, lhs = left-hand side.

projects, and intellectual property (providing robust protections for innovators in one country licensing their technologies in other countries), and incentives to deploy new technologies.

International diffusion of low-carbon technologies, which are often developed in advanced economies and reach developing countries through trade and foreign direct investment, could also be promoted by agreements to lower tariffs and non-tariff barriers on low-carbon technologies. Tariffs are not actually that large, averaging between 2 percent in advanced economies and 6–8 percent in middle- and low-income countries, and are somewhat smaller than average tariffs on other traded products (see Figure 9.10)—but combining mitigation policies with a reduction in tariffs can significantly increase the inflow of low-carbon foreign direct investment.[13] And applying the same standards to products across countries (such as adopting the same type of charger for ensuring interoperability and tradability of electric vehicles) could address a key non-tariff barrier.

Additional mechanisms for transferring low-carbon technologies might include capacity-building programs (for example, training local engineers, technicians, and policymakers on technology implementation and maintenance or creating networks to exchange information and best practices), collaborations between foreign and local companies to develop and deploy technologies, demonstration projects promoting public–private partnerships, and sharing of designs.

Various plurilateral initiatives to promote international diffusion of low-carbon technologies have recently emerged. For example, the International Partnership for Hydrogen and Fuel Cells in the Economy, established in 2003,

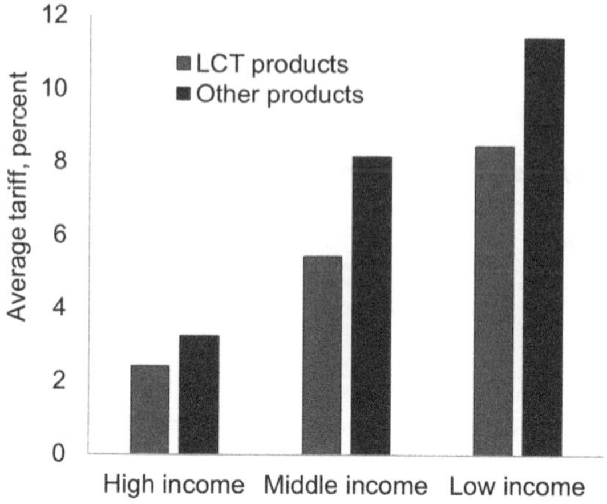

Figure 9.10 Average Tariffs on Low-Carbon Technologies and Other Products by Country Income Group, 2015–21.

Source: Black et al. (2023).

comprises 24 member countries to advance the development and deployment of hydrogen and fuel cell technologies. The Global Methane Initiative brings together governments, the private sector, and non-governmental organizations to implement methane recovery and abatement technologies more effectively in extractives, agriculture, and waste management through coordinated efforts and unified technical standards.

Are Policies Needed to Address Supply Concerns for Critical Minerals?

Minerals such as copper, nickel, cobalt, and lithium are critical inputs used in electric vehicles, batteries, wiring, solar panels, and wind turbines. Demand for these critical minerals could increase substantially in coming years with low-carbon energy transitions, but supply responses may be limited given the geographical concentration of production (see Figure 9.11) and the difficulty of scaling up mining. Consequently, global prices for these critical mineral prices could become more volatile and rise substantially, about 90 percent by 2030 according to IMF estimates. Moreover, if commodity markets become fragmented, price rises could reach 300 percent for countries in mineral-scarce blocs (from IMF 2023, Chapter 3), which could hinder low-carbon energy transitions.

Ideally, mineral-rich blocks should keep open trade in critical minerals (for example, clarifying rules for critical minerals at the World Trade Organization); foster domestic investment in mining, exploration, and recycling of these minerals; develop synthetic alternatives to critical minerals; and diversify supply sources.

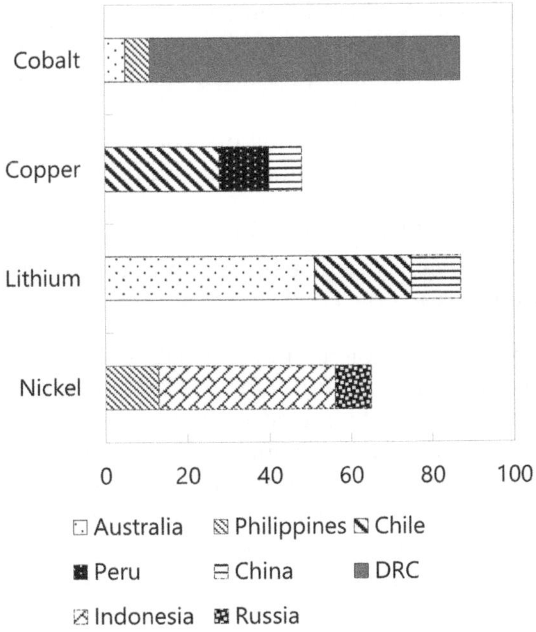

Figure 9.11 Share of Top Three Producers in Global Mineral Supply.

Source: IMF (2023), Online Annex 3.2.

Note: Figure is for unrefined production.

What Is the Role of Geoengineering?

Geoengineering technologies seek to reflect incoming sunlight back into space. Most attention has been focused on solar radiation management (SRM) which involves using high-flying aircraft to inject reflective sulfur aerosols (or other chemicals) into the stratosphere.[14] By some estimates, roughly 2 million tons of sulfur would be needed to suppress average global temperatures by 1°C at a cost in the order of $20 billion a year (for example, Smith 2020), a small fraction of the costs of achieving the same temperature control through cutting emissions.

Key concerns with geoengineering, however, include:

- *Climate risks.* SRM reflects light more effectively at low latitudes, in the summer, and only during daytime, so may have little benefit across certain latitudes and seasons (which could exacerbate changes in local precipitation patterns);
- *Rapid reversal.* If, for some reason, SRM is stopped, the cooling effect would cease within 1–3 years, leading to large, extremely rapid warming with risks, for example, to biodiversity and the water cycle;
- *Moral hazard.* Geoengineering could take the pressure off countries to achieve temperature goals through cutting emissions;

- *Unilateral deployment.* There is some risk (especially given current geopolitical tensions) that one or several countries may deploy SRM unilaterally without proper precaution, research, or international consultation, or use it for strategic purposes;
- *Ocean acidification.* Geoengineering does not affect absorption of CO_2 in the oceans which is causing acidification and threatening the marine food chain; and
- *Ozone depletion.* SRM might also amplify chemical reactions that slow recovery of the ozone layer, thereby allowing more cancer-causing ultraviolet radiation to reach the Earth.

In short, SRM may have a role in a global risk diversification strategy, particularly for potential deployment to limit the risks of crossing tipping points in the global climate system, failing adequate action on emissions mitigation. It should, however, be viewed as a complement to, not a substitute for, reducing emissions. International coordination could focus on (1) advancing research on the technical feasibility and effects of geoengineering; (2) establishing permitting systems for outdoor experiments; (3) procedures for deployment and monitoring of technologies; and (4) cost-sharing arrangements.

Offsets

What Are Emissions Offsets?

Carbon offsetting is a carbon trading mechanism enabling firms, governments, individuals, or other organizations to offset their emissions by paying for projects reducing emissions elsewhere. Under ETSs, firms are often allowed to cover some of their emissions through offsets rather than allowance purchases—analogous provisions could, but rarely do, apply under carbon taxes. International or independent organizations[15] manage registries of certified offset projects which are traded through various carbon exchanges—collectively known as voluntary carbon markets—or bilateral government exchanges. The markets are dominated by trades for meeting legal compliance obligations, though a small portion of trades are from firms, individuals, and other organizations meeting voluntary emissions targets (see https://www.respira-international.com/what-is-the-difference-between-the-compliance-and-voluntary-carbon-market). A variety of projects can be used to generate carbon offsets, though the two largest sources to date have been renewable investments and afforestation/reduced deforestation (Haya et al. 2023).

There are two rationales for offset markets:

- *Cost-effectiveness*: Offsets can promote cost-effectiveness by reallocating emissions reductions away from countries or entities with relatively high incremental abatement costs (for example, advanced economies with relatively aggressive mitigation targets) to countries or entities with relatively low incremental costs.
- *Finance*: Offsets can be a source of finance for countries selling them.

Between 2021 and 2023, voluntary carbon market prices have been relatively low at about $4–7 per ton (https://carboncredits.com/carbon-prices-today) though prices might become more robust over the next decade as countries (and ICAO) scale up mitigation policies.

Do Offsets Increase Emissions?

Offsets do not reduce global emissions, unless they indirectly encourage countries (for example, those facing high incremental costs from domestic abatement) to tighten their mitigation targets. Indeed, there are several reasons why carbon offsets may *increase* global emissions:

- *Additionality*. Offsets may not always be additional, that is, a project might have gone ahead anyway even without the offset payment for economic reasons (like renewables being more competitive);
- *Permanence*. Offsets may not be permanent (for example, new forests may subsequently burn down or be logged, releasing the sequestered carbon);
- *Emissions shortfalls*: Offset projects may not fully achieve the promised amount of emissions reductions;
- *Leakage*. Emissions reductions from an offset project might be offset by increased emissions elsewhere in the country selling the offset (for example, if forestry preservation in one region leads to increased deforestation elsewhere); and
- *Double counting*. Governments of both the buyer and the seller of the offset may count it toward meeting their mitigation targets.

It can be difficult to fully address all the factors mentioned above—indeed the EU no longer allows firms covered by its ETS to purchase offsets in place of surrendering allowances.[16] Organizations with offset registries have programs attempting to certify offset additionality, though the validity of current procedures is subject to dispute. Article 6 of the Paris Agreement confirms the role of offsets in achieving global emissions reduction targets and seeks to establish universally accepted standards for certifying and trading credits, thereby consolidating currently fragmented voluntary markets—its primary focus is on government-to-government trades termed "internationally traded mitigation outcomes" (ITMOs).

How Might Offset Markets Be Reformed?

Reforms might include:

- *Permanence/shortfalls*. Sellers of forestry offsets might be required to take out insurance in case they become liable for repayment in the event of forests being destroyed or emissions reductions falling short of contracted levels.

- *Additionality/leakage/double counting.* These issues might be addressed by a focus on nationwide emissions and if the offset-selling country already has in place validated policies to achieve its NDC commitments, with the offset further reducing emissions below this level (see the discussion on climate finance allocation). In principle, when offsets are transferred, corresponding adjustments are made to avoid double counting of emissions reductions toward NDCs.
- *Advancing direct air capture.* This technology avoids additionality. The technology is expensive at present (see the previous section) but might stimulate future offset markets with progress in cutting its costs.

A further concern with offsets is that they may increase mitigation costs for developing countries if they sell low-cost ITMOs to other countries. Ideally, developing countries would use their low-cost abatement opportunities to help meet their domestic emissions target and sell more costly ITMOs to other countries.

Suggestions for Further Reading

- *Global policies needed for temperature goals.* For a recent discussion, see Ekins (2024). A large modeling literature assesses global carbon price trajectories consistent with aligning global GHGs with global temperature goals. Stern and Stiglitz (2017) provide a good overview of this literature.
- *Global ambition gaps.* The United Nations Environment Program produces an annual report assessing the gap between pledged GHG reductions and reductions required to get on track with global temperature goals, and the opportunities for bridging the gap (the latest version is UNEP 2024). IMF staff also produce an annual update of the global mitigation ambition gap and equitable scenarios for closing it, based on the latest available data for over 200 countries (recent examples include Black et al. 2022, 2023, 2024). Another source is Climate Action Tracker (see https://climateactiontracker.org/global/cat-emissions-gaps) which rates over 40 countries on whether their emissions targets and current policies are sufficient or not for meeting global temperature goals. The Mercator Research Institute on Global Commons and Climate Change provides annual updates on the "carbon budget," that is, the remaining emissions that can be released subject to meeting global temperature goals (see https://www.mcc-berlin.net/en/research/co2-budget.html).
- *International coordination regimes for carbon pricing.* Nordhaus (2015) proposed an alternative to the Paris Agreement based on a "Climate Club" where participants coordinate over uniform carbon pricing. The IMF staff proposal for an ICPF among large emitters is designed to work alongside and reinforce the Paris Agreement, allows for minimum pricing requirements to differ by development level, and allows for alternative mitigation approaches at the national level achieving emissions outcomes equivalent to

those under the pricing requirements. For further discussion of international carbon price coordination regimes, see Chateau, Jaumotte, and Schwerhoff (2024), Cramton et al. (2017), IMF (2022), Weitzman (2014, 2016), and Global Climate Policy Project Working Group on Climate Coalitions (2025).

- *International regimes for coordinating emissions targets.* Parry et al. (2022) describe, and implement for G20 countries, an operational methodology for comparing emissions reductions implied by current and envisioned mitigation policies at economywide and sectoral level.
- *Coordination regimes for international transport fuels.* For discussions of the rationale, design, and effects of policies to reduce international aviation and maritime emissions, see Keen, Parry, and Keen (2013) and Black et al. (2024). On maritime specifically, see Baresic et al. (2022) and Dominioni and Englert (2022). For more details on the emissions offset program for aviation, see ICAO (2018).
- *Coordination regimes for reducing methane emissions.* Parry et al. (2022) provide a brief discussion of design features for coordinating methane pricing plans.
- *Options for mobilizing climate finance.* For discussions of different options for mobilizing revenues for climate finance, see AGF (2010), de Mooij and Keen (2012), Hirsch, Argueta, and Gück (2023), or (for more general revenues) IMF (2024). Jaumotte et al. (2024) discuss policies to promote low-carbon foreign direct investment.
- *Technologies for transferring low-carbon technologies.* Pigato et al. (2020) provide an in-depth discussion of how most of the emissions reductions needed to meet global temperature goals can be reached through the global deployment, particularly from developed to developing countries, of existing and commercially proven low-carbon technologies.
- *Offsets.* For further discussion of emissions offsets and principle for designing them, see Black (2018) and Axelsson et al. 2024).
- *General discussions of international climate change policy.* See, for example, Chan, Stavins, and Ji (2018).

Annex 9.1 Precedents for International Coordination Mechanisms for Reducing CO_2

Previous Agreements

Previous environmental and other multilateral agreements provide some precedent for international coordination regimes for reducing CO_2 emissions, including:

- *Montreal Protocol.* Ozone-depleting substances (ODSs), particularly chlorofluorocarbons, react in the stratosphere to deplete the ozone layer, thereby allowing more ultraviolet light to penetrate to ground level causing skin cancers and damage to crop production and ecosystems. After the surprise discovery of the Antarctic ozone hole in 1985, North America and Europe took the lead in developing a global system to control ODSs under the 1987 Montreal Protocol, which has (along with subsequent agreements) almost eliminated production of ODSs. The success of the Protocol reflected the concentration of ODS production by a small number of firms, mostly in industrial countries, and the rapid development of ODS substitutes. The EU and the United States reduced emissions through a mixture of taxes, ETSs, and bans on certain applications (see Hammit 2010).

- *Kigali Agreement*. Unlike other GHGs in the Paris Agreement, hydrofluorocarbons (HFCs), the main fluorinated gas, have other international negotiations. HFCs are mainly used as refrigerants, or in foams, aerosols, and fire extinguishers and were largely developed in response to the phase-out of ODSs. Although HFCs do not deplete the ozone layer, they are a potent GHG and can reside in the atmosphere for centuries. Under the Kigali Agreement advanced economies are required to reduce use of HFCs by 85 percent (relative to 2011–13 levels) by 2036 and developing countries by 80–85 percent by 2045–47 (see Mulye 2017).
- *EU Energy Tax Directive (ETD)*. Introduced in 2003, the ETD sets minimum tax rates for motor fuels (making a distinction between on- and off-road uses), electricity, and heating fuels that member states need to incorporate in their national tax systems. The ETD is motivated by concerns about the environment and energy dependence, as well as containing tax competition (for example, the risk of one country lowering tax rates to attract mobile tax bases from other countries). Most states tax most energy products and, in some cases, electricity above the ETD minimum rates. Recent reforms to the ETD include taxing fuels according to their energy and carbon content rather than their volume and phasing out various exemptions (such as fuel used in intra-EU air and maritime transport; see https://www.eceee.org/policy-areas/product-policy/energy-taxation-directive).
- *Base Erosion and Profit Shifting (BEPS) Agreement*. BEPS refers to tax planning strategies that exploit gaps and mismatches in tax rules to (legally or illegally) shift corporate profits to tax-favored locations where there is little or no economic activity or to erode tax bases through deductible payments such as interest or royalties. The OECD/G20 Inclusive Framework on BEPS brings together over 145 countries and jurisdictions to collaborate on addressing corporate tax avoidance through a 15 percent minimum rate and tools to ensure that profits are taxed where economic activities generating the profits are performed and where value is created (see https://www.oecd.org/tax/beps).

Discussion Fora

Beyond the G20 and the United Nations Framework Convention on Climate Change, other international fora where coordination mechanisms for CO_2 mitigation might be discussed include (see https://www.bmwk.de/Redaktion/

EN/Pressemitteilungen/2022/12/20221212-g7-establishes-climate-club.html; https://www.financeministersforclimate.org/; https://pmiclimate.org):

- *Coalition of Finance Ministers for Climate Action.* This brings together fiscal and economic policymakers from over 90 countries in leading the global climate response and securing low-carbon energy transitions. Activities are guided by six principles: (1) aligning policies with the Paris Agreement; (2) sharing experiences and expertise; (3) promoting carbon pricing; (4) mainstreaming climate in economic policies; (5) mobilizing climate finance; and (6) progressing on NDCs.
- *G7 Climate Club.* This seeks to foster implementation of the Paris Agreement, accelerate net zero emissions transitions, and boost sectoral decarbonization. The Club's three pillars are to advance: (1) climate mitigation policies through emissions monitoring methodologies and measures to limit emissions leakage; (2) industrial decarbonization; and (3) international climate cooperation and partnerships.
- *Canada's Global Carbon Pricing Challenge.* This calls for a partnership of carbon pricing champions from around the world to expand the use of carbon pricing by strengthening existing systems and supporting emerging ones toward a collective goal of covering 60 percent of global emissions by 2030. The Challenge also creates a forum for dialogue and coordination to better understand policy design choices and to support other countries, especially developing countries, in adopting carbon pricing.

Annex 9.2 International Aviation and Maritime: Further Details[17]

Need for Pricing Emissions

Although there are a variety of shorter-term responses for reducing fuel intensity in aviation and maritime[18] and reducing travel demand for aviation (fuel costs are a significant share of ticket prices for aviation but are a small share of landed import prices for shipped products), sustainable fuels are ultimately needed in both industries. A possibility for ships is hydrogen or ammonia (produced from hydrogen), with hydrogen produced with zero emissions from renewable-generated electrolysis or natural gas with carbon capture. But advances are needed to lower the cost and improve the safety of onboard technologies for storing these fuels and converting them to propulsion, and new infrastructure is needed to transport and disburse the fuel.[19] Hydrogen-based fuels are further from market for aviation, but other near-term possibilities include biofuel blending which could cut emissions up to 60 percent (biofuel production would, however, require substantial diversion of land away from forestry or agriculture). Electrification has some potential for both industries, but it is constrained by limited battery range. A robust price on CO_2 emissions will be needed to close lifecycle cost gaps between zero emissions planes and ships and their oil-based counterparts, because the former come closer to market.

The economic case for carbon pricing is reinforced by uniquely favorable treatment of both industries from a broader tax perspective.[20] Specifically:

- *Fuel excise/carbon pricing*. International transportation fuels are not subject to excises or (aside from in the EU) carbon pricing. For aviation, the 1944 Chicago Convention and subsequent ICAO resolutions prohibit taxation of fuel already on board an aircraft by the state where the aircraft lands, as does widespread country practice codified in numerous bilateral Air Service Agreements providing similar exemptions. For maritime, it reflects long-standing practice and (especially) the extreme mobility of the tax base.
- *Consumption taxation*. For aviation, where leisure-related travel is about 70 percent of international air travel, services are mainly a consumer product and in principle should be subject to taxes applying to other consumer goods. International air travel is, however, almost unique in being "zero-rated" under the VAT, meaning those providing the service charge no tax on sales but receive a full refund of VAT charged on the inputs used to provide those services. Applying VAT would be complex, however—for example, ticket purchasers could be taxed differentially according to where they live but the ticket seller would need to remit the tax to the consumer's government—a domestic ticket tax, or extension of the Air Solidarity Levy would be more feasible.[21]
- *Business taxation*: In principle maritime should be subject to corporate profit taxes applying to other industries—instead, however, shipping is commonly subject to tonnage taxes that amount to only about 10 percent of normal corporate income taxes.

Aviation and maritime emissions are included in the EU ETS. All airlines operating flights within the European Economic Area (EEA), Switzerland, and the United Kingdom are required to monitor, verify, and report their emissions and to surrender allowances against those emissions, whereas for flights between the EEA and other countries CORSIA (potentially) applies rather than the ETS. For maritime, the EU ETS covers 50 percent of emissions from voyages starting or ending outside the EU and 100 percent for trips within EU ports. Administering authorities of EU Member States ensure compliance using similar rules as for the other ETS sectors.[22]

Need for Price Coordination

For maritime, international price coordination regimes need to be global from the start because of the extreme mobility of the tax base, which greatly limits the scope for differentiated pricing of maritime emissions across countries. High-volume ships can undertake long voyages on a single bunkering of fuel (using it for ballast initially and replacing it with water as fuel is used), which enables them to re-tank at ports (or from tankers and platforms on the high seas) that have lower fuel prices, without significantly adding to operational costs. For aviation, the tax base is also internationally mobile, though to a lesser degree than for maritime, given costs of diverting planes to other airports for refueling and carrying more fuel than otherwise optimal—for aviation there is more scope for sequentially expanding pricing across countries.

Compensation Programs

Aviation. Although the burden of pure carbon pricing for aviation is likely to fall mostly on travelers from higher-income countries and relatively well-off domestic travelers, effects on low-income countries and tourist destinations are a concern. Compensation mechanisms might include:

- Allowing low-income countries to impose charges on, and retain the revenues from, fuel disbursements within their own borders for international flights (and exempting these disbursements from ICAO-collected charges).
- Rebate ICAO-collected revenues to low-income countries based, for example, on inward passenger kilometers traveled to that country as a share of global passenger kilometers traveled.

The first program is simpler, less demanding in its information requirements, and seems likely to deliver adequate compensation in most cases.

Maritime. For maritime the concern is low-income countries and (remote) small island developing states, where imports and shipping costs are disproportionately high relative to GDP. Compensation options might include:

- Reimbursing vulnerable countries for charges on their maritime fuel sales which would be reasonable in most cases but with some exceptions—countries with hub ports (where ships frequently refuel prior to offloading cargo in other countries) would be overcompensated whereas small islands where ships offload cargo without refueling would be undercompensated.
- Basing compensation on countries' shares of global import values is another possibility though import value tends to be negatively corrected with CO_2 (for example, light electronic equipment has a low ratio of CO_2 to import value) and poor countries importing low value/high CO_2 products may be disadvantaged.
- Compensation could also be based on cross-country incidence studies by external experts.

Some form of acceptable compensation program should be feasible, however, especially given the modest effect of carbon pricing on landed import prices—for example, even a \$75 per ton of CO_2 price would only increase imported food prices by about 0.5 to 3 percent.

Feebates

In the context of aviation and maritime, the emissions rate in a feebate formula (see Chapter 3) would be defined with respect to passenger or plane miles and ton miles of freight, respectively. In maritime, where emissions rates for bulk shipping (for example, oil products, steel, iron ore, coal, grain) substantially exceed those for container shipping it may make sense to have separate pivot points for the two segments to improve acceptability for bulk shippers. The feebate price can be aligned to close projected cost gaps between zero emissions and oil-based planes and ships, whereas the pivot point can be aligned with revenue objectives. Procedures for administering feebate programs at ICAO and IMO would be the same as those for carbon taxes—the main difference is that data on operators' output, as well as emissions, is needed. The lack of a demand response under a feebate would be a notable limitation for aviation but not for maritime.

Notes

1 See Sievert, Schmidt, and Steffen (2024) and Toman et al. (2024). Capturing CO_2 from the air is more energy intensive (and therefore more expensive) than capturing it from an industrial smokestack, given the much smaller concentration of CO_2 in the atmosphere—costs may, however, decrease as the technology matures and scales.

2 See https://www.iea.org/reports/global-energy-review-2021/co2-emissions. Indeed, to date there are few examples of where countries have managed to increase GDP, while reducing absolute GHG emissions (Haberl et al. 2020).

3 The study is by van der Berg et al. (2020) which considered several alternatives (for example, based on per capita income, convergence of per capita emissions, and equalization of incremental mitigation costs across countries)—the results here are from Black et al. (2023) who infer, and average over, the emissions reductions from these approaches that would be consistent with temperature goals.

4 Indeed, this was recognized early on, because the original agreement allowed for supplementary mechanisms among subgroups of countries to raise mitigation ambition.

5 Or more generally slower implementation timetables for developing countries (as in the Kigali Agreement—see Annex 9.1). Imposing a uniform price across countries has theoretical appeal (given the contribution to future climate change from a ton of CO_2 emissions is the same, regardless of where the emissions are produced) but it places the onus of addressing international equity entirely on international support, which is difficult, for example, because of budgetary constraints in advanced economies.

6 See Parry et al. (2022) or, for an earlier, similar proposal, Nordhaus (2015).

7 Operational methodologies are available for measuring EECPs. The calculation involves eliminating all fuel taxes/subsidies and carbon pricing programs and, starting with the new baseline, simulating an economywide carbon price that returns nationwide emissions to their level in the original baseline.

8 The Global Methane Pledge seeks to cut global methane emissions by 30 percent by 2030 relative to 2020 levels—more than 150 countries have so far signed the pledge (notable large emitting exceptions include China, India, and Russia). See https://www.globalmethanepledge.org.

9 Multilateral sources are mostly from development banks, but also the Green Climate Fund, Global Environmental Facility, and other climate investment funds. Just Energy Transition Partnerships are an example of bilateral support from countries in the Global North to help transitions away from coal use in emerging markets like Indonesia, South Africa, and Vietnam.
10 Authors' calculations using CPAT.
11 The financial transaction tax could increase the cost of capital with negative growth effects, whereas the financial activities tax would help offset distortions caused by the exemption of financial services under value-added tax.
12 Most strikingly, the 90 percent decline in the costs of solar power between 2010 and 2020 was pushed by strong incentives in countries like China and Germany (Black et al. 2023, Annex G).
13 See Hasna et al. (2023) for more discussion. For example, a legally binding trade agreement between Costa Rica, Iceland, New Zealand, and Switzerland was signed in 2024 that removes tariff and other barriers on more than 300 environmental and energy-saving goods, with the hope of encouraging other countries to join.
14 Another possibility is marine cloud brightening which involves spraying fine seawater to whiten high-level clouds, thereby increasing cloud reflectivity.
15 For example, The Gold Standard, Climate Action Reserve, American Carbon Registry, and Verra.
16 This decision was influenced by a study suggesting 85 percent of previous offsets allowed in the EU ETS were not additional (Cames et al. 2016).
17 The discussion and statistics in this Annex are taken from Black et al. (2024) and Keen et al. (2013).
18 Such as use of lighter construction materials and more efficient engines in new builds, faster turnover of plane and shipping fleets, better maintenance of existing ships, and optimizing shipping speeds.
19 Unlike for oil, however, most countries could potentially produce hydrogen, implying a diversified international market.
20 See Keen et al. (2013) for more details.
21 Aviation tickets are subject to various fees, but these are generally user charges for services, such as security, that on net do not raise government revenues. Several countries impose the Air Ticket Solidarity Levy (including Cameroon, Chile, Congo, France, Madagascar, Mali, Mauritius, Niger, Korea, and Norway) on airline tickets for outbound international flights, with proceeds remitted for health improvements in low-income countries. As of 2023, levies for economy or business flights in the European Economic Area were €3–8 or €20–63 for flights terminating within or outside of the Area, respectively. See http://unitaid.org/how-we-work/donors/#en.
22 Free allowance allocations for plane and ship operators are set to phase out by 2027.

References

Advisory Group on Climate Change Financing (AGF). 2010. *Report of the Secretary General's High-Level Advisory Group on Climate Change Financing*. New York: AGF, United Nations.

Aligishiev, Zamid, Emanuele Massetti, and Matthieu Bellon. 2022. "Macro-Fiscal Implications of Adaptation to Climate Change." IMF Staff Climate Note 2022-002, International Monetary Fund, Washington, DC.

Axelsson, Kaya, Audrey Wagner, Injy Johnstone, Myles Allen, Ben Caldecott, Nick Eyre, Sam Fankhauser, et al. 2024. "Oxford Principles for Net Zero Aligned Carbon Offsetting (Revised 2024)." Smith School of Enterprise and the Environment, University of Oxford.

Baresic, Domagoj, Isabelle Rojon, Alison Shaw, and Nishatabbas Rehmatulla. 2022. *Closing the Gap: An Overview of the Policy Options to Close the Competitiveness Gap and Enable an Equitable Zero-Emission Fuel Transition in Shipping*. London: University Maritime Advisory Service.

Black, Simon. 2018. *Carbon Markets under the Kyoto Protocol: Lessons Learned for Building an International Carbon Market under the Paris Agreement*. Washington, DC: World Bank Group.

Black, Simon, Jean Chateau, Florence Jaumotte, Ian Parry, Gregor Schwerhoff, Sneha Thube, and Karlygash Zhunussova. 2022. "Getting on Track to Net Zero: Accelerating a Global Just Transition in This Decade." Staff Discussion Note 2022/010, International Monetary Fund, Washington, DC.

Black, Simon, Antung A. Liu, Ian Parry, and Nate Vernon. 2023. "IMF Fossil Fuel Subsidies Data: 2023 Update." IMF Working Paper 23/169, International Monetary Fund, Washington, DC.

Black, Simon, Ian Parry, Sunalika Singh, and Nate Vernon. 2024. "Pricing Policies for Decarbonizing International Aviation and Maritime." IMF Staff Climate Note 2024/003, International Monetary Fund, Washington, DC.

Cames, Martin, Ralph O. Harthan, Jürg Füssler, Michael Lazarus, Carrie M. Lee, Pete Erickson, and Randall Spalding-Fecher. 2016. *How Additional Is the Clean Development Mechanism? Analysis of the Application of Current Tools and Proposed Alternatives*. Freiberg: Öko-Institut.

Chan, Gabriel, Robert Stavins, and Zou Ji. 2018. "International Climate Change Policy." *Annual Review of Resource Economics* 10: 335–60. https://doi.org/10.1146/annurev-resource-100517-023321

Chateau, Jean, Florence Jaumotte, and Gregor Schwerhoff. 2024. "Global Climate Policy with Differentiated Carbon Price Floors." *Climate Policy* 24 (4): 515–28.

Clausing, Kimberly A., Luis Garicano, and Catherine Wolfram. 2023. "How an International Agreement on Methane Emissions can Pave the way for Enhanced Global Cooperation on Climate Change." Policy Brief 23-7, Peterson Institute for International Economics, Washington, DC.

Cramton, Peter, David MacKay, Axel Ockenfels, and Steven Stoft, eds. 2017. *Global Carbon Pricing: The Path to Climate Cooperation*. Cambridge, MA: MIT Press.

de Mooij, Ruud, and Michael Keen. 2012. "Fiscal Instruments for Climate Finance." In *Fiscal Policy to Mitigate Climate Change: A Guide for Policymakers*, edited by Ian Parry, Ruud de Mooij, and Michael Keen. Washington, DC: International Monetary Fund.

Dominioni, Goran, and Dominik Englert. 2022. *Carbon Revenues from International Shipping: Enabling an Effective and Equitable Energy Transition*. Washington, DC: World Bank.

Ekins, Paul. 2024. *Stopping Climate Change: Policies for Real Zero*. New York, NY: Routledge.

Global Climate Policy Project Working Group on Climate Coalitions. 2025. *Building a Climate Coalition: Aligning Carbon Pricing, Trade, and Development*. Cambridge, MA: Global Climate Policy Project at Harvard and MIT.

Haberl, Helmut, Dominik Wiedenhofer, Doris Virág, Gerald Kalt, Barbara Plank, Paul Brockway, Tomer Fishman, et al. 2020. "A Systematic Review of the Evidence on Decoupling of GDP, Resource Use and GHG Emissions, Part II: Synthesizing the Insights." *Environmental Research Letters* 15 (6): 065003. https://doi.org/10.1088/1748-9326/ab842a

Hammit, James. 2010. "The Successful International Response to Stratospheric Ozone Depletion." In *Issues of the Day: 100 Commentaries on Environmental, Energy, Transportation, and Public Health Policy*, edited by Ian Parry and Felicia Day. Washington, DC: Resources for the Future.

Hasna, Zeina, Florence Jaumotte, Jaden Kim, Samuel Pienknagura, and Gregor Schwerhoff. 2023. "Green Innovation and Diffusion: Policies to Accelerate Them and Expected Impact on Macroeconomic and Firm-Level Performance." IMF Staff Discussion Note 2023/008, International Monetary Fund, Washington, DC.

Haya, Barbara K., Aline Abayo, Ivy S. So, and Micah Elias. 2023. *Voluntary Registry Offsets Database v10*. Berkeley: Berkeley Carbon Trading Project, University of California. https://gspp.berkeley.edu/faculty-and-impact/centers/cepp/projects/berkeley-carbon-trading-project/offsets-database

Hirsch, Thomas, Bertha Argueta, and Martin Gück. 2023. *New Resources for Public Climate Finance and for the Loss and Damage Fund: Exploring Taxes and Levies at EU and Multilateral Level*. Brussels: Climate Action Network Europe.

Intergovernmental Panel on Climate Change (IPCC). 2022. *Climate Change 2022: Mitigation of Climate Change*. Working Group III contribution to the Sixth Assessment Report of the Intergovernmental Panel on Climate Change. Geneva.

International Civil Aviation Organization (ICAO). 2018. *What Is CORSIA and How Does it Work?* Montreal. https://www.icao.int/environmental-protection/Pages/A39_CORSIA_FAQ2.aspx

International Civil Aviation Organization (ICAO). 2022. *Report on the Feasibility of a Long-Term Aspirational Goal (LTAG) for International Civil Aviation CO2 Emissions Reductions*. Montreal.

International Energy Agency (IEA). 2021. *Net Zero by 2050*. Paris.

International Maritime Organization (IMO). 2023. *2023 IMO Strategy on Reduction of GHG Emissions from Ships*. London.

International Monetary Fund (IMF). 2022. *Fiscal Monitor April 2022: Chapter 2: Coordinating Taxation Across Borders*. Washington, DC. https://www.imf.org/-/media/Files/Publications/fiscal-monitor/2022/April/English/ch2.ashx

International Monetary Fund (IMF). 2023. *World Economic Outlook: Navigating Global Divergencies*. Washington, DC.

International Monetary Fund (IMF). 2024. *G20 Note on Alternative Options for Revenue Mobilization*. Washington, DC.

Jaumotte, Florence, Jaden Kim, Samuel Pienknagura, and Gregor Schwerhoff. 2024. "Policies to Foster Green FDI: Best Practices for Emerging Market and Developing Economies." IMF Staff Climate Note 2024/004, International Monetary Fund, Washington, DC.

Keen, Michael, Ian Parry, and Jon Strand Keen. 2013. "Ships, Planes, and Taxes: Charging for International Aviation and Maritime Emissions." *Economic Policy* 28: 701–49.

Mulye, Manjiri. 2017. "Kigali Agreement: Simplified." Cearias. https://www.clearias.com/kigali-agreement

Nordhaus, William D. 2015. "Climate Clubs: Overcoming Free-Riding in International Climate Policy." *American Economic Review* 105: 1339–70. https://doi.org/10.1257/aer.15000001

Organisation for Economic Cooperation and Development (OECD). 2024. "Developed Countries Exceeded the $100 Billion Annual Goal for the First Time in 2022." Paris. https://www.oecd.org/en/about/news/press-releases/2024/05/developed-countries-materially-surpassed-their-usd-100-billion-climate-finance-commitment-in-2022-oecd.html

Parry, Ian, Simon Black, Danielle Minnett, Victor Mylonas, and Nate Vernon. 2022. "How to Cut Methane Emissions." IMF Staff Climate Note 22-008, International Monetary Fund, Washington, DC.

Pigato, Miria A., Simon J. Black, Damien Dussaux, Zhimin Mao, Miles McKenna, Ryan Rafaty, and Simon Touboul. 2020. *Technology Transfer and Innovation for Low-Carbon Development*. Washington, DC: World Bank.

Powis, Carter M., Stephen M. Smith, Jan C. Minx, and Thomas Gasser. 2023. "Quantifying Global Carbon Dioxide Removal Deployment." *Environmental Research Letters* 18 (2): 024022.

Sievert, Katrin, Tobias Schmidt, and Bjarne Steffen. 2024. "Considering Technology Characteristics to Project Future Costs of Direct Air Capture." *Joule* 8: 979–99.

Smith, Wake. 2020. "The Cost of Stratospheric Aerosol Injection through 2100." *Environmental Research Letters* 15: 114004. https://doi.org/10.1088/1748-9326/aba7e7

Stern, Nicholas, and Joseph Stiglitz. 2017. "Report of the High-Level Commission on Carbon Pricing." Paper of the Carbon Pricing Leadership Coalition, World Bank Group, Washington, DC.

Toman, Michael, James Boyd, Alan Krupnick, and Emily Joiner. 2024. *Policies for Scaling Up Carbon Dioxide Removal in the United States*. Issue Brief 24-01, Resources for the Future, Washington, DC.

United Nations Environment Program (UNEP). 2023. *Adaptation Gap Report 2023*. Nairobi.

United Nations Environment Program (UNEP). 2024. *Emissions Gap Report 2024: No More Hot Air ... Please! With a Massive Gap between Rhetoric and Reality, Countries draft new Climate Commitments*. Nairobi.

van der Berg, Nicole J., Heleen L. van Soest, Andries F. Hof, Michel G. J. den Elzen, Detlef P. van Vuuren, Wenying Chen, Laurent Drouet, et al. 2020. "Implications of Various Effort-Sharing Approaches for National Carbon Budgets and Emission Pathways." *Climatic Change* 162 (4): 1805–22. https://doi.org/10.1007/s10584-019-02368-y

Weitzman, Martin L. 2014. "Can negotiating a uniform carbon price help to internalize the global warming externality?" *Journal of the Association of Environmental and Resource Economists* 1 (1/2): 29–49. The University of Chicago Press.

Weitzman, Martin L. 2016. "On a World Climate Assembly and the Social Cost of Carbon." Discussion Paper 16–72, Harvard Environmental Economics Program, Cambridge, MA.

10 Conclusion

Dispelling 50 Myths about Climate Mitigation

This closing chapter reiterates some of the main messages from the volume by dispelling some common myths about climate mitigation.

Myth 1. Factors other than greenhouse gas emissions have caused observed warming to date of 1.2°C.
No. There is consensus among scientists that the warming to date above preindustrial levels (observed at weather stations and confirmed by satellite data) is from atmospheric accumulations of human-induced, heat-trapping gases, rather than other factors like changes in solar radiation and volcanic activity or urban heat absorption (see Chapter 2).

Myth 2. Global warming is not a major concern because people can adapt, for example, by adopting air conditioning, drought-resistant crops, and moving to cooler climates.
No. Global warming is causing a diverse range of climate risks such as greater frequency and intensity of heat waves, shifting precipitation patterns (which puts at risk water systems, agriculture, and ecosystems), droughts, wildfires, floods, and hurricanes—these risks are escalating because warming causes more energy and water vapor in the atmosphere. Higher atmospheric CO_2 concentrations also eat away at the minerals used by marine life to build their shells and skeletons. And there is an escalating risk of crossing (poorly understood) tipping points in the Earth's climate system such as permafrost melting (which could turn on an unstoppable gas tap of CO_2 and methane), long-term collapse of major ice sheets (which could raise global sea levels several meters), changes in ocean circulation (which could radically change temperature and precipitation patterns around the world), and forest dieback (which could transform the Amazon into dry savanna) (see Chapter 2).

Myth 3. Near-term mitigation action in advanced economies can largely get global emissions on track with temperature goals.
No. Global emissions need to be cut 25–50 percent below 2019 levels by 2030 to get on track with limiting warming to 2°C and 1.5°C, respectively. This will not be possible without substantial emissions reductions

DOI: 10.4324/9781003755012-10
This chapter has been made available under a CC-BY-NC-ND license.

in developing countries given they account for nearly 70 percent of global baseline CO_2 emissions in 2030 (see Chapter 2). Proportionate emissions cuts should however be larger in advanced economies, and international climate finance should support low-carbon energy transitions in low-income countries.

Myth 4. The Paris process is on track for achieving global temperature goals.
No. Even if fully achieved, current mitigation targets in Nationally Determined Contributions would only reduce global greenhouse gas emissions by 12 percent below 2019 level by 2030. Put another way, new measures equivalent to a global carbon price upward of $80 per ton are needed by 2030 to be on track with keeping warming below 2°C (the current global average carbon price is $5 per ton). If the required emissions reductions are not achieved by 2030, emissions will need to be cut even more drastically after 2030, rapidly raising the costs of low-carbon energy transitions and potentially putting temperature goals permanently beyond reach (see Chapters 2 and 9).

Myth 5. Low-carbon technology subsidies and mandates can mimic many of the mitigation responses from carbon pricing.
No. Carbon pricing can promote the full range of behavioral responses to cut emissions across fuels, sectors, firms, and households—and cost-effectively, because it equates the cost of the last ton reduced across responses. Low-carbon technology subsidies and mandates promote a much narrower range of responses. For example, in the power sector carbon pricing will reduce electricity demand, encourage operational efficiencies, promote switching from coal to gas and from fossil fuels to nuclear and hydro, adoption of carbon capture technologies, and switching from fossil fuels to wind and solar. In contrast, subsidies or generation share requirements for renewables promote only the last response. In addition, under technology subsidies and mandates there is no automatic mechanism for equalizing the cost of the last ton reduced across firms and sectors (see Chapter 3).

Myth 6. Carbon pricing is not practical for developing countries.
Not necessarily. Carbon taxes, that is, charges on the carbon content of fossil fuel supply, are a straightforward extension of fuel taxes, which are among the easiest of all taxes to collect and are well established in more than 160 countries. Alternatively, in energy-producing countries, carbon taxes can be integrated into existing fiscal regimes for extractive industries (combined with rebates/charges for exported/imported fuels). Emissions trading systems (ETSs) can be more administratively challenging, however, and may not be practical for capacity-constrained countries. ETSs require new capacity for monitoring emissions, given they usually apply downstream to emissions from power generators and industrial facilities. They also require supervision of allowance trading markets and enough participants to create fluid trading markets (see Chapter 3).

Myth 7. ETSs are preferable to carbon taxes given the focus of mitigation targets on emissions rather than prices.

Not necessarily. Carbon tax trajectories can be set such that projected future emissions are aligned with an emissions target for a given future year (perhaps with occasional interim adjustment). Trading systems can achieve annual emissions targets with greater certainty, but the flip side is uncertainty over future emissions prices which can deter low-carbon investments (whose lifecycle returns can be highly sensitive to future emissions prices). Indeed, trading systems are usually combined with mechanisms, like price floors and ceilings, to limit price volatility, sacrificing some of the certainty over emissions (see Chapter 3).

Myth 8. Carbon pricing obviates the need for sector-based mitigation instruments.

No. Leaving aside the possibility of sectoral mitigation targets and technology policies, sectoral-based mitigation instruments are still needed. This is because of likely constraints on the political acceptability of carbon pricing from its significant effect on energy prices, which in turn burdens households and firms. Complementary sectoral instruments should, insofar as possible, mimic the behavioral responses of pricing, while they avoid energy price increases and significant fiscal costs. Furthermore, extra high explicit, or implicit, carbon prices may be needed, even in the near term, to kick-start investment in certain hard-to-abate sectors if they are to be decarbonized by mid-century. For example, it is less costly to make new buildings net zero emissions (through insulation, electric heating, and rooftop solar), rather than building an emissions-intensive structure and subsequently retrofitting it to become net zero—and this may require strong upfront explicit or implicit carbon price signals (see Chapter 3).

Myth 9. Low-carbon technology subsidies or mandates can substitute for carbon pricing when the latter is politically constrained.

Not necessarily. There are more efficient alternatives to carbon pricing than low-carbon technology subsidies and mandates. In particular, feebates (sliding scales of fees/rebates on activities or products with above/below average emissions intensity) or tradable performance (or emissions rate) standards can cost-effectively promote the full range of behavioral responses for reducing emissions rates in different sectors, while they avoid both fiscal costs on the government (unlike low-carbon technology subsidies) and significant increases in energy prices (unlike carbon pricing). See Chapter 3.

Myth 10. Feebates and tradable performance standards (TPSs) require large numbers of firms.

Not necessarily. Feebates can be applied when the number of firms (for example, in a particular industry like steel or cement) is small (or even one). The feebate specifies a pivot point emissions rate above/below which fees/rebates apply, and the pivot point is set exogenously by the government. TPSs do, however, require significant numbers to lubricate credit trading markets—if the number of participants is very limited, a feebate would be better in this regard. See Chapter 3.

Myth 11. Market-based mitigation instruments cannot be used for the power and industrial sector where governments are reluctant to significantly raise electricity prices or industrial production costs.

Not necessarily. Feebates or TPSs can cost-effectively exploit all mitigation options for reducing the emissions intensity of the sectors. They do not raise government revenues, but they limit increases in electricity prices and production costs by avoiding charges on unabated emissions for the average firm. Capacity requirements for these instruments are, however, similar to those for ETSs and they do little to reduce electricity demand or industrial production levels (see Chapter 4).

Myth 12. Subsidies for low-carbon technology adoption in industrial firms confer a large competitiveness advantage.

Not necessarily. In quantitative terms, the effects of technology adoption subsidies on relative competitiveness are likely modest. The base of the subsidy is the emissions reduction, or a proxy for it, which is generally smaller than remaining emissions (the relevant base for carbon pricing), and the subsidy payment is at least partly offset by extra abatement costs. Auction mechanisms for allocating subsidies to lowest-cost bidders can also limit subsidy payments in excess of mitigation costs (see Chapter 4).

Myth 13. Fuel taxes can promote decarbonization in transportation.

Probably not. For many countries, fuel taxes may be at, or close to, maximum politically acceptable levels because of the unpopularity of higher taxes at the pump. And lifecycle costs (including fuel costs at current fuel taxes) are generally smaller for internal combustion engine vehicles than their electric vehicle counterparts—promoting transitions to the latter likely requires additional incentives. Rather than dramatically raising fuel taxes, this can be achieved with a feebate, which alters relative vehicle prices without a new tax burden on the average motorist. Alternatively TPSs might be applied to vehicle sellers (see Chapter 4).

Myth 14. Decarbonizing buildings will be fiscally costly for the government.

Not necessarily. Incentives are needed for insulation upgrades, heat pumps, and rooftop solar and these could be financed through taxes on building fuels or fossil-based heating equipment. Another possibility is to integrate feebates linked to energy or CO_2 performance ratings for buildings into existing property taxes. All these revenue-neutral possibilities limit fiscal burdens on the general budget, strengthen mitigation incentives, and promote efficient allocation of resources between the building and other sectors (see Chapter 4).

Myth 15. Project-based approaches are needed to promote forest carbon sequestration.

Not necessarily. Funding projects to slow deforestation, or promote afforestation, promotes a limited range of responses because they only affect carbon storage on land parcels enrolled in the program, there is no automatic mechanism for prioritizing cost-effective projects, budgetary constraints may limit the number of projects, and there could be risks of leakage (if higher commodity prices lead to forest clearance in land not under contract). All these issues would be addressed under a nationwide system of subsidies/fees for landowners increasing/reducing carbon storage on their land over time, though capacity needs for this approach are substantial (including carbon storage monitoring, well-defined property rights at the forestry/agricultural border, and subsidy/fee administration). An interim possibility might include forest commodity taxes (with rebates for sustainably produced products) (see Chapter 4).

Myth 16. Methane fees for extractives are not practical because governments cannot monitor the emissions.

Not necessarily. Governments can require that coal, oil, and gas extractors monitor and self-report their emissions (subject to third-party verification) and remit taxes accordingly. Alternatively, these firms can be subject to methane fees based on their reported production levels and default emissions factors (related to observable on-site features and technologies) with firms allowed to petition for rebates if they validate their emissions rates are significantly below the default. Methane fees can be integrated into fiscal regimes that are routinely applied to extractive industries (see Chapter 4).

Myth 17. Emissions fees for livestock products are not practical on administrative or acceptability/competitiveness grounds.

Not necessarily, at least for high-capacity countries where large farms account for most emissions. Livestock farmers (above a size threshold) can be required to assess their emissions (based on farm-level characteristics like type and size of herd and feed and default emissions factors). Administration for fee collection may already be in place where farmers are already subject to business tax collection. And acceptability/competitiveness might be addressed through recycling revenues within the sector or using revenue-neutral feebate approaches instead of emissions fees. Where administration at farm level is not practical, fees might be levied at processor level scaled by default emissions factors for different products (or perhaps the difference between emissions factors and a pivot point to limit new tax burdens on food) with side payments for suppliers demonstrating their products come from farms with emissions rates below the default. See Chapter 4.

Myth 18. Evaluating mitigation strategies requires sophisticated models with substantial detail on sectors and technologies.

Not necessarily. Economic-engineering models with details on existing and emerging technologies for different sectors can provide state-of-the-art projections of emissions with, and without, mitigation policies. Streamlined models built up from a few key underlying relationships can, however, be parameterized so they approximately behave like a much more sophisticated model in terms of key variables like fuel use and emissions. Streamlined models can be highly flexible, being readily transferable to different countries, accommodating a range of different policy instruments and different metrics for comparing policies, as well as allowing for easy sensitivity analysis. And results can be explained in terms of underlying concepts familiar to policymakers (like the responsiveness of fuel use in different sectors to prices and income) (see Chapter 5).

Myth 19. Establishing unbiased projections of future baseline emissions is very challenging.

No. Future emissions in the baseline (with no new or tightening of existing mitigation policies) can be projected from currently observed fuel use and emissions by sector (which is publicly available for all countries) and a few key underlying factors for which there are solid data. One is future GDP forecasts (which are regularly updated for each country by IMF staff and can be extrapolated to longer time horizons). Another is parameters indicating how the demand for different energy products responds to higher income (a large empirical literature provides estimates of these parameters by energy product and country income level). Less important are assumptions about annual rates of improvement in energy efficiency (for example, as capital stocks turn over). For the power sector, more accurate emissions projections can be obtained using country data on planned investments in different types of generation capacity (see Chapter 5).

Myth 20. The responsiveness of emissions to carbon pricing or other mitigation policies is difficult to project.

Not necessarily. The effects of carbon pricing on emissions largely boil down to emissions factors, proportionate changes in fuel prices because of carbon pricing, and the price responsiveness of fuel use. Emissions factors for fossil fuels are given, while proportionate fuel price changes depend on carbon prices, emissions factors, and baseline fuel prices. And there is a large empirical and modeling literature providing information on the responsiveness of different fuels in different sectors and countries to carbon pricing and changes in fuel prices—this information is reasonably reliable for moderately scaled carbon pricing (though uncertainties escalate for higher levels of carbon pricing). Similarly, there is ample evidence and modeling results to inform behavioral responses to other mitigation policies like feebates and electric vehicle or renewable subsidies (see Chapter 5).

Myth 21. Clean energy transitions impose large economic costs.

Not necessarily, because the costs (largely reflecting extra expenses from using cleaner technologies) of achieving required emissions reductions in the medium term should be manageable, at least if efficient mitigation policies are used. Mitigation costs are about 0.05 to 0.3 percent of GDP across G20 countries for a 20 percent reduction in CO_2 emissions below baseline levels in 2030 and 0.3–0.9 percent for a 30 percent reduction See Chapter 5.

Myth 22. Recycling revenues from carbon pricing can offset some, but not all, of the costs on the economy from mitigation.

This generally applies for advanced economies but not necessarily for developing countries. If the bulk of carbon pricing revenues are used productively, say for investment projects with benefit–cost ratios of about 1.3, up to a point carbon taxes can imply net benefits, rather than net costs, for developing economies (see Chapter 5).

Myth 23. Carbon pricing adversely affects GDP.
GDP effects from carbon pricing are more difficult to estimate than mitigation costs. In addition to aggregate consumption losses (which mainly reflect mitigation costs), GDP effects also depend on changes in economy-wide investment and net exports as well as the state-of-the business cycle and additional consumption effects from changes in the distribution of income (to the extent there are differences in people's propensity to spend out of additional income). These factors will depend on how carbon pricing revenues are recycled (for example, investment may increase if some revenue is used to lower taxes on capital), whereas accompanying trade measures (like free allowance allocations), as well as mitigation policies in trading partners, will affect net exports. Ex ante modeling simulations do not account for all these factors—ex post empirical studies do, but it is difficult to disentangle the effects of carbon pricing on GDP from other macroeconomic shocks. On balance, however, studies suggest GDP effects are generally modest and could be either positive or negative (but the latter will be more likely at deeper levels of decarbonization). See Chapter 5.

Myth 24. Methane emissions are unresponsive to pricing.
Not necessarily. In the extractives sector, there can be a preponderance of low-cost mitigation opportunities, and a \$70 CO_2-equivalent fee in 2030 would on average cut emissions 50 percent below baseline. In agriculture, however, methane emissions are costlier to reduce—here a \$70 CO_2 equivalent fee in 2030 cuts emissions by about 20 percent on average. See Chapter 5.

Myth 25. Carbon pricing imposes disproportionate burdens on low-income households.
Not necessarily. Prior to recycling of revenues, carbon pricing tends to be, at most, only moderately regressive (imposing a moderately larger burden relative to consumption for low- than high-income households). Although low-income households may spend a larger portion of their budget on energy, much of the burden comes indirectly through higher prices for general consumer goods and services and these indirect burdens are fairly evenly distributed (in proportion to consumption) across households. Moreover, carbon pricing revenues can be recycled in ways that can make carbon pricing pro-poor and progressive on net (for example, using some revenues to compensate low-income households and the rest for broad reductions in labor taxes or public investments). See Chapter 6.

Myth 26. Holding down electricity prices is an efficient way to limit the burden of carbon pricing on low-income households.
No. Holding down electricity prices is an inefficient way to help low-income households because most of the benefits leak away to higher-income households and it does not compensate for burdens from higher prices for other energy products and consumer goods. It also foregoes fiscal revenues and undermines incentives to reduce electricity demand. Targeted measures (like stronger social safety nets, earned income tax credits, or other

adjustments to the tax system) can provide more comprehensive assistance for poor households, with lower fiscal cost, and without undermining emissions objectives (and their practicality is improving with digitalization) (see Chapters 6 and 8).

Myth 27. Compensation schemes for low-income households absorb a large portion of carbon pricing revenues.

Not necessarily. For example, compensating the bottom three income deciles typically requires about 15 percent of carbon pricing revenues, at least in countries with comprehensive social safety nets. See Chapter 6.

Myth 28. Mitigation policies cause significant losses in industrial competitiveness.

Not necessarily. Production cost increases, and reductions in production, from carbon pricing can be significant for some energy-intensive, trade-exposed industries (like cement and chemicals) but in other cases (like steel) they are more moderate. Countries can also take measures to limit competitiveness effects, for example, keeping revenues from carbon pricing within the sector, using non-charging instruments like feebates or TPSs instead of carbon pricing, or combining carbon pricing with border carbon adjustments (BCAs). And competitiveness is less of a concern if other countries are also moving forward with mitigation policies for the industrial sector (see Chapters 6 and 9).

Myth 29. Carbon mitigation policies cause significant emissions leakage.

Not necessarily. Emissions leakage could be substantial in some industries (for example, about 30–50 percent or more for cement and chemicals). Leakage is, however, much smaller if other instruments like feebates or TPSs are used, or as typically happens, countries combine carbon pricing with measures like free allowance allocation or BCAs. And leakage will be largely neutralized if trading partners are also pricing industrial emissions or, more generally, meeting binding emissions targets (see Chapter 6).

Myth 30. BCAs harm the competitiveness of trading partners.

Not necessarily. BCAs preserve a level playing field for carbon pricing by imposing the same price on emissions embodied in imported products as on domestic producers. In the EU and the United Kingdom, BCAs are being phased in, while compensation schemes (free allowance allocations) for trade-exposed industries are being phased out, so on net there may be little change in competitiveness. BCAs can however impose disproportionate burdens on trading partners with emissions-intensive production (for example, relying primarily on coal blast rather than electric arc furnaces for steel production), and they impose the same emissions price on advanced and developing countries, which might be viewed as inconsistent with differentiated responsibilities under the Paris Agreement. Most of the incidence of BCAs, however, is passed forward to domestic consumers (rather than borne by trading partners in lower prices) and some revenue collected from BCAs might be remitted for climate finance or to governments of low-income trading partners (see Chapter 6).

Myth 31. As more countries impose BCAs, this will effectively scale up global mitigation.

Not necessarily. BCAs can facilitate robust carbon pricing in the domestic economy. They only price emissions embodied in imports to the domestic economy, however, which are a small fraction of nationwide emissions in trading partners—BCAs may therefore provide little incentive for trading partners to introduce or scale up economywide carbon pricing (though they may encourage pricing of emissions from the industrial sector). International coordination to progressively scale up comprehensive carbon pricing would be more effective at reducing global greenhouse gas emissions (see Chapters 6 and 9).

Myth 32. Investment needs for low-carbon energy transitions are daunting.

Not necessarily. Annual investment needs are put at about $5 trillion globally in 2030 on pathways to net zero emissions by mid-century. Much of this investment need, however, is redirected away from fossil-based investments that would otherwise have occurred, whereas for energy efficiency investments there is a partially offsetting savings in future energy costs—net investment needs are therefore much lower than gross investments. Moreover, much of the investment could be efficiently mobilized from private markets with the right price signals on carbon emissions (see Chapter 7).

Myth 33. Clean energy transitions impose significant burdens on government debt.

Not necessarily. Clean energy transitions require government outlays for low-income households and low-carbon technology infrastructure networks (like power grid upgrades), but these outlays are modest relative to potential revenues from carbon pricing. Moreover, public spending on infrastructure is more efficiently financed by user fees at the sectoral level than the general budget. Fiscal costs are significant if the mitigation strategy largely relies on low-carbon technology subsidies rather than carbon pricing, but this approach is much less efficient at promoting, and cost-effectively balancing, all potential behavioral responses for reducing emissions. Revenue losses from the erosion of road fuel taxes as transportation is decarbonized can be significant, but ideally these revenues are replaced by phasing in charges on kilometers driven for all vehicles (which ultimately can be fine-tuned to efficiently manage road congestion). See Chapters 7 and 8.

Myth 34. Combining carbon pricing with R&D subsidies is sufficient to advance critical mitigation technologies.

Not necessarily. A wider portfolio of measures—to complement explicit or implicit carbon pricing—is needed to address various obstacles at different stages in the development and diffusion of low-carbon technologies. For advanced and large emerging market economies, this includes funding basic research in low-carbon energy and (in limited cases) large demonstration projects. But a balance between patents, technology prizes, and subsidies is needed to promote applied R&D into the full range of potential emissions-saving technologies (rather than R&D subsidies alone). And at the deployment stage, appropriate measures can include a balance of transitory/technology-specific and permanent/technology-neutral incentives, public awareness campaigns (about energy efficiency), and novel financing mechanisms to address household borrowing constraints See Chapter 7.

Myth 35. For state-owned enterprises (SOEs), mitigation policies will have little effectiveness and excessive costs.

Not necessarily. Where SOEs are subject to strict government control over production and investment decisions, and market competition is restricted, carbon pricing policies may have limited effects on emissions in the sector and automatic mechanisms are lacking to promote cost-effectiveness across mitigation responses. However (leaving aside the possibility of governance and market reforms), regulatory approaches like performance standards can force emissions reductions for the SOE and shadow carbon pricing (perhaps supported by external technical studies) can guide cost-effective mitigation responses within the SOE (see Chapter 7).

Myth 36. Finance for mitigation investment can be largely mobilized through financial sector policies.

No. Financial sector policies—for example, requiring firms to disclose their carbon footprints, facilitating green bond markets, using government-backed instruments like loan guarantees to leverage private finance—can enhance the effectiveness of carbon pricing and other mitigation policies. But in the absence of emissions mitigation policies, financial market policies will have limited effects because there is no market incentive for firms and investors to pay extra for emissions-reducing investments (see Chapter 7).

Myth 37. Fossil fuel-producing countries should levy a carbon tax on exports to appropriate revenues from energy-consuming countries.

Not necessarily. If imposed unilaterally, these taxes will be largely passed backward in lower prices for domestic producers. Initiating and maintaining coordination over carbon taxes among large energy exporters (to exploit market power in international markets) may be difficult because individual countries have incentives to free ride and benefit from higher international prices without levying carbon taxes. And even if they did levy formal carbon taxes, their effects might be neutralized through (difficult to monitor) adjustments to fiscal regimes for extractives (to maintain the same rent sharing between governments and investors See Chapter 7).

Myth 38. Emissions fees for stationary sources of local air pollution are not feasible for developing countries.

No. Emissions fees are the most efficient instrument for reducing local air pollution from power generators and industrial firms because they cost-effectively exploit all mitigation opportunities, such as switching away from emissions-intensive fuels like coal and adopting control technologies in smokestacks at both new and existing facilities. For high-capacity countries, it is feasible to require firms to self-report emissions (using continuous emissions monitoring systems) and remit fees accordingly. Where this is not feasible, taxes might be imposed on fuel supply and default emissions rates, and downstream firms may petition for rebates (subject to third-party verification) if they can demonstrate that their emissions rates are below the default (see Chapter 8).

Myth 39. Traffic congestion can be efficiently managed through expanding road and transit infrastructure and fuel taxation.

No. For given road and transit infrastructure, drivers do not account for their effect on adding to congestion and slowing speeds for other road users and, consequently, traffic congestion is excessive. And fuel taxes penalize all driving, regardless of whether it is in urban or rural areas, or at peak and off-peak periods. Instead, congestion can be efficiently managed by charging kilometer-based fees on busy roads that rise and fall during the rush hour (see Chapter 8).

Myth 40. Preexisting fuel taxes reduce the need for carbon mitigation.

Not necessarily. Fuel taxes were imposed historically for non-climate reasons, principally to raise revenue while also (albeit bluntly) reducing domestic environmental problems (like local air pollution and congestion). And current CO_2 emissions reflect the effect of fuel taxes. Ideally, fuel taxes are aligned with domestic environmental costs and a carbon price imposed on top to help eliminate the difference between projected and target CO_2 emissions (see Chapter 8).

Myth 41. Fuel taxes should not reflect traffic congestion, accidents, and road damage because there are better policies for addressing these problems.

Not necessarily. Besides congestion fees, kilometer-based charging systems can efficiently address accident risk and road damage, in the former case through, for example, pay-as-you-drive auto insurance schemes and in the latter case through fees on trucks scaled by axle weight. No country, however, has comprehensively implemented the most efficient policies for addressing congestion, accidents, and road damage (in part because these schemes have only recently become feasible administratively with satellite tracking of vehicles). For the interim, it is entirely appropriate to fully reflect these environmental costs in fuel taxes (see Chapter 8).

Myth 42. The benefits to energy price reform are limited.

No. Across G20 countries, full energy price reform would reduce annual CO_2 emissions by 25–60 percent below baseline levels in 2030, reduce annual global fossil fuel air pollution deaths by 15–50 percent, raise revenues of 2–10 percent of GDP, and generate net economic benefits of up to 10 percent of GDP (see Chapter 8).

Myth 43. Countries are necessarily worse off from climate mitigation (leaving aside benefits of limiting global climate change)

No. A substantial reduction in use of fossil fuels like coal can be in countries' own interests, especially in some densely populated developing countries with high local air pollution concentrations, because of the reductions in air pollution deaths and other domestic environmental co-benefits. These fuel reductions can complement and reinforce other measures (like requirements for emissions control technologies at new and existing plants) to address local environmental problems (see Chapter 8).

Myth 44. Aligning global emissions with temperature goals will burden developed and developing countries alike.

Not necessarily. Global CO_2 emissions can be aligned with 2°C with manageable mitigation costs at the global level of about 0.5 percent of GDP. And costs can be largely progressively distributed (higher relative to GDP in high-income countries and lower in low-income countries) and for developing countries, costs may be offset by domestic environmental co-benefits. Costs will, however, be larger if inefficient mitigation strategies are adopted (see Chapter 9).

Myth 45. Supplementary international coordination mechanisms to reduce CO_2 emissions and reinforce the Paris Agreement are too challenging politically.

Not necessarily. All participants benefit collectively from enhanced mitigation action and limiting risks of destabilizing the global climate system. For low-income countries, participating in a supplementary coordination mechanism provides an opportunity for securing robust and transparent support for low-carbon energy transitions. Regional coordination schemes may emerge sooner or later (for example, as countries in Asia progress on carbon pricing) and these could be a stepping stone to a broader international agreement. Precedents for international climate mitigation mechanisms include global agreements to phase out ozone-depleting substances and hydrofluorocarbons, global coordination of corporate income taxes, and floors for energy taxes and VAT in the EU (see Chapter 9).

Myth 46. Coordination mechanisms should be negotiated among all countries not subgroups.

Not necessarily. Small numbers of participants are needed to facilitate negotiation, ideally including large emitters (like China, EU, India, G20) to cover most global emissions. A larger number of countries could be initially represented by negotiating blocs (for example, EU, African Union) or subsequently accommodated through entry provisions negotiated by the initial group (others may follow the lead of the larger economies). The Paris Agreement explicitly allows for supplementary mini-lateral agreements among subgroups of countries (see Chapter 9).

Myth 47. All countries should put the same (explicit or implicit) price on carbon.

No. The contribution to future global climate change from a ton of CO_2 emissions is the same, regardless of where the emissions are released, because emissions assimilate and persist in the global atmosphere—hence, there is some conceptual appeal for putting the same explicit price on emissions, regardless of which countries release them. This would, however, sidestep the mitigation targets countries have already made for the

Paris Agreement, whereas it would place the entire burden of addressing international equity issues through financial and technical support from advanced to developing countries. More realistically, current mitigation targets could be reinforced by minimum mitigation requirements (like carbon price floors) with equity issues addressed through a combination of stricter minimum mitigation requirements for higher-income countries and international assistance (see Chapter 9).

Myth 48. The international aviation and maritime sectors can be decarbonized without a price on carbon.

No, this seems unlikely. A robust carbon price can close the gap in lifecycle costs between low- or zero-emissions fuels and oil-based fuels. Global pricing schemes are needed (especially for maritime) because of the international mobility of the tax base and could be supervised centrally by the regulatory bodies for the industries (evolving, in the case of aviation, from the existing emissions offsetting scheme) with tax collection by specialized funds or national tax authorities (see Chapter 9).

Myth 49. Advanced economies are solely responsible for achieving climate finance goals of the Paris Agreement.

No. Advanced economies have (belatedly) achieved a commitment to mobilize $100 billion a year in climate finance for developing countries, and the new commitment is to scale this finance up to $300 billion by 2035. A potentially large portion of these flows (for mitigation) could come from private capital markets, and the key to promoting these flows is for developing countries to implement robust carbon pricing signals. Charges on international transportation fuels could be a game-changing source of public climate finance (see Chapter 9).

Myth 50. Offset schemes can cost-effectively reduce global emissions.

No. Offsets do not reduce global emissions on net and could increase them if they are not additional, for example, if they credit a mitigation project (like an investment in a renewables plant) that would have gone ahead anyway (without the offset) for economic reasons. In addition, offset projects may not be permanent (for example, new forests receiving offset credits may subsequently burn down or be logged) or might also cause emissions leakage (for example, if forestry preservation in one region leads to increased deforestation elsewhere). Moreover, there are no automatic mechanisms to ensure that the most cost-effective projects are those receiving offset payments (see Chapter 9).

Glossary

Afforestation Planting of forests on lands that historically have not contained forests.

Atmospheric greenhouse gas (GHG) concentration Measured at a particular instant in time, it is equivalent to the cumulative total of all past inflows of GHGs into the atmosphere less uptake of gases by the oceans and other sinks.

Baseline projection Projections of future emissions and other outcomes that would occur in the absence of new, or changes to existing, mitigation policies.

Biofuels Fuels that contain energy from recent production of carbon in living organisms like plants.

Border Carbon Adjustments (BCAs) or Carbon Border Adjustment Mechanisms (CBAMs) These measures impose charges on the embodied carbon content of certain products imported into a country and (in some proposals) provide rebates for domestic carbon pricing for categories of exported products.

Building codes Minimum requirements for how structural systems, plumbing, heating, ventilation and air conditioning, natural gas systems, and other aspects of residential and commercial buildings should be designed and constructed.

Burden or incidence Refers to whose economic well-being is reduced by a policy and by how much. It is quite different from the formal or legal incidence—gasoline suppliers, for example, may be responsible for remitting tax payments to the national tax authority, but they may bear little economic incidence if taxes are passed forward to motorists in higher prices.

Carbon capture and storage (CCS) An (as yet unproven) technology for extracting CO_2 emissions from smokestacks and transporting them through pipelines to underground geological storage sites. Alternatively, captured gas might be used in industrial processes (for example, by conversion into plastics, concrete, and biofuels).

Carbon dioxide (CO_2) A naturally occurring gas and also a by-product of burning fossil fuels and biomass, as well as land-use changes and other industrial processes. It is the main gas causing global warming. CO_2 has an average atmospheric residence time of hundreds of years or more.

Carbon Offsetting and Reduction Scheme for International Aviation (CORSIA) CORSIA is the centerpiece of International Civil Aviation Organization's strategy for reducing international aviation emissions. Under this program, which will be mandatory for about 90 percent of international flights from 2027 onward, operators are required to purchase international offsets for any emissions above 85 percent of 2019 levels.

Carbon pricing Policies that put an explicit price on CO_2 emissions, including carbon taxes and ETSs.

Carbon sequestration The process of removing carbon from the atmosphere and absorbing it in forests or other sinks.

Carbon tax A charge on the carbon content of coal, oil, and natural gas, which can be levied midstream (after fuel processing) or upstream (at the point of fuel extraction). The tax applies to fuel imports but not exports.

Climate mitigation Actions taken to reduce GHG emissions, thereby slowing down the rise in global temperatures and associated climate changes.

Climate Policy Assessment Tool (CPAT) A model developed by IMF and World Bank staff, implemented in a spreadsheet, that provides—on a country-by-country basis for 200 countries—projections of fuel use and GHG emissions by sector and the environmental, energy, fiscal, incidence, and other impacts of a wide range of alternative mitigation instruments. The model is available for use by governments.

CO_2 equivalent The warming potential of a GHG expressed in terms of the amount of CO_2 that would yield the same amount of warming over a long time period.

Common but differentiated responsibilities and respective capabilities in the light of national circumstances A principle of the UNFCCC calling for developed countries to bear a disproportionately larger burden of mitigation costs (through more stringent mitigation targets and policies and supportive climate finance), given they are relatively wealthy and contributed most to historical GHG accumulations.

Comprehensive mitigation strategy A diverse package of elements including: (i) medium- and long-term emissions commitments; (ii) fiscal and other instruments to reduce GHG emissions at economy-wide and sectoral level; (iii) measures to enhance acceptability by addressing distributional and competitiveness concerns; (iv) supportive technology policies, public infrastructure investment, energy and financial market reforms, and (for energy exporters) revenue diversification; (v) complementary reforms to reduce domestic environmental costs of fossil fuel use; (vi) participation in international fora to foster greater ambition and policy coordination; and (vii) use of modeling toolkits to inform dialogue and design of all these elements.

Conference of the Parties (COP) The supreme body of the UNFCCC that meets annually to promote and review implementation of the UN Framework Convention on Climate Change.

Continuous emissions monitoring systems A technology that continuously measures flue gas emissions (for example, CO_2, SO_2) from a stationary source caused by fuel combustion in power plants or industrial processes.

Cost-effective mitigation policy A policy achieving a given emissions reduction at least economic cost. This requires that the cost of the last ton reduced is equated across firms, households, fuels, and sectors.

Credit trading In ETSs, credit trading allows firms with high abatement costs to do less mitigation by purchasing allowances from firms with low abatement costs. In other regulatory systems, credit trading allows firms with high compliance costs to fall short of an emission rate or other standard by purchasing credits from firms that exceed the standard.

Direct air capture A technology extracting CO_2 directly from the atmosphere by passing air through a filter with a sorbent material. The CO_2 can be permanently stored in deep geological formations or used for industrial applications. Direct air capture is costlier than CCS (because of the lower concentration of CO_2 in the atmosphere than smokestacks) but (unlike CCS) can be installed at any location.

Distribution-neutral policy A policy imposing approximately the same burden as a proportion of consumption (or some other measure of household well-being) on all different income groups.

Downstream policy A mitigation policy imposed at the point at which emissions are released from stationary sources, primarily from smokestacks at coal plants and other facilities.

Economic welfare cost A measure of economic cost routinely used in cost–benefit analysis of investment projects and environmental and other public policies. In the context of climate mitigation, it largely corresponds to integrals under marginal abatement cost curves, with adjustments for pre-existing taxes or subsidies (mainly on fuels) which shift up, or shift down, these curves.

Electric vehicles (EVs) A vehicle powered by an electric motor drawing electricity from a battery charged from an external source.

Emissions factor The emissions (for example, of CO_2) released per unit of fuel combustion. For coal and natural gas, emissions factors are usually expressed in tons per unit of energy, and for liquid fuels, tons per liter.

Emissions leakage Refers to a possible increase in emissions in other countries in response to an emissions reduction policy in the domestic country. Most focus is on potential leakage from the international migration of energy-intensive, trade-exposed industries in response to higher domestic production costs.

Emissions Trading System or Scheme (ETS) A market-based policy to reduce emissions sometimes referred to as cap-and-trade. Covered sources are required to hold allowances for each ton of their emissions or (in an upstream program) embodied emissions content in fuels. The total quantity of allowances is fixed, and trading allowances in market exchanges establish a market price for emissions. Auctioning allowances can provide a valuable source of government revenue.

Energy-intensive, trade-exposed (EITE) industry Industries like steel, cement, and chemicals that compete in international markets and use fossil fuels intensively and/or produce significant process emissions. Concerns about competitiveness and leakage impacts of mitigation policies focus on these industries.

Energy paradox The observation that some energy-efficient technologies are not adopted by the market even though they appear to pay for themselves through discounted lifetime energy savings that exceed the upfront investment cost.

Externality A cost imposed by the actions of individuals or firms on other individuals or firms (possibly in the future, because of climate change) that the former does not consider. Externalities can be positive when they confer benefits to others.

Feebate Imposes a sliding scale of fees on firms with emissions rates (for example, CO_2 per kilowatt hour) above a "pivot point" level and corresponding subsidies for firms with emissions rates below the pivot point. Alternatively, the feebate might be applied to energy consumption rates (for example, gasoline per kilometer driven) rather than emissions rates. Feebates are the fiscal analog of a tradable performance standard but can better accommodate uncertainty.

Feed-in tariff Provides a guaranteed above-market price for producers either through a price floor or a subsidy per unit of production.

Flaring The open-air burning of natural gas or methane. The practice is commonly used by oil drillers, refineries, and natural gas processing plants as a means of disposing of excess stocks, which can be an important safety measure.

Fluorinated (F-) gases Potent, synthetic GHGs used in various applications like refrigeration, air conditioning, and industrial processes. The most important F-gas is HFCs.

Forest management In a climate mitigation context, management practices affecting carbon sequestered in a forest, such as conversion of forestland to plantations, postponing timber harvests, planting trees rather than allowing natural regeneration, thinning trees and undergrowth to enhance forest growth, controlling forest fires and other disturbances, and fertilizing.

Fossil fuels Natural resources, such as coal, oil, and natural gas, containing hydrocarbons. These fuels are formed in the Earth over millions of years and produce CO_2 when combusted.

Fuel economy (or efficiency) standard Policy regulating the allowable fuel use per unit of distance (or distance per unit of fuel use) for new transportation vehicles, often averaged over a manufacturer's vehicle fleet.

Gigajoule (GJ) A metric term used for measuring energy use. For example, 1 GJ is approximately equivalent to the energy available from 278 kWh of electricity, 26 cubic meters of natural gas, or 26 liters of heating oil.

Global Methane Pledge (GMP) Seeks to cut global methane emissions by 30 percent by 2030 relative to 2020 levels. Over 150 countries have so far signed the pledge.

Global warming The rise in observed globally averaged temperature from preindustrial levels (1.2°C to date) attributed to rising atmospheric accumulations of GHGs (as opposed to other factors like changes in solar radiation).

Global warming potential (GWP) Of a non-CO_2 GHG refers to the cumulative change in warming over time (for example, a century) caused by an extra ton of the gas relative to a ton of CO_2.

Greenhouse effect Trapping and buildup of heat in the atmosphere near the Earth's surface. Some of the heat flowing back toward space from the Earth's surface is absorbed by GHGs in the atmosphere and then reradiated back toward the Earth's surface. Because the atmospheric concentrations of GHGs rise, the average temperature of the lower atmosphere increases.

Greenhouse gas (GHG) A gas in the atmosphere that is transparent to incoming solar radiation but traps and absorbs heat radiated from the Earth. CO_2 is easily the most predominant GHG followed by methane. Other gases include nitrous oxide and F-gases.

Green hydrogen Hydrogen (potentially used as a fuel for industrial heating or powering ships) produced by water electrolysis using renewable electricity.

Group of Twenty (G20) An international forum comprising 19 countries and the EU, and more recently the African Union. It works to address climate change and other major issues related to the global economy.

High-income country Countries with annual per capita income above $14,005 in 2023.

Hydrofluorocarbons (HFCs) An F-gas, with especially high GWPs, used, for example, in refrigeration and air conditioning.

Income elasticity Indicates the percent increase in demand for a product in response to a 1 percent increase in income.

Input–output table These tables provide detailed information on fuels, electricity, and other inputs per unit of output across industries producing both intermediate goods and final consumer goods. The tables can be used to trace through the effects of carbon pricing (via higher energy prices) on the price of final goods.

Intergovernmental Panel on Climate Change (IPCC) Established in 1988, the IPCC is a body providing regular scientific assessments of knowledge about the drivers of climate change, its impacts, and future risks, and how mitigation and adaptation can reduce those risks. For its reports, thousands of experts from across the world assess the latest scientific literature on global warming—to date, the IPCC has produced six Assessment Reports (the last in 2023) and various special reports. The IPCC consists of three Working Groups dealing with (1) the physical science basis of climate change; (2) climate change impacts, adaptation, and vulnerability; and (3) climate change mitigation. In addition, an IPCC task force refines methodologies for assessing and reporting national GHG emissions.

Internal combustion engine vehicle (ICEV) A vehicle that is powered by gasoline or diesel which combust inside a chamber with the help of oxygen.

International carbon price floor (ICPF) A proposal for an international mechanism to complement the Paris Agreement and facilitate a scaling up of global mitigation action. It would focus on (1) a small number of large emitters to facilitate negotiation; and (2) a minimum carbon price that each participant should implement. Equity issues could be addressed through differentiated floors and climate finance.

International Civil Aviation Organization (ICAO) A UN agency responsible for supervising and regulating international aviation.

International Maritime Organization (IMO) A UN agency responsible for supervising and regulating international shipping.

Kigali Agreement Under this agreement, advanced economies committed to reduce use of the main F-gas by 85 percent (relative to 2011–13 levels) by 2036 and developing countries by 80–85 percent by 2045–47.

Kilometer-based taxes Taxes that vary directly in proportion to how much a vehicle is driven, for example, on busy roads at peak periods.

Land use, land-use change and forestry (LULUCF) A GHG inventory sector that covers emissions and removals of GHGs resulting from direct human-induced land use, land-use change, and forestry activities.

Low-income country Countries with annual per capita income below $4,515 in 2023.

Methane (CH_4) The second most important source of GHGs. Sources from human activities include leaks from fossil fuel extraction, livestock operations, and waste sites. Methane is a powerful heat-trapping gas but has a relatively short atmospheric lifespan—substantially cutting emissions could slightly cool global temperatures and limit the risk of tipping points.

Middle-income country Countries with annual per capital income between $4,515 and $14,005 in 2023.

Midstream policy An emissions policy applied at the point where fuels enter the economy after processing (for example, at the refinery gate). The policy might build off existing capacity for fuel tax collection.

Nationally Determined Contribution (NDC) Commitments to climate mitigation and adaptation submitted by parties for the Paris Agreement. Countries are required to report progress on implementing NDCs every two years and to submit revised NDCs which ratchet up over time.

Net zero emissions Implies cutting a country's GHGs to as close to zero as possible, with remaining emissions offset, for example, through direct air capture or forest carbon sequestration.

Net zero emissions building An energy-efficient building that produces its own carbon-free electricity (through rooftop solar or geothermal) or procures carbon-free electricity from the grid.

Nitrous oxide (N_2O) A GHG generated primarily from livestock manure and soil tilling for crops. In contrast, nitrogen oxides (NO_x), which react to form fine particulates, are local air pollutants.

Non-CO_2 GHGs These gases, which include methane, nitrous oxide, and F-gases, have relatively high GWPs.

Offset A reduction in emissions in other countries or unregulated sectors that is credited to reduce the tax liability or permit requirements for emissions covered by a formal pricing program, or to help meet an emissions or emission rate target.

Paris Agreement An international agreement (ratified in 2016) from within the UNFCCC, on climate mitigation, adaptation, and finance. A total of 195 UNFCCC members originally signed the agreement. The agreement's central objective is to contain global average temperature increases to 1.5–2°C above preindustrial levels.

Pass-through (of climate mitigation policies) The extent to which a carbon tax or other mitigation policy is reflected in higher prices for energy consumers (rather than lower prices for producers).

Payment for Environmental Services (PES) programs These programs provide compensation to landowners for achieving environmental objectives (such as carbon storage, sustaining biodiversity, soil conservation, preventing floods, and land degradation) and mostly operate in African, Asian, and Central/South American countries.

Preindustrial levels of CO_2 Levels of CO_2 in the atmosphere prior to the start of the Industrial Revolution, which were about 280 parts per million (ppm). The current level is about 420 ppm.

Process emissions Emissions released from the chemical transformation of raw materials, such as limestone used to produce clinker (an input in cement).

Progressive policy A policy imposing a smaller burden as a proportion of consumption (or some other measure of household well-being) on lower-income households than higher-income households.

Rebound effect The increase in fuel use (or emissions) resulting from increased use of energy-consuming products after an improvement in energy efficiency, which lowers their operating costs.

Reducing Emissions from Deforestation and Forest Degradation (REDD) An effort to create a financial value for the carbon stored in forests and thereby offer incentives for developing countries to reduce CO_2 emissions from deforestation and forest degradation. "REDD+" goes further and rewards forest conservation and management practices that sequester carbon.

Reforestation Replanting of forests on lands that have previously contained forests but that have been converted to some other use.

Regressive policy A policy imposing a larger burden as a proportion of consumption (or some other measure of household well-being) on lower-income households than higher-income households.

Renewable portfolio standard (RPS) Requires that a specified percentage of electricity production comes from renewable fuels.

Research and development (R&D) Innovative activities undertaken by firms or governments to develop new or improved technologies or products.

Revenue recycling Use of carbon pricing revenues to, for example, lower other distortionary taxes or fund government investment.

Sustainable Development Goals (SDGs) A collection of 17 goals set by the UN General Assembly in 2015 covering global warming, poverty, health, education, gender equality, water, sanitation, energy, urbanization, environment, and social justice. Each goal has a set of targets to achieve, and in total there are 169 targets.

Tipping points Refer to risks of crossing thresholds in the Earth's climate system beyond which abrupt (or nonlinear) changes occur. These risks are not well understood but likely rise exponentially with warming. Potential risks include, among others, runaway warming because of emissions releases from permafrost melting, collapse of major ice sheets, and flipping of ocean circulatory systems (with potentially dramatic effects on local temperature and rainfall).

Ton A metric ton is a unit of mass equal to 1,000 kilograms. Metric tons are the standard unit for measuring CO_2 emissions (rather than short tons, which are 2,000 pounds or 907 kilograms).

Tradable performance standard (TPS) Under this program, firms are required to meet a standard for their emissions rate (for example, tons of CO_2 per kWh averaged across their plants, or CO_2 per km averaged across vehicle sales fleets). Their emissions rates can however exceed the standard if they buy credits for their excess emissions from firms that go beyond meeting the standard. Emissions reductions are cost-effective across different firms so long as credit trading markets are fluid.

United Nations Framework Convention on Climate Change (UNFCCC) An international environmental treaty produced at the 1992 Earth Summit. The treaty's objective is to stabilize atmospheric GHG concentrations at a level that would prevent "dangerous interference with the climate system." The treaty itself sets no mandatory emissions limits for individual countries and contains no enforcement mechanisms but instead provides for updates or "protocols."

Upstream policy An emissions policy applied to fossil fuels at the point of extraction (for example, at the mine mouth or wellhead), which might be integrated into existing fiscal regimes.

Index

Pages in *italics* refer to figures and pages in **bold** refer to tables.

For Product Safety Concerns and Information please contact our EU representative GPSR@taylorandfrancis.com Taylor & Francis Verlag GmbH, Kaufingerstraße 24, 80331 München, Germany